Koreans in America

Koreans in America

in

America

최봉윤

Bong-youn Choy

Nelson-Hall ｎｈ Chicago

Choy, Bong Youn,
    Koreans in America.

    Bibliography: p.
    Includes index.
    1. Korean Americans—History. 2. United
States—Foreign relations—Korea. 3. Korea
—Foreign relations—United States. I. Title.
    E184.K6C48   973'.04'957   79-9791
    ISBN 0-88229-352-4

Manufactured in the United States of America

10   9   8   7   6   5   4   3   2   1

Contents

Foreword

SINCE THE CONCLUSION of the Korean American Treaty of 1882, Korea has deeply penetrated the American consciousness. Certainly there are few nations in the world where recent American military and economic as well as political commitments have been so substantial. The tragic Korean War lies in the past, but the 38th parallel, which divides the Korean people, still remains with us as one of the unsolved dramas of postwar politics.

The history, culture, and traditions of Korea are both old and rich, but her economics and politics are still in a developing or "emergent" stage by Western standards. Korea, as a nation, faces tremendous internal and external problems: unification of the divided country, installation of a single democratic government, and reconstruction of a self-supporting economy. As in the past, United States policy will influence Korea's future. In addition, the influx of Korean immigrants to the United States after 1965 will have a social and political impact on America's multi-ethnic society in general and on the Korean-American community in particular in the years to come.

Against this setting, Professor Choy's book—*Koreans in America*—assumes a significant position. I have known the author, who also wrote *Korea: A History,* for many years. His long residence, study, and teaching both in Korea and the United States, together with his constant research, qualify him to present a balanced, scholarly account of Koreans in this country. To my knowledge Professor Choy's book is the first authoritative book written by a competent scholar who is acquainted with both Eastern and Western ways. It is a book that will be very useful to all people, especially scholars and the general public interested in Koreans in the United States.

Dr. Chang Lee-wook
Former President of Seoul National University
and Korean Ambassador to the United States

Preface

THERE HAS BEEN a need for a detailed and scholarly book on Koreans in the
United States since at least the mid-1960's, when there was an influx of
Korean immigrants and a rapid expansion of ethnic studies. The author
hopes this book will meet the need by presenting the socio-economic, cultural, and political activities of Koreans in America from 1882 to 1976, together with an account of Korea's domestic and external conditions during
the same period.

The book is addressed to American college and university students in
courses on ethnic studies; to elementary and high-school teachers (to be used
as a guide for bilingual and multi-cultural programs); to American-born
Koreans and to Korean immigrant school-age children; to the American
public interested in Korean-American developments; and to school and
public libraries. In addition, this book might be useful to students of history, political science, sociology, and anthropology as a supplementary or
reference reader.

Until the Korean War, many Americans were unaware of the land and
people of Korea. Hence, this study has attempted to sensitize the audience to
the growing number of Korean immigrants and to their problems. This book
is divided into three parts: the first provides the historical background of
Korea and of American-Korean relations; the second deals with the history
of early Korean immigrants and their economic, social, and political activities; the third is an analysis of postwar Korean immigration and its characteristics and problems. The last two chapters contain an account of
Korean contributions to America and tape-recorded interviews with early
immigrants.

This book introduces a "new" method: the analytical and objective
interpretation of the socio-economic, cultural, and political development of
Korean-American history. This method differs from those in existing books.
Koreans in America by Warren Y. Kim (Kim Won-yong) is a summary
translation of his Korean language book *Chaemi Hanin Osipnyon-sa* (A

ix

Fifty Year History of the Koreans in America). It concentrates on the political activities of Koreans in America, and uses the traditional historian's method of descriptive writing. *The Koreans in America: 1882—1974* by Kim Hyung-chan and Wayne Patterson contains only detailed chronologies, some documents of important events in the Korean community, and an editor's foreword. *The Koreans in Hawaii* by Arthur Gardner is an annotated bibliography on Koreans in Hawaii and includes some material about the mainland. *Han'kook Imin-sa Yonku* (A Study of the History of Korean Emigration) by Koh Sung-che covers only the early part of Korean migration to Hawaii. *Chemi Hanin Saryak* (A Short History of Koreans in America) by Noh Chae-yon contains chronologies from 1882 to 1957.*Chaemi Hanin Chilsipnyon-sa* (A Seventy Year History of Koreans in America) by So Kwang-woon is a brief history of Korean migration to the United States. It, too, uses the descriptive method.

This author bases his text on primary Korean-language sources, original tape-recorded materials, personal interviews, and his own experience in the Korean American community since 1938. A selected bibliography and extensive notes provide the scholarly apparatus for information hitherto unavailable to the English-speaking world.

I wish to express my sincere gratitude for the valuable suggestions and editing of Mrs. Evelyn B. McCune, Korean-born member of a distinguished family of American missionaries and scholars, and the author of *The Arts of Korea,* whom I have known for more than thirty-five years. My thanks also go to my daughter-in-law Sharon, my daughter Sunnie, and my son-in-law, Dong Ku, for their help in reading my manuscript, typing some of the chapters, and translating some articles. I am grateful to Professor Kim Hyung-chan, author of many articles and books on Asian-American studies, for his help in giving me his published and unpublished materials on the subject of Korean community matters.

Notes

In the text, most Korean names are written with the family name before the personal name, as they are in their native land. The few exceptions, such as Syngman Rhee and Younghill Kang, are names that are usually inverted in the Western language sources. General guidelines to the pronunciation of Korean words are explained on page 9 of this book. The omission of diacritical works on the Korean names is the publisher's decision.

1

Historical Background

1.

Korea: The Land, the People, the Culture, and the History

THE LAND

The Korean peninsula is strategically located in the heart of the Far East. Because it is surrounded by three powerful countries—China, Russia, and Japan—Korea has, since the late part of the nineteenth century, been a battleground for power politics. The islands of Japan lie only one hundred and twenty miles away to the southeast. China lies approximately twice as far away to the west. Manchuria, the northeastern province of China, shares most of Korea's northern boundary, the Yalu and Tuman rivers. Finally, Korea shares eleven miles of its northern boundary with Soviet Siberia.

The Korean peninsula comprises 85,285 square miles, roughly the size of Minnesota, New York or Great Britain. Elongated and irregular in shape, it stretches about six hundred miles from the Manchurian border to the island of Cheju, off the southwest coast. In width, the Korean peninsula varies from one hundred and twenty miles to a more uniform width of one hundred and sixty miles.

Because it is a natural bridge between Japan and the Asian mainland, Korea has always been considered of great strategic importance. It has been likened to a "dagger pointed at the heart of Japan."[1] From the north, the Mongols during the thirteenth century and the Manchus during the seventeenth century swept through the peninsula to attack Japan. The Japanese themselves on numerous occasions (such as Toyotomi Hideyoshi's invasion in the sixteenth century) occupied the Korean peninsula as a base from which to attack other parts of the Asian mainland. The struggle for control of Korea was a direct cause of the Sino-Japanese War of 1894-1895, the Russo-Japanese War of 1904-1905, and the Korean War of 1950-1953.

In addition, during times of peace, Korea served as a cultural link between China and Japan. For example, Confucianism and Buddhism, along with other aspects of Chinese culture, were introduced to Japan through Korea. Despite the fact that the Korean people were forced to accept much

3

of China's culture, they managed to maintain their own cultural identity over the centuries.

Korea has many mountains and rivers. The famous Paektu-san, White Head Mountain, situated in northeastern Korea, is the highest mountain, rising to an elevation of over 9,000 feet. The Kumgang-san, Diamond Mountain, located in central Korea, has long been a mecca for tourists from all parts of Asia because of its spectacular scenery. On Cheju Island, the Halla-san (6,398 ft.) is the highest point in South Korea. Northeast of Seoul (capital of the Republic of Korea) is another important mountain, the Ta'ebaek-san. West of this range are the drainage basins of the Han and Kum rivers, which supply water to rice fields for southern Korean farmers. Southwest from the Ta'ebaek range is another range, the Sobaek, which culminates in the massive range of Chiri-san. The Naktong River basin is in southeastern Korea. The Chungchon and Taedong rivers, which run through P'yongyang, capital of the Democratic People's Republic of North Korea, are important sources of water for northern Korean farmers. Korea's two longest rivers, the Yalu and the Tuman, run along the boundary with China and the Soviet Union. The Yalu flows west for four hundred and ninety-one miles into the Yellow Sea, and the Tuman flows east for three hundred and twenty-four miles into the Sea of Japan.

The Korean peninsula has fifty-four hundred miles of varied coastline. The east coast is relatively straight and rocky, with a tidal range of not more than two feet, whereas the west coast is flat and has long stretches of winding mud flats, with a tidal range of more than seventeen feet. The important ports of the south coast are Pusan, Masan, and Mokpo. On the west coast, they are Inchon and Chinnampo, and on the east coast, Ch'ongjin and Wonsan.

There are about three thousand offshore islands, of which some two hundred are habitable. The largest is Cheju Island, which has become one of the provincial administrative units of the Republic of Korea.

As previously stated, much of the eastern coast of the peninsula has mountains that rise abruptly from the seashore. Thus, it is well suited for the production of hydro-electric power. On the other hand, the western half of the country, being flat, is well suited for farming, especially rice production. Because of this, northern Korea is referred to as an industrial zone, while southern Korea is referred to as an agricultural zone. Only one-fifth of the Korean peninsula can be cultivated, though, largely because of the mountainous terrain. It is estimated that a little over twelve million acres are cultivated today.

Korea's climate, in general, is humid and monsoonal in nature, although there is a definite distinction between the four seasons. The warm springs, hot summers, cool falls, and cold winters have a strong influence on the Korean peasant's choice of crops and on his daily activities. The clear fall weather is the most pleasant time of year.

The soil of Korea is not particularly fertile, and a major portion has been changed by human activities through the centuries. Thus, "the working and reworking of the soils of the land used for crop cultivation has produced man-made, rather than natural soils."[2]

In general, the Korean peninsula can be characterized as a mountainous, hill-and-valley country of natural beauty with rich natural resources.[3] The location, climate, soil, and vegetation have influenced the economic, political, and social activities of the Korean people for centuries.

THE PEOPLE

The traditional view about the origin of the Korean people is based on legend. Korean tradition places the founding of the tribal state in the year 2333 B.C. by a spirit king of divine origin named Tan'gun. One of the stories about his birth is the following: Long, long ago, a lovely maiden rested beside a clear stream. She thought deeply upon the gods of the heavens. She pondered upon the spirits of the mountains and seas. Finally, a god in the heavens saw her and fell in love with her. Disguised as a gentle breeze, he descended from the heavens and caressed her with his breath. From this caress, a son was conceived and born. This son was named Tan'gun, and he became the first ruler of the Korean peninsula. His successors reigned for more than twelve hundred years. Although no archeological evidence can be found to support this traditional story, some Korean historians nonetheless write about Tan'gun.[4]

According to anthropologists, the Korean people are descended partly from the Mongolian race, and partly from the Tungus and Proto-Caucasoids who arrived in the Korean peninsula in waves from the plains of Manchuria or central Asia. Professor Cornelius Osgood has summarized the matter thus: "In any case, the basic population of both Korea and Japan was almost certainly built up by successive small migrations from northeast Asia, over a period quite possibly exceeding fifty thousand years. . . . Before the beginning of recorded history, therefore, we can imagine the Korean peninsula sparsely populated by a few thousand people, mostly Mongoloids from the cold northeast section of Asia. We can guess that these first Koreans lived as separate tribal groups occupying the eight or ten principal river valleys."[5]

Early Chinese records indicate that, in the second century B.C., various clans and tribes inhabited the peninsula.[6] All the tribes in Korea were a mixture of the Tungus and Proto-Caucasoids. In the northeastern area, the most powerful tribal group, the Puyo (in Chinese Fuyu), lived in the Sungari river coastal area. The Puyo tribes were classified into four groups: the horse, the dog, the pig, and the cow. The supreme chieftain over all the Puyo was elected by the four group chiefs. These chiefs wore fox furs, sables, silk, and hats decorated with gold and silver. In addition to the Puyo, there were three other tribal groups living in the northeastern section of Korea. The Okoho tribes occupied the area known today as Hamkyong Province and the Tuman river valley. The Yemaek tribes lived along the upper section of the Yalu River, and the I-Lou tribes occupied the forested mountains of the far northeast (even Chinese records fail to indicate a definite area). Eventually all these smaller tribes merged under the leadership of the Puyo people, and established the Koguryo kingdom in northeastern Korea and eastern Manchuria.

The southern section of the peninsula was occupied at this time by three Korean Han tribal groups (this Han differs from the Chinese Han). They were the Mahans, the Pyonhans, and the Chinhans. The Mahans, who occupied the southwestern portion, were composed of fifty-five different tribes, of which the Mokchi were the most important. These people, who were strongly influenced by the Chinese, engaged in agriculture. They held two major sacrificial ceremonies a year, a spring festival to celebrate the end of planting and a fall festival to celebrate the harvest. These celebrations involved singing and dancing to honor the spirits of nature. The Pyonhan tribes, who occupied the Naktong river valley, lived in close contact with the Chinhan in the Han river valley. Although their dress and dwelling places were similar, their languages differed. This can be partially explained by the fact that the Pyonhan engaged in maritime trade and eventually crossed over to the Japanese islands of Kyushu and Honshu. Some Pyonhan settled there, while others joined the Koguryo people and migrated southward down the Korean peninsula. In contrast, the Chinhan had closer contacts with the Chinese and, in fact, considered some of their leaders to be "descendants of refugees from the Chinese state of Chin (255-205 B.C.).[7] Even their musical instruments resembled the Chinese five-stringed instruments. These Chinhan tribes also were farmers and used ox- and horse-powered carts to cultivate their land. Eventually, the Chinhan built a strong tribal state, later known as the Silla.

Recorded Korean history begins with the period from 57 B.C. to 668 A.D. known as the period of the Three Kingdoms. The peninsula was divided into three parts. Most of northern Korea was under the rule of the kingdom of Koguryo. Southeastern Korea was occupied by the Silla, and the southwestern section was dominated by the Paekche. Thus, all the smaller tribes in the peninsula had been integrated into one of these three dominant groups. When the Silla unified the peninsula into one political entity in 668 A.D., the people of the three kingdoms emerged as one nationality. This is to say that over the centuries Koreans developed as a distinctive people, different from their neighbors, the Chinese and Japanese. The Koreans became a nation of one language, one culture, and one proud past.

In terms of physical characteristics, Koreans are midway in height between the shorter Japanese and the taller northern Chinese. The average male, according to a recent study, is five feet, five inches tall; the average female is five feet, one inch. The skin is generally light yellow-brown. The hair is usually black or brown-black, except for a minority who have reddish-brown hair. The texture of the hair is usually smooth and straight, although it is sometimes very curly. The eyes are usually dark-brown, with a comparatively small iris. The nose is medium, with nostrils neither flat nor bulging. The lips are of medium thickness.

THE CULTURE

A Summary of Korean Cultural Development

The earliest Korean people possessed a Neolithic culture.[8] Modern archaeological and linguistic hypotheses show that primitive hunting and fishing people moved into the peninsula from the northeast during the fourth millennium B.C. These early peninsula people had a shell-fish diet and lived in pit shelters.

From the Neolithic stage, the early Koreans progressed to a bronze and iron culture. During the *Sam Han* ("Three Han") period, the Korean people developed certain unique customs and engaged in farming and the manufacture of primitive handicrafts. When the Chinese established colonies in northern Korea (the best known one being Nangyang), their civilization began to influence the Korean people. The influence of China's Han dynasty can be seen in the lacquer ware, pottery, jewelry, bronze mirrors, and farming and battle tools that have been discovered in Korean tombs.

Buddhism reached the peninsula from China in the fourth century A.D. It was introduced into Koguryo in 327 A.D., then into Paekche about 384 A.D. About one hundred and fifty years later it took hold in Silla. Eight large monasteries were constructed on the peninsula, and Buddhism became the state religion. When Silla unified the peninsula and ruled the country for almost three hundred years (668-935 A.D.), a high level Buddhist civilization developed. It was called the Golden Age, and its center was the capital, Kyongju. Many Buddhist temples, monasteries, and giant pagodas were built during this period. Some of them still remain.

Despite the Mongol invasions and constant warfare against Japanese piracy, the Koryo kingdom (935-1392) also reached a high level of cultural achievement. Craftsmen produced more than eighty-thousand carved wooden plates used to print Buddhist scriptures. Scholars made great progress in literature. And artists perfected the well-known celadon pottery, with its delicate forms and watergreen color, that still remains one of the most coveted art treasures of the world.[9]

The first two and one-half centuries of the more than five-hundred year rule of the Yi period (1392-1910) were considered the brilliant years in terms of cultural development. As we will discuss later, an alphabet was developed; movable metal type for printing was invented, fifty years before Gutenberg printed the Bible; and a one hundred and twelve volume encyclopedia was compiled. Confucianism became the new creed of the Korean government in place of Buddhism. During the Japanese invasion under Toyotomi Hideyoshi's command, the first ironclad warship was invented by Admiral Yi Soonshin. Although the Japanese forces were forced to withdraw from the peninsula after seven years of war, the invasion brought an end to the prosperity of Korea, and the Yi dynasty began to decline.

Unique Characteristics of Korean Culture

One of the unique characteristics of Korean culture is its language. The Korean language belongs to the Ural-Altaic group, which also includes Mongolian, Turkish, and other lesser known languages scattered around the world. Despite the fact that the official writing system of the Korean government for many years was the Chinese one, the Koreans never adopted the Chinese language, although they did borrow many words from it. There are dialectal differences between Korea's north and south, but they are not sufficiently large to provide a barrier to understanding.

Before the fifteenth century, Koreans who desired to become government officials had to master the Chinese language, because the Confucian classics were a requirement for the civil service examinations. Until the Korean alphabet, called *hangul*, was devised, Korean books and official documents were written in Chinese characters, but for their sounds rather than their meanings. Koreans had their own pronunciation of the characters and sometimes their own meanings. This extremely inefficient method of writing hampered the spread of education for many centuries, since only the children of wealthy families and men of leisure had time to master the thousands upon thousands of Chinese ideographs.

At long last, during the enlightened reign of King Sejong (1397-1450), a royal commission of scholars, after many years of study, developed a Korean phonetic alphabet composed of ten vowels and fourteen consonants. This phonetic system was credited to the personal leadership of the king and was called *hunmin jongum*. Today it is named *hangul*. The Korean alphabet, as judged by many scholars, is one of the simplest, most concise, and most efficient means of writing in the world.

The fourteen consonants are generally pronounced as they are in

English, the ten vowels as in Italian. The alphabet has no *f, v,* or *l* sounds as the English alphabet does. The basic vowels, *a,e,i,o,* and *u,* are pronounced as follows:

> a, as in f*a*rm
> e, as in *e*nd
> i, as in k*i*ng
> o, as in m*o*ss
> u, as in *u*p

Other vowel sounds are:

> o, as in the a in *a*bove
> u, as in the oo in f*oo*t
> ae, as in b*a*g
> oe, as the German umlaut ö

Because of the euphonic changes upon the consonants, there is a plurality of romanization of each of the consonants, To Koreans, these euphonic changes are so natural that they consider them as self-evident. A simple example is the name of the Korean kingdom, spelled Sin-ra, but pronounced Silla. Therefore, in order to romanize the consonants correctly, it is necessary to take into consideration their position in relation to other (the following) consonants. This could be easily done by treating each consonant separately as an initial, medial, and final letter. It should be noted that *k, p, t,* and *chi* are pronounced without appreciable aspiration.

According to common Korean usage, personal names usually consist of two or three names, with the surname appearing first. A hyphen is used between first and middle names because they are always pronounced together, with a few exceptions like Syngman Rhee.

Koreans all speak, write, and understand the same language in basically the same manner. After the liberation of Korea from Japanese domination in 1945, *hangul* became used nation-wide. South Korea still uses Chinese characters occasionally: North Korea eliminated Chinese characters altogether. Because the Korean alphabet is so simple and easy to learn, the rate of literacy in Korea is over 90 percent, one of the highest in the world.

The traditional Korean house is another unique element of Korean culture.[10] Korean houses differ from Japanese and Chinese ones. Except for old or primitive huts with thatched roofs that are found in remote mountain villages, most Korean houses have tile roofs. The flowing lines of the tiles on the roofs are never angular or straight, but run in graceful curves from the high ridges out to the wide sheltering eaves.

The heating system, called *ondol,* is the most distinctive characteristic of the structure of a Korean house. This heating system, which works through flues beneath the floor, was invented by the Koguryo people about

500 A.D. Every Korean house, even a newly built Western-type home, retains this heating system. The preparation of the *ondol* floor begins before the house is set up. A platform of dirt and stones is built two or three feet above ground level. The dwelling rooms of the house stand above this platform, and its smoothed and leveled top becomes the floor of the dwelling rooms. A special mortar of prepared clay (in recent times concrete) is spread over the floor, and over this a thick strong oiled paper, almost like parchment, is pasted down. This heating method is economical and ideal for the cold winters on the peninsula. In the hot summer months, only enough fire is burned under the cauldrons to keep the platform free from moisture.

The structure of the kitchen is also unique. The floor is dug several feet below ground level at one end of the platform that supports the dwelling rooms. It is always necessary, therefore, to go up several steps to pass from the kitchen to the dwelling rooms. The great iron cauldrons in which Korean food is cooked are set in masonry that extends into the kitchen from the platform on which the dwelling room stands. Fire doors are placed in the masonry below each cauldron. The flues from the kitchen fires are led as tunnels through the platform to a chimney at the opposite end of the house. Therefore, whenever meals are cooked, the fires beneath the cauldrons warm the platform floor of the dwelling rooms for the entire length of the house. Smoke passes through the tunnels below the platfrom and comes out of the chimney, which is located at the opposite end of the house.

Because Koreans remove their shoes before entering their homes, floors are kept clean and highly polished. Mats, cushions, and sometimes rugs are also used for the convenience of the family and guests. Usually guest rooms are separated from family rooms.

Clothing

Perhaps the most distinctive characteristic of traditional Korean dress is color. The apparel of both adult men and women is white, while that of children varies from blue to red to grey. White clothing has been traditional among the common Korean people throughout their long history. Special colors were used to designate court rank as early as 517 A.D. In the Silla kingdom, purple, red, and blue formed a graded hierarchy. This system was elaborated in the Koryo kingdom, and purple, red, deep red, and blue respectively represented positions of official rank. During the Yi dynasty, palace hats and embroidered insignia depicting such animals as the stork and the tiger were characteristic of high government officials. A very pale tint of blue was worn for ancestral worship, while red designated a Confucian scholar who had passed the National civil service examination.[11]

With respect to materials, animal skins were gradually replaced by woven fabrics, such as silk and cotton. For economic reasons, cotton and hemp became the dominant clothing resource among the peasants.

Men wore wide trousers, called *baji*, bound tightly at the waist and gathered at the ankles by colored bands. Jackets were short and loose and were usually fastened by a tie with a single bow. Over the jacket men wore a large, pocketed vest in winter time. They usually wore hats made of horsehair and tied their hair in topknots to indicate that they were married. Confucian scholars and high government officials wore different types of hats representing their social rank. Today, of course, no Korean wears his hair in a topknot, and many wear Western-style hats or caps. Men's shoes varied according to wealth or social position: poor people wore rubber or straw shoes with or without stockings. When men went out, they usually wore a Korean version of an overcoat, called a *durumagi.*

The traditional women's dress, like the men's, consisted of two pieces: a *choguri,* which is a short, flared blouse that fits tightly to the shoulders, and a *chima*, which is a long, high-waisted, pleated skirt that resembles a lotus leaf. It is made of anything from coarse hemp or cotton to lavish, colorful silk brocade. Sometimes the upper garment contrasts with the lower skirt, one being white and the other red or blue. In the countryside, a woman sometimes wears her hair in a braid around her head, particularly if her household duties require her to carry a load on top of her head. In the old days, Korean women wore a little cap. They also wore straw sandals or rubber shoes, which were narrow and canoe-like. Today, Western-type leather shoes with high heels are often seen in urban areas.

Children's clothing and wedding dresses were made of brilliantly colored and expensive materials. In contrast, clothing worn at the time of a funeral was simple and made of less expensive material, usually hemp. Men wore a hempen coat and completed their costume with a large wicker hat. Today, many Koreans wear Western-type clothes, especially in the cities, but resurgent nationalism has resulted in a revival of the wearing of the traditional dress, particularly among the women.[12]

Diet

Koreans have developed their own cooking methods and many unique dishes. Their daily meals, though, are simple and usually include a bowl of rice, a meat or fish soup, and a dish of *kimchi. Kimchi* is the Korean version of hot pickles. It consists of sliced napa cabbage or turnip, mixed with green onion, red pepper, salt and other ingredients. It is a fermented vegetable and is served at every meal. *Bul kogi* is barbecued beef and is sliced and charcoal-cooked over a brazier at the table. The beef is marinated in a complex mixture of soy sauce, sesame oil, green onion, sugar and other spices prior to cooking. It is a year-round dish and is considered the most popular Korean meat dish. Another favorite is called *sin sullo,* named after the cooking pot used in its preparation. It is a regal casserole of vegetables, meat, fish, and eggs that is prepared in a cooker with a charcoal chimney in the center. The food is brought to the table for final cooking and is a winter favorite.[13]

Korea does not grow tea, so people, especially peasants, drink a brew made from rice or barley. After they have cooked rice, they transfer it from the pot, leaving four or five tablespoons. This rice is browned over a flame, then boiled with added water.

Traditionally, a Korean meal is prepared in the kitchen and carried into the dining room where it is served on a low table, sometimes on individual tables. Today, one large table is more common, so that members of a family may eat together.

Music

There are two kinds of music in Korea. Court ceremonial music is solemn and dignified, and is written. Its long, elaborate melodic lines tend to evoke rich imagery. The second type is folk music, which is usually fast and lively. A traditional folk song is the farmer's song, which is basically a prayer for good harvests. There is also a traditional form of performing art, called *pansori.* The story of Chunhyang is a well-known and popular *pansori.*

A typical Korean musical instrument is the *kayageum,* invented during the Silla period. It is a twelve-string harp-type instrument played with the fingers. It is usually played by women and produces a melancholy sound.

Korean dances are expressions of wishes for good luck, fortune, and harvests. There are many kinds of dances, of which the drum dance is typical. It is performed by a woman who beats a drum that is slung across her shoulder. Today there is another type of drum dance in which a number of drums, sitting on stands in two rows, are beaten by the dancer in various tempos and rhythms.

Korean folk songs are different from those of other Asian countries. First of all, women are credited with the writing of many folk songs. The songs are an emotional outlet for them and express their feelings about being repressed by men. Another characteristic of Korean folk songs is the humor that is used to turn a sad occasion into a lighter event. Of all Korean folk songs, the best known is "Arirang," which is the name of a mountain pass. It was very popular with Korean underground patriots when the Japanese dominated Korea. Japanese authorities banned the singing of the Korean national anthem, so freedom-loving Koreans expressed their patriotism by singing "Arirang." One version of the song is as follows:

Arirang, Arirang, Ara-ri-yo	He (or she) walks over Arirang Hill
Arirang kogye-rul nomo kanda.	My lover who in deserting me
Narul porigo ksinun nimun	Shall have hurt feet ère he (or she)
Simnido Motkaso Palbyong nanda	goes even ten-ri.
Arirang, Arirang, Araryo	
Arirang kogye-rul nomo kanda.	

THE HISTORY

Korean tradition dates the founding of the Korean tribal state in the year 2333 B.C. by Tan'gun, a mythical character. Recorded history begins in 57 B.C. During the past two thousand years, the Korean people have had four native dynasties, that of the Three Kingdoms (57 B.C.-668 A.D.), the Silla (668—935), the Koryo (935—1392), and the Yi (1392—1910). Thereafter, Korea was under Japanese rule for thirty-five years (1910-1945). After the Second World War, the Korean peninsula was divided into two zones by the Allied powers. Southern Korea is now the Republic of Korea, and northern Korea is now the Democratic People's Republic.

Legendary History

According to Korean legend, the founder of the country was a spirit king of divine origin named Tan'gun. One version of the legend holds that a bear and a tiger met upon a mountain side and wished they could become human beings. They heard the voice of the Creator say, "Eat a lot of garlic and retire unto a cave and fast for twenty-one days and you shall become men."[14] They ate and sought the gloom of the cave, but the tiger, becoming restless, did not last out the ordeal. The bear, however, with greater patience waited the allotted time and changed into a woman. The master of this metamorphosis was attracted to this female, and she bore a grandson of the Creator known as Tan'gun. Tan'gun's dynasty ruled over the wild people for twelve hundred years, teaching them agriculture and the rudiments of civilization. The dynasty lasted from 2333 B.C. to 1122 B.C. Then, again according to legend, Kija, a Chinese political refugee at the time of the fall of the Shang dynasty, came to the Korean peninsula and established the kingdom of Choson, "Morning Calm." The Kija dynasty ruled for a thousant years and consisted of forty-two kings. The capital of the kingdom was Pyongyang, the present capital of the Democratic People's Republic of North Korea. Although no archeological evidence substantiates the existence of the Kija kingdom, the tomb of Kija could have been seen in Moranbong, in P'yongyang, until the 1940s. The author often visited the tomb when he attended high school.

Then there was another Chinese legendary character called Wiman, also a fugitive, who crossed the Yalu river in 193 B.C. He and his followers were given political asylum by King Kijun, the last ruler of Kija Choson. Eventually, though, Wiman managed to establish himself as the ruler in northern Korea and forced Kijun to flee to southern Korea with a few followers. Wiman's rule lasted only eighty years, until the kingdom of Koguryo was established by the native tribal chief Chu Mong in 37 B.C. Here ends the legendary history of Korea.[15]

The Three Kingdom Period (57 B.C.-668 A.D.)

The Korean peninsula was divided into three parts. The northern section was ruled by the Koguryo, the southeastern part by the Silla, and the southwestern area by the Paekche. Of the three, the Koguryo were the most powerful, extending their control over a great part of Manchuria. Buddhism was introduced into the kingdom in 327 A.D. along with other aspects of the Chinese culture, including Confucian ethics. The Koguryo ruling class, which was composed of five clans, was very warlike: these aristocrats were the most aggressive on the peninsula. The common people, the ruled, engaged in hunting and farming.

Paekche, a small communal city-state, was under constant attack from both the Koguryo and the Silla. Therefore it never became strong militarily or economically, although it possessed rich agricultural land and warm weather, and had an advanced culture. The Paekche ruling class was composed of political refugees from the Koguryo kingdom. Throughout its entire existence, Paekche never seems to have had a native ruler.

The Silla kingdom was the youngest of the three kingdoms. It was established in the village of Kyongju and gradually extended its jurisdiction over the southeast coast. Six aristocratic clans ruled the kingdom and developed indigenous political, military, and economic institutions. This was possible because of Silla's geographical isolation from the rival northern kingdom of Koguryo. In particular, the Taebaek mountains acted as a protective wall against the aggressive Koguryo. The warm climate and rich soil of Silla were suitable for the development of an agrarian economy that made the kingdom self-supporting. Silla's ruling class practiced a primitive democratic procedure in selecting its chiefs. Tradition states the conferences of the six communal chiefs were held either at a riverside or on a hilltop, and that their first order of business was to elect one chief as head of all the clans. Then they decided upon important affairs that concerned the community, such as declaring war and making peace. Of the three kingdoms, Silla was the least influenced by early Chinese civilization, although it eventually adopted Chinese political institutions and made Buddhism the state religion.

The social structure and the agrarian economic systems of the three kingdoms were similar. Two sharply distinctive social classes existed, the rulers and the common people. The rulers were non-productive but monopolized the means of production: the land, the handicraft industries, and the slaves.

The general characteristics of the primitive agrarian economic systems of the three kingdoms can be summed up as follows: all the land belonged to the king, who gave it away to his retainers and to members of the royal family. No landlord class existed; hence, no economic and social relations between landlords and tenants developed. Instead, a primitive type of collective farming under the supervision of government officials was common. One of the main economic problems was a shortage of laborers. The total population of the three kingdoms was estimated at about two million. Subtracting the old, young, and disabled, fewer than a million were active workers. The ruling class, including the members of the royal family and the warriors, was estimated at sixty thousand. Therefore, in order to solve the labor-shortage problem, the rulers demanded more from the common people and waged war against weak neighboring states to capture more workers.

During the period of the Three Kingdoms, Chinese culture was successfully assimilated into the native culture, and, in due time, Buddhism and farming methods as well as other cultural habits were transmitted to Japan. Thus the Korean peninsula began to serve as a cultural bridge.

The Unified Kingdom of Silla (668-935)

In the middle of the seventh century, constant attacks against Koguryo by the Sui emperors of China caused gradual deterioration of the primitive agrarian economy and of the people's will to fight the invaders. In addition, the ruling class of the Koguryo became divided into two factions over a controversy regarding succession to the throne.

In the meantime, a significant change took place in the Silla kingdom. The Hwarang group, one of the ruling groups of the Silla, shifted its attention from social and religious concerns to political and military ones. Religious and social ceremonies were replaced by prayers for victory in wars with neighboring kingdoms. Bravery and loyalty to the Silla kingdom became of new importance to the members of the Hwarang. They became a well-trained and devoted military group, and produced many outstanding military leaders.

In the latter part of the seventh century, the Silla formed an alliance against the Koguryo with the Paekche and later with the T'ang dynasty of China. First, the combined forces of the Silla and the T'ang invaded the southwestern part of the peninsula, conquering Paekche in 660. Then they invaded Koguryo territory simultaneously from both the north and the south. Finally, in 668, P'yongyang, the capital city of Koguryo, fell to the invaders. Thus the Koguryo kingdom came to an end. The T'ang army did not withdraw from the peninsula until 676 when Silla, in close cooperation with the remaining forces of Koguryo, drove the Chinese out.

Silla then extended its jurisdiction over the northeast and northwest, including the Taedong river area, and became the sole ruler of Korea. The unification of the peninsula by the Silla is historically important for three reasons. First of all, the native tribes in the peninsula were unified into one nationality, known as the Korean nationality. Second, the system of a kingdom as a political institution was upheld, and lasted until the Japanese annexation. And third, a unified national history, language, and culture began to develop, and the Korean people became a homogeneous society.

Buddhism became the political ideology of the ruling class and served as a state religion. It influenced the rulers' way of life and the mentality of the intellectuals. The Mahayana branch of Buddhism was popular during the Silla period, because it preached the doctrine of "blessing and happiness" for the ruling class and protection of the state. The Silla government sent many scholars to China and India to study Buddhism. The capital of Silla, Kyongju, became the center of Buddhist intellectual activity and the model of Buddhist culture on the Korean peninsula. Many temples, monastaries, pagodas, sculptures and paintings were made throughout the country by slaves and peasants under government supervision. Some of them still remain.

The Silla rulers, who included the Kim, Park, and Suk clans, reorganized the administration set up by the T'ang dynasty of China, that is, the centralization of power in the hands of the ruling class in the capital city. The territory of Silla was divided into nine provinces, each of which was subdivided into four administrative units. Thirteen administrative departments were created in the capital, including the Department of Ceremony and Construction.

According to the *Samguk-sagi* (History of the Three Kingdoms), the Silla kingdom introduced land reform by creating new land systems.[13] One of the interesting features of the new systems was the limited recognition of private ownership of land. In conformity with the land reform measures, every adult peasant was entitled to receive from the government a fixed amount of land with the right of cultivation. He could use the land for his own benefit without interference from the government until he reached the age of sixty. Then he had to return the land to the government for redistribution to other peasants. There is no record of how long this practice was continued.

Handicrafts and commerce were monopolized by the government. Textiles, silk, cotton fabrics, gold, silver, and copper were produced by slaves, who also made articles of clothing, simple weapons, and horse saddles. Under the supervision of government officials, only licensed persons were allowed to do business in the public markets. China was the principal outlet for external trade, although there was also some minor trade with Japan.

The Koryo Kingdom
A Centralized Feudal State (918-1392)

Factional strife and corruption among the ruling class, combined with revolts by the peasants—who resented their social and economic exploitation by the aristocrats—caused the gradual downfall of the Silla kingdom. One of the strongest rebel military men, Wang Kon, made a political deal with some of the ruling aristocrats and, in 918, seized power and formed the new kingdom of Koryo (from which we get the name "Korea"), with himself as king. He made his capital at Kaesong (then called Songdo), above the 38th parallel of the peninsula. By 935 Wang Kon had conquered the last king of Silla.

Buddhism continued as the state religion and as the political ideology of the aristocrats. The Buddhist scripture, called *Tripitaka Koreans,* was printed from more than eighty thousand carved wooden plates. In the meantime, Confucian teachings also became popular, and a national civil service examination based on the Confucian classics was adopted. The social structure, influenced by Confucianism, began to divide into four distinctive groups. Glazed celadon pottery became the finest art achievement in Korean history. Koryo celadon has been imitated but never matched in terms of color and craftmanship.

The political and economic structure of Koryo can be characterized as that of a centralized feudal state. Politics, economics, and military strength were all centered at the capital. Local administrative units were established to facilitate control of the people. The state-owned land system provided an economic foundation for the feudal ruling class.[17]

During the last two centuries of the Koryo period, the peninsula suffered military attacks from outside. These attacks included the invasions of the Chi-tans, or Tartars, as well as almost constant thrusts by Japanese pirates. Finally, in 1258 the entire Korean peninsula was conquered by the Mongols. The Koreans were forced to join the Mongols in their unsuccessful invasions of Japan in 1274 and 1281. Koryo kings had to marry Mongol princesses, and court life followed the pattern established by the conquerors. Koreans suffered from almost unbearable exploitation and humiliation imposed upon them by the Mongols, and national strength and resources were gradually exhausted.

Toward the end of the fourteenth century, the Mongols faced violent revolts from the Chinese. Finally, the Ming dynasty of China came to power by ousting the Mongols. In Korea, General Yi Song-ge, a pro-Ming leader, also revolted against the Mongols and founded a new dynasty, the Yi dynasty, in 1392.

In summary, the economic foundation of the Koryo kingdom was agriculture. Primitive handicrafts and commerce held subordinate positions. Buddhism was the state religion, as well as a way of life for intellectuals. In general, there were two social classes, the ruling aristocrats and the mass of the people. The political structure was that of a centralized feudal society. Because of the foreign attacks, especially the Mongol invasions, the Koryo kingdom began to decline. General Yi Song-ge set up the Yi dynasty after the Mongols were ousted from China.

The Yi Dynasty (1392-1910)

In 1392, General Yi Song-ge, later known as King T'aejo, sought from the Ming emperor of China authorization to rule the Korean peninsula. The emperor complied, confirming Yi as the king of the new government, and suggested that the country be called "Choson," which had been the name of the country when the legendary ruler, the Chinese political refugee, Kija, governed the peninsula. Yi Song-ge adopted this name. He also moved the capital from Songdo (presently Kaesong) to Hanyang (or Seoul, as it is called today), and instituted Confucianism in place of Buddhism as the creed of the new government. He modeled his administration after that of the Ming government.

The rapid change of state political ideology from Buddhism to Confucianism was implemented for the following reasons. During the Koryo period, Buddhist priests controlled a great portion of the land and thus of the national economy. They were essentially the rulers in many local areas. When Yi seized power, he needed to shift the power held by these priests to those he wanted to become the new ruling class, the Confucian aristocracy. Hence, under the guise of a new land reform act based on public ownership, Yi confiscated the property of the Buddhist temples and gave it to the Confucian aristocrats.[18]

Under the Yi Dynasty, two social groups existed: members of the royal family and the Confucian *yangban* on one hand, and the vast number of underprivileged peasants, handicraft laborers, and slaves on the other.[19] According to Confucian ethical principles, each person's social status was fixed by his occupation. The scholar was at the top, followed by the farmer, the artisan, and the merchant.

Confucianism as a state creed discouraged progress, preserved the established order, and assured power and position for the literate and educated. The concentration of power and wealth in the hands of a small elite class fostered the development of an authoritarian society. Confucian scholars justified a doctrine of inequality as follows. They said that as soon as there was a heaven and an earth, there was a distinction between that above and that below (superior and inferior). Therefore, everyone and everything should be under someone's control. Responsibility and benevolence descended from above, from heaven and the ruler. Obedience, loyalty, and filial piety came from below, from the common people. This Confucian concept was a convenient political ideology for the Yi dynasty and allowed the establishment of an absolute monarchy. The concept of a paternalistic government allowed no room for the voice of the people. The government of the Yi dynasty can be characterized as a "government of the ruler, by the ruler, and for the ruler."

The Yi dynasty was in power 518 years, from 1392 to 1910. The first two hundred years of the dynasty were relatively peaceful, and the people made brilliant cultural, technical, and military progress. Perhaps the most notable achievements were the development of the Korean phonetic alphabet called *hangul*; the invention of movable metal type for printing; the use of astronomical instruments, compasses, and cannon; and the invention of the ironclad turtle ship. However, in 1592, the first big-scale Japanese military attack, Toyotomi Hideyoshi's invasion, put an end to the prosperity of the Yi dynasty, even though Japanese forces were forced to withdraw from the peninsula following the naval victories of Admiral Yi Soon-shin. It was he who was credited with the invention of the ironclad turtle ship. In 1627 and 1636, the Manchus invaded the peninsula, and Korea suffered from both physical and mental destruction. As a result, Korea entered into a self-imposed isolation for the next two and one-half centuries, during which it was known as the "Hermit Kingdom." However, throughout this period of isolation, the Yi dynasty maintained contact with the Chinese Ching dynasty.

During the seventeenth and eighteenth centuries, there was considerable factionalism (*tang-jaeng*) within the ruling class, based on southern versus northern provincialism, and fights over the division of land developed. There was also tension between those who espoused traditional Confucianism and those who championed the "progressive" or Neo-Confucian doctrine (Chu Cha doctrine). The ultimate objective of these factional fights was, of course, the monopoly of political power by one group. For years these party struggles were a dominant factor in Korean court life. The factionalism weakened the government and hindered social and economic progress.

In the meantime, the ruling class developed a reliance upon a big power as a safeguard for independence. This idea of *sadae sasang* was another product of Confucian teachings. As previously stated, the early relationship between the Ming dynasty of China and the Yi dynasty was that of superior and inferior. Thus China treated Korea as a tributary state, although it did not interfere with internal affairs. Because of this concept of reliance upon a big power (China) to safeguard national independence, the Yi dynasty did not develop a foreign policy of its own.

Attempts by the French in 1866 and the Americans in 1871 to open the doors of the Hermit Kingdom failed, but isolation was broken when Korea was forced into a friendship and commercial treaty with Japan in 1876. This treaty was followed by another with the United States in 1882, and, within the next five years, by treaties with Russia, France, and England.

With the end of isolation, Korea became a battleground of power politics in the Far East. As its age-old social, economic, and political feudal system disintegrated, revolts took place, in 1882, 1884, and 1894. The last revolt led to a Japanese invasion, which in turn resulted in the Sino-Japanese War of 1894-95. Ten years later, Russian and Japanese interests in Korea collided, and the result was the Russo-Japanese War of 1904-05. Japan won both wars and, with the approval of the British and American governments, finally annexed Korea in 1910.[20] The Yi dynasty ceased to exist, and Korea remained under Japanese rule for the next thirty-five years.

2.

Korea in the 19th and Early 20th Centuries: A Pawn of Power Politics

GENERAL BACKGROUND

The Yi dynasty was a centralized feudal regime in the pattern of the Confucian absolute monarchy. Both land and people belonged to the king in theory, and the Confucian-trained *yangban* class (aristocrats) became powerful landlords in place of the Buddhist priests. This change was attributed to the adoption of Neo-Confucianism in place of Buddhism. All government appointments from top to bottom were made by the king from among those who passed the civil-service examinations, which were based on the Chinese classics. Thus only landlords could afford for their children the Confucian education necessary to pass the civil service examination. Once obtained, the title of *yangban* was passed on by inheritance and was lost only if the head of the family was charged with treason. The *yangban* class was divided into two groups: the central or Seoul *yangban*, and the local *yangban*. The latter group settled in central and southern provinces after having incurred royal disfavor. The Seoul *yangban* had been the privileged ruling class because they were the sole repository of Confucian learning and acted as the brain trust of the king. They enjoyed the highest social status in the country. The number of Seoul and local *yangban* was estimated at 3 percent of the total population during the Yi period.

For public identification, the *yangban* wore different garments, hats, and shoes from the rest of the population. Their residential sections were also segregated from those of the commoners. In the capital, the southern and northern sections of the city were reserved for the central *yangban* class; in the provincial cities, the inner sections of the castles were reserved for the local *yangban*. From the economic point of view, the *yangban* were parasitic: they considered manual labor inferior, and made a sharp distinction between it and mental labor. They wore long gowns and let their finger nails grow long as a sign that they did not engage in manual labor. They cultivated extreme conservatism and hindered social and economic progress.

They emphasized formalism, setting up correct ceremonies for marriage, funerals, and ancestor worship. They also preached asceticism, which involved purity of scholarship based on the idea of loyalty to the state and the avoidance of material gain. They stated that responsibility and authority should be in the hands of the superior, virtuous man, the Confucian scholar-ruler, whereas filial devotion and unconditional obedience should be the duty of the inferior, the ruled. Thus they created the authoritarian feudal society controlled by the Confucian aristocrats.

The ruled class was divided into three groups. The *chung-in* ("middle-man") included those in medicine, the arts, and mathematics, that is, the skilled professions. The *sang-min* ("commoners") were divided into various sub-groups such as farmers, merchants, artisans, and fishermen. The third group, the slaves, were also divided into two groups: public slaves who were assigned work in public offices, cleaning and doing janitorial jobs, and private slaves who worked in private homes (*yangban* families). Their status was inherited. Slaves were one of the basic productive forces of Korean feudal society.[1]

Factionalism (*tang-jaeng*) and the concept of reliance upon a big power (*sadae sasang*) were always present in the *yangban* class during the Yi dynasty.[2] The origin of the factionalism was seeded by Yi Song-ge himself. Although a northerner by birth, when he became the first king of the Yi dynasty, he appointed only southerners to important central government positions. He did so because he thought northerners were trouble-makers and rebels. This practice continued throughout the Yi dynasty. This meant that the southern *yangban* were the core of the ruling clique for more than five hundred years.

The conflict of landed interests among the *yangban* was another basis of factionalism. Often no land was available for those who passed the civil service examinations and became *yangban*. Disputes between the latecomer "have-nots" and the older, propertied *yangban* then broke out. The winners of the struggle took the property of the losers, and the losers were usually exterminated.

Another basis of factional dispute was the split between traditional Confucianism and the "progressive" Chu Cha doctrine, or Neo-Confucianism. The latter emphasized "purity" in politics and economics on the one hand, and the attainment of knowlege through reason on the other. This school was represented by the younger and more progressive elements of the local *yangban*. Traditional Confucianism was represented by the central *yangban*, who were in power. No fundamental differences in political ideologies divided these two groups, however, because both believed in Confucianism and were loyal to the king. The ultimate objective of the factionalism was the control of political power in the central government.

Korea's foreign policy during the nineteenth century was still based on the concept of reliance on a big power as a safeguard of national independence. This policy was adopted on the assumption that the big power, then China, would not interfere in Korea's domestic affairs. The relationship between the Yi dynasty and the Chinese Ching dynasty was that of a younger brother to an older one. The Korean king annually sent a good-will tributary envoy to the Chinese emperor, illustrating the nature of the relations between the two countries.

The geographical location of Korea and its history of repeated foreign invasions promoted a policy of national seclusion that isolated the peninsula from the rest of the non-Chinese world. This self-imposed policy of isolation continued until the Korean-Japanese Treaty was concluded in 1876. During the preceding decade, however, several attempts were made to break Korea's isolation. In 1866 a French squadron of seven warships and about six hundred men attacked Kanghwa Island, located about sixteen miles from the capital of Seoul. The French demanded the reason for the persecution of French missionaries who had landed in Korea a few years before. But the Korean government refused to reply, and the French forces withdrew. In 1871 a similar military expedition of five American warships, protesting the destruction of an American trading ship, the *General Sherman*, also failed to open the doors of Korea.

During the period of these Western attempts, Korea was under the rule of Daewongun, father of the reigning monarch. Daewongun became regent in 1864 because the crown prince (named Yi Hyong and later referred to as King Kojong) was only twelve years old. Daewongun soon set himself up as dictator. He was noted for his vigorous enforcement of the policy of isolation and for his persecution of Christians and the killing or driving off of foreigners who landed on Korean soil. He allowed only minimum contact with China and completely closed the door to Japan. Then he concentrated on internal political "reform." But his reform measures did not succeed, partly because his main concern was to terminate factionalism rather than to introduce a two-party system based on competing policies and political ideologies.[3] His principle of equal opportunity in public employment was feasible so long as no particular group was strong enough to overthrow the others. Daewongun's new land and tax systems did not release the common people from the heavy burden of taxation. On the contrary, he imposed more taxes and even required compulsory labor service from the peasants in order to reconstruct Kyongbok Palace, which had been destroyed by the Japanese in the 1590s.

Because of Daewongun's unrealistic attitude toward "foreign barbarians," he and the Korean people were not aware of what had been happening in neighboring countries. Japan and China had opened their doors to

Western powers and had begun to modernize their countries politically and economically, albeit under unequal treaties. But Daewongun refused even to renew relations with the new Meiji government of Japan. His attitude irritated the Meiji oligarchy and led to their support of the *seikan ron* ("conquer Korea argument") advanced by Saigo Takamori of the Satsuma faction in 1872.[4]

In 1874, when King Kojong reached the age of twenty, a new political faction emerged under the influence of Queen Min. First, the king assumed full responsibility for royal affairs and forced Daewongun into semi-retirement from politics. Then a coalition of the Min family, headed by the ambitious queen, and another group, known as the Noron faction, produced a new powerful ruling group. These new coalition leaders adopted a more conciliatory policy toward Japan and other foreign countries, including Western states.

Conclusion of the Korean-Japanese Treaty (The Treaty of Kanghwa in 1876)

Soon after the Meiji Restoration, the new Japanese government adopted a Western-type treaty policy as a means of forcing the Korean government to open Korea to Japan. In September 1875, the Japanese government dispatched a military mission to Korea and a diplomatic mission to China. The Japanese gunboat *Unyoko*, under the command of Lieutenant-General Kuroda Kiyotaka, surveyed the Korean coast. The ship was fired upon by the Koreans, and the Japanese retaliated by destroying both the bastion and the defenders of Kanghwa Island.

In the meantime, the Japanese special envoy to China opened diplomatic negotiations with Li Hung-chang, the governor-general of Chili Province and the de facto foreign minister of China. The Sino-Japanese negotiations were inconclusive at best, but the Japanese envoy did inform China that a treaty mission was already on its way to Korea, and that should it not be received in a good manner, or should its demands for friendship and commerce be refused, Japan was ready to risk a war with Korea.

The main objective of the Japanese government was, however, to obtain from the Chinese government a formal declaration of Korea's freedom to deal with non-Chinese powers. The Japanese envoy, Mori Yurei, argued that Korea was not a Chinese dependency. He pointed out that China had never levied taxes upon Korea nor interfered in its internal affairs. But Li Hung-chang, well aware of Japan's political motives, avoided any formal declaration concerning Korea's status as a sovereign state, and the conversations seemed to be at a deadlock for a few days.

Finally a compromise was reached. Japan tacitly recognized the special position of China in relation to Korea. In return, China agreed to use its influence to get a courteous reception from the Korean government for the Japanese treaty mission. As later events show, the so-called compromise was a victory for Japan, because it became the first country to secure from the Korean government a Western-type commercial treaty.

In short, three factors—Japanese determination to risk a war against Korea, Chinese "counsel", and a conciliatory attitude on the part of the Korean government under the Min family's leadership—led to the signing of the Korean-Japan Treaty, known as the Treaty of Kanghwa, on February 26, 1876, by Shin Hong of Korea and General Kuroda Kiyotaka of Japan. The treaty was comprised of twelve articles. The first provided that "Chosen (Choson, or Korea) being an independent state enjoys the same sovereign rights as does Japan." Other articles of the treaty provided for the exchange of diplomatic emissaries (article 11), the opening of two ports other than Pusan (article 4), Japan's right to survey Korean coasts without restriction (article 7), and the extraterritorial rights for Japanese citizens in Korea (article 10).[5]

The treaty was interpreted in different ways. One Western observer, J. H. Longford, stated that the treaty not only brought Korea's isolationist policy to an end, but also "terminated forever, theoretically at least, its dependence on China." In contrast, China felt no change had occurred. The traditional Confucian relationship between countries was maintained with Korea continuing to report to the Peking government all events in its external relations, including those with Japan. The Japanese government, however, made every effort to have the treaty with Korea appear to be a treaty between equals. The Japanese wanted Korea to appear independent of China so that they could remain in Korea without further approval from the Chinese government.

As expected, the Treaty of Kanghwa brought many political and economic consequences for Korea. The self-imposed two-hundred-and-fifty-year isolation came to an end. Similar unbalanced commercial treaties were concluded thereafter with Western countries. This meant, among other things, that the feudalistic native economic structure began to collapse under the influence of Japanese and Western imperialism. By the end of 1881, a permanent Japanese diplomatic mission was established in Seoul, and detailed agreements about trade and commerce were signed.

The volume of trade with Japan increased rapidly, with Japanese merchants obtaining the right to use both Japanese and Korean currency for their trade in Korea. Many Japanese businessmen engaged in moneylending and in running pawn shops. Some of them later became absentee landlords. Japanese merchants formed monopolistic import-export businesses, im-

porting Japanese goods into Korea and exporting Korean agricultural products—especially rice and raw materials—to Japan. During this period, no
native merchant class existed to compete with the Japanese.

In 1881 the Korean government sent a ten-man study group, headed by
Kim Ok-kyun, to Japan to study various aspects of the modernizing
Japanese society. All the group's members came from *yangban* families and,
as we will see later, most of them became leaders of a progressive or independent party. They advocated the modernization of Korea by means of
economic, military, and political reforms similar to those adopted by the
Japanese. However, a reaction against such reform movements by the Confucian conservatives, led by the Daewongun faction, became strong. The
conservatives denounced the reform programs as "the wicked learnings"
from abroad.

In China, Li Hung-chang began to worry about the steady growth of
Japanese influence in Korea since the Kanghwa treaty. He now realized that
Japan could become a major threat to Korea and eventually to China. He
felt Korea should build its own military power at once, and should conclude
treaties of friendship and commerce with Western powers as a means of
checking Japanese influence. Li also believed that of the Western countries,
the United States was the first and best choice as Korea's treaty partner because it had no territorial desires in Korea and could therefore be trusted.[6]

The Japanese government began to take strong measures to end
Chinese influence in Korea. Two internal revolts took place in Korea. In
1882 Korean veterans revolted against a Japanese military reorganization
program as well as against the pro-Japanese native cabinet ministers. This
revolt, which was called *Imo-gunran*, was suppressed with the aid of Chinese
soldiers. Thereafter, five thousand Chinese remained in Seoul. This was a
victory for the Chinese and the pro-Chinese native government. In 1884
another political coup, *Kapshin Chongpyon*, occurred. It was led by the
Japanese-oriented progressive group, who were impressed by the rapid
modernization of Japan after the Meiji Restoration. Kim Ok-kyun, Park
Young-ho, and So Chae-p'il (Philip Jaisohn) organized a party in opposition
to the pro-Chinese conservatives in power. With the aid of the Japanese legation in Seoul, they seized power through a coup d'etat and formed a pro-
Japanese government. But it lasted only three days, because the Chinese
soldiers and the native armed forces took the side of the conservatives. The
defeated progressive leaders either went into political exile or were killed.
The Japanese minister in Seoul was recalled.

The Japanese government sent a new envoy, Count Inoue Kaoru, with
two army divisions to demand a new treaty. In this treaty the Korean
government agreed to pay an indemnity, made land grants for the construction of Japanese army barracks around the Japanese consulate, and offered

an apology to the Japanese emperor. Nevertheless, Japanese leaders felt that they were not strong enough to make war against China. So they attempted a workable compromise. Japan sent a special envoy with Ito Hirobumi to Peking to negotiate with the Chinese government about the Korean issue. The main objective of the Japanese was still to secure recognition of Korea's independence from China.

In 1885, Ito and Li Hung-chang signed a treaty known as the Treaty of Tientsin. Some of its main points were: (1) Chinese forces and the Japanese legation guard were to be withdrawn from Korea; (2) the Korean government was to organize a Korean army in which neither Chinese nor Japanese were to be employed; and (3) in case disturbances or revolts in Korea made it necessary for China or Japan to send troops to the peninsula, the country sending them was to notify the other beforehand and document in writing its intention to do so, and the troops were to be recalled when the matter was settled.

THE SINO-JAPANESE WAR OF 1894-1895

After the signing of the Tientsin treaty between Japan and China in 1885, Li Hun-chang sent Yuan Shi-kai, the future president of the Chinese republic, to Seoul with the title of resident of Korea. Yuan took charge of Korea's diplomatic and commercial affairs during the decade of Chinese dominance between 1885 and 1894. Korean foreign policy had to be approved by Yuan before the Korean government took action. The Korean customs service was integrated with that of China by the appointment of Henry F. Merrill as inspector general of Korean customs, as recommended by Yuan. Chinese troops were stationed in Seoul to guard the Chinese legation and the Korean palace. Thus, the Chinese resident became the de facto ruler of the Korean peninsula.

Chinese economic penetration was also impressive. In 1885 the Chinese government constructed Korea's first telegraph line, linking Inchon with Seoul, and a Chinese official was appointed to supervise its operation. The Japanese wanted a Seoul-Pusan line, which was also finally constructed by Korea with a loan obtained from the Chinese Merchant Marine Company. In order to modernize Korea, the Korean government had to borrow great sums of money from foreign countries. The king and his close advisers solicited foreign loans on their own without going through regular government channels. By the middle of 1889, Korea's indebtedness was estimated at 1.3 to 1.5 million yen. The principal creditors were China, America, Germany, and Japan.[7] The Korean government needed still more money to maintain its operations, but no foreign country was willing to lend, partly because the Chinese government blocked loans out of its own political interests, and partly because of the unstable conditions within Korea caused by economic hardship and social unrest. However, in 1892, when the national treasury was almost empty, the Korean government finally obtained a loan of 200,000 taels from China.

Chinese trade with Korea increased from 19 percent of the total in 1885 to 45 percent in 1892, while Japanese trade during the same period declined from 81 percent to 55 percent.[8] If this trend had been allowed to continue, China's trade would soon have surpassed Japan's. Japan accordingly prepared to act to end China's supremacy in Korea at the first opportunity. The Japanese minister in Seoul, Oishi Masami, delivered what amounted to an ultimatum to the Korean government requesting a reply within fourteen days regarding the bean-export controversy, which had started in 1883. Briefly, the bean-export controversy was as follows. Japanese merchants had bought grain from Korean peasants before the harvest at a very high interest rate. When autumn came, the peasants resented their Japanese creditors for having charged such high interest rates, and some peasants refused to pay. In 1889, the governor of the northern province of Hamkyong issued an embargo decree, which technically violated the trade agreement. The Japanese government demanded damages. The United States offered to help arbitrate the matter, but it was settled mainly through Chinese mediation, with the Korean government paying 50,000 yen to the Japanese merchants as compensation.

There were two other similar incidents, one involving a dispute over fishing rights off the coast of Korea in 1888, and the other, a rice-export trade incident with China in the fall in 1893. Both cases could be considered power contests between China and Japan over Korean affairs. The fishing rights dispute was never resolved, but the rice trade contest was won by the Chinese government. The Korean government agreed not to remove the prohibition against exporting rice to Japan.

To sum up, from 1885 to 1894, China succeeded in converting the Korean peninsula into a semi-protectorate under the rule of Resident Yuan Shi-Kai with the cooperation of the native pro-Chinese Min family. Japan lost much of its influence but was ready to challenge Chinese supremacy by force if necessary.

Two dramatic events took place on the eve of the Sino-Japanese War. One was the murder of progressive leader Kim Ok-Kyun in Shanghai on March 28, 1894, by a pro-Chinese Korean youth. The other was the revolt of the Tonghaks, a semi-religious nationalist group opposed to all foreign interference, which developed in the wake of large-scale peasant uprisings in southern Korea.

The assassination of Kim Ok-kyun and the subsequent attempt on Park Yong-ho's life, inspired by the Li Hung-chang clique, had the effect of clarifying for Korea the extent of the growing popular feeling in Japan that that nation's "weak" foreign policy should be amended. Japanese liberals, under the leadership of Fujizawa Yukichi, and the liberal press condemned the Chinese and Korean governments for welcoming Kim's death on the one hand, and urging the Japanese government (which had forced Kim to leave Japan) to take strong action against China on the other. As soon as the news of Kim's assassination reached Japan, Oi Kentaro, Inoue Kakugoro, and others organized the Society of the Friends of Kim Ok-kyun, and launched a fund drive. They hoped that Kim's body could be brought to Japan for funeral services to be held at a mass meeting in Tokyo. This plan never materialized, however, because of the negative attitude of the Japanese government. In the meantime, a Japanese reactionary group, *Genyosha* (Black Ocean Society), joined the protest but for a different reason. *Genyosha* members proclaimed the "imperial honor offended" and urged whatever action was necessary to restore Japanese prestige in Korea. Under these circumstances, the Japanese ruling oligarchy, who had been cautious about military action before, now felt that they had the necessary support for war from the Japanese people from extreme reactionaries to left liberals. No individual or group in Japan seemed likely to oppose future strong action in Korea. Some Japanese authorities, like Aoki Shuzo (foreign minister in 1890), even stated that "Korea should be made a part of the Japanese map."[9] Finally, the Japanese Army General Staff, led by Generals Yamagata Aritomo and Kawakami Soroku, made the ultimate decision to take military action by proposing to the Japanese cabinet that it send troops to Korea.

When the Tonghak revolution broke out in June 1894, the Korean government requested China's assistance. The Chinese government promptly complied, dispatching fifteen hundred troops from Tientsin, with seven hundred more to follow. In conformity with the Tientsin treaty, the Chinese government notified the Japanese government of its actions, taken at the request of the Korean king, and assured Japan that "these troops shall be withdrawn at once, upon the cessation of hostilities." The first troops landed at Asan, about eighty miles south of Seoul, on June 8, 1894. But the first phase of the Tonghak rebellion ended before the Chinese forces were ready to move out to rebel territory.

The Japanese government immediately replied that it was likewise sending troops to protect the Japanese legation and Japanese residents in Korea. Japan sent six times as many soldiers as China had sent. Alarmed by the presence of the two rival foreign armies, the Korean government announced the recovery of the rebel-held provincial territories and demanded the withdrawal of all foreign troops. Li Hung-chang, concerned by Japan's aggressive move, notified the Japanese government of China's willingness to recall its troops from Korea. Ignoring Li's notification, the Japanese government sent additional troops to Korea in the last days of June. This was a definite sign of Japan's determination to risk war with China. The Korean king again begged the Chinese and Japanese governments to leave Korea since there was no further danger of revolt.

Unexpectedly, the Japanese government asked the Chinese government for cooperation in introducing "reforms" in the Korean government. The Chinese rejected this proposal, saying that "even China, whose vassal Korea has always been, would not interfere in the internal affairs of the kingdom. Japan, having from the beginning recognized Korea as an independent state, cannot claim any right to interfere."[10]

The Japanese government disregarded the Chinese objection and concentrated on the establishment of a pro-Japanese Korean government under the pretext of reforms. On June 26, the Japanese minister in Seoul, Otori, held a conference with the Korean king and presented the following memorandum. Japan found it necessary, for the mutual welfare of the two countries, to ask that certain radical changes be made in the government and policy of Korea, in consultation with the Japanese authorities. Until these changes were made in a manner satisfactory to Japan, Japanese troops would not be withdrawn. Two days later, Otori demanded an answer within twenty-four days to the question of "whether or not Korea was a tributary of China." To this the Korean government replied by quoting the first article of the Kanghwa Treaty of 1876: "Korea, being an independent state, enjoys the same sovereign right as Japan." The reply also contained a quotation from the Korean king's letter to the president of the United States stating that in both internal administration and foreign intercourse, Korea enjoyed complete independence.

On July 4, Otori presented an ultimatum to the Korean government, demanding that Korea, an independent state, should order the Chinese troops to leave the peninsula at once, and that the unequal Sino-Korean treaty be abolished. Without even waiting for a reply from the Korean government, Japanese troops in Seoul attacked the royal palace and seized the king. A virtual Japanese prisoner, the king thereupon organized a Japanese-dominated Korean government, excluding members of Queen Min's family. Kim Hong-jip became prime minister. Park Yong-ho, one of the chief conspirators of the 1884 coup who had escaped to Japan, was invited back and appointed minister of home affairs. And Cho Pyong-jik became minister of foreign affairs.

On July 24, the new Korean government issued a decree denouncing the treaties with China and asking Japan's aid in driving Chinese troops from Korea. On the following day a temporary agreement between Korea and Japan was signed. Some of the main points were: that the Korean government would accept the Japanese reforms, that the Japanese government would build a railroad from Pusan to Seoul, and that more commercial ports would be opened to the Japanese. In return, Japan agreed to render assistance toward the complete restoration of Korea's national independence. On July 26, a treaty of military alliance was signed with Japan which provided that the Korean government give every facility for the movement of Japanese troops as soon as Japan started war against China. Japan promised "to maintain the independence of Korea on a firm footing."[11]

The war actually started when, on July 25, the Japanese sunk the British steamer *Kowshing*, which was transporting Chinese troops. An official declaration of war was proclaimed on August 1 by both the Chinese and Japanese governments. The war lasted from August 1894 to April 1895 and ended in the defeat of China. The peace treaty was signed at Shimonoseki on April 17, 1895. China recognized the "full and complete independence" of Korea and agreed that "the payment of tribute and the performance of ceremonies and formalities by Korea to China, in derogation of such independence and autonomy, shall cease." China also agreed to pay an indemnity to cede Taiwan (Formosa) and the Liaotung Peninsula to Japan. Thus the age-old Confucian relationship—Korea's tributary status with China—was ended and the national independence of Korea was guaranteed by the Japanese government.[12]

On August 20, 1895, the Japanese government asked Korea to sign what was called a provisional agreement. Among other things, it obligated Korea to accept Japanese advice on Korea's internal reforms. The task of advising the Korean government was entrusted to Count Inoue Kaoru, who had been one of the powerful members of the Japanese Meiji oligarchy. But the Japanese victory over China did not bring about all the changes Japan wanted. The Min influence on the Korean court was not removed by any means, while the diplomatic intervention of Germany, Russia, and France forced Japan to give up the Liaotung Peninsula. The latter event caused considerable controversy among the Japanese ruling factions and reduced Japan's prestige in international politics. Faced with such an unfavorable international development, the Japanese government also retreated from a strong policy in Korea by giving up the projected internal reform measures. The Japanese minister in Seoul, Inoue, was recalled. He admitted the failure of the Korean reform policy and offered three main reasons: Japan's selfishness in looking after Japanese national interests only; disunity within the Korean cabinet; and the unexpected intervention of Germany, Russia, and France.

AMERICA'S ATTITUDE ON THE KOREAN ISSUE

The first task of the American minister in Seoul was to prevent the war, or, failing that, to put an end to it as soon as possible. The American, Russian, French, and British representatives in Seoul asked the Japanese and Chinese governments to withdraw their troops from Korea simultaneously. But the effort failed. Dr. Horace N. Allen and the American minister, John M. Sill, wanted to help Korea but received no encouragement from Washington. Richard O. Gresham, then the secretary of state, instructed his minister in Seoul "to use every possible effort in the cause of peace, and ask Japan to move with moderation." However, the American government at the time believed that a Sino-Japanese war would not endanger its policy in Asia.[13]

As soon as the joint effort of the four powers (Russia, America, Britain, and France) failed, the American minister, Sill, "did not conceal his feeling that the Japanese should be supported in their policy." According to Sill, "Japan seems only to desire, once and for all, to throw off the yoke of Chinese suzerainty and then to assist her small neighbor in strengthening her position as an independent state, by aiding her in such reforms as shall bring peace, prosperity and enlightenment to people—a motive which pleases many Korean officials of the more intelligent sort, and which, I imagine, will not meet with disapproval in America."[14]

That was in September of 1894. About two months later, Minister Sill observed that "the Japanese-introduced reforms had little effect outside of Seoul, where magistrates disregarded the orders of the king, saying he was a helpless prisoner of the Japanese minister." Early in December, Sill reported that the new Japanese minister in Seoul, Inoue, "was disappointed that Park Yong-ho, the Japanese entrusted cabinet member, was still listening to the queen's group (pro-Chinese) and had done nothing to secure the confidence of the king."[15] Sill expressed his views on the new Korean government as follows: Park Chung-yang (minister of education) and Yi Wan-yong (vice-minister of foreign affairs) were representatives of a pro-American party. Park Yong-ho and So Kwang-pum were pro-Japanese. Only the vice minister of internal or home affairs was pro-Chinese.

On March 1, 1895, Sill reported on Inoue's difficulties in Seoul as follows: "Political deadlock in the cabinet took place: Park Yong-ho was the chief villian. He has been raised up to the position of minister of internal affairs by the Japanese, but the queen, who is very clever, has made him 'quite her tool.' He was refusing to accede in order to obtain great concessions for railways proposed by Count Inoue. The anti-Japanese hated him. Now the Japanese might desert him. The Daewongun party was plotting and becoming stronger. The king was insisting confidentially that Russia come to his assistance."[16]

On April 3, Sill made another report: The Korean government needed a Japanese loan of three million yen in silver, but "the Japanese gave them 1.5

million yen in silver." The Japanese government demanded concessions in return for loans: "railroads for fifty years, telegraphs for twenty-five years, postal services for five years." But Park Yong-ho, the home minister, was giving the Japanese trouble. He had now emerged as a "virtual ruler of Korea" and seemed to "have a sincere regard for his own country" and to "resent Japan's attempt to take everything for herself."[17]

Sill joined with the representatives of other Western nations in Seoul in sending a strong note to the Korean government aimed against the attempts of the Japanese to obtain economic concessions in Korea. But Sill placed primary responsibility for Korea's difficulties on Korean government officials. He believed that there would have been no Tonghak rebellion against the government in the countryside, and hence no Sino-Japanese War, had the Korean government been willing to initiate the needed reforms.

Allen did not despair about the Korean government. He believed efficiency and patriotism could be developed, and that Korea could become an independent country. Yet he also knew that the "Koreans were so oppressed, officially, that they don't care who rules them as they think their conditions could be no worse."[18] He met men who would not work because they knew the squeeze was getting worse and the magistrates would take all they earned.

RUSSO-JAPANESE RIVALRY, 1895-1904

After the Sino-Japanese War, a coalition cabinet of the queen's faction and a newly emerging pro-Russian group was formed under the leadership of Kim Hong-jip as prime minister. A cordial relationship developed between the two groups, and the pro-Japanese prime minister had no power in the court. After Japan was forced to renounce possession of the Liaotung Peninsula by Russia, France, and Germany on the grounds that Japanese possession of it "would be a perpetual obstacle to the peace of the Far East," the Korean government began preparations for disbanding a Japanese-trained Korean infantry regiment in the capital. The Korean coalition government believed that Japan was too weak to challenge Russia's aggressive policies in Manchuria and Korea, and the Korean court became "pro-Russian."

Japan recalled Inoue and replaced him as minister in Seoul with Lieutenant-General Miura Goro. Miura was a professional soldier with no diplomatic experience. He thought he had to act swiftly to remedy the Korean situation, even without consent from his own government. Miura immediately consulted Sugimura Fukashi, who had been the Japanese legation secretary for seven years, and Okamoto Ryunosuke, Japanese advisor to the Korean war and household ministers. The three agreed that the

Korean queen should be killed because of her anti-Japanese stand and her overwhelming influence in the court. They also thought that Daewongun could be a useful but very slippery ally. In order to hold him, the Japanese insisted that he sign a statement promising the Japanese special privileges if he secured control of the government.

At the instigation of Miura, Japanese civilians prepared to enter the palace to dispatch the queen. The *kunrentai*, the Japanese-trained soldiers of the Korean army, fell into line because of their dissatisfaction with the treatment accorded them by the court. Finally, success was assured when the Japanese troops stationed in Seoul offered their support.

The threatened disbandment of the *kunrentai* furnished an excellent opportunity to strike. The Japanese moved on the palace in the early morning hours of October 8, 1895, two days earlier than planned. Japanese troops escorted Daewongun from his country residence into Seoul. Simultaneously, the *kunrentai*, the *soshi* (adventuresome Japanese civilian extremists), and Japanese soldiers advanced on their prey. Miura stayed at his legation to avoid the appearance of participation, but was ready to enter his sedan chair if the situation demanded his presence. The Korean palace guards were overcome and the palace was entered. The queen was murdered and her body burned. Shortly before daybreak, Miura and Sugimura went to the palace and "feigning innocence, ordered the withdrawal of the invaders."[19]

Within a few days the king was coerced into appointing pro-Japanese leaders to key government positions and issuing a decree that demoted the late queen to commoner status. At this time, no mention of her death was made to the public. The king became a prisoner in his own palace and lived in daily fear of his life.

The Japanese government received its first news of this incident from its legation in Seoul. Acting Foreign Minister Saionji Kimmochi inquired about the incident, but Miura denied any Japanese involvement in the murder of the queen. He stated that the incident was a clash between Korean soldiers and the palace guards, and that the Japanese army unit had become involved only in order to guard the palace and to "calm things down." However, all the evidence was against his explanation, and he finally conceded that Japanese troops had aided the rebellious Korean soldiers and that some of the *soshi* invaders had, in fact, taken an active part in the incident. On October 17, the Japanese government recalled Miura to face trial. Komura Juntaro was appointed to succeed him, and Inoue Kaoru was sent to Seoul as a special envoy to settle the sensitive Korean issue.

This incident touched off popular resentment in Korea against the Japanese. Working on this sentiment, anti-Japanese leaders planned a counter-revolution. The plan was to take back the palace on November 28,

1895. Allen knew of the plan for this anti-Japanese coup and opposed it. His main concern was for the safety of the king. With Sill's tacit consent, Allen asked some missionary friends to stay close to the Korean king during the counter-revolutionary coup. So Mr. Underwood, Mr. Avison, and Mr. Hulbert, with revolvers in their pockets, went to the palace and obtained admission by the use of a card from the American legation.

The anti-Japanese coup failed completely because of the stiff resistance of the newly trained palace guards. But the leaders of the unsuccessful attempt did not give up their project. They awaited another opportunity. The anti-Japanese leaders drew their strength primarily from the Korean people. The Koreans deeply resented the news of the queen's murder by the Japanese. They were also angered to hear that although a Japanese court found Miura and his aides guilty of plotting against the queen, it freed them on a technicality.

Another distressing incident involved the outlawing by the Japanese of the Korean topknot, which was declared to stand in the way of activity and health. Koreans prized the topknot as a symbol of Korean manhood. The cutting of their hair went against the principle of filial piety. Outlawing this age-old social custom meant national humiliation. The general feeling against the Japanese-ordered social reform was expressed by the action of one father who committed suicide when his two sons accepted the hair-cutting law. Soon after this incident, provincial officials began ignoring the orders of the central government. Instead of going to work, farmers stayed home in protest against the decree. The price of rice in Seoul jumped. General social unrest was common in the rural areas, and another Tonghak-type of mass revolution was imminent.

The native anti-Japanese leaders, including the king, as well as some of the foreign envoys, especially Allen and the Russian minister, Waeber, were aware of the anti-Japanese feelings throughout the country. The first thing they wanted to do was to rescue the king from his palace prison, thus enabling him to defy Japanese authority.

The king's escape from his palace happened as follows. On February 9, 1896, the guard at the Russian legation was increased by more than one hundred and fifty soldiers. The following day, the king asked Allen if it would be wise to seek the aid of Russia. This was, of course, just what the American legation secretary was waiting for. Allen endorsed the king's suggestion and personally assisted in perfecting the plans. That night Allen took the Russian minister to the house of a Korean officer entrusted with the plans. "There he left the two, conferring; and the next morning His Majesty fled from his palace to take refuge in the Russian legation."[20]

The escape had been carefully planned. The palace women had been going in and out of the palace for weeks. At first the guards challenged each one and searched them, but that grew tiresome. The women seemed quite harmless, and they were friendly, too. They brought hot dishes to the guards on chilly mornings, and such treatment had its effect. The better known females were soon allowed to pass through the gates at will. On the morning of February 11, 1896, a palace woman left the grounds, and with her went the king, dressed as a coolie, and the crown prince, clad in woman's clothing. Once outside the walls, the royal fugitives dashed to the Russian legation not far away, and there they stayed for a full year.

This meant that Russia, not Japan, was giving orders to the Korean king about how to govern the Korean people. Russia was on top and Japan was out. The Japanese, in driving out the Chinese, had found another and stronger foe. Soon after, the Korean king "sent an envoy to St. Petersburg to file a request for the formal protection of the Tsar."

THE RUSSO-JAPANESE WAR OF 1904
AND THE AMERICAN ATTITUDE

During the period of Russian influence from 1896 to 1898, the Japanese government could do little in Korea. It therefore limited itself to preserving its economic interests in the peninsula by means of direct agreements with the Russian government. Russia's interest in Korea was well expressed by Tsar Nicholas II: "Russia absolutely needs a port free and open throughout the whole year. . . This port must be located on the mainland (in the southeast of Korea) and certainly, connected with our possessions by a strip of land." The Russian envoy to China also said: "Japan undoubtedly is an undesirable neighbor for us on the mainland."[21] Therefore the job of the Russian minister in Seoul was to get an ice-free port and head off Japan before it could dominate the peninsula.

While the Korean king was still in the Russian legation, the first Russo-Japanese agreement was reached. It was known as the Waeber-Komura memorandum of May 14, 1896.[22] In this agreement, the two governments pledged to leave the matter of the Korean king's stay in the Russian legation to his own discretion, but said they would recommend the king's departure when there were no further doubts about his safety. To insure such safety, the Japanese government promised to control those subjects who were known to favor violent action. The Japanese government also agreed to recognize the new Korean cabinet as the legitimate government organized by the king of his own free will (in fact all its members were recommended by the American envoy, Allen). The number of troops as well as the number and location of Japanese telegraph guards in Korea were limited. This agreement constituted a Russian victory over the Japanese.

The second agreement was the Yamagata-Lobanov Treaty of June 9, 1896. Under this contract, Russia and Japan pledged to respect each other's position and rights and agreed that only "by mutual accord" would the governments lend money to Korea. They also agreed to permit the creation and maintenance of an armed force and a native police sufficient to maintain internal order without foreign aid.

Under the Yamagata-Lobanov Treaty the Japanese government recovered somewhat from its loss of influence in Korea.[23] This treaty, however, became the cause of controversy between the two powers. The Japanese government argued that a subsequent loan from Russia and the dispatch of Russian military personnel to Korea were not in conformity with the agreement. The Russian government, however, declared that a Russian agreement with Korea to furnish financial and military aid had been signed before the Yamagata-Lobanov Treaty.

A secret agreement between the tsar and the Korean government was signed when the Korean envoy, Min Yong-whan, attended the coronation ceremony. Among other things, the agreement provided Russian protection for the Korean king. A more important provision called for Russia's supplying of military and other assistance to Korea in case of serious internal disturbance or the violation of Korean independence by a foreign power. In the summer of 1896, the Russian government sent to Korea two representatives of the newly created Russo-Chinese Bank, together with a small group of Russian military personnel. The Japanese government viewed Russia's actions as contrary to the Yamagata-Lobanov Treaty.

Fortunately for the Japanese, an incident involving the Russian representative in Korea occurred in 1897. This became known as the Masan incident. Russia demanded a coaling station at Masan, near the port of Pusan. The real objective of the Russian government in the area was a military one. By securing Masan, Russia's naval defense line could be extended from Vladivostok to Pusan and from Pusan to Port Arthur. Thus the Russians could easily block or restrict Japanese sea power.

While the Masan lease was being secretly discussed by Russia and Korea, a Japanese private citizen, Hakuma Fusataro, purchased some of the Russian-claimed lease land and turned it over to the Japanese army. The new Russian envoy, de Speyer, was now determined to legalize the lease agreement, and he pressed the Korean government for formal approval. The Korean foreign minister presented the lease agreement to the cabinet. But the cabinet refused to approve it. The Russian government then threatened to withdraw its financial and military aid. This threat led to vigorous protests from many Korean officials as well as from the Korean people. The Independence Club, under the leadership of Dr. So Chae-p'il, was especially opposed to any foreign intervention or foreign concession. The members of the Club were the nation's leading reformers and intellectual nationalists. They advocated absolute national independence without foreign control. They promptly staged anti-Russian demonstrations in major Korean cities.[24]

It should be pointed out here that the personal relationship between the new Russian envoy, de Speyer, and the American minister, Allen, was not cordial. Allen, who had just been promoted to the position of minister, called Karl L. Waeber, the previous Russian envoy, a "very able and courteous representative who suits us all right." But he thought that de Speyer was "an impudent person, a most arrogant and boisterous man, and a bitter enemy of the United States." When Allen was sworn in as minister, he pledged to be "absolutely neutral . . . . to say or do nothing that can in any way be construed as taking sides with or against any of the interested parties." But de Speyer was an ardent expansionist, one who wanted Korea linked with Russia. He told the Korean king to "take Russian advice upon all matters and advise only with Russia. Russia will see that he is not troubled, and that he will have ample funds for his enjoyment."[25]

The Russian minister allowed the Korean king to take the title of emperor in October, 1897. The Russian envoy then announced that "no Korean entertaining friendly sensations for America shall have a place in the government." This meant that American advisors would lose their power in the Korean court. Then de Speyer attacked the new native political force, the Independence Club, as being pro-American. Offended by the actions of the Russian envoy, Allen told him that the Russians "have received more sympathy and support from Americans in Korea than you are aware of." The Russian envoy shot back by saying: "Oh yes . . . . When the Japanese controlled everything, they were very willing to come to us to get their Korean friends out of trouble, but lately, no." Then he attacked So Chae-p'il as the head of the pro-American party, who was always crying for independence. "I shall force the Independence Club out of Korea, they shall cease to exist." Allen replied: "It seems to me you are taking a great deal upon yourself, especially since this idea of independence was born in your legation and nurtured by your predecessors." The Russian envoy retorted: "I do not approve of Mr. Waeber. I like not many things he has done. You will find me a true Russian. Mr. Waeber is not."[26]

Such an arrogant attitude, combined with the threat of financial and military controls over Korea, produced nothing but anti-Russian feelings among Koreans and personal dislike between the Russian and American representatives in Seoul. So the Korean government accepted the withdrawal of Russian financial and military aid. Thus the Russian envoy fell into his own trap. Russian influence in Seoul, which had been skillfully and patiently cultivated by Waeber, was destroyed overnight.

The Japanese government was quick to take advantage of the Russian diplomatic setback and proposed the Nishi-Rosen Treaty on April 25, 1898. Under it the Russian and Japanese governments agreed to recognize "the sovereignty and independence of Korea" and "to take no measure in respect to the appointment of military instructors or financial advisors, without arriving beforehand at a mutual agreement on the matter." The Japanese government secured Russian recognition of its interest in the "development of the commercial, industrial, and financial relationship between Japan and Korea." Finally, the Russians pledged themselves "to refrain from direct interference in the internal affairs of Korea." The Russian government's formal acknowledgment of Japan's economic interests in Korea left the Japanese a monopoly of the Korean economy.

After 1898 the Japanese concentrated on three areas of economy. The financial area was the first. The Japanese established a bank with branches in major Korean cities and industrial districts. These banks obtained the right to purchase gold and silver, to lend money to the Korean government, and to issue bank notes. And under a new currency agreement between Korea and Japan, the Korean monetary system was integrated into the Japanese system.

Second, the Japanese undertook the construction of modern communication and transportation systems. The right to build a Chemulpo (Inchon)-Seoul railroad, which had originally been granted to an American company, was sold to the Japanese following the withdrawal of American capital. A Pusan-Seoul line was also completed by the Japanese, and a Seoul-Shinuiju line was finished by the Japanese army engineer corps (it had been granted originally to a French company). Thus, three important railroad lines connecting Manchuria and Korea were under Japanese control.

Third, the Japanese concentrated on Korea's import and export businesses. Between 1892 and 1905, Korean imports from Japan increased from 50.2 percent to 73.7 percent, while those from China and Russia decreased from 49.8 percent to 18.9 percent. During the same period, however, Korean exports to Japan decreased from 90.9 percent to 78.8 percent, and those to Russia, from 1.2 percent to 0.2 percent.[27]

Both the Japanese and Russian governments began to violate their treaty agreements. The Japanese government demanded reforms from the Korean government, and sent Japanese military and civilian advisors to Korea. The Russian government attempted to obtain a new economic concession. In 1902, the Korean king agreed that no more mining concessions would be granted to any foreigners except Russians. In return, the Russian government promised to furnish capital for the construction of railroads by Koreans. In addition, the Russian government notified the Korean government of its intention to exercise its option of cutting timber in the Yalu Valley. It later sent "frontier guards" to the area.

The Japanese viewed this Russian move into northern Korean territory as an indication that the Russians had no intention of leaving Korea to Japan. Hence, Japan began to strengthen its military forces. It also moved to strengthen its diplomatic defenses by signing the Anglo-Japanese Alliance of 1902, in which Great Britian recognized Japan's political and economic interests in Korea. In response, the Russian government declared that the Russo-French Alliance of 1895 would be extended to the Far East.

The Japanese minister at St. Petersburg expressed his government's concern over the Russian advance in the Korean peninsula as follows: "Russia, stationed on the flank of Korea, would be a constant menace to the separate existence of that empire, and in any event it would make Russia the dominant power in Korea. Korea is an important outpost in Japan's line of defense, and the Japanese consequently consider the independence of Korea absolutely essential to her own repose and safety. Japan possesses paramount political as well as economic and industrial interests and influence in Korea which, having regard to her own security, she cannot consent to surrender to, or share with, any other power."[28]

Political deals, based on the Korea-Manchuria trading formula (Russia's freedom of action in Manchuria in exchange for Japan's freedom of action in Korea), continued for six months between the representatives of the two countries. Finally, the Russian government rejected the Japanese offer, negotiations broke down, and a war started.

The Korean government announced Korea's neutrality on January 21, 1904,[29] but it was too weak to avoid involvement in the war. The Japanese government severed diplomatic relations with Russia on February 6, 1904, and two days later, Japanese forces attacked Port Arthur. The next day Russian ships in the Korean port of Inchon were attacked by the Japanese navy. On February 10, the Japanese government formally declared war. Ignoring the Korean declaration of neutrality, Japanese troops soon occupied the Korean peninsula. After two weeks of resistance, the Korean government was compelled to sign a treaty of alliance with Japan in which the Japanese government obtained the right to use Korean territory as a base for military operations. In return, the Japanese government again "guaranteed the independence and territorial integrity of Korea." The Korean government also agreed to accept Japanese advisors and reform proposals in the reorganization of the administration.

The Russo-Japanese War ended officially on September 5, 1905, with the signing of the Treaty of Portsmouth, negotiated through the mediation of the American president, Theodore Roosevelt. The defeated Russian government acknowledged Japan's paramount interests in Korea. As we will see later, even before the war was over, Great Britian and the United States had approved Japan's domination of Korea as a means of checking Russian expansion in East Asia. Thus, once again, Korea became a victim of international power politics.

3.

The Korean-American Treaty

THE FIRST TREATY WITH THE WEST IN 1882

The signing of the Korean-American Treaty of 1882, also known as the Treaty of Chemulpo (Inchon), was initiated and directed by Li Hung-chang and Commodore Robert W. Shufeldt. Li Hung-chang, who carried the burden of Chinese foreign relations for many years, was in charge of Korea's foreign policy behind the scenes from 1881 to 1894. The Chinese imperial edict of February 23, 1881, "symbolized a change in China's policy toward Korea and was calculated to pave the way for a Korean-American treaty."[1] According to the edict, a Chinese representative was to render his "advice," or guide Korea's foreign policy.

Li sent a message to the Korean court in which he explained why Korea should conclude a treaty with the United States. He asked the Korean court to send a high official to Tientsin in the name of the "office in charge of students," in order to avoid any possible unexpected intervention by Japan or Russia. In the meantime, Li instructed Ma Chien-chung and Chen Tsao-ju to prepare a draft of a Korean-American treaty, because the Korean government lacked experience in matters of diplomacy with Western powers.

The Korean government set up a new department to handle foreign and national defense matters. The prime minister was head of the department, with high-ranking staff officials as his subordinates. This meant that the new ruling group was ready to open the door to Western powers. It was at this time that the reactionary political faction led by semi-retired Daewongun launched an unsuccessful coup to denounce the "wicked learnings from abroad." Because of the power struggle between the two factions, the departure of the Korean mission to China was delayed a few months. The seventy-man mission, headed by Kim Yun-sik, arrived in Tientsin in the winter of 1881. Thirty-seven members of the mission were assigned to receive military training from the Chinese officials.

Upon his arrival, Kim delivered a written statement to Li Hung-chang. It contained two major points: the reason for the delay of the mission, and a request that the Chinese government "command Korea to send a plenipotentiary to negotiate a treaty with the American envoy." Kim explained that a command from China was needed in order to overcome any opposition to the treaty from the Daewongun faction. He also pointed out that any further delay in treaty-making would bring possible Japanese and Russian intervention.

Li, however, did not accept Kim's view, and asked Kim to stay in Tientsin to observe treaty negotiations closely. This meant that Li Hung-chang himself would negotiate with the American envoy on behalf of the Korean government. Since the Korean-Japanese Treaty of 1876, China had formulated three definite policies in order to maintain traditional Confucian relations with Korea. The first policy was that Korea was to build up its military strength to defend itself against non-Chinese attacks. The second policy was that China should take a more active role in establishing diplomatic relations with Western powers on Korea's behalf since the latter had no experience in dealing with foreign powers. Third, Korea was to conclude a treaty with the United States—which had no territorial designs on Korea—in order to protect itself against possible Japanese and Russian aggression.[2]

The story of American attempts to conclude a treaty with Korea goes back to 1871. An American ship, the *General Sherman*, reached the Taedong River in May, only to be fired upon by the Koreans. After firing back, the American captain requested an apology from the Korean government but received no response. Recognizing the futility of attempting to secure a treaty, the expedition withdrew, leaving the government and the people of Korea with the impression that another Western nation had been forced to retreat under the pressure of Korean military power.

However, the signing of the Korean-Japanese Treaty of Kanghwa in 1876 encouraged the United States Senate on April 8, 1878, to appoint a commission to negotiate a treaty with Korea through Japan. It is said that although a formal resolution never emerged from the Committee on Foreign Relations, the Navy Department decided to send Commodore Robert W. Shufeldt with the U.S.S. *Ticonderoga* to the Korean peninsula. The Navy Department instructed Shufeldt to explain to the Korean government the reason for the 1871 incident and to say that the American government was ready to negotiate a commercial treaty with Korea. In the meantime, the State Department directed the American minister in Japan, John A. Bingham, to seek a letter from the Japanese government facilitating Shufeldt's plan. But the letter was rejected by the Korean government, partly because it was addressed to "Corai" instead of "Choson," and partly because the Korean government had no desire for relations with Western powers at that time.[3]

Shufeldt then made contact with the Chinese consul at Nagasaki and received through him an invitation from Li Hung-chang to come to China to a personal interview on the treaty matter. It was reported that Li was willing to use his influence to induce the Korean government to undertake treaty negotiations with the United States. At this point, Shufeldt persuaded Secretary of State Blaine to send him as an attache to the American legation in China. The Chinese government, under the leadership of Li Hung-chang, was finally able to obtain assurances from the Korean government that it was willing to negotiate a treaty. Thus, by Li's intercession, the American naval officer Shufeldt was to be rewarded for his long wait.

On March 25, 1882, formal negotiations began between Li Hung-chang and Shufeldt. As previously mentioned, although the Korean "representative" Kim Yun-sik was in Tientsin, he never attended any of the meetings. Li and Shufeldt worked out the treaty agreement themselves. First Shufeldt presented the American version of the treaty draft. It contained ten articles, similar to those contained in the American treaties with China and Japan. Li then presented his draft, which had been prepared by his two trusted subordinates, Ma Chien-chung and Chen Tsao-ju.

The main difference between the Chinese and American drafts was the question of Korean status vis-a-vis China. In short, Li was determined to have the American government acknowledge Chinese suzerainty over Korea, and he forcefully expressed his resolve that "the mistake" of the Japanese-Korean Treaty of 1876 should be avoided.[4] For his part, Shufeldt maintained that "no acknowledgement of Korea's inferiority should be included in the treaty itself." Shufeldt did not challenge the Chinese claim of suzerain rights, but he argued that an explicit statement to that effect did not belong in the treaty. After much debate, the issue of China's suzerainty was compromised. Pending further instruction from the United States government, the controversial statement of Chinese suzerainty over Korea was deleted from "the provisional text for the time being." That was to say that should the United States government agree to its inclusion in the treaty, it was to be restored in article 1 as follows: "Korea is a vassal state of China, but has always enjoyed autonomy in both its internal and external affairs." Should the United States government disapprove, it would remain deleted, providing that Shufeldt would forward to the American president a separate letter from the Korean king acknowledging Korea's inferior status vis-a-vis China.

Based upon this compromise, the two representatives signed the provisional treaty on April 19, 1882. Shufeldt waited for several days for the United States government to reply. When no reply was forthcoming, Shufeldt decided on his own to go to Korea to execute the treaty. Li Hung-chang, also ready to consummate the project, sailed for Korea on a special ship. He also sent a personal letter to the Korean prime minister, Yi Che-ung. In the letter Li described in detail the Tientsin proceedings, the forthcoming visit of the American envoy to Korea, and the need for the Korean king's letter to the American president acknowledging Chinese suzerainty. The reply from the Korean prime minister reached Tientsin three days prior to the last Li-Shufeldt session. The reply contained the needed statement that Korea had been under Chinese suzerainty and that the Korean king would write a letter to the American president to that effect.[5]

Thereupon Li dispatched a squadron of three Chinese battleships under the command of Admiral Ting Ju-ch'ang to the Korean port of Chemulpo (Inchon). Li also sent one of his trusted subordinates, Ma Chien-chung, to Seoul in order to handle political problems with the Korean court. The next day Commodore Shufeldt left for Korea on the U.S.S. *Swatara*.

On May 22, 1882, a formal signing of the Chemulpo treaty, also known as the Treaty of Amity and Commerce, took place aboard the Chinese warship. The Korean representatives, Shin Chen and Chin Hong-chi, American representative Shufeldt, and two Chinese "observers," Admiral Ting Ju-ch'ang and Ma Chien-chung, were present.

The treaty was almost identical to the provisional treaty text signed by Li and Shufeldt at Tientsin.[6] There was no explicit statement regarding the status of Korea vis-a-vis China. Instead, the first article stipulated that "There shall be perpetual peace and friendship between the President of the United States and the King of Choson (Korea) and the citizens and subjects of their respective governments. If other powers deal unjustly or oppressively with either government the other will exert good offices, on being informed of the case, to bring about an amicable arrangement, thus showing their friendly feelings."

The treaty, similar to those Japan and China had made with Western states, was "unequal". Some of its important provisions were: (1) the establishment of diplomatic and trade relations as well as trading ports and foreign settlements (articles II and III); (2) protection of American citizens by extraterritorial rights which provided that "citizens of the United States, either on shore or in any merchant's vessel, who may insult, trouble, or wound persons, or injure the property of the people of Choson, shall be arrested and punished only by the Consul or other public functionaries of the United States" (article IV); (3) traffic and customs regulations including the most favored nations clause (article V); (4) freedom of residence and purchase of real estate for citizens of both governments. "Subjects of Choson

(Korea) who may visit the United States shall be permitted to reside and to rent premises, purchase land, or to construct residences or warehouses, in all parts of the country. They shall be freely permitted to pursue their various callings and avocations, and traffic in all merchandise, raw and manufactured, that is not declared contraband by law." The citizens of the United States were given the same rights and privileges (article VI); (5) a ban on the import and export of opium (article VII); (6) a ban on Korean export of grain and "red ginseng" (article VIII); and (7) "all possible protection and assistance to the students of both countries" (article XI).

It is interesting to note that the Korean king's letter to the president of the United States was dated May 15, 1882, one week before the signing of the treaty. But it was handed to American envoy Shufeldt for transmission to Washington on May 24, two days after the signing of the treaty. The letter read:

> The Cho Hsien country (Korea) is a dependency of China, but the management of her government affairs, home and foreign, has always been vested in the sovereign.
>
> Now, as the Government of the United States and Korea are about to enter into treaty relations, the intercourse between the two nations shall be carried on in every respect on terms of equality and courtesy, and the King of Korea clearly asserts that all the articles of the treaty shall be acknowledged and carried into effect according to the laws of independent states.
>
> In the matter of Korea being a dependency of China (in) any question that may arise between them in consequence of such dependency the United States shall in no way interfere.
>
> The King has accordingly appointed commissioners for the purpose of negotiating the treaty, and now, as in duty bound, addresses this communication for the information of the President of the United States.[7]

Another English translation of the king's letter published by the Chinese office reached Secretary of State Frelinghuysen on June 26, 1882, but no substantial differences between the two translations can be found. The meaning of the Korean king's letter could be viewed as follows. Korea had always been a self-governing state in its internal and external matters, although it asked for Chinese help when national emergencies occurred. The relations between the two states had been that of elder and younger brothers in the Confucian tradition: this was the meaning of "a dependency on China." Korea and the United States should treat each other on equal terms as independent states, the way Korea and Japan did under the Treaty of Kangwha. Therefore "the duties that devolved upon Korea as a nation dependent on China were not the concern of the United States."[8]

It should be pointed out that the king's letter was written under pressure from two directions: from Li Hung-chang, the strong man of China, and from the native antiforeign reactionary faction led by semi-retired Daewongun, who denounced any Koreans who favored foreign intercourse. It was this group who plotted an abortive political coup in 1881 to replace King Kojong with the forty-year-old son of Daewongun (a half brother of the king). Although the leaders of the conspiracy, including the would-be king, were executed, anti-foreign political forces were still strong in the Korean court. Under these circumstances, the king and the ruling Min faction were cautious in dealing with both China and the United States.

The text of the treaty and the letter of the Korean king were contradictory at best in the eyes of Western students. The treaty contained nothing that could have been interpreted to mean that Korea was not an independent state like China or Japan. But the king's letter acknowledged the fact that Korea was a Chinese dependency. Therefore Western observers, who were trained to accept legal concepts of sovereignty, had difficulty reconciling the two documents. In contrast, Eastern students, who were familiar with the Confucian concept of state systems, understood that the two documents represented the centuries-old Sino-Korean relationship.

As might have been expected, the gap between the Chinese and American views as to the status of Korea became controversial. The United States took the position that Korea was a sovereign independent state, as stipulated by the Korean-American Treaty. On March 17, 1883, Secretary of State Frederick T. Frelinghuysen wrote to Minister Lucius H. Foote in Seoul. Among other things, Frelinghuysen quoted the Korean king's letter as follows: "The Cho Hsien country is a dependency of China, but the management of her governmental affairs, home and foreign, has always been vested in the sovereign." He went on to say that "it appears also that the King of Corea asserts that the Treaty be acknowledged and carried into effect according to the laws of independent states and that in questions between Corea and China this Government shall in no wise interfere. The relations of the United States towards Corea are therefore clear. As far as we are concerned Corea is an independent sovereign power, with all the attendant rights, privileges, duties and responsibilities: in her relations to China we have no desire to interfere unless action should be taken prejudicial to the rights of the United States."[9]

A similar view was expressed by Minister Foote in his letter to the secretary of state on September 4, 1884: "Fortified as Corea is, by the Treaties lately concluded here, it has seemed to me that China would, in time, voluntarily relinquish her claim to suzerainty; that this is the earnest desire of the King and his people there is no doubt."[10]

In short, as far as the United States was concerned, the Korean-American Treaty was concluded between two independent and sovereign countries, and the Chinese officials, Li Hung-chang and Ma Chien-chung, who were familiar with Sino-Korean relations, had rendered their services to the representative of the United States. To American government authorities the letter from the Korean king to the president had no validity. Thus, as Tyler Dennett stated, the treaty was "one of the great mistakes of his [Li's] career."

Li Hung-chang, of course, refused to accept the official interpretation of the American government. In his view, the letter of the Korean king justified Chinese intervention should Korea be attacked by any foreign power or should Korea refuse to acknowledge its subordinate status to China. Li further argued that the reason for the omission of the clause regarding Chinese suzerainty over Korea was done to save the "dignity" of the Western power, who did not understand the Confucian state system. However, it would seem that the underlying reason for Li's compromise was to use the treaty to protect Korean territory from aggressive neighbors, namely, Japan and Russia. Li knew that China was not strong enough militarily to protect Korea alone, and the United States had no territorial designs on Korea.

It should be mentioned here that the Japanese government supported the Korean-American Treaty indirectly for its own interests. The Japanese wanted Korea to become "independent" of traditional Chinese protection because that would make Korea an independent state in Western international law. Then future relations and agreements between Korea and Japan would not need the approval of the Chinese government. Such independence of the Korean government would certainly be advantageous to the Japanese.[11]

AMERICAN INTERESTS: ECONOMIC CONCESSIONS

At the end of the nineteenth century, Korea was a backward feudal state, dependent upon primitive agriculture and handicrafts. More than 90 percent of the working population was engaged in farming; of these, 85 percent were tenants or "slave farmers." Government officials from top to bottom were corrupt, squeezing money from the people. Public offices and titles were sold like commodities. Thus, the Korean ruling class can be characterized as a decayed product of the authoritarian Confucian government. The government was financially irresponsible. No one in the capital knew who owed what to whom. The king, the queen, and other high officials borrowed heavily without consulting one another. After 1885, most of the money was supplied by China, directly by the telegraph loan and indirectly through the China Merchant Steamship Company. But there were other creditors as well. Japanese and German merchants lent substantial sums at interest running up to 10 percent. Townsend's American concern also extended credit, and there were many unpaid bills. Korean customs brought in a quarter of a million dollars annually, but Korea was plunging further into debt every month.

After the 1884 political coup led by Japanese-oriented progressives failed, the Chinese government realized that its suzerain claims would be strengthened if it could keep Korea financially dependent. One Chinese official even wanted his country to lend Korea interest-free money to show Chinese generosity and, presumably, to keep the non-Chinese countries out.[12]

Seeing the difficulties the Korean govenment had with its economy, Allen devoted his attention first to the franchise field. But he soon found that he could not separate loans from concessions. Korea wanted money in return for grants, and China used its control over the Seoul government's finances to fight would-be concessionaries. Allen thought that he could become a "Christian envoy and a dollar diplomat—making Korea the best and most satisfactory missionary in the world and give Americans their undeniable predominance in the Korean investment field." He felt this could be accomplished because he had been the royal physician and one of the most trusted advisors of the Korean king since 1884. He also knew that working with businessmen paid off in cash and jobs.

The American president, Chester A. Arthur, said that Korea "needs the implements and products which the United States is ready to supply." The field of finance was promising, for Korea wanted to borrow money. And franchise prospects appeared even better, particularly in the fields of mineral exploitation, communication, and transportation. Allen kept his eyes on these fields, his first choice being the gold mines. He obtained information on the gold mining resources of the peninsula from Korean friends, Japanese engineers, and his close friend Walter D. Townsend, the only American trader to have a trading house in Korea. Allen's chance came when the king asked him how the Korean government could interest the United States government and its people in Korea, and secure American help in keeping China out. Immediately Allen answered: "Give the gold mining to the Americans," and he proposed that the king grant him a monopoly of the Unsan gold mine in P'yongan puk-do.[13]

Allen asked the king to grant a mining franchise to his friend James Morse, head of the American Trading Company and a former partner of Townsend. The mining concession of Unsan was granted on July 15, 1895, to Morse, although he knew nothing about the negotiations. With the approval of the king and queen, the contract was signed, delivered, and deposited in the American legation safe. The American minister called the contract "as broad as possible," because the terms were very favorable to the grantee. The concession was to run for twenty-five years and was to cover the whole Unsan area. A newly created American company, the Korean Development Company, was to have exclusive rights of exploitation and be able to choose which mines it wanted to develop. The company was immune from all taxes. In exchange, it agreed to use Korean labor whenever possible and to teach Koreans Western methods. It promised to refrain from opening or removing graves without consent. Allen presented the king with $25,000 and said that "the advantage to the Koreans in this matter was chiefly to be the greater interest America would take in the country."[14]

Nevertheless, Morse lost interest in the mining franchise after he obtained a railroad franchise to build a Seoul-Inchon line in the spring of 1896, again through Dr. Allen's efforts. Hence, Allen looked for other friends who might be interested in the Unsan mines. Two American capitalists, Leigh S.J. Hunt of Seattle and Solat J. Fassett of New York, were seeking business openings in Asia. They met Morse in Yokohama, Japan. Morse sold the Unsan gold mining concession to Hunt and Fassett for $30,000. Actually Morse did nothing to earn the money because Allen did all the work on his behalf. Morse had not even been present for the signing of the original contract papers with the Korean king.

Hunt and Fassett formed a $5 million firm called the Oriental Consolidated Mining Company, incorporated in West Virginia on September 29, 1897. The company invested huge sums of money in equipment and built up a large staff. By 1903, there were seventy Occidental employees at the mines, almost as many Japanese, nearly seven hundred Chinese, and more than two thousand Korean workers. These employees were operating eight different mines and three cyanide plants. They handled two hundred thousand tons of ore. They brought in an operating profit of three quarters of a million dollars which led to the declaring of the first dividend of 12.5 percent.

Hunt and Fassett paid back their debt to Allen by helping him obtain a promotion. Fassett had political connections in New York and with the State Department, and Allen was appointed Minister to Seoul in 1897. Allen also received a cash present from Hunt and Fassett on two occasions, but the amounts were not revealed.

Allen eventually secured a fifteen year extension of the concession with an option for fifteen more years of mining rights. This meant that from a legal point of view, the Oriental Consolidated Company could operate the Unsan mines until 1954. The Korean king received very little consideration: a total of less than $250,000 for more than fifty years of mining rights. The new concession was signed by the foreign minister as well as by the household secretary. The contract secured interior passports for mine employees and free passage for supplies, and eliminated inspection of dynamite shipments by the custom house. Allen also persuaded the king to keep P'yongan government officials from squeezing the American investors.

The sixteen native mine owners in the Unsan district wrote a protest letter to the Amercan minister which read:

> We are gold miners who have been engaged in opening quartz mines in the Li Tap Mountains. . . but in the 7th moon last year, American miners took away from us by force all the mines without a single payment, under the pretense that they had purchased the same while we are working them.
>
> Also, big and small fir trees which we planted and cared for for several hundred years in the neighborhood of our homes and our fathers' graves were cut down leaving only the bare hills, by the American miners without any compensation. . . . Is it in an accordance with international law that any one can take away by force the property of another without payment?
>
> We trust you will immediately let us have 6,000,000 (yen) cash or more for the price of the mines, crushers and trees, and do not let us be ruined to our destruction.
>
> Also, coolies from Seoul and P'yongyang who are employed in the gold mines are looking at the native people and committing wicked acts under the pretense of mine work, therefore every native of said district will become a beggar, as they give up their farming work because of the hindrance of the said coolies. If they are coerced by their officials great disturbance and collisions will occur between the coolies and natives.
>
> We trust you will instruct the overseer (manager) of mines in our district to expel these evil coolies of Seoul and P'yongyang and give the work to the native people.[15]

The American minister in Seoul paid no attention to the protesting Koreans. As long as the Korean government was satisfied with the contract, the Korean people did not matter. Allen, in fact, had attempted to get more concessions for the American investors. By 1898, he was urging that Hunt be given the management of all Korean mines in return for a loan of two and a half million dollars. But this plan eventually failed because of Japanese and Russian intervention.

Americans also obtained coast-wide navigation privileges. The American Trading Company won the right to cut timber on Dagelet Island, and the Thomas Edison Company secured a contract to install electric lights in the royal household. The former American envoy, Foote, obtained a pearl and fishing grant after his retirement from government service.

The Unsan mine made the most money of all the mines in Korea. Even after Korea was annexed by Japan in 1910, the Oriental Consolidated Mining Company held on. Allen's work on the concession was so well done from a legal point of view that the Japanese could find no flaw in the legality of the mine grants. It is reported that the net dividends averaged 12 percent a year from 1903 to 1917. There was a small drop after the First World War, but profits rose again during the depression years to make the average annual dividend more than 9 percent. Dividends totaled more than fourteen million dollars through 1938.

After Japan became more militaristic in the early 1930s, Hunt's company could no longer export gold. By 1939, the company decided to sell its rights to Japanese concerns for $8 million, and Hunt's money-making mining business in Korea came to an end.

The story of railroad franchises is likewise a story of Allen's work. Allen had considered railroad possibilities ever since his first journey from Inchon to Seoul in 1884. Allen's backstage work with the Korean court in securing the railroad franchise for his friend Morse was nothing but clever. Although some Korean progressives, especially So Chae-p'il (Philip Jaisohn), tried to thwart Allen's plan, Allen finally won over the Korean court and informed them that Morse had priority over other Americans in receiving a franchise. The Japanese minister in Seoul, Komura, objected to giving the railroad franchise to an American. However, you will recall that during a period of political turmoil. the Russian legation gave the Korean king asylum. This put Allen in an excellent position to obtain the franchise because he was a close friend of the Russian envoy, Waeber. Here is Allen's memo: "I spoke to Waeber to know if Russia would object to seeing America get that road. . . . Waeber is under some obligation to me and we went together last fall during the trouble (murder of the Korean Queen). He shrugged his shoulders and said that as for himself it would be all right but he could not answer for his government."[16] After about a month, the Russian government approved with some conditions. Allen agreed to everything that Waeber asked and offered to toss in a clause granting Russian troops free transportation on the new railroad. But Waeber rejected this offer. Instead, he asked that Morse's American Trading Company turn over its Dagelet Island timber-cutting privileges to the Russians. Allen agreed. At this point, the Japanese foreign officer, Hara, chief of the Commercial Bureau, told the American minister in Tokyo that "since Japan could not obtain the railroad line concession from the Korean government, it was well to have Americans in charge."[17] So Allen now was able to ignore the Japanese minister's objection.

The Korean king then formed a new cabinet, most of whose members were friends of Allen's. An exception was Cho Yong-chik, the minister of public works, who objected to the giving of railroad concessions to any foreign power. But the king settled this issue in favor of Allen by making Yi Wan-yong the new foreign minister and Yi Chae-yun the vice-minister of public works. Allen suggested that Morse give about fifteen thousand dollars worth of stock to Yi Won-yong and ten thousand dollars worth of stock to Yi Chae-yun but none to Jaisohn, who was then advisor to the privy council, because he opposed concessions to foreigners. Finally, on March 29, 1896, Morse received the railroad franchise for a line from Seoul to Inchon. Morse had a full year to start operation and three years to complete the work. Labor provisions favored the employer, and the railroad was exempted from taxes of every kind.

As in the case of the mine concession, Morse had trouble getting money. His financial resources and contacts back home were limited because American investors were suspicious of enterprises in countries as turbulent as Korea. So Morse mortgaged his concession to the Japanese Specie Bank and, in 1898, was forced to sell out to the Japanese. Allen was unhappy, because he felt the Russians would regard it as dishonorable if the Japanese got the railroad, and the Koreans would consider it a low-down and unprincipled thing to do. Even the Japanese would think Morse had not been square with the Koreans.

In March 1898, Morse's telegram to Allen read: "Seoul-Chemulpo (Inchon) railroad franchise sold to Japanese syndicate. I have associated with them as a member."[18] Sadly, Allen had to accept the announcement. In the meantime, the Japanese minister in Seoul, M. Kato, asked Allen's help in obtaining a franchise for a line from Seoul to Pusan. Although Allen refused at first, he later agreed because Kato promised, "If you help me, I will do my best to see that things manufactured in America are purchased, and American interests are promoted through Mr. Morse."[19] Allen rendered his help, and the Japanese obtained the franchise.

Later that day, Allen could not figure out the situation he had gotten into, but one thing seemed clear. He had perhaps unintentionally played into the hands of the Japanese. Allen knew that he had gone too far with Morse, and it had all ended in benefits for Japan. But Allen could rejoice in the fact that Morse had made a million dollars profit in the railroad deal, and that Collbran and Bostwick, the American contractors for the Seoul-Inchon railroad, had also made handsome profits. The American company's first franchise was for a streetcar and lighting system in Seoul early in 1898. Other merchants and investors were Walter Townsend and David W. Deshler. Townsend, already an established merchant, gained additional power when he became an official distributor for the Standard Oil Company. Deshler, who took a Japanese girl for his bride, was born in Ohio and became a close friend of Allen. His interests were broad, but in due time he concentrated on shipping. As we will see later in more detail, in November 1902, Deshler, with the help of Allen, was given authority by the Korean government to recruit Korean laborers for Hawaiian sugar and pineapple plantations.

Deshler was permitted to set up a number of agents in strategically convenient places throughout the peninsula and, within a short period, he secured
some 121 persons. On December 22, 1902, the first shipload of Korean mi-
grants left Inchon for Hawaii.

After the Russo-Japanese War of 1904 broke out, however, Allen and
other Americans began to realize that it would become increasingly difficult
to properly protect and advance American interests. A month after the war
began, the Japanese were talking about the "white menace." The Japanese
representative, Ito Hirobumi, told the Korean king that "the countries of
Asia must stand together as brothers . . . otherwise the Western powers
will devour them." He continued: "Korea must stop issuing concessions to
Americans and must regret that an American flag flew over the . . . building
in Seoul." Then he suggested that "Korea must lean upon Japan alone."[20]
Allen thought that Americans "will be protected in their vested interests and
might be able to supply the Japanese with capital they lacked." There was no
question that a few Americans, mainly his friends, had become rich from
franchises he negotiated, but the final profits ended up with the Japanese.
Allen himself conceded this point in his letter to William W. Rockhill, the
State Department's Far Eastern expert: "I have favored the Japanese
entirely—after Korea herself and the United States. I have all along held that
Japan should have the paramount influence [in Korea]."[21]

AMERICAN MISSIONARIES IN KOREA

The general position of American Christian missionaries of this era was
well expressed by the Rev. Frank Ellinwood of the Presbyterian Board of
Foreign Mission: "Our missionary work in coming decades, whether we will
like it or not, and whether for good or bad, will be more and more closely related to the influence of diplomacy and commerce." Allen believed that he
had two religious tasks in Korea: to protect the missionaries, and to counsel them in keeping free from harm. If these two tasks had been neglected,
the Christian cause in Korea might have failed. But Allen handled both skillfully, and Korea became the "banner mission field of all the world." Allen
further stated that since he possessed both monetary influence and influence
over the church, he could be called "a Christian envoy and a dollar diplomat." Thus he had much to do with making Korea the "best and most satisfactory missionary station in the world, and with giving Americans their undeniable predominance in the Korean investment field" until the outbreak of
the Russo-Japanese War.

American missionaries in Korea provided a market for Western goods,
and by example they stimulated the natives' desire for these products. Some
of the missionaries in Korea engaged in various business activities. For
example, missionaries in Wonsan developed a commercial orchard. One

brought in a hundred sewing machines. Other missionaries, like Mr. Underwood, imported kerosene, coal, and agricultural implements. Mr. Graham Lee and Mr. Samuel Moffett became interested in Yalu River timber and obtained a contract to take lumber from that region.

In defense of their economic activities, the missionaries claimed that they were doing a service for humanity. Having little overhead, they could sell their products more cheaply than professional businessmen. Sometimes they disposed of their stocks at cost, getting satisfaction in the knowledge that Koreans were obtaining the benefits of Western civilization. However, in many cases, commercially minded missionaries bought land in urban areas at cheap prices and resold it when prices went up, thus making huge sums of money. Sometimes they built missionary schools and hospitals on the land they purchased.

Here is a story of a land dispute between the Korean king and the American missionary, Mr. Underwood. The king liked the man and was grateful for the advice and comfort he gave during political coups and wars. But in 1903, the king's eyes fell on the Underwood establishment, a section of land surrounded and protected on three sides by the American legation. The king wanted to build a home for his own safety on the site, but Mr. Underwood rejected the king's request. The king called Allen and asked him to order Mr. Underwood to sell. Allen explained the American concept of private property rights by saying that neither he nor the American government had authority to force an American citizen to sell his private property against his will. Still, the king wanted to buy the land. Finally, Allen went to Mr. Underwood and asked him to yield as a voluntary act of friendship. Mr. Underwood agreed to sell his land to the Korean king for a handsome profit.

During the years from 1897 to 1909, the American missionary population increased dramatically. In 1904 there was a total of 174 Western missionaries in Korea from fourteen denominations, 85 percent of whom were Protestant. This number increased to 205 in 1909, 77 percent of whom were Protestant. Almost all the Protestant missionaries were Americans.

Some missionaries and native Christian leaders, including active ministers, were anti-Japanese and worked for Korean national independence. But on the whole, neutrality was the accepted policy of the American missionaries. George L. Paik observed: "As far as we can discover in the private letters of the missionaries, a large number favored and cooperated with the Japanese and made an effort to quiet the restlessness of the Christians."[22]

Their policy of neutrality was maintained with difficulty. The problem was to win the confidence of the Japanese and at the same time to hold the faith and trust of the Koreans, who declared the Japanese to be their enemies. When the Japanese armed forces landed in Korea in 1904, many missionaries welcomed them because they believed that the "Japanese would help to better things" for the Koreans. When Ito became resident-general in Korea, "the prevailing sentiment was that it would be better for the people to submit and to make the best of existing conditions, in the hope that the harshness and injustice of Japanese rule would pass."[23]

Ito announced his views on religious matters in order to win missionary support: "Civilization depends on morality and the highest morality upon religion. Therefore, religion must be tolerated and encouraged."

However, when the Japanese in Korea began to mistreat the Koreans, many missionaries openly expressed their disapproval. The Rev. Elmer M. Cable reported to his mission as follows: "Our church at Annai burned to the ground by the Japanese soldiers, and at Sajackhoe three of the Christians were seized and tied to a stake and ordered to be shot. Two of them were killed, but one escaped, and his almost miraculous deliverance made a deep impression on the people."[24] Korean converts often turned to the missionaries for advice and assistance. Failure to respond to this call would hurt the work of the mission, but supporting Korean appeals would bring ill feelings from the Japanese authorities. The Japanese felt that the Christian church, as the country's largest non-governmental organization, was a threat to Japanese rule and a source of anti-Japanese sentiment. The general anti-Japanese feelings among the native Christians was a result of their awareness of group strength and their knowledge of Western concepts of the individual, God-given political rights. Some missionaries, like the Rev. George McCune, felt that their duty was to fight with native Christians against the injustice of Japanese rule.

American Christian missionary work extended into the educational, medical, and social fields. Hundreds of missionary schools from primary to college levels, hospitals, medical schools, YMCAs and YWCAs were established. Almost every town and village had a church building, and within a short period Korea became one of the most Christian nations in the Far East.

THE AMERICAN POLICY TOWARD KOREAN POLITICS
BEFORE THE RUSSO-JAPANESE WAR OF 1904-1905

The Korean royal family, especially the king, had been pro-American and depended upon American advisors and aides (military as well as financial) ever since Allen became the king's personal advisor and loyal physician. On the fateful day of October 8, 1895, Allen awoke at dawn to the sound of firing. He was greatly concerned, for Minister Sill was on vacation and he was in charge, responsible for the safety of the Americans in Seoul.

Furthermore, he also felt morally responsible for the safety of the Korean king and queen.

Soon the minister of public works of the Korean government, Yi Pumchin, dashed in with a communication from the king, who wanted Allen to "hurry to the palace."

Allen described the incident of the queen's murder as follows:

> First he and the Russian envoy, Waeber, went to the Japanese legation, but the Japanese envoy Miura had left already. They followed rapidly, pushing their way through the gathering crowds of natives. As they entered the royal grounds and approached the palace, they saw "30 very evil looking Japanese with disordered clothes, long swords and sword canes, coming away." These men were Japanese civilian residents of Seoul, Soshi, who sometimes did the dirty work for the Japanese legation.[25]

As Allen saw it, the "chief devil in the trouble" was the king's father, Daewongun, who devised this plot for power with the Japanese. Allen felt that America, like Russia, had good reason to check the Japanese. The loss of the queen was irreparable. "She had been a strong character and one of the great personages of Asia." Allen thought her death meant that Korean progressives would be out of power and that opportunities for American penetration would disappear. Only strong, quick action could prevent this unfortunate development.

Allen's rank being limited, however, meant that any important decisions had to be made by Sill. Moreover, the State Department prohibited interference in the domestic politics of Korea. Diplomatic instructions made this point clear, as did a dozen messages on file in the legation. But Allen decided to protect American interests as he conceived them: he threw his entire weight against the Japanese. He openly accused them of having caused the incident intentionally. In the meantime, he refused to deal with Daewongun's pro-Japanese Korean government. He gave aid and comfort to the king when the Japanese envoy attempted to make him a mere puppet ruler and encouraged counter-revolution by supporting the progressives.

Allen sent telegrams and letters to Washington. He said that "the murderers were Japanese in civilian dress. The Japanese legation was involved, no doubt of that; evidence of Miura's participation was overwhelming."[26]

The foreign diplomatic corps in Seoul, including Waeber, held a conference and presented the facts to the Japanese envoy. But Miura denied any involvement on the part of the Japanese. He said that "evil had been done by Koreans dressed as Japanese in European clothes." The Japanese government in Tokyo also asserted that their government had "nothing to do with the incident." This was echoed by Dun, the American pro-Japanese minister in Tokyo.

Without consulting his superiors in the State Department, Allen took an open stand against the new pro-Japanese government. The Korean government issued decrees in order to eliminate the remaining anti-Japanese leaders who supported the queen. The edict of October 11, for example, attacked and degraded the queen for her "extreme wickedness" in helping her relatives dull the king's senses "by their evil counsel." Allen resented this decree and attacked the pro-Japanese Korean government for speaking as though the queen were still alive. He flatly refused to recognize this decree as coming from the king.

Allen consulted with the diplomatic representatives of Russia, England, France, and Germany, who formed a united front against the Japanese. They adopted Allen's proposal denying recognition to the new Korean government decrees. The European diplomats sympathized with the imprisoned monarch, made sure he was not abused by the Japanese authorities, and gathered as much information as the king dared whisper in their ears. Generally, he pleaded for aid. The diplomats responded by sending marines to Seoul. Allen himself brought fifteen from the U.S.S. *Yorktown*.

The American diplomat was determined to protect the Korean king's life. He even asked American missionaries to cooperate by taking turns staying in the palace, thus cheering the king and reducing the danger of assassination. The European legation ladies prepared food for the king in order to avoid any possibility of his being poisoned by pro-Japanese Korean palace ladies. Allen also protected anti-Japanese leaders. Although he was cautioned by his superiors not to accept political refugees, half a dozen of them were granted asylum in the American legation. Allen said, "I cannot drive them out to their death now." Allen believed that "the king literally depends on me like a child on his father" and that the anti-Japanese leaders looked "on him with great devotion."[27]

Later, even Daewongun asked Allen's help. Although he had disposed of his enemy, the queen, the new cabinet he hoped to dominate was controlled by the Japanese. Furthermore, the new Japanese envoy, Inoue, also asked Allen's help in developing friendly relations with European diplomats in Seoul and in securing the confidence of the king.

Allen believed that the queen's assassination had forced Russo-Japanese relations into a crisis. He pictured himself as the person who could prevent a war between the two powers in Korea. He also thought that such a war would involve England and France, as well as Germany. In his opinion, the American government could control it. But Washington did not consider rendering its services as a mediator. Therefore, the only alternative was a "joint commission of Japanese and Russians to conduct Korean affairs. Neither would allow the other to gain ascendancy, but together they might bring order in Seoul."[28]

The Japanese envoy, Inoue, finally took a conciliatory attitude and expressed his regret about the queen's murder. Inoue told the diplomatic corps that he "could not but express his strong condemnation of outrages that had been committed, and he failed to find words strong enough to describe his disapprobation of the assassination of the Queen and the indecent and outrageous decrees, the blackest . . . in Korean history with reference to her degradation." He went on to say that he "had no doubt that his government would accept the suggestion of Sill and others that Japan assume responsibility for getting rid of the present native government and providing for the safety of the King."[29] Miura was recalled, and Inoue's conciliatory attitude reduced the crisis. Beyond that, however, little was accomplished. The degrading decrees were withdrawn, but in other respects conditions remained unchanged. The king was still virtually a prisoner of the Japanese authorities, and the pro-Japanese Korean government remained in power.

Allen's firm stand faced a setback because Washington repudiated all his work. President Grover Cleveland and Secretary of State Olney sent a cable to Allen which read: "It was no part of his duty to refuse to recognize the dead Queen's degradation—diplomatic instruction 64 forbade intervention in political concerns of Korea." Moreover, Allen's cooperation with European diplomats was "open to serious objections on account of our consistent policy . . . of abstaining from cooperating with other persons of whatever nature . . . our strength lies in our independence and the knowledge all countries possess that we never seek anything beyond what our treaties clearly entitle us to, and only do what disinterested friendship naturally suggests." But Allen stood by his decision, saying he was sorry that his superiors in Washington did not see the light. His immediate superior, Sill, defended his work. However, another angry cable came from the secretary of state to Allen. "Continued intermeddling with Korean political affairs in violation of repeated instructions noted with astonishment and emphatic disapproval. Cable briefly any explanation you have to make: also answer whether you intend to comply with instructions given." Sill cabled back saying that Allen "apologized profusely and promised to do better in the future."[30] But the truth was that Sill was not able to control his aide who had the utmost confidence of the Korean king. Therefore, Allen's activities during this period can be characterized as "one man's diplomacy."

Allen had been watching the Japanese gain strength in Seoul since 1898, when Russia yielded power to Japan. He thought that there had been an amazing increase in Japanese influence in the peninsula, with many native politicians being controlled from Tokyo. As early as 1899, Allen reported that "gradually Japan has become aggressive here until they now seem to regard Korea as their own peculiar sphere of action and all others to be mere interlopers." He believed that eventual Japanese domination of Korea was inevitable.

But Russia provided the severest competition for Japan. As pointed out earlier, the Russians wanted Masan, which lay midway between Vladivostok and Port Arthur and was the key to the Strait of Japan. The Russian envoy Matunin, de Speyer's successor, was personally associated with the lumber enterprise backed by the pro-Russian native government official Yi Yong-ik. The Russian envoy was seeking more concessions from the Korean king. But this time native progressive leaders opposed any concessions to foreign powers. Independence Club members, led by American-educated So Chae-p'il and Yun Chi'-ho, advocated national independence without concessions and without the interference of foreign powers. They preached democracy and proposed the establishment of a parliamentary form of government under a constitutional monarch. They launched a movement for popular rights, local autonomy, and equal representation of Independence Club members in the central government. They also published the first private newspaper, *Toknip Sinmun*, printed in Korean phonetics instead of Chinese characters.[31]

This was the first genuine political reform movement influenced by Western political ideology, and Allen and many American missionaries gave it sympathy and aid. But the movement was soon outlawed, and Dr. So Chae-p'il, founder of the Independence Club, was forced to return to the United States a second time. The pro-reform Korean king once again became a "prisoner of the native conservative political faction." The Japanese government gave no support to the Independence Club because it opposed all kinds of concessions and interference by foreign powers, including Japan The Japanese envoy stood by calmly as Dr. So was dismissed, and voiced no protest when reactionary peddlers' guild members beat up independence demonstrators. What Japan wanted was Korea's independence from Russia but not from Japan.

Allen threw his weight behind the Independence Club, although the street fight between the Independence Club supporters and the reactionary peddlers threatened the peace of Seoul. In the fall of 1898, when agitation reached its peak, Allen secured a royal promise that Korea's army would not fire upon the independence demonstrators. But Allen fought for a lost cause. The reactionary faction regained political control, and the members of the Independence Club were put completely out of power.

When the reform movement failed, Allen lost some of his influence. Many of his personal friends, like Yun Ch'i-ho, president of the Independence Club, were ousted from the government, and some were put in prison. However, Allen still retained his good relationship with the Korean king, then called emperor. He had such important privileges as the right to sit down in the royal presence. Whenever the Korean emperor was in trouble, he always turned to Allen for his help and advice.

On many occasions, Allen had to choose between Russia and Japan. Years back, in the Manchu period, he had been pro-Japanese. Then, with Japan on top, he had befriended Russia. Later, de Speyer had made him shift again, over to Japan. And in 1898 he was not sure just where he wished to go. But one thing was always clear. Allen had fought for the interests of Americans in Korea, especially in the fields of economic concessions and missionary work. He wanted to prevent one power from having a monopoly in Korean affairs. He joined forces with the Japanese and English representatives to block a projected Franco-Russian customs loan in 1901. He worked with other diplomats to force the opening of north Korean ports, thus preventing the Russians from taking over.

Eventually Allen favored Russia. This was directly contrary to the position taken by President Theodore Roosevelt. Allen expressed his pro-Russian view after he made a trip to Russia in 1903. He thought that since Russia was backward, "even not nearly so good as the Korean peasant huts, having vasts of territory and population growing, the opportunity of the American trader will be great." He thought that Russia and Manchuria would be a "splendid and growing field for American commerce" in the Far East. [32] Therefore he felt that the American government should avoid supporting Japan in Russo-Japanese disputes, and should remain aloof unless Russia turned against American traders.

President Roosevelt followed the view of William W. Rockhill, the State Department's Far Eastern expert. Rockhill believed that the United States should support Japan, and let the Korean peninsula check Russian expansion in Manchuria. Allen was convinced that the United States should aid Russian interests in Manchuria, because Russia had opened up a "great commercial field" by pacifying Manchuria and constructing roads and railroads there, and "75 percent of this great and growing trade was coming to us."[33] Allen thought that the United States should not sacrifice such an opportunity. Roosevelt took issue with Allen on every point, and Rockhill backed up his chief by arguing that "anti-Russian action would not impair our chances in Manchuria, because the Russian government had fully sanctioned all our attempts to secure the Open Door and . . . they favored our getting the open ports." Allen said that the Russians might oppose American traders there. Roosevelt replied, "No, our government had assurance on that point too."[34]

Finally, Roosevelt asked Allen: "Who would win if Russia and Japan should meet at war?" Allen replied, "Japan on the sea, but perhaps also on land too." The president said, "Well, then, why back a loser?" Allen replied that Russia "wanted us to have all her trade we could handle, while the Japanese were just the opposite and would make us increasing trouble until we might have to cross swords with her."[35]

Allen thought it was useless to try to convert Roosevelt. He returned to Seoul, realizing he could never work in harmony with his superiors in Washington.

The Korean king asked for protection in case war should take place. As a personal friend, the American envoy wanted to give him legation protection, but Washington would not approve such action. The new palace of the king was built close to Allen's residence, and almost every day the king visited the American legation and created the impression that he was under Allen's protection.

When the Korean king failed to receive American legation protection, the Korean government wanted neutralization of the country. This proposal was submitted to Washington and Tokyo, but neither gave much attention to it. On the eve of the Russo-Japanese War, the pro-Japanese American president was "almost contemptuous of Korea and was perfectly willing to have the Korean kingdom ruled from Tokyo."[36] Both Rockhill and Roosevelt believed that the United States government "cannot see any possibility of this government using its influence to bolster up the Empire of Korea in its independence." Rockhill said: "I fancy that the Japanese will settle this question when the present war is finished. The annexation of Korea to Japan seems to be absolutely indicated as the one great and final step westward of the extension of the Japanese Empire. I think when this comes about it will be better for the Korean people and also for the peace in the Far East." When the Korean envoy in Washington told the American secretary of state that his government was in serious trouble and wanted some assistance from the United States, Secretary Hay replied in "carefully guarded phrase, expressing our friendship and good wishes, but added that our interests were rather commercial than political."[37]

Allen noticed that the American general public also sympathized with Japanese expansion. He asked Morse's view about Russia and received the following answer, that the Russians were "rotten to the core . . . unprincipled, tyrannical and brutal, and I hope the Japanese will knock their heads off."

Allen finally had to go along with the idea that "Japan should have the paramount influence in Korea." But he knew that the Japanese would seek an Asia not for the Asian people but for Japan. Thus, a Japanese triumph in Korea would cripple American interests, which he had built up with "love and care" over the past twenty years. The Japanese special envoy, Ito, had told the Korean king that the countries of Asia must stand together as brothers in order to check "the White Menace" in Asia and "Korea must lean upon Japan alone." Allen believed that Roosevelt and Rockhill were wrong in backing the Japanese to check Russian expansion in East Asia. In March 1905, Allen was recalled from Korea and replaced by Edwin V. Morgan, a friend of Roosevelt.

Even before the Russo-Japanese War was over, Great Britian and the United States approved Japan's plans in Korea. The British government gave tacit consent to Japan's intention of establishing a protectorate over Korea. Lord Lansdowne's dispatch to the British ambassadors in Russia and France on September 6, 1905, contained the statement that Korea, "owing to its proximity to the Japanese empire, its inability to stand alone, and danger arising from its weakness, must fall under the control and tutelage of Japan."[38] As early as January 1905, President Roosevelt told the Japanese minister to the United States that Japan had the right to place Korea in its sphere of influence. When the Japanese envoy communicated Japan's wish to provide "protection, supervision, and guidance" to Korea, the American president fully concurred. The reason for Roosevelt's approval was that "we [United States] cannot possibly interfere for the Koreans against Japan: they [Koreans] could not strike one blow in their own defense."[39]

Six months later, the American government gave additional assurance of its approval of Japanese domination of Korea. William H. Taft, the secretary of war, and Katsura, the prime minister, concluded what is known as a secret memorandum. Japan promised not to interfere with American domination of the Philippines in exchange for complete freedom of action in Korea. Taft stated that "the establishment by Japanese troops of suzerainty over Korea to the extent of requiring that Korea enter into no foreign treaties without the consent of Japan was the logical result of the present war and would directly contribute to permanent peace in the East."[40] Thus, international approval was given to Japan's complete dominance over Korea prior to the signing of the Treaty of Portsmouth.

THE AMERICAN POLICY TOWARD
KOREAN POLITICS AFTER THE RUSSO-JAPANESE WAR OF 1904-1905

Before the Korean government was forced to sign the protectorate agreement by the Japanese government, the Korean king sent two personal letters to the American president.[41] The first letter, conveyed secretly in October 1905, was read by President Roosevelt but no action was taken by the American government. The Korean king mentioned the Korean-American Treaty of 1882, which provided that "if other powers deal unjustly or oppressively with either government, the other will exert their good offices, on being informed of the case, to bring about an amicable arrangement, thus showing their friendly feelings." The letter also stated: "The American representatives have always shown themselves to be in sympathy with the welfare and progress of Korea. Many teachers have been sent from America who have been much for the uplift of our people." Then the king pointed out that although Japan had promised to respect Korean independence and territorial integrity before and after the Russo-Japanese War, now "Japan proposes to abrogate their part of this treaty and declare a protectorate over our country in direct contravention of her sworn promises in the agreement of 1904. . . . The destruction of Korean independence would injure both Koreans and Japanese because Japanese oppressive measures would cause hate, social, and political unrest between the two countries. Furthermore, it would destroy international peace in the Far East." The letter concluded by saying: "We beg of you to bear upon this question the same breath of mind and the same calmness of judgement that have characterized your course hitherto, and, having weighed the matter, to render us what aid you can consistently in this our time of national danger."

The second secret letter was carried by H. B. Hulbert, because the American legation, headed by E. V. Morgan, refused to forward it to Washington. According to Hulbert, Morgan cabled the State Department that he was coming with the letter. Within thirty minutes of the time Hulbert arrived in Washington, "the Japanese went to the palace and by threats of death and torture, forced three men in the king's cabinet to sign away their country. The king never surrendered to the Japanese. He bent, but would not break. At the risk of his life he sent me to America."[42] Hulbert said that the letter was not accepted by the American government, and he was told that in any case the letter had arrived too late to be considered. The contents of this letter have never been made public, and nobody knows what was in it.

In November 1905, Ito Hirobumi arrived in Seoul and presented Japan's new policy, the protectorate treaty.[43] The Korean king and the majority of his cabinet ministers at first refused to sign the treaty. But when armed Japanese soldiers were placed around the palace and Prime Minister Han Kyu-sul was dragged out of the conference room by Japanese officers, the remaining ministers signed the treaty at gun point. A few ministers, including Min Yong-whan, former minister of war, committed suicide.

Korea then became a protectorate of Japan, and Ito assumed the post of resident-general in February 1906. At this time, most Europeans and Americans, especially missionaries and intellectuals, welcomed the Japanese. The reason was that they knew the tyranny and abuse of the Korean government and believed that the Japanese would bring better things to the Koreans.

George Kennan, a well-known writer and intimate friend of Theodore Roosevelt, described his impression of the Korean government as follows: "The government officials corrupt and demoralize its subjects by setting them examples of untruthfulness, dishonesty, cruelty, and cynical brutality in dealing with human rights and that is almost without parallel in modern times." Then he wrote about the people:

> As one's field of observation widens, so as to take in country as well as town, and to include moral as well as physical and intellectual characteristics, one's first impression hardens and one's bad opinion of the people settles into a conviction. They are not only unattractive and unsympathetic to a Westerner who feels no spiritual or religious interest in them, but they appear more to be lazy, dirty, unscrupulous, dishonest, incredibly ignorant, and wholly lacking in the self-respect that comes from a consciousness of individual power and worth . . . they are the rotten product of a decayed oriental civilization.[44]

Kennan then suggested that Japan take over all Korean affairs, since the Koreans were inferior to the Japanese. He said: "Suppose that they had brought over from Japan a hundred intellectual samurai policemen and twelve or fifteen police inspectors; then there would have been a very considerable improvement in Korean administration and a very desirable change for the better in the feelings and attitude of the Korean people toward the Japanese."[45]

Perhaps the most serious fault in Kennan's appraisal of the Korean government and people was that he was completely ignorant of the new social and political forces arising within the Korean people.[46] These forces might eventually have brought about Korea's liberation from a corrupt despotism, as happened in other states such as China, Russia, Mexico, and Japan. But the rivalries of three powerful neighbors made it impossible for the Korean people to liberate themselves from exploitation.

The United States government sided with Japanese imperialism for its own national interests. And Kennan distinguished himself as one of the prominent apostles of this imperialism.

2

Early Korean Emigration to America

4.

The Pioneer Period

The history of Koreans in America can be divided into four periods: (1) the pre-emigration period from 1883 to 1900, during which a Korean diplomatic mission, political exiles, students, and a small number of merchants came to the United States; (2) the official emigration period from 1902 to 1905 when seven thousand Koreans went to the Hawaiian Islands as plantation laborers; (3) the semi-official emigration period between 1905 and 1940, when a few hundred political refugees from Japanese rule, "picture bridges" planning to marry earlier male immigrants, and approximately three hundred students with passports from the Japanese government landed in America; and (4) the postwar emigration period after the 1950s, when the Korean population in America increased rapidly.

THE KOREAN DIPLOMATIC MISSION TO WASHINGTON AND OTHER EARLY KOREAN ARRIVALS

On September 2, 1883, the first Korean good-will mission, headed by Min Yong-ik, visited the United States. Min's official title was Special Envoy Extraordinary and Minister Plenipotentiary of Korea. He was accompanied by four secretaries (Hong Yong-sik, So Kwang-pum, Pun Soo, and Hyun Hung-taik) and one American advisor (Frederik F. Low).[1] They visited Washington, D.C., where they met President Arthur, and made a nation-wide tour before returning to Korea on May 31, 1884.

In 1887, Dr. Horace H. Allen persuaded the Korean king to send an envoy to Washington to obtain American advisors and a $2 million loan for

the modernization of Korea. The king decided to send a mission headed by
Park Chung-yang as Envoy Extraordinary and Minister Plenipotentiary and
including Allen. At first the Chinese resident in Seoul, Yuan Shi-kai, acting
under the instructions of Li Hung-chang, objected. The Chinese government wanted to show that Korea was a dependent state and that its foreign
affairs should be handled through Chinese foreign officials. Later, under
pressure from Japan and Russia, the Chinese government withdrew its objection, but Li Hung-chang attached the following three conditions in order
to demonstrate Chinese suzerain claims over Korea.

First, upon arriving at their posts, the Korean representatives had to
call the Chinese legation to introduce themselves and to ask the assistance of
the Chinese minister, after which they were allowed to call where they liked.

Second, at official gatherings, the protocol was that the Korean representatives should always take a lower place than the Chinese representatives.

Third, when important questions were to be discussed, the Korean
representatives had first to consult secretly with the Chinese minister before
talking to other diplomats. However, as this rule did not concern other
governments, they were not able to inquire into the situation.[2] According to
Allen, the Korean king apparently accepted these three points. In addition,
he apparently agreed to withdraw Park Chung-yang after he presented his
credentials, thus leaving the Korean legation in Washington in the hands of
a low-ranking charge d'affaire.

The American government was deeply concerned about the Chinese
intervention in Korean diplomatic matters and expressed its disapproval.
Knowing the American government's official attitude, Allen decided to follow his own independent course when he arrived in Washington with the
Korean mission. In theory, Allen ranked below Park Chung-yang, since he
was just an employee of the Korean government, but in practice Park was
nothing but a figurehead without any experience in foreign affairs. The
strong-minded Allen thought that his duty was to check Chinese interference in Korean foreign relations and to assert the independence of Korea.
Upon reaching Washington, he found that the Chinese minister expected to
control Park Chung-yang and that the Korean envoy, fearing retaliation
after his return to Seoul, was satisfied to follow Chinese instructions. Park
wanted to call upon the Chinese minister before presenting his credentials to
the American president. At this point, Allen tried threats: "He would resign
if Park called on the Chinese representative or sent his card before he saw
the American officials." He also warned that "the King would surely de-
capitate him: I mean cut off his physical head."[3]

Allen thought that if Park called on the Chinese minister before seeing
the American president, the United States would feel insulted. At the same

time, making such a call would defeat the goal of establishing Korea's independence. Allen's strong stand on this matter left poor Park in a miserable position: he feared Li Hung-chang and Yuan Shi-Kai, but he needed Allen. In fact, he needed Allen more than he feared the two Chinese officials, at least at the time. So on January 3, 1888, Allen had the honor of presenting the Korean envoy to President Cleveland.

On the whole, Allen felt the mission was successful. By instituting a permanent legation in Washington (in spite of Chinese opposition), the Korean government had finally been able to establish its independent status in international affairs. Allen wrote: "I regarded the outcome as owning entirely to my efforts and thus giving me the unique advantage of having been chiefly, if not wholly responsible for securing for the country the independence she had long striven for."[4]

Allen's independent action[5] in Washington forced the European-bound envoy, Cho Shin-hi, to return home on the pretext of poor health. His replacement, Park Chae-sun, never left Korea because of pressure from the Chinese government. It was not until after China had been defeated by Japan in 1895 that the Korean government appointed another envoy to Europe.

These incidents caused further damage to the traditional ties between Korea and China, in that Korea's submission to China no longer stemmed from willingness to recognize Chinse superiority, in accord with their traditional relationship. By 1890, Korea was forced to submit, thus subverting the Confucian relations between the two nations that hinged upon "the personal allegiance of the lesser ruler" to the Chinese throne. In the face of China's superior power, Korea could not openly defy that nation, but its will to defy was manifested clearly in various actions toward Yuan, the strong man in Seoul. In 1888, and again in the following year, the Korean government had the courage to request Yuan's recall. The requests were rejected by Li Hung-chang, and Yuan remained in Seoul until the Japanese virtually forced him out in 1894.

One of the members of the first goodwill mission, Yu Kil-jun, stayed in America. In 1884, he enrolled at the Dammer Academy in Massachusetts to study Western civilization and the American political system. Upon returning to Korea, he wrote a book entitled *Soyu Kyon Mun* (What I Saw and Heard in My Visit to the West), in which he described briefly the people, civilization, and various government structures of the West. Many Korean intellectuals read the book and were inspired to go to the West to learn about other nations.

Following the unsuccessful political coup led by the leaders of the Korean progressive party in 1884, three political refugees arrived in San

Francisco in 1885 seeking asylum. They were So Chae-p'il, Park Yong-ho, and So Kwang-pum. So Chae-p'il, the youngest of the three, remained in the United States to study. The first two went to Japan and later returned to Korea. After the Sino-Japanese War, So Kwang-pum was appointed Korean Envoy Extraordinary and Minister Plenipotentiary to Washington, D. C. As we will see later, So Chae-p'il graduated from an American college and a medical school and became one of the most respected leaders in the Korean community in America. He adopted the American name of Philip Jaisohn and married an American girl.

The second group of Korean students who came to the United States for more advanced studies included Yun Chi'-ho, who later became one of the leaders of a reform movement in Korea. He served as president of the Independence Club, founded by So Chae-p'il in 1896, and was an advisor to the Korean Privy Council. Ahn Cha'ng-ho, a young reformer and patriot, arrived in San Francisco in 1899. Syngman Rhee, who had just been released from jail after having served seven years for anti-government activities, landed in the United States in 1904. Park Yong-man, another reformer who also served a prison term for anti-government action, entered the United States as a student in 1905. The last three men, as well as Dr. So, emerged as leaders in the Korean community and launched a national independence movement among Korean immigrants in the United States.

The first group of Korean merchants in Hawaii arrived in 1899. They were five in number. They arrived by way of China and were registered as Chinese.[6] According to available information, the first individual Korean merchant registered as Korean was Paik Jang-hing, who landed in Hawaii in 1898. Kim Ii-yoo and Young Paik-hin arrived in Honolulu on January 15, 1900,[7] Kim with $400 and Young with $180. Although there is no accurate information as to their occupation, they were probably ginseng merchants. A few weeks later, three more Korean ginseng merchants landed in Hawaii from China. They went into business selling ginseng to the local Chinese, who considered it a panacea.

According to the Bureau of Immigration and Naturalization Services, the first Korean immigrant was named Peter Ryu. He landed in Hawaii on January 9, 1901, from a Japanese ship called *Hongkong Maru*.[8] On June 30 of the same year, five more Korean laborers landed in Hawaii. It is also reported that in June 1902, twelve Korean laborers arrived in Hawaii, presumably via Japan. This meant that before the first shipload of "official" immigrants arrived in Hawaii on January 13, 1903, there were fewer than fifty Koreans living in the United States, including diplomats, students, merchants, and laborers.

THE OFFICIAL EMIGRATION PERIOD (1902-1905)

The Korean people in general have not been adventurers. For more than two centuries, until the conclusion of the Korean-Japanese Treaty of 1876, the Korean government adopted a policy of isolation. The ruling class became very exclusive and had no contact with other peoples except for the Chinese. In addition, the traditional Confucian ethical principles of filial piety, ancestor worship, and absolute obedience to elders blocked the common people from accepting such new ideas as the equality of men and individual liberty. Thus, a family-centered, feudal social system prohibited Koreans from leaving their native land.

Against this background, there are three factors that encouraged the emigration of Koreans to Hawaii at the beginning of the twentieth century. The first factor was the economy. After Korea opened its doors to foreign powers, the peninsula became a semi-colony of Japan and the West. The country was divided into zones of influence of the various foreign powers. The United States obtained mining concessions and communication and transportation franchises. Japanese merchants began to monopolize Korean import and export businesses. Russians were interested in timber concessions. The native handicraft industries and the primitive agricultural economy faced bankruptcy, and the national treasury became empty. As an old Korean saying goes, "Misfortune seldom comes singly." In 1901 a nationwide famine took place, caused by an unusual drought followed by floods. The Korean government imported large amounts of grain from foreign countries, but many people faced starvation. By then the Korean government was willing to relax its traditionally tight restriction on emigration.

The second factor was the fact that Hawaiian plantation owners needed the Korean laborer. With the annexation of Hawaii by the United States, the importation of Chinese labor and official contract labor came to an end. This caused Oriental immigrants to shift from one plantation to another in an attempt to obtain higher wages and better working conditions. Plantation workers' strikes became common. Between 1900 and 1905, Japanese workers alone conducted thirty-four strikes. Many workers simply quit their jobs and left for urban areas or went to California. More than one thousand Japanese plantation workers left Hawaii in 1902 alone. The plantation owners then decided to recruit Korean laborers in order to meet the labor shortage on the one hand and to check Japanese predominance on the other.[9]

The third factor was the influence of the American Christian missionaries and of Dr. Horace N. Allen, then the American minister in Seoul. The Reverend George H. Jones told his fellow Christians and the Korean people that America was a Christian country and that Hawaii was the paradise of the Pacific, where the weather was good and working conditions, excellent. If one wanted to, one could work all year around. Other missionaries, like Dr. and Mrs. H. G. Underwood and the Rev. Henry G. Appenzeller, encouraged Koreans to emigrate to the Hawaiian Islands be-

cause they believed it was an opportunity for the Koreans to better themselves financially and acquire knowledge of Western civilization.

Allen, one of the trusted advisors of the Korean king, also encouraged
Koreans to emigrate to Hawaii. Allen performed a lot of backstage maneu-
vering to insure this. Returning to Korea after a visit home in March of
1902, he was met in San Francisco by a representative of the Hawaiian plantation owners. He also had a meeting with the Hawaiian Plantation Association in Honolulu. There is no doubt that Allen, who was familiar with
Korean politics and the general condition of the people, gave information to
the plantation owners on the capacity of the Koreans for work and on existing conditions in Korea. Allen also had a business friend, David W. Deshler,
then a junior partner in the American Trading Company in Seoul. Since
Deshler had been the first to support Allen in his ambition to become the
American minister to Korea, Allen owed him a political debt. Deshler, who
had married a Japanese girl and had a home in Kobe as well as in Seoul,
owned a steamer service from Inchon (then called Chemulpo) to Kobe.[10]

In the meantime, Allen wrote a letter to the governor of Hawaii,
Sanford E. Dole, which read:

> My reason for sending you these copies is that I learn it is the inten-
> tions of a number of Koreans to try the experiment of emigrating to the
> Hawaiian Islands during the coming winter, with the idea of bettering
> their conditions and preparing the way for others to follow in case the
> conditions are found to be satisfactory. . . . The severe famine of the
> past winter made the matter seem all the more attractive to the people,
> while the fact that the Government had to import large quantities of rice
> to feed the starving seems to have turned the attention of the officials
> favorably to the subject of emigration. It is probable however, that the
> pride of the Emperor in learning that his people might go where the great
> Chinese are excluded, had much to do with the matter. . . . The
> Koreans are a patient, hard-working, docile race, easy to control from
> their long habit of obedience. They are usually very keen on the getting
> of a foreign education, and this has taken quite a number to the United
> States where a few have become naturalized, while those who have re-
> turned are doing well and are a credit to their American educa-
> tion. . . . If the Koreans do get to the Islands in any numbers it will be a
> God-send to them (Koreans) and I imagine they will be found to be un-
> objectionable and of good service as laborers.[11]

Allen told the Korean king that emigration to Hawaii would relieve
some of the burden on the government of feeding the starving people. He
also hinted that the emigrants might be able to send money back to their
families in Korea. This would certainly help the domestic situation and
would lessen social unrest. The king finally accepted Allen's suggestion and
in November 1902 authorized Deshler to be in charge of taking Koreans to
Hawaii. In the same month, the Korean government established the *Su Min-*

Won (Bureau of Peoples' comfort) headed by Min Yong-hwan, who was in charge of issuing passports and rules and regulations concerning emigration. Deshler had already set up an organization called *Kaibal Hoesa* (Development Company) in Inchon to recruit Korean emigrants. He hired a Korean, Kim Jae-ho, as his interpreter, and organized branch offices of his company in Pusan, Chinnampo, Wonsan, and Seoul. Deshler's company advertised for recruits in the following manner:

> The climate is suitable for everyone and there is no severe heat or cold. There are schools on every island. English is taught and the tuition is free. Jobs for the farmers are available all the year around for those who are healthy and decent in behavior. Monthly payment is fifteen dollars in American money (sixty-seven won in Korean money). There are ten hours of work a day with Sunday free. The expenses for housing, fuel, water, and hospital will be paid by the employer.[12]

In the meantime, the Korean government also made a similar public announcement as follows:

> (1) Any person desiring to go to the Hawaiian Islands will receive government help. (2) The climate in Hawaii is warm, and there is no severe temperature change. (3) The educational system is very generous, and free public education is provided on every island; English can be learned without difficulty. (4) Farmers will be able to find jobs year around, and a healthy and honest person will be able to find permanent employment; the working people's rights will be protected by law. (5) Monthly salary will be fifteen dollars, which is equal to thirty yen in Japanese money and sixty-seven won in Korean money: the working hours will be ten hours a day with no work on Sundays. (6) The plantation owners will provide living quarters and will be responsible for the medical expenses of the employees.[13]

Deshler started actively to recruit Korean immigrant laborers on behalf of Hawaiian plantation owners. Within a short period, he secured 121 persons and on December 22, 1902, the first shipload of emigrants set out from Chemulpo (Inchon). Because Korea lacked modern medical facilities at this time, formal physical examination of the Koreans was performed by Japanese physicians at Kobe. Twenty of the group failed to meet the physical qualifications. The remaining 101 emigrants, consisting of 55 males, 21 females, and 25 children, sailed for Hawaii on the merchant ship S. S. *Gaelic*, which arrived in Honolulu on January 13, 1903. Eight Koreans were barred from landing because their eyes were found to be diseased. Thus, the exact number in the first group of Korean laborers was only 93. After resting a few days in Honolulu, they were sent to work at the Waialua sugar plantation at Mokola, Oahu.

According to the records of the U. S. Immigration and Naturalization Service in Honolulu, 7,226 Korean immigrants arrived on sixty-five different ships between 1903 and 1905. However, of these, 479 failed to pass their physical examinations and were sent back to their homeland. Therefore, an actual total of 6,747 Koreans[14] arrived in Hawaii before the Korean government terminated its emigration policy in November 1905. Also, from October 1904 to January 1905, over a thousand Korean emigrants, including children, went to Mexico.

There were two basic reasons for the cessation of Korean emigration to other countries: the Korean government was concerned and distressed over the suffering of its people in Mexico, and the Japanese government exerted pressure to block the continued exodus of Korean workers.

These two reasons were clearly expressed in Deshler's letter to Huntington Wilson, the American charge d'affaires in Tokyo. In part, the letter read:

> On or about the 4th day of April, in the year 1905, an order was given under the name of the Korean Government, but with the consent and advice of His Excellency, the Japanese Minister to Korea, prohibiting the further emigration of Koreans, no matter what their destination might be.[15]

The letter also stated that Korean Foreign Minister Yi Ha-Yung said that the reason for stopping the emigration was the fact there had recently come to Korea an irresponsible company, which, by promising high wages and other advantages, had induced some nine hundred Koreans to take passage to Mexico on a specially chartered vessel; that the management of this company did not meet with government approval; that the company had misrepresented Yi's views with respect to Korean emigration to Mexico: that he, Yi, did not consider Mexico a suitable place for Koreans to go in any numbers; and that in order to stop this undesirable movement, he had originally intended to prohibit the emigration of Koreans to Mexico but after consulting with the Japanese minister to Korea, the latter had pointed out that it would be unfair to discriminate against a particular company or country and that if one were stopped, all must stop. This meant that although the Korean government wanted to continue the emigration of Koreans to Hawaii, the Japanese government did not favor it on the basis that it was "unfair to discriminate in favor of any emigration company or country."

It should be noted here that the Koreans went to Hawaii as free laborers, and not as contract laborers. The 1882 Treaty of Amity and Commerce between the United States and Korea had a provision pertaining to the emigration of Koreans to America proper. The Korean immigrants possessed passports issued by the Korean government, and article VI, paragraph I of the treaty stipulated:

> Subjects of Choson (Korea) who may visit the United States shall be permitted to reside and to rent premises, purchase land, or to construct

residence or warehouses in all parts of the country. They shall be freely permitted to pursue their various callings and avocations, and to traffic in all merchandise, raw and manufactured, that is not declared contraband by law.[16]

However, the Korean immigrants were not even aware of the existence of the treaty. Most of them came to Hawaii to stay only temporarily. They wanted to return to their homeland as soon as they made enough money or the political climate of the Korean peninsula permitted them to go back. From 1905 to 1910, the Korean population in the Hawaiian Islands declined steadily. Nearly one thousand returned to Korea, forty died, and more than one thousand went to the mainland, mostly to California. The Korean National Association reported that in 1910 about four thousand Koreans, including about one hundred Hawaii-born Korean-Americans, remained in Hawaii.

The classification of the immigrants by sex, age, education, and occupational background was roughly as follows: 90 percent were males, 10 percent were females; 93 percent were adults, 7 percent were minors; about 35 percent were literate, 65 percent illiterate. Their previous occupations varied. As expected, farmers comprised the majority, followed by manual laborers, soldiers, Christian church workers, and a small number of students and highly educated Confucian scholars. About 40 percent were Christians, and gradually most of the Koreans became church-goers.[17]

During the early years, most immigrants came from the northern provinces. There were three reasons for this. First of all, during the Yi dynasty, northern Koreans were discriminated against by the southern *yangban* ruling class and were denied high positions in the government. Such discriminatory policies eventually led to a revolt against the central government. This meant that northern Koreans became less conservative and comparatively receptive to new ideas, while the traditional conservative southerners wanted to retain the status quo. Therefore, more northerners than southerners accepted Christianity, and more northern Koreans joined in the emigration to Hawaii than southerners did.

Second, northern Korea is mountainous, with rich natural resources and has now become an industrial zone, whereas southern Korea is predominantly an agricultural area with rich land. Historically, because of the shortage of cultivated land, northern Koreans developed a more flexible social structure. Southern Koreans retained a rigid, feudal, family-centered social structure.

Third, both the Sino-Japanese War and the Russo-Japanese War were fought mostly in the northwestern region of the peninsula. The wars destroyed not only national independence but also property. The suffering northern Koreans desperately needed a new place to live, and emigrating to Hawaii provided them with hope for a better life.

The early Korean emigrants to America concentrated on how to survive by physical labor; how to educate their children without losing their Korean heritage; and how to help restore national independence. They never thought that the United States was their permanent home. On the matter of racial discrimination, they believed they were helpless human beings living in the white people's society, and they dreamed of going back to their homeland as soon as Japanese domination ended. The Korean community leaders purposely did not take action against discrimination because they did not wish to harm their chances of getting American support for the cause of Korean national independence.

THE SEMI-OFFICIAL EMIGRATION PERIOD (1905-1940)
FIVE POLITICAL REFUGEES

The history of Korean emigration cannot be separated from the story of Korean political refugees and students who came to the United States for freedom and advanced studies. According to the report of the education committee of the Korean National Association of Hawaii, the total number of Korean students in America from 1882-1940 was estimated at 891.[18] This number can be divided into three groups: the first group of sixty-four who came to America between 1884 and 1909; the second group numbering over five hundred, who came between 1910 and 1924 by way of China and Europe after Japan's annexation of Korea; and the third group, estimated at fewer than three hundred, who came with Japanese-issued passports. Of the sixty-four in the first group, forty-five completed college and university studies. A few of them, including Philip Jaisohn, Kim Kiusic, and Syngman Rhee, obtained doctoral degrees. But only one hundred out of the five hundred in the second group were able to graduate from American colleges and universities because of financial hardships. Most of the third group of students finished their advanced studies and returned to Korea. Fewer than a hundred remained in the United States until 1945.

The leaders of the Korean community in America emerged from the first and second groups and became the nucleus of an independence movement outside of Korea. In the meantime, Korean community leaders maintained traditional Korean values by establishing Korean schools and religious and cultural institutions wherever Korean immigrants lived. The Korean leaders in America believed they could make a contribution toward the eventual independence of their homeland by working with other Korean immigrants, even though their numbers were small. The leaders regarded other Korean immigrants as water and themselves as fish; in other words, they could not be separated from each other, and should work together to achieve a common goal, the restoration of Korean independence.

The leaders, like the early Korean immigrants, faced many hardships because they had not prepared themselves for a new life in the United States. Because of the language barrier, cultural conflicts, and a lack of skills, as well as racial discrimination, many Korean intellectuals had to take back-breaking jobs as physical laborers. They worked as house workers, field laborers, janitors, dish washers, or busboys at hotels and restaurants. In the evenings and on Sundays, they taught Korean culture. At the same time, they planned and worked with the immigrants for the cause of national independence.

Among the many intellectuals in the early Korean community in America, perhaps the most prominent leaders were Philip Jaisohn, Ahn Cha'ng-ho, Dr. Syngman Rhee, and Park Yong-man. All of them had participated in the political reform movement against the native Confucian conservative authoritarian government in the latter part of the nineteenth century. They came to the United States for political freedom as the Puritans did for religious freedom. They also searched for new political ideologies, a knowledge of Western technology, and American help in their struggle against the Japanese domination of Korea. Before coming to the United States, they all belonged to the upper middle class. They were neo-Confucian intellectuals and anti-conservative and anti-Japanese patriots.

Jaisohn was the son of a wealthy aristocratic family. He took part in the political coup of 1884 against the corrupt, pro-Chinese reactionary party then in power. Unfortunately the coup collapsed after three days. So Jaisohn fled, first to Japan and then, with his three friends, to the United States. His account stated: "We did not know anybody; we did not have any money; we don't speak English. . . . Nobody recognized us and nobody paid any attention to us. . . . We felt that we were the lonely and pitiable abandoned orphans from the ship which carried us across the Pacific Ocean."[19]

Jaisohn worked for several months as a delivery boy for a used furniture store in San Francisco, where his daily wage was two dollars for a ten or twelve hour day. His memo said: "I did not realize until now the American businessmen make their employees work so hard with so little wages." Fortunately, he made an American friend at his church, a Mr. Hellenbeck, who promised to support him through college if he would go with him to Pennsylvania. This Jaisohn did. He finished at a small private college within three years and was chosen valedictorian of his graduating class. He then decided to go on to medical school, despite his sponsor's advice to become a theological student in preparation for missionary work in Korea. Jaisohn enrolled at George Washington Medical School where he completed his medical training within eight years by earning money as a medical-school librarian.

Jaisohn returned to Korea after the Sino-Japanese War and advocated political reforms based on a democratic parliamentary system. He organized the Independence Club as a progressive party in order to challenge the conservative forces in power. He served as advisor to the king's privy council. He and other members of the Independence Club erected the Independence Arch in Seoul as a symbol of national independence. He also established a newspaper called *Toknip Shinmun* (Independence Newspaper). However, when the conservative clique seized power again, he was forced to leave Korea for the second time.

After returning to the United States, Dr. Jaisohn played an elder statesman's role in the Korean independence movement. When the March First nation-wide independence uprising took place in Korea, he convened a Liberty Congress of the Korean people in Philadelphia. Thereafter, he acted as advisor on diplomatic affairs for the Korean provisional government, which came into being in Shanghai in 1919. He had no personal political ambitions, and worked for the interests of the Korean people and the restoration of national independence. He stayed out of factional struggles during his entire life in Korea and in America. Jaisohn was a true gentleman and political leader in the Korean community in America.

After the Second World War, he was recalled to Korea in 1946 by General John R. Hodge, the commander of American occupation forces, to serve as a special political advisor. Upon the establishment of the Republic of Korea in 1948, he returned to the United States for the third time. He passed away in 1951 at the age of eighty-five. Dr. Jaisohn seeded democratic ideas in Korean soil, but the fruit of his efforts have not been made public until this writing.

Ahn Cha'ng-ho, another ardent national leader, landed in San Francisco in 1899. He was twenty-two years old and had come to America to learn Western civilization. One day, he observed an unexpected scene. Two Koreans wearing native clothing fought each other in the street while some Americans looked on. Ahn stopped the fight and asked the reason for it. He learned that the two Koreans were ginseng peddlers in Chinatown, and one of them had overstepped the other's marketing district.

This incident shocked Ahn. He felt he had to do something to improve the situation among the Korean peddlers in the Bay Area, because such behavior would give the American public a bad impression of Koreans. The Americans might think that Koreans were "uncivilized" and not able to govern themselves. After much consideration, Ahn decided to postpone future study in order to work for the improvement of the Korean community in the Bay Area.[20] He discussed this matter with his friends, and they agreed to provide Ahn's living expenses while he served the Korean community.

Ahn started his community service program by visiting all the Koreans in the Bay Area. He found the following: (a) their living quarters had no curtains and the windows were dirty; (b) there were no flowers or trees of any kind; (c) every house was dirty and filled with unpleasant smells; and (d) most Koreans were loud and disturbing to their neighbors.

Ahn also heard that some Americans wanted to sell their houses because they did not wish to live with the "unclean Koreans" next door. Of course, Ahn realized that this attitude was based on racial discrimination, but he did not want Koreans to be used as scapegoats. Hence, he began his community services with house cleaning. He visited Korean homes and cleaned the windows, rooms, and front and back yards. Some Koreans suspected his motives and sometimes refused his free services. However, as time passed, they began to understand his motives and cooperated with him. Within a few months, they had changed their life style drastically. Every Korean residence looked clean from inside and out. Flowers and trees had been planted in every yard. In addition, the Koreans became more courteous and respectful to each other. Ahn won respect from his fellow countrymen and became their friend as well as their advisor.

Ahn's next project was to set up a Korean employment agency. He organized a Korean labor-supply service center and supplied Korean laborers to American employers who needed them. Through this agency, most Koreans in the Bay Area were employed and obtained reasonable wages.

Ahn always wanted to work behind the scenes, without recognition as a leader in the Korean community. Here is a beautiful story about how much the Korean community in San Francisco improved within a short period because of his influence. One American landlord, who rented his house to a Korean, said to his tenant: "I think that the Korean people must have a wonderful leader recently . . . because your life style has changed drastically, and it would seem impossible to have such changes without a community leader." The tenant told his landlord about Ahn, and the landlord asked to meet him in person. The landlord was surprised to find out that the man who had such a fine program for the improvement of the Korean community was so young. As a token of his appreciation of Ahn's work, the landlord offered one month's free rent to his tenant. He also offered a rent-free meeting place for the Korean people in San Francisco. This was the first Korean mass-meeting place in San Francisco, and it also became the first Christian worship place for Koreans in the Bay Area.

Under Ahn's leadership, the first Korean social organization, called *Chin'mok-hoe* (Friend's Society), was organized in 1903. Two years later the first Korean political organization, *Kongnip Hyop Hoe* (Mutual Assistance Association), was formed.

In 1907 Ahn returned to Korea, where he took an active part in the national independence movement by organizing secret societies and establishing schools. But he was forced to flee Korea before the annexation of the country by the Japanese in 1910. When he came to Los Angeles by way of Europe in 1911, he found that his wife had been working as a housemaid in order to support herself and their two children (the first son is Philip Ahn, who became the first Oriental actor in Hollywood). Ahn immediately started to work as a general construction worker, but his physical condition did not allow him to continue his job. Then he got a job as a hotel room cleaner, which he left after one year because of the great demand for his services in the Korean community.

Here, again, is a beautiful story. The owner of the hotel said to Ahn: "Since you have been working so diligently for me, I would like to do something for your service, and what do you want most?" Ahn replied: "The only thing I want is that one of my countrymen take my place after I leave." The owner promised to do so, and it is said that Koreans have been working in that hotel for many years.

In 1913, Ahn organized a long-term national independence movement and formed the *Hung Sa Dan* (Young Korean Academy) in San Francisco. Ahn spelled out his theory of Korean nationalism as follows.[21] He believed that the Korean independence movement must begin with national regeneration. The cultivation of the character of the Korean people could be achieved through four principles and three disciplinary measures. The four principles were truth-seeking, deeds (practice what you preach), loyalty, and courage. The three disciplinary measures were knowledge, virtue, and health. According to Ahn, Korean nationalism had three objectives: the restoration of independence (rejection of Japanese domination), the establishment of a national state based on utilitarianism (expression of totality of national welfare), and the development of a progressive nationalism (political and economic democracy).

Ahn believed that individual interest must be sacrificed for the benefit of national interests. Therefore, every Korean should realize that he had a mission to serve for the cause of independence. In his later years, Ahn also advocated four equalities—racial, political, economic, and educational—as well as the establishment of communities on a cooperative economic basis. The idea of the four equalities and the concept of utilitarianism were influenced by Western political ideologies, but Ahn's main political philosophy was influenced by traditional Confucianism. He did not separate politics from ethics. The four principles and three disciplinary measures roughly corresponded to the five Confucian virtues (benevolent love, righteousness, propriety, wisdom, and faithfulness). Confucian political philosophy, to "cultivate personal virtue, rule the family, govern the state, and pacify the world," was accepted by Ahn.

When the March First independence movement broke out in Korea in 1919, Ahn was sent to Shanghai as the representative of the Korean National Association in America. He became secretary of the interior and later secretary of labor in the Korean provisional government, and served as acting prime minister until Syngman Rhee arrived and took over the presidency. In 1935, Ahn was arrested by the Japanese police in Shanghai and charged with anti-Japanese activities. He was sentenced to four years imprisonment and died in 1938 after being released because of poor health suffered while in jail.

The story of Ahn's arrest by the Japanese police is an example of his belief in practicing what you preach.[22] Ahn had always told Koreans to be honest and to keep the promises they made. Ahn promised a birthday present to the son of a friend. He was warned by informed Koreans that he should not go to the party because he might be arrested by a Japanese secret agent. Nevertheless, Ahn went because he did not want to break his promise to the boy. Today Ahn is considered one of the most respected patriots in Korean national history. A memorial park in his honor was opened in Seoul in 1974.

Syngman Rhee was familiar with both Eastern and Western culture and politics.[23] He was born in 1874 into an upper-class Korean family and received a classical Confucian education. As a young man, he participated in the political reform movement against the Yi dynasty. Rhee's early political life was influenced by the principles of the Independence Club. Because of his anti-government activities as a member of the Independence Club, he served seven years in prison before coming to the United States as a student in 1905. Rhee graduated from Harvard with an M.A. and from Princeton with a Ph.D. in politics. Rhee returned to Korea, where he served as general secretary of the YMCA in Seoul for about one year, and in 1911 he came back to the United States.

In 1913, Rhee was invited to Hawaii by his prison mate from Korea, Park Yong-man, to work in the Korean community. Rhee became a teacher at the Korean Community School, also called the Korean Compound School, and soon assumed the principal's position. The school, which had been established for the children of Korean plantation workers, offered Korean history, culture, and language as well as English and Western civilization.

From 1919 on, Rhee went on numerous trips to international conferences and capitals, seeking to gain Korea's independence from the Japanese. For more than forty years he was a leader within the Korean community in America. He became the first president of the Korean provisional government in 1919, and he was chairman of the Foreign Commission of the Korean Overseas Association (United Korean Committee in America) in Washington, D. C. during the Second World War.

Rhee never engaged in physical work in the United States, but one time he spent about a year in Hawaii aiding a Korean business enterprise. The enterprise was established by members of the *Tongji-hoe* (Comrade Society), which became Rhee's political group in 1921. Later Rhee formed the Korean Christian Church (*Hanin Toknip Kyo Hoe*) and published a magazine called *Pacific Weekly*.

Everybody was surprised when Rhee brought his new wife, Francesca Donner, to Hawaii. He had met her at an international conference in Geneva, in 1932. One of Rhee's friends said: "At first he did not have a car—but the garage was put to good use as a library for mountains of National Geographic magazines." He went on to say that "Rhee was loved by his students and that his head was scratched daily by the daughters of the Korean immigrants."[24] Another one of Rhee's American friends described him by saying that "the only hobby Dr. Rhee had was trying to do something for Korea . . . that's all the hobby he had."

Rhee published two books, *Toknip Chongsin* (The Spirit of Independence) in 1910 and *Japan Inside Out* in 1941. Until 1945, he was a frustrated national leader, similar to Nehru of India. Rhee concentrated on diplomatic agitation against the Japanese as a lobbyist, petitioner, or unofficial delegate to international conferences. But his personal political future began in October 1945, when he left Washington for Seoul as a top political advisor to Lt. General John R. Hodge, then the commanding general of the American occupation forces in South Korea. This was his first return to Korea after more than thirty years in the United States.

Rhee's authoritarian character in politics was well expressed in the 1954 amendment to the constitution of the Republic of Korea, which made him the "life-time ruler". Again, it shows in his theory of *ilmin-juii* ("the one-people principle").[25] Having had a Confucian aristocratic background, followed by a study of Western politics in the United States, Rhee's basic political thinking and tactics were a mixture of an authoritarian outlook, a patriarchal flavor, and a belief that the end justifies the means. He became the first president of the Republic of South Korea, but the eventual fall of the twelve-year-old iron-fisted Rhee regime was caused by official corruption, favoritism, political oppression, and fraudulent elections. All these were practiced in the name of anti-communism and under the guise of patriotism and democracy.

During Rhee's rule, many Koreans in America had a tough time. Rhee took a passionate interest in all Koreans in America, even if they were naturalized citizens of the United States. He and his official representatives did their best to discredit anti-Rhee Koreans and even have them deported. If deported, execution awaited them in Korea. One young Korean writer in America was forced to flee the long arm of Rhee by going to Europe. He returned only after Rhee was out of power. The Rhee regime ruined the careers of many Korean intellectuals in America, just as many American liberals had their careers ruined during the McCarthy era.

After the sudden collapse of the Rhee regime, brought about by the student revolution in 1960, Rhee became a political exile for the second time. He went to Hawaii, where he died in June of 1965 at the age of ninety. The *Star Bulletin* in Hawaii reported that Rhee "wanted to return to Korea to die—the last wish, but the saddened Rhee had to bow to the military junta's rule—do not return." The message of the governor of Hawaii, John A. Burn, read: "Because of his long association with our land—where he spent important periods of his life and where he found a haven of rest in his final years—we in Hawaii had a special affection for President Rhee." But none of the Korean authorities, including President Park Chung-hee, mentioned Rhee's patriotism and his contribution for the cause of national independence. "Thus, a nice old man died like any other nice old Korean immigrant disappearing in a strange land."[26]

Park Yong-man was another ardent patriot who emerged as one of the leaders in the Korean community in Amercia. Park also participated in the anti-government reform movement before he came to the United States as a student in 1904.[27] He was a prison mate of Rhee in Seoul. By nature, Park was a man of action who believed that Korean national independence could never be achieved except through direct military action against the Japanese. Park majored in political science at the University of Nebraska and studied military science as a minor subject. Upon graduation in 1909, he established a Korean Youth Military Academy in Hastings, Nebraska, with the permission of the university president. There he started training twenty seven Korean cadets. These young men worked on farms during the day and received military training in the evening. The military training program consisted of drill and field exercises for three evenings and class lectures for two evenings. Because American law did not permit aliens to have real rifles, the cadets used wooden guns for their drills.

The influence of Park's military training program in Hastings caused four other military centers to be established by Korean immigrants who had served in the Korean army before emigrating to the United States. The centers were in Claremont and Lompoc, California; Kansas City, Kansas; and Superior, Wyoming. Each center had about twenty cadets. Later, a pilot training center was also established at Willows, California. The expenses for this last training center were paid by a rich Korean farmer, Kim Jong-lim, known as the rice king.

In 1910, the Korean National Association in Hawaii set up military training centers on the islands of Oahu, Maui, and Hawaii, and recruited about two hundred trainees. Park Yong-man went to Hawaii in 1912 as

editor of the Korean weekly newspaper *National Herald*. In 1913 he consolidated all military training centers into one by organizing the Korean National Brigade. The Ahumanu Plantation in Kailua, Oahu became the headquarters of the Korean National Brigade. Korean military billets were built
by the cadets, while materials and ground space were donated by the plantation owners. The total number of cadets was 311. On August 29, 1914, opening ceremonies were held and were attended by about six hundred
Koreans.[28] The trainees worked on plantations during the day and drilled at
night, with wooden rifles. Park took charge of the Korean National Brigade
as commanding officer. He published a military drill text book for the class,
and translated a *History of American Revolution* into Korean. He became
the publisher and editor of *Taepyongyang Shi-sa* (Pacific News) and also
attended many international conferences as a delegate for the Koreans in
America. He organized a political group, the Korean Independence Party, in
1919.

The first ideological dispute between Syngman Rhee and Park Yong-
man seeded factionalism in the Korean community in America. Rhee rejected Park's military training programs on the grounds that military action
to restore national independence was not realistic and wasted both energy
and money. Rhee advocated educational and diplomatic means as the surest
and most reasonable avenue for eventual realization of independence. These
two different policies proved to be irreconcilable, and factional fights continued for many years in the Hawaiian community, as we will see later.

Park was elected the minister of foreign affairs of the Korean provisional government, while Rhee became president in 1919. Park did not
stay in his position, however, but instead concentrated on the establishment
of military training centers in northern China, especially in Manchuria. On
October 17, 1928, Park was assassinated by an unknown Korean youth in
Peking.

To sum up, the early Korean community in America had four leaders:
the Western-oriented *yangban*-type of gentlemen, Philip Jaisohn; the
Machiavellian-type of politician, Syngman Rhee, the Joseph Mazzini
(Italian patriot) type of patriot, Ahn Cha'ng-ho; and the Oriental-type military activist, Park Yong-ho. Their ultimate objectives were the same, the restoration of national independence from Japan, but their methods were different. In general, one group emphasized military action: the other,
education and diplomacy. Dr. Jaisohn did not take sides and did not involve himself in Korean community issues, whereas Ahn established himself
as an unchallengeable leader on the mainland. Rhee and Park contested for
leadership in Hawaii, with the latter being the loser and the former the winner. But Rhee eventually ended up a loser in history, labeled a dictator.

In addition to the four men mentioned above, there were many other devoted Korean community leaders in the United States. It is impossible to write about all the pioneers who made contributions. Therefore, it should be noted that the Korean community in the United States was the product of the common labor of the early Korean immigrants. However, there was one individual who literally sacrificed his life for the services of the Korean community and who should be mentioned.

The Rev. Mr. Lee Dae-wii (David Lee) came to the United States as a political refugee in 1905. He was a graduate of Soong Sill College (American Missionary Institute) in P'yongyang, and attended the Pacific School of Religion in Berkeley.[29] He settled in San Francisco and became one of the founders of the early Korean social and political organizations, like *Chin'mok-hoe* (Friends Society) and *Kongnip Hyop Hoe* (Mutual Assistance Association). He was one of the original·members of the Korean National Association, which came into being in 1909. He also served as editor of the *New Korea*, the first Korean community weekly newspaper, which is still (1976) in existence. Between 1910 to 1928, he served as a minister of the Korean Methodist Church in San Francisco, the first Korean church in the United States. Established in 1906, it has been situated on Powell Street since 1928.

It was the Rev. Mr. Lee who helped hundreds of Korean political refugee students come to the United States without passports. After Korea was annexed by Japan, many Korean intellectuals and patriots participated in anti-Japanese activities, and many of them fled to China to avoid persecution by Japanese authorities. From China, some of them took American steamships, hoping to enter the United States. Some of them possessed Chinese passports, but many had no passports at all.

One time, thirteen Koreans arrived on Angel Island from China without passports. The Rev. Mr. Lee attempted to persuade the immigration authorities to grant the Koreans permission to land in San Francisco. He argued that they were political refugees and that since no Korean government existed, the Korean National Association would sponsor them. But Mr. Lee's efforts were turned down by the immigration authorities, and the thirteen Koreans faced deportation to either China or Korea. At this critical moment, Mr. Lee hired a lawyer and sent a petition to Secretary of State Bryan. The main point of the petition was the question "where were these thirteen Korean political refugee students to go?" They were not able to go back to China because they were not Chinese. They were not able to return to Korea, because execution by the Japanese awaited them. They were not allowed to come to this "free country" of America because they had no passports. The only thing they were able to do was jump into the Pacific Ocean. The secretary of state permitted them to land. Over the next eight years, 1910 to 1917, a few hundred Korean political refugees entered the United

States without passports by way of China and Europe. Many became successful leaders in the Korean community and worked for the welfare of Koreans in America.

Perhaps one of the greatest contributions of the Reverend Mr. Lee was his invention in 1915 of a type-setting machine for the Korean phonetic alphabet. Since then, all Korean publications in America have used this machine and have not employed Chinese characters.

According to one of his closest friends, Yang Choo-en, the only surviving Korean immigrant from 1902, the Rev. Mr. Lee worked day and night for the benefit of the Koreans in the Bay Area ever since he arrived in San Francisco. Because of his hard work, he took sick with tuberculosis and died in 1928. His body was buried in San Francisco, and the ninety-seven-year-old Yang still (1976) visits the grave at least once a year.

THE PICTURE BRIDES

The story of the picture brides is a mixture of tragedy and comedy in the history of Korean immigration into America. About 80 percent of the nearly seven thousand immigrants who entered Hawaii were bachelors. Their lives in the strange land were lonely, dull, and monotonous. They worked from dawn to sunset on the plantation fields and spent their nights in the camps. Their only enjoyments were drinking, gossiping, gambling, and sometimes fighting among themselves when holidays or Sundays arrived. Practically speaking, there were no available Korean women in Hawaii, and interracial marriage was unthinkable at this time. Most of the bachelors were approaching their thirties, and some were older. Thus the marriage problem was not only an individual problem but also a social issue within the Korean community in terms of population increase and individual happiness. The importation of Korean women was necessary to build a healthy Korean community. A healthy and happy community would in turn improve the quality of work performed on the plantations.

Finally someone suggested the idea of picture brides: sending the bachelors' pictures to prospective brides in their home towns, and letting the girls choose their mates. The plan was approved by the plantation owners, and the United States immigration authorities agreed to grant the brides permanent residence. The first picture bride was Sara Choe, who arrived in Honolulu on November 28, 1910. She became Mrs. Lee Nai-soo.[30] Between 1910 and 1924, when the Oriental Exclusion Act was passed, more than eight hundred picture brides came to Hawaii and more than one hundred to the mainland, especially to San Francisco, Los Angeles, Sacramento, and Portland, Oregon.

A majority of the picture brides were much younger than their bridegrooms. This was the beginning of the comedy as well as the tragedy in the lives of the early Korean immigrants. The young brides were under the impression that their chosen mates would be exactly what their pictures depicted. Unfortunately, many men sent deceivingly young pictures of themselves. The girls thought the men's ages would not be too different from their own. When the ship carrying the picture brides arrived in Honolulu, the bridegrooms, dressed in their best suits, greeted them at the dock. According to eye witnesses, some of the brides fainted because their bridegrooms were so old and much uglier than they expected. Some of the brides were bewildered and cried "*Aigo omani*," which means "O dear me, what shall I do?" A few of the brides refused to land, and some of them returned to their homeland. The confused bridegrooms did not know what to do and stood on the dock, their hands clasped behind their backs, absolutely speechless in front of the disappointed brides.

As time passed, most of the brides were able to adjust to their new husbands. Many of the brides had better educations than their husbands. A great number moved into Honolulu after they married. Some bought farm land with their accumulated capital and began to operate their own farms. A few opened family-operated small businesses, such as shoe repairing shops, laundry shops, restaurants, and used-furniture stores. Thereafter, the Korean community in America gradually became happier in terms of individual lives and economic betterment.

5.

The Koreans in Hawaii

THE HIDDEN STORY OF KOREAN EMIGRATION TO HAWAII

As a background for understanding the importation of Korean workers into Hawaii, it might be useful to look at economic conditions before and after the annexation of the islands in 1898. Five big plantation companies had been the de facto rulers of Hawaii. They were J. F. Hackfield and Company, C. Brewer and Company, Alexander and Baldwin Company, Davids Company, and Castle and Cook Company. Robert M. Little said: "To think of Hawaii in an economic sense is to think of sugar. That territory is ruled by financial oligarchy around which is built the business and social structure of the islands. Hawaii is thus a territory with a very strong and powerful propertied class and a very numerous and heterogeneous nonpropertied class. There are very few middle-class people between."[1]

Of the five, Hackfield and Company, a German concern headquartered in Bremen, was responsible for the financing of plantation operations and the procuring of plantation labor. In addition, Hackfield and Company was the agent for the Pacific Mail Steamship Company, which provided the transportation for the majority of the Japanese immigrants who came to Hawaii to work on the plantations. Hackfield was the first man to suggest the possibility of importing Korean labor, not only because the plantations needed more labor, but also because he would get revenue from transporting Koreans to Honolulu on his steamships. It should be pointed out that Hackfield was made an honorary Russian consul in Honolulu. Thus he could contact the Russian minister in Seoul through the Russian consulate in Honolulu.

The national affairs of Korea at this period were quite unusual. King Kojong had taken up residence (exile, in reality) at the Russian legation in Seoul as a result of Japanese intervention into Korean internal affairs after the Sino-Japanese War of 1894-1895. During the year that the Korean king remained in the Russian legation, the influence of the Russian minister was paramount, as the king was virtually a captive.

The Russian minister, Karl L. Waeber, had very cordial relations with Horace N. Allen, then the secretary to the United States legation. The Russian government thought that one way to offset the predominant Japanese position in Korea was to encourage Koreans to emigrate to Hawaii, so that the United States government would pay attention to Korean issues.

In 1902, Japanese plantation workers in Hawaii were estimated at 31,029. This was 73.5 percent of the total of 42,249 workers and constituted the highest percentage of any one racial group. Chinese workers numbered only 5,299, or 9.3 percent of the total plantation labor force. Other ethnic groups represented were Filipinos, Portugese, and Puerto Ricans.[2]

In spite of the continuing influx of Japanese and other national groups, the shortage of labor became more acute as the sugar business became more prosperous. This continuing shortage of labor stemmed from the conditions on the plantations. First, the wage scale was low, averaging sixty-five cents a day for ten hours of work in the hot sun. This drove the workers from the plantations, either by desertion or by a failure to renew contracts. Second, the Japanese resented the harsh treatment they received from their white bosses and did not remain "docile workers." They complained about the low wages and demanded better living conditions. They united to protest and often went on strike. Third, the contract labor system came to an end soon after the annexation of Hawaii, and plantation workers were then free to leave the plantations whenever they wanted. In addition, strikes were legalized.

Because of frequent strikes by the Japanese workers—thirty-four strikes between 1900 and 1905—the plantation owners began to dislike the Japanese and decided not to depend on one racial group. So they worked out a policy of drawing workers from a number of different sources, particularly from Asia, because, whereas recruiting and transporting one Caucasian laborer cost about $250, the cost for one Asian was only $70.

About this time, the plantation owners received very favorable reports about Koreans as good, hard-working people. Some Americans who had business establishments in Korea reported that "the Korean is the pick of all the Orientals as a worker. Besides, the Korean coolies are more obedient and respectful to their employers than any other Orientals." As mentioned previously, Allen, who had just been elevated to the post of minister in Seoul, held a conference with the representatives of the Hawaiian plantation owners in March 1902 on his way back to Korea. After he returned to Seoul, he did a lot to encourage Korean emigration.

Allen persuaded the Korean king to permit his subjects to emigrate to Hawaii for economic betterment. He pointed out that the Korean king might be proud to send his subjects to a place from which Chinese were now excluded. Allen also suggested that the Korean government should organize an emigration bureau modeled after the one in Japan. Accordingly, the *Su Min Won* was established to take care of emigration and passport matters. Allen then chose his friend David W. Deshler as the representative of the Hawaiian Plantation Association. At this time, Deshler was a junior partner of the American Trading Company, and his steamship line more or less monopolized sea transportation services between Inchon and Kobe, Japan.

In September 1902, the Hawaiian Sugar Plantation Association sent E. F. Bishop, the owner of Brewer and Company, to Japan with $25,000 to recruit Korean immigrants. Bishop met with Irwin, the American consul in Japan, and they discussed transportation, medical examination, and other problems concerning Korean immigrants arriving in Kobe. Bishop then sailed to Korea to meet Deshler. They worked out the recruiting plan in detail.

Deshler chose to become involved with the Korean immigrants for two reasons: there was money to be made by transporting the immigrants from Inchon to Kobe on his steamship, and the Hawaiian Sugar Plantation Association promised to pay him on a per capita basis. On the other hand, Allen's advocacy of Korean emigration to Hawaii can be seen in the light of a political motive. Allen wanted the United States to become interested in Korean affairs. After the Anglo-Japanese Alliance was signed in 1902, Japan appeared determined to take over the Korean peninsula step by step. Allen thought that by promoting the Korean immigration project, the United States government would have a greater stake in the independence of Korea, and at the same time would provide a check to the expanding Japanese influence.

One of the major obstacles to recruiting Koreans was the fact that they hesitated to leave their ancestors' graves. They felt guilty about not performing the duties of ancestor worship. This obstacle, however, was overcome by the efforts of the American missionaries. They told the Korean Christians that they would become better Christians away from home, and would have a better opportunity to improve their economic lives and to learn Western civilization.

The last problem was how to finance transportation fees. None of the Koreans who desired to emigrate to Hawaii could afford the steamship fare, which amounted to roughly one hundred dollars. The problem was solved in the following manner. The Hawaiian Sugar Plantation Association instructed Deshler to set up a bank in Inchon. It was called Deshler's Bank, but was actually the Hawaiian Plantation Association's bank since they were the only depositors. The bank lent one hundred dollars to every Korean immigrant with the understanding that the immigrants would pay back their loan by deducting a sum from their pay check every month for a three-year period. But none of the Korean immigrants actually paid back their loans. When Deshler came to Hawaii to collect the money, the immigrants not only refused to pay but asked him to leave the plantation, arguing that the wages were low and the living quarters very poor. Finally, Deshler gave up and left the plantation.

PLANTATION CAMP LIFE OF THE EARLY KOREAN IMMIGRANTS

Plantation camp life for the early Korean immigrants differed greatly from the kind of life Koreans have today on the Hawaiian Islands.[3] During those days, the immigrants lived in one big camp on the plantation, in a manner similar to collective farmers' lives in Communist countries or the commune life style in America today. Everybody worked and ate together in one place. Single men lived in big barracks, which consisted of one big square sleeping room where no privacy existed. Married men were given a small house for themselves or, in some cases, a private room in one of the barracks. On one plantation, the barracks were segregated racially: The Japanese occupied one building, the Chinese another, and the Koreans still another. Usually, however, everybody ate in the same place, in a big kitchen. Some plantations provided different kitchens according to nationalities. Chinese, Japanese, and Korean food were prepared by members of the respective groups. Living quarters were free, but everyone had to pay for meals. On the average, meals cost about $6.00 per month. Laundry cost an additional $1.00. Fortunately food was cheap during this period. A hundred pound bag of rice, for example, cost only $1.50.

The working day on a plantation followed the same pattern day in and day out, six days a week and seven days during harvest time. Usually the cooks were the first to arise at about three o'clock in the morning to prepare breakfast and lunch for their fellow workers. The cooks got free meals for their services. General plantation workers got up at five o'clock. They had only half an hour to eat and get ready to go to work. Trucks or a small locomotive train would take them to their place of work in the fields. Foremen (called *lunas* in Hawaiian) got assignments for the day's work from the boss, who ran the plantation on behalf of the landlord.

One foreman was in charge of 250 workers, divided by sex into 200 men and 50 women. Work began at six o'clock. Workers spent ten hours a day in the blazing sun (more than 100 degrees) and sometimes in the rain, with half an hour for lunch. There were two kinds of working patterns, based either on piece work or on a monthly salary. In the former case, which paid according to the amount of work the individual did, wages sometimes were $1.25 a day. In the latter case workers got between $16.00 and $18.00 a month, averaging from sixty-five to seventy cents a day. Women's wages ran from fifty to sixty-five cents a day. The foreman's wage averaged between $50 and $75 a month. Interpreters were paid about the same as foremen.[4]

When the workers got to the fields, the foreman lined them up with the fastest workers at the head of the line. Every worker had a number; no name tags were used. During working time, no private conversation was allowed, and no smoking either. Anyone who failed to obey these rules was subject to a beating or a slapping by the foreman. Usually the foreman belonged to a different race than his workers. For example, Korean workers were under the supervision of a German foreman; Filipinos, Puerto Ricans, and Portuguese were under Korean, Japanese, or Chinese foremen. Naturally, some foremen were very strict with their workers, while others were mild. According to experienced plantation workers, mild foremen usually produced more work, because workers resented a harsh foreman's attitude and worked poorly.

Every day, the boss inspected the camps after the workers left for the fields. Then he went out to see how the workers performed their work. The laborers quit at half-past four and returned to their camps. On the way back, the foremen recorded the workers' time. They then ate dinner, bathed, and retired directly to bed. This was their everyday routine, except for Sundays and holidays. Except during the harvest season, Sunday was the day off. Some workers just slept through the day, while others gambled and drank. Some visited friends or went to church.

The plantation owners did not provide any amusement or sports facilities for their employees. There were no public parks either at that time. Essentially, plantation workers were isolated from the outside world and the white society. The overwhelming majority did not speak English and did not know the customs of the American people. They were treated not as human beings but as a means of production. But they could not complain because nobody would listen. They could not communicate with anybody except their own countrymen. Although there were seven different nationalities (Korean, Chinese, Japanese, Hawaiian, Filipino, Puerto Rican, and Portuguese) in one plantation camp, they hardly spoke to each other because of language differences. If they got sick, they were dependent upon an interpreter, who communicated with the English-speaking physician. But many interpreters did not speak English fluently, which made an accurate diagnosis difficult.

The following story was told by Lee Hong-ki, who was ninety-five years old in 1971. One of the early Korean immigrants to Hawaii in 1903, he worked on the Kolora Plantation on Kaui Island. Lee said:

> I got up four-thirty in the morning and made my breakfast: I had to be out to the field at five o'clock and work started at five-thirty. I quit work at four-thirty in the afternoon and had a half an hour for lunch. I worked ten hours a day with a sixty-seven cents a day wage. . . . The

supervisor or foreman was called luna in Hawaiian language and my luna was German. He was very strict with us. . . . He did not allow us to smoke and did not allow us to stand up straight once we started to work. He treated us like cows and horses. If any one violated his orders, he was punished, usually a slap on the face or flagellating without mercy. We couldn't protest against the luna's treatment because we were in fear that we would be fired. . . . We carried our number all the time as an identification card, and we were never called by name, but number. I lived in the camp: it was just like the army barracks; wooden floors and we slept on wooden beds or just on the floor, with one blanket over the body. Usually four single men lived in one room. . . . Sometimes I could not sleep at all due to the hot air.[5]

According to Lee, the average number of working days per month was twenty-five. The monthly income was $16.00 for men and $12.50 for women. The wages were not enough to cover the monthly expenses of the plantation workers, because some of them had families and many had to send money back home to Korea.

An editorial in the *Hapsong Shinpo* stated: "Often the Korean immigrants felt that their life of bewilderment and hardship was far from the vision of paradise they had expected when they applied for emigration."[6]

The life of an immigrant's wife was no better than that of her husband. Here is the life story of a lady who was eighty-six years old in 1973. Mrs. Kim Tai-youn came to Hawaii in 1905 at the age of seventeen. She described her early life experiences as follows:

When I landed from the ship I felt very gloomy and I did not expect any bright hope for the future in this strange land of Hawaii. When I looked at the living quarters provided by the plantation owners, I was disappointed and began to worry, because I had to live in this camp under the Hawaiian hot sun. But seventy years later now I can say that I came here for my own good. I was a little different from most other Korean women. I joined my husband: we married in Korea before my husband came to Hawaii, whereas most of the other women came here as "picture brides" to marry the man whom they saw only by picture. . . . My husband was an object of envy and jealousy by many unmarried single men at that time.[7]

Mrs. Kim's first job was operating the rooming house for single men who worked on the plantations. She remembers that she charged each man six dollars per month for room and board, and one dollar extra for laundry. The total of seven dollars was not enough to cover all her expenses, but she said, "What could you do, since the wages of the plantation workers were so low?" Most of the workers had to send money home to Korea to support members of their family.

In order to supplement her meager income and meet her expenses, Mrs. Kim planted corn in a vacant lot. She also planted red peppers and other vegetables in order to make *kimchi* (Korean hot pickles). Sometimes she picked up the intestines of cows and pigs from slaughter houses to make soup for the plantation workers.

Mrs. Kim had to prepare food for twenty-one people, including her husband. She prepared breakfast, lunch, and dinner for them every day. She had to be up by half-past three every morning to cook a Korean-style breakfast, which consisted of soup, rice, and *kimchi*. The lunch boxes usually contained rice and salted dry fish. Dinner was not very different from breakfast, except for an additional vegetable or sometimes a fish dish. During the day time, she would wash work uniforms and sacks for all twenty-one people at the nearby river and dry them under the sun. At night, after washing dishes, she would iron the washed clothes for the next day. So her working hours lasted from half-past three in the morning until almost midnight. She thought her living conditions were a little better than those of most other immigrants at that time. Mrs. Kim operated the rooming house for seven years. Later she and her husband moved to Honolulu, where they opened a used-furniture store and also repaired shoes. Mrs. Kim has been a Christian from childhood and attended the Korean Methodist Church in Hawaii. According to her memory, on every immigrant ship that carried Koreans to Hawaii there was at least one Christian minister who gave inspiration and hope to the despairing immigrants and led them toward a meaningful life.

Mrs. Kim continued: "Wherever Korean immigrants lived there was always a Christian church," and the Christian church-goers became the center of the Korean community. Every Korean wanted to live near the church, and almost every Korean went to church on Sundays to meet each other and to help those in trouble. She concluded by saying that "I did not learn how to speak English because everyone spoke Korean in our community."

Mrs. Kim's life story is just one of the stories about early Korean immigrants in Hawaii. Today her nick-name in the Korean community in Hawaii is "our grandma." Mrs. Kim was honored at the celebration of the Seventy Year Korean Emigration Anniversary, held in January of 1973.

In contrast, American businessmen and missionaries saw the working and living conditions of Korean immigrants in Hawaii quite differently. James W. Hunt, then vice-manager of the Wonsan gold mine in northern Korea, said when he visited Hawaii that he had been working the past seven years with Koreans, Japanese, and Chinese and found that of the three nationals, the Koreans were the best workers. He further stated that the Wonsan mines had about two thousand five hundred workers. Their daily wage was twenty-five cents in Korean money, and they were very happy with that wage. This implied that the Korean immigrants in Hawaii were well paid and treated well by the plantation owners compared to the mine workers in Korea.

Another observer, the Rev. Mr. George Heber Jones, one of the most influential missionaries to encourage Korean emigration to Hawaii, came to the islands and visited various work camps there. Then he wrote a long article entitled "The Koreans in Hawaii" in *Korea Review* in 1906. This is one of the major English language articles about the Koreans in Hawaii at that period and is therefore quoted here at length.

> It is in Hawaii the Korean (nearly seven thousand including women and children) is at his best. At first he had some difficulty in adjusting himself to his surroundings. Everything was new and strange and he had to learn how to handle himself. He did not know how to live, but it did not take him long to learn how to do so. He had to learn what to wear and where to eat, where to buy it, and how to cook it: how to work and how to take care of himself. The Korean, when placed in favorable circumstances, is wonderfully quick to learn and in a marvelously short length of time, he learned his lessons and today the universal testimony is that the Korean is a very desirable plantation hand. . . . I had many a meal with Koreans, which, though homely, was well cooked and as good as any man might wish. As a result, the Koreans live well. They wear American clothing, eat American food, and act as much like Americans as they can. Under such conditions the Koreans grow and develop very rapidly. Hawaii is the land of great possibilities for him. Being farm laborers, he gets the very training he needs to fit himself for usefulness in his native land. Hawaii becomes to him a vast School of Agriculture where he learns something of the character and treatment of different soils; method of irrigation and fertilization; care and system in the handling of the crops. He learns how to work according to system, and also the value and obligation of law and regulation. If a thousand selected Koreans a year could be permitted to emigrate to Hawaii in a few years, they would return and develop the natural resources of Korea, adding manyfold to the value and financial resources.[8]

According to Mr. Jones' findings, Koreans ranked second in number on the sugar plantations, and played no small part in the production of Hawaii's great crops. The distribution of Koreans on the sugar plantations according to occupation was as follows:

Administration (clerical workers)	10
Cultivation (plantation workers)	4,384
Irrigation	1
Manufacture	19
Superintendents (*lunas*)	4
Transportation	248
Unclassified	17
	4,683

Mr. Jones argued that judging from the above figures, about 75 percent of the Koreans worked on the plantations. The remaining 25 percent consisted of women and children. By tradition, Korean women were not compelled to work with their husbands in the fields. The children went to school.

Mr. Jones' observations were far from the real situation that prevailed on the plantations. Every Korean who worked on the plantations agreed that the work demanded by the plantation owners was extremely difficult and unreasonable, while the financial return scarcely provided enough to avoid starvation. As mentioned previously, the average daily wage was about sixty-nine cents for men and fifty cents for women for a ten-hour day under the hot sun. As Mrs. Kim Tai-youn's testimony indicated, she wasn't able to charge more than six dollars for room and board since "the wages of the Korean laborers on sugar plantations were so low." As a way of supplementing her rooming-house business, she had to plant vegetables in a vacant lot. She also had to work fifteen to seventeen hours a day. It is also a fact that most of the plantation workers were sometimes unable to sleep at night because they suffered from the pain of sunburn.

The Korean weekly newspaper reported that nearly one thousand Koreans left Hawaii for the mainland between 1904 and 1907, when a presidential executive order banned any further movement of Orientals from Hawaii to the mainland. During the same period, over one thousand Koreans returned to their native land because their life of bewilderment and hardship was far from "the vision of paradise they had expected when they had applied for emigration." Thus, the Korean population in Hawaii steadily declined between 1907 and 1912.

The idea of "a vast School of Agriculture" where Koreans could learn new methods in farming, as Mr. Jones suggested, was not a valid idea. The truth of the matter was that the Korean immigrants in Hawaii did not need to learn how to raise sugar because the Korean peninsula does not produce sugar. Therefore, the Korean plantation workers felt they had nothing to learn in Hawaii.

THE KOREAN COMMUNITY IN HAWAII: YESTERDAY AND TODAY

An overwhelming majority of the almost seven thousand Korean immigrants in Hawaii were unmarried men and, with few exceptions, were not educated or of a socially prominent class. But soon after they settled down on a plantation, they formed a self-governing social organization known as the *dong-hoe*, or village council. The origin of *dong-hoe* goes back to the Silla kingdom. The ruling class of the Silla practiced a primitive form of democracy in selecting their ruler and in governing their people.[9] Important affairs of a village were decided upon by a majority of the village members. This practice was carried on throughout the centuries, and was kept intact even under Japanese rule. In the United States, the *dong-hoe* was organized as a means of maintaining law and order among the Korean immigrants. Koreans on each plantation elected a headman, called the *dong-chang*. Law violators or disorderly persons were punished in conformity with rules set forth by the *dong-hoe* under the supervision of the *dong-chang*. Thus, the *dong-chang* acted as the ruler of the local Korean immigrant community.

In 1907 the *dong-hoe* of the various plantations united in a single organization called the *Hanin Hapsong Hyop-hoe*, or the United Korean Society. Every Korean in Hawaii was supposed to become a member of the United Korean Society and to obey its regulations. The Society acted as a self-governing body on behalf of the Koreans in Hawaii until 1909. In February of that year, representatives of the Society and delegates from the *Kongnip Hyop-hoe* (Mutual Assistance Society) in San Francisco held a joint conference and organized the *Kook-min-hoe*, or Korean National Association. The Korean National Association became a self-governing body for the Koreans in the United States. Every January, delegates were sent from each plantation or settlement of Koreans to the annual meeting in Honolulu. There were seventy-eight local branches of the Association in the Hawaiian islands alone. The delegates from each branch would submit new proposals or discuss and legislate on matters having to do with their own communities. They would also vote on a budget, raised by collecting individual dues of three to five dollars a year. This money provided an education for their children, welfare work for their members, support for the independence movement, a weekly newspaper, and textbooks for the Korean language schools.

Until 1915, before factionalism between the Syngman Rhee group and the Park Yong-man followers started, the Koreans in Hawaii were able to handle their own disciplinary problems and to maintain law and order without help from the Hawaiian local government. Unfortunately, this homogeneous and self-governing Korean community was disrupted when the first ideological struggle emerged between the two groups. Some Koreans supported educational and diplomatic means to achieve national independence, whereas others supported military action.

Within six months after the Korean immigrants landed in Hawaii, the first Korean church was established. The first church service was held under the leadership of Kim Ii-je on July 4, 1903, on a sugar plantation in Mokuleia, Oahu.[10] There were already about four hundred Koreans who had been converted to Christianity prior to their departure from Korea, and more than thirty had taken part in church work in their homeland. The Reverend Mr. Jones stated: "One third of all the Koreans in Hawaii were professing Christians, and they dominated the life in the camps on the sugar plantations in Hawaii."[11] In 1918 it was estimated that nearly three thousand were converted to Christianity, and thirty-nine churches of various denominations were established.

A rapid progress of the Korean community in Hawaii, in terms of quality as well as quantity, began about the time of the arrival of the picture brides. Between 1910 and 1924, more than eight hundred young women, mostly from Korea's southern provinces, came to Hawaii to marry single Korean immigrants. According to one source, in 1905 there were about seven hundred women out of almost seven thousand Koreans. This meant that only 10 percent of the Korean men married and had family lives. The Korean bachelor's life was lonely and sometimes miserable. Traditionally, Korean society was family-centered, and marriage was one of the most important events in one's life. Therefore, the marriage problem became very serious in terms of individual happiness, as well as in terms of increasing the Korean population.

When the picture brides settled in Hawaii, the Korean community gradually changed from a rural society to an urban one. The picture brides encouraged their husbands to change their occupations, and many of the plantation workers moved to the urban areas, particularly Honolulu. With the accumulation of a little capital, the Koreans established small family-operated businesses or purchased real estate. Later many of the women ran rooming houses and bought homes and apartment buildings.

The Korean population began to increase as time passed. Children received American educations and obtained white-collar jobs. Some became professionals: lawyers, doctors, and teachers. Present statistics show that second and third generations of Koreans moved very rapidly into professional fields as compared to other ethnic groups. Had the picture brides not emigrated to Hawaii, the Korean community today might be quite different from what it is.

As Arthur L. Gardner stated: "Koreans (in Hawaii) rank proportionately high in representation in the business and professions. This is a noteworthy achievement for those immigrant families of relatively modest social background who made their way to a new and strange country less than seventy years ago."[12]

In 1976 there were more than twelve thousand Koreans in Hawaii, of whom eighty-five hundred were American citizens. This means that only thirty-five hundred Koreans have immigrant status. Proportionately, the Korean population in Hawaii has never been large. The number of Koreans is estimated at 1.1 percent of the total population. Japanese residents in Hawaii comprise 28.3 percent; Filipinos, 12.2 percent; and Chinese 6.8 percent. About 38 percent are Caucasians, and the rest come from other ethnic groups.[13]

Koreans in Hawaii have a relatively high rate of intermarriage with other ethnic groups. Nevertheless, the Korean community has constantly resisted erosion of its separate identity. In general, the Koreans possess resilient, individualistic personalities. They are hospitable and forgiving. They also have dynamic individual intellectual resources to compete with other ethnic groups. On the other hand, they are factious, idealistic, and sometimes mild and/or dependent on others.

The early Korean immigrants laid the foundation for the Korean community in America through their back-breaking physical labor. As mentioned previously, they concentrated on three things: how to survive; how to educate their American-born children; and how to work together for the restoration of national independence. They made a great contribution toward the achievement of these objectives. Most Koreans in Hawaii today live comfortably. There are ten Korean millionaires, and a considerable number of the older generation draw their income from rental properties. Many young people of the second and third generations received higher educations and moved quickly into professional positions. American-born Koreans have been especially successful in the legal and medical professions. The state attorney general is an American-Korean, and the first person of Oriental extraction to be appointed a federal circuit court judge is also an American-Korean. There are a few well-known physicians who are of Korean ancestry. The early Korean immigrants never lost their hope for Korean national independence, and each considered himself a freedom fighter for national liberation from Japanese domination. This hope came true at the end of the Second World War in 1945.

At present only a handful of original Korean immigrants, perhaps fewer than twelve, are still alive in Hawaii. But the Korean community there has been growing in terms of quality and quantity. The number of Korean immigrants has increased since 1968. According to official reports, between 1959 and 1968 only 3 Koreans emigrated to Hawaii. In 1969, however, 284 arrived and in 1973, 1,305. In 1974 and 1975 more than two thousand five hundred entered Hawaii. Since the Korean War, many young Korean scholars have engaged in research projects at the University of Hawaii.

In 1971, the Center for Korean Studies was established "to coordinate and develop the resources for the study of Korea at the University of Hawaii." The primary objectives of the Center have been "to enhance faculty quality and performance in Korean studies, to develop comprehensive and balanced academic programs, to stimulate research and publications, and to coordinate the resources of the University with those of the Hawaiian community."[14] The Center's building, which is near completion in 1978, is designed after the traditional Korean palace. If everything goes as planned, Hawaii will become an intellectual center for the Korean community in the

United States. At present, more than a dozen faculty members, mostly Korean, engage in teaching and research work at the Center. Dr. Suh Deasook has been director of the Center since it was established.

Things are not entirely bright in Hawaii's Korean community today. The people face leadership problems. The traditional leaders have gone, and the remaining early Korean immigrants will soon disappear. Only four traditional organizations remain: the *Tongji-hoe*, the Korean National Association, the Patriotic Women's Association, and the Yong Nam Women's Society. The principles of these organizations are obsolete, membership has declined, and they are no longer socially or politically important. Nor do the second and third generations have active organizations like the Japanese-American Citizen's League. In other words, no meaningful social, cultural, or political organization exists within the Korean community in Hawaii.

The newly arrived Korean scholars seem to avoid direct involvement in Korean community affairs. It is quite clear that without new intellectual leadership, the Korean community cannot make real progress toward a healthier and better society.

The new immigrants face many problems similar to those their predecessors faced: a language barrier, cultural conflicts, and problems of employment. The gap between the old and new generations is another problem because of the lack of communication between them. Hundreds of immigrant children who do not speak English are denied an opportunity to learn in the public school system because of the total inadequacy of bilingual facilities. On the other hand, Korean immigrant parents hesitate to send their children to Korean language schools. In 1971, for example, a Korean language school remained open during summer vacation but fewer than thirty children enrolled.

At present, Koreans in Hawaii do not avail themselves of existing public and private services. This is caused partly by the absence of Korean influence in organizations that take charge of public services, and partly by public and private ignorance of Korean needs.

6.

Koreans on the Mainland

COMING TO CALIFORNIA

Koreans from Hawaii came to the West Coast of the mainland because the railway companies needed manpower and offered slightly higher wages than Hawaiian plantation owners. In addition, job opportunities for Orientals were better and more varied on the mainland; agricultural work in California, railroad and mining jobs in Oregon, Washington, Montana, and Utah were wide open. General housework, cleaning, restaurant work, janitorial work, and other underpaid jobs involving hard physical labor were available in the urban areas.

Between 1904 and 1907, just before the formal immigration of Orientals to the mainland was banned by a presidential executive order, about one thousand Koreans entered San Francisco. From there, they scattered up and down the West Coast, although most remained in California. Dinuba and Reedley, in the San Joaquin Valley, and Sacramento and Delano became the centers for the Korean immigrants. In addition, San Francisco and Los Angeles emerged as focal points of Korean social, religious, and political activities.

There were fewer than fifty Koreans living in San Francisco before 1904. Most were engaged in selling ginseng to the Chinese residents; some were students. They had already organized social clubs under the leadership of Ahn Cha'ng-ho, a respected patriot who came to the United States in 1899. They had also formed an informal Christian church and held worship services on Sundays in private homes.

When the newcomers from Hawaii arrived in San Francisco, they faced all sorts of difficulties. Many of them had no money and often owned nothing more than one suitcase. Most of them did not speak English since they had no opportunity to learn the language while working on Hawaiian plantations. Practically all of them were plantation workers who were not prepared to handle other jobs such as house-cleaning, gardening, or cooking.

All the newcomers were required to take physical examinations and deposit a certain sum of money with the Immigration Service. Fortunately, these two requirements were solved without much difficulty. Dr. Drew, who had worked as a physician at an Amercian mission in Korea, took care of the physical examinations, and none of the immigrants were barred from landing in San Francisco. Also, the *Kongnip Hyop-hoe* (Mutual Assistance Association) became the sponsor for the newcomers, so the financial deposit was waived.

Some of the leaders of the *Kongnip Hyop-hoe* acted as employment agents for the newcomers. For example, Ahn Cha'ng-ho made personal visits to Chinese farms and businesses to let the Chinese know that Koreans were ready for work any time they were needed. In this way, some of the Koreans were able to acquire jobs. A few went to Utah and Wyoming to work for mining companies, and some were hired for railroad construction work in Arizona. The remaining Koreans went to farms in Riverside to pick oranges.

Perhaps it might be worth telling the story of how Koreans were able to secure orange-picking jobs on Riverside farms, which were operated by white people. Orange-picking was hard work, and the American orchard owners preferred Orientals to white laborers. The wages of the Orientals were lower but they produced more work. They were willing to work longer hours without overtime pay, and they obeyed the instructions of the employer without any complaints. At this period, orange-picking was more or less monopolized by the Japanese. Therefore the members of the *Kongnip Hyop-hoe* worked out detailed plans for securing orange-picking jobs in competition with the Japanese.

The plan was as follows. Physically strong and experienced Koreans were to be sent to the Riverside orchards as a sample labor force. They were told to construct their own living quarters as soon as they arrived, without asking for any money from the Americans. Then they were to organize a working team of ten men. Each man on the team was supposed to follow these working guidelines: "Our only capital today in this land is nothing but honesty; therefore, work diligently without wasting time whether your employer watches you or not; then you will be working not only today but tomorrow and even the whole year round. If your employer has confidence in you, then your friends, Kim, Lee, or Park will also get jobs, because of your hard and honest work. In this way, eventually all Koreans will get jobs anywhere and at any time."[1]

With these instructions, the newcomers were sent out to the Riverside orchard farms. Most of then did not have money and did not speak English. So the members of the *Kongnip Hyop-hoe* collected money and bought train tickets for their fellow Koreans. They also prepared lunch boxes. When the working team got on the train, the leaders of the *Kongnip Hyop-hoe* told the conductor the name of the station where they were to get off. This is one of the examples of how a minority ethnic group like the Koreans worked out tactics for survival in a strange and hostile land.

The "Yellow Peril"
and Korean Experiences with Racial Discrimination

After 1900, American hostility against Orientals—Chinese, Japanese, and Korean—steadily increased. Hostile groups claimed that the Orientals were evil and dirty, an inferior people who would eventually take over all the jobs from white working-class people because they were working longer hours for lower wages. This concept of a "yellow peril" spread all over the United States. It was most intense, however, in California, where most of the Orientals lived. In 1906, for example, the San Francisco School Board decided that American-born students of Korean and Japanese ancestry could not attend the same school as white children but had to attend Oriental schools with the Chinese. A local judge named Robinson made a public statement that "Puerto Ricans and Koreans were immoral and religious fanatics."[2] At that time, the Japanese population in California was estimated at 110,000; the Chinese, close to 45,000; and the Korean, a little over 1,000.

The concept of a "yellow peril" was based on racism, the idea that white people were superior to non-whites. Cultural conflicts and misunderstandings between whites and non-whites were also a factor. In addition, the economic interests of white people versus Orientals played an important role in the "yellow peril" hysteria.

In 1913, the California state legislature passed the Webb-Heney Land Law. This law prevented immigrants who were not allowed to become naturalized citizens from owning land. This meant that Koreans, Japanese, and Chinese alike could not buy land or other real estate such as houses, apartments, and commercial buildings. After passage of the Oriental Exclusion Act of 1924, no Koreans were allowed to enter the United States with the exception of students who were admitted to American universities for advanced studies. As a result of this act, many Korean immigrants suffered because there was no way they could reunite with members of their families in Korea. The Korean immigrants in the United States did not receive the basic human rights and protections that white European immigrants received.

Curtural conflicts were another cause of racial discrimination. For example, Japanese males tied samurai-style bands around their heads and wore only *fundoshi* (loincloth) in the summertime. Sometimes males and females took baths together. They ate *sashimi* ("raw fish") with chop sticks, and they bowed several times when greeting one another.

However, the economic issue was the underlying cause of anti-Japanese feeling among white people. The Japanese were hardworking and diligent. They worked from ten to twelve hours a day for lower wages than most white people would accept. Some Japanese leased farm land and sold their products below the general market price. Furthermore, the Japanese produced much better rice, vegetables, and fruits than white farmers did.

How about the Chinese? They were famous for keeping their own traditions and customs no matter where they lived. Some male Chinese wore black caps and smoked long-stemmed pipes. Chinese women wore Chinese dresses at all times, and some still practiced the custom of foot-binding. Sometimes, opium-smoking and gambling could be seen in the Chinese community. The Chinese spoke loudly in the home as well as in the street. They did not appear friendly, and it took time for them to become real friends with non-Chinese. They were very money-minded: they saved all they could and sent their savings to their homeland. They stuck together and lived in their own communities. They also established afternoon or evening schools and taught Chinese history, culture, and language to their children. Most second and third generation Chinese speak their parent's tongue and therefore there is no language barrier between generations.

During the period under study, the American public was not ready to accept such Chinese attitudes, nor did they attempt to understand them. Instead, many Americans looked down upon the Chinese as an uncivilized people.

Koreans were about the same. They retained their own traditions. Some wore native clothing and smoked long pipes. They also talked loudly, both in private and public. They ate *kimchi* (Korean hot pickles), which have a strong odor that was noticeable in any Korean residential area. However, the Korean population in America was very small compared with that of the Japanese or Chinese. The total number of Koreans in the United States never exceeded ten thousand, including students, until the end of the Second World War. Koreans were sometimes called "invisible Americans." Often they were regarded as being either Chinese or Japanese because their family names were the same as the Chinese and their physical appearance resembled both. Koreans in America were a forgotten people indeed until the Korean War.

In the early days, Koreans were refused service in restaurants, barber shops, and public recreation facilities. White landlords often refused to rent them houses or to lease them farming lands. American-born Koreans, although they were citizens, could not get white-collar jobs even if they had college or university degrees. They were treated as second-class citizens. After Korea became a colony of Japan in 1910, Koreans suffered even more from racial discrimination. They rejected the protection of the Japanese government and became anti-Japanese. They organized their own self-governing body, the Korean National Association, which became an official organ of the Koreans in dealing with American authorities. Under such social and political conditions, the Koreans had to depend largely upon their own personal strength and power.

In the midst of the "yellow peril" scare, Koreans experienced an explosive racial riot, known as the "Steward Incident." Mrs. Mary E. Steward, a native of Missouri and a Christian, owned an orange orchard in Upland, California. She employed Koreans as orange-pickers, and they camped on her property. One night, white farmers and workers attacked the Korean camp with stones and rocks, threatening to kill the Koreans if they did not leave the camp at once. The frightened Koreans had no other place to go and no other prospect of employment. They stayed at the camp site, afraid to move for fear of being killed by the rioting white mob. At this critical moment, Mrs. Steward got in touch with the police and was given permission to buy guns so the Koreans could defend themselves. She told her Korean employees that if anyone attempted to invade their camp, they were to shoot. At the same time, she contacted the local newspapers and made the incident as well as her actions public.

The white farmers in the neighborhood sent Mrs. Steward threatening letters demanding that she fire all the Koreans from her orchard at once. But she rejected their demands, saying: "The minority Korean people in this great country of America have a right to live and work just as other nationalities. They are hard working, diligent and honest people who are struggling for a decent life. Therefore, your hostile attitude toward these people cannot be justified."[3] The camp was saved from further trouble by Mrs. Steward's firm stand. After the situation had subsided, Mrs. Steward introduced Koreans to her neighbors as excellent workers. Thereafter, many Koreans, including students looking for summer jobs, were able to find employment as orange-pickers in southern California.

The Korean intellectuals, who came to the United States as political "student" refugees after their anti-Japanese activities, faced as much hardship and racial discrimination as the other Korean immigrants had. Job opportunities were almost nil in the fields for which they were qualified, so they had to work as houseboys, janitors, dishwashers, or busboys. They had bitter experiences with racial discrimination. Dr. Chang Lee-wook, former president of the Seoul National University and former ambassador to Washington, D. C., described his personal experiences with racism in America.[4] Among other things, he stated that in Los Angeles one day, "I entered a restaurant and sat down in order to have lunch. Although there were not many customers, the waitress did not come to my table. After awhile, a young receptionist came to me and said with a low voice that, 'we can't serve you lunch, because if we start serving lunch to the Orientals, white Americans will not come here.' "

The same year, 1918, Dr. Chang saw another ugly incident on the train to Dubuque University. At dinner time, a black passenger entered the dining room. The waiter led him to a seat and then pulled a curtain around him to prevent anyone from seeing him eating in the same dining room as the white passengers.

Dr. Chang concluded by saying that after fifty years, "I could see with my own eyes some of the great changes that took place in the matter of human relations in America, although racial discrimination still exists and many problems remain to be resolved."

Dr. Chang wrote an article entitled "There Is an Unforgettable Generation." Since this is the only major statement written by a well-known Korean educator who experienced American life and was involved in Korean community affairs for many years, it might be well to quote from his article at length.

> Seventy years have passed since the Korean immigrants came to the United States: during which period the first generation have almost gone and the second and third generation (American-born Koreans) together with the new immigrants have settled down in America as masters of the Korean community.

Dr. Chang then mentioned the rapid increase of the Korean population in Los Angeles.

> I wonder how many Koreans today will remember the early immigrants who laid the foundation of the Korean community? The life of all early Korean immigrants—pioneers of the Korean community—had been the same everywhere; of loneliness, hardship, and fatigue. The first generation suffered more mentally and physically than the succeeding generations, because Korea was annexed by Japan; they became men without country. Nobody cared for and looked after them. Nevertheless, more than two thousand Koreans, including the political refugees, did not lose their hope, and thought that their first duty was to work for the cause of the restoration of national independence from the Japanese domination.

Dr. Chang pointed out that every Korean in the United States participated in activities for independence. Some donated a large part of their earnings to the independence movement. Some did not hesitate to sacrifice their lives. He cited the assassination of Durham Stevens, whose statement that Japanese control of Korea was working for the good of the Korean people was printed in the *San Francisco Chronicle* in March 1908. All the legal expenses for the defense of the two Koreans who took Stevens' life were met by the Korean residents in America.

It was at this time that all existing Korean social and political organizations, both in Hawaii and on the mainland, merged into the Korean National Association. The purpose of the Association was to protect the interest of Korean residents in the United States. The Association established its headquarters in San Francisco. There were overseas chapters in Siberia, Mexico, and Manchuria. The Korean community leaders, including Ahn Cha'ng-ho, Park Yong-man and Syngman Rhee, traveled all over the United States for the cause of national independence. All their expenses were met by the Korean residents in America. When the March First independence demonstration took place in Korea, many Korean residents in America donated "patriotic money". The Korean provisional government in Shanghai was able to carry out its activities because of the financial support of the Koreans in America. Dr. Chang said, "I still remember when Mr. Kim Jong-lim and Lim Jun-ki donated $1,000 cash and Shin Kwang-hi and two others, $500 as patriotic money." Dr. Chang considers this "patriotic money" a different kind of money from the money of today's Korean residents in America. He argues that the idea behind the financial drive and the manner in which the money was earned are different, as is the way in which the money was spent. "Patriotic money" was the fruit of the sweat and blood of the early immigrants, and it was used for national independence.

Dr. Chang suggested that although most of the early immigrants have gone, their noble idea of patriotism should be inherited by the present Korean community. He further said that Korean residents should work out fresh principles for the advancement of the Korean community. He concluded, "I miss the early immigrants who were my dear friends . . . and it is about time to do something for the memory of the early Korean immigrants—the pioneers of the Korean community—as a token of respect for their unselfish services for the development of the Korean community and the cause of national independence."[5]

THE LIFE STORY OF MRS. ROH JUNG-SOON

One wintry morning in January 1923, Jung-soon was at her neighbor's house to meet her long-awaited fiancé from America. It was the first time she would see her fiance in person, even though she had been engaged to him for nine years. She had received a letter from him several months earlier but was not informed of his arrival. She was overly anxious to see him since she had only seen him in pictures. When she saw him, however, she was quite disappointed, for he was dark and differed a bit from what she had expected. Yet she could not do anything since she was already twenty-eight years old and also had a younger sister to worry about. (In Korea in those days, young girls were usually married before the age of twenty. Also, girls were married in order, that is, the oldest one first.) So finally Jung-soon married and started a new life as the wife of Roh Shin-tae.

Nine years earlier, everything had been arranged by Jung-soon's aunt in Sacramento. Roh, who was originally from Ko-sung, had left Korea in 1905 to seek financial opportunities in Hawaii. Both the Sino-Japanese War and the Russo-Japanese War had been fought in Korea, and the resulting severe famine and semi-colonial status had forced young Roh to leave his homeland.

Roh worked on a sugar plantation in Hawaii for one year. He had to work extremely hard to earn a living. He rose at three o'clock in the morning to cook breakfast for his fellow plantation workers, toiled on the farm during the day, and in the evening returned to cook dinner again. For this routine he received fifty cents a day. After one year, realizing that his hard work was not paying off properly, he decided to move to the mainland. He arrived in San Francisco just after the great earthquake, so work was impossible to find. He was forced to move to Sacramento and work on a farm again. Because of his limited English, it was the only job available. It was while working in Sacramento that he met Jung-soon's aunt. He remained on the Sacramento farm for seventeen years before returning to Korea to marry his fiancée.

Jung-soon was engaged when she was nineteen years old. She wanted to marry Roh because she was fascinated by the idea of going abroad. She was born and raised in Pusan, the biggest harbor city of Korea, and she had hardly been out of her home town.

After the Rohs were married in Pusan, they left Korea on March 3, 1923. Mrs. Roh remembered the day well, for it was the day on which, Koreans say, the swallows return from the south after the long winter. The couple went to Japan, where they underwent a physical examination that took a week. They finally arrived in San Francisco on May 15, 1923, but had to stay in quarantine for three days. Then, at long last, they went to Sacramento to see Mrs. Roh's aunt.

It was a very long trip from Korea to Sacramento, and Mrs. Roh had much time to think about and plan for the future. She did not like the idea of her husband working on a farm and wanted him to learn a skill. Her new life in America, she discovered, was very difficult. For awhile, she stayed with her aunt while her husband worked on the farm. He earned about five dollars a day. During the winter rainy season, however, work was not to be found. Roh would return empty-handed, not being able to find work for the day. Life was truly miserable. Unable to support themselves, they were dependent on her aunt's family. She again pressured her husband to learn a skill in a field where a job was available.

About two years later, on a rainy day when farmwork was still nil, Roh decided to become a barber. He borrowed $125 from a friend to attend school to learn the trade. It was very difficult at first because of the language problem, but he studied hard for three months and managed to finish with good results. He decided to move to Oakland where his friend had a barber shop. He worked there for two months and then, in June, 1926, opened a shop of his own on Seventh Street in downtown Oakland. He paid $40.00 a month rent for the shop. The cost of a haircut in those days was thirty-five cents; a shave, twenty-five cents. At first customers were few, and Roh could not earn enough to pay the rent. He also had to pay a monthly rent of $12.50 for the place in which they lived. After both rents were paid, nothing was left over for food. The Rohs were starving and had no place to turn to but a Korean church in Oakland. They asked the minister there, Lim Jung-ku, for help. Mr. Lim got in touch with public welfare agents, and the Rohs received some free food for their children. They lived on welfare for a few months. Mrs. Roh could never forget those days. Being so limited in funds, she cooked nothing but cabbage soup and rice with sometimes a little bit of hamburger meat.

At last, their life began to look up a little. The barber shop business finally started paying off after three or four years. Roh charged seventy-five cents per haircut while his competitors charged a dollar. Now he had regular customers, although most of them were old. By 1941, he was earning $35 to $45 per day. That same year Jung-soon started her own business, a public shower-and-bath business. Since the shop was close to the harbor, a lot of crewmen from the ships came to take a shower. She made about $30 a day by charging fifty cents for a shower and forty cents for a bath.

By 1942, the Rohs were finally able to save some money. In fact, they saved enough to buy a small hotel. It was the building in which Mrs. Roh's public bath was located. Even when money was very tight, Roh had paid his rent regularly, so the owner of the building had a good impression of him. The building was estimated to be worth $15,000 but the owner was willing to sell for $9,500. Furthermore, he accepted the measly down payment of $300 that was all Roh could afford. He bought the building in his daughter's name, for in those days real property could only be bought by an American citizen.

By 1945, the family's income had jumped to almost $2,000 a month. They earned $500 from the hotel, $500 from the bath business, and $700 from the barber shop. They were economically secure now and in return for what they had received many years earlier, they worked for the Korean community. Mr. and Mrs. Roh were good Christians, and they attended the Korean church regularly, contributing to it both physically and financially. They joined the Korean National Association, paid dues, and gave many special donations.

Today, Mrs. Roh Jung-soon is eighty years old. Her husband and eldest son have passed away, but she has four daughters and one son living. To her

earlier regret, only one daughter married a Korean man. Her other daughters are married to a Chinese-American, a black, and a Caucasian. Her son is
married to a Chinese-American and is a board member of the Berkeley
Unified School District. She had hoped that all her children would marry
within their ethnic group. At one time, she had even refused to see one
daughter for three years because she did not marry a Korean. But now she
feels no regret and is extremely proud of all her children's success.

Mrs. Jung-soon was one of the hundreds of picture brides who came to
this country between 1910 and 1924. Since most were better educated than
their husbands and wanted more out of life, these picture brides helped
Korean men get away from the farm. As can be seen from the story of Mrs.
Roh, it was she who pressured her husband to move away from the farm
where he had spent twenty years of his life.[6]

KOREAN COMMUNITY ORGANIZATIONS IN THE EARLY PERIOD

As mentioned in the previous chapter, the first Korean community organization was the *dong-hoe*, or village council, a self-governing body established on every plantation in the Hawaiian islands in 1903. That same
year, *Sinmin-hoe* (New People's Society) was formed in Honolulu to protest Japanese interference in Korean affairs. Between 1903 and 1907,
Koreans in Hawaii organized more than twenty different social and political as well as cultural organizations. One of the main objectives of the organizations was opposition to Japanese domination of Korea. The leaders of
the organizations realized the necessity of unity, and in September 1907 the
various groups emerged into one organization named the *Hanin Hapsong
Hyop-hoe* (United Korean Society). It had headquarters in Honolulu, with
branch offices throughout the Hawaiian islands.

On the mainland, the *Chin'mok-hoe* (Friendship Society) was organized in 1903 by Ahn Cha'ng-ho. It was the first social organization of
Koreans in San Francisco. The first political organization was formed in
1905; it was called *Kongnip Hyop-hoe* (Mutual Assistance Society), and all
the members of the *Chin'mok-hoe* joined it. It published *Kongnip Sinpo*
(News of the *Kongnip*). the first Korean language newsletter in the United
States. In 1907, another political organization, *Taedong Pokook-hoe*, was
established by Chang Keng. Its newsletter was called *Taedong Kongpo*. The
membership of each political organization was not more than thirty. The
Kongnip Hyop-hoe, however, had more members than the *Taedong
Pokook-hoe* and had branches in Los Angeles, Riverside, and other places.[7]

Most of the early Korean community organizations were influenced in
terms of principles, functions, and structure by the Korean Christian
Church. This was only natural because most of the leaders of the community were members or ministers. As will be discussed later, the Church

was the center of the Korean community. When it faced trouble, the community was involved in the same trouble.

When news of the 1905 Protectorate Treaty between Korea and Japan reached the Korean community in America, community leaders saw the necessity of unifying all the existing organizations. The unity movement was accelerated by an unexpected event, the assassination of Durham Stevens on March 23, 1908, in San Francisco. In order to mobilize the financial and moral resources of the Koreans in America to defend the two Koreans who killed Stevens, the *Kongnip Hyop-hoe* in San Francisco and the *Hanin Hapsong Hyop-hoe* in Hawaii merged. The Korean National Association (*Taehan Kookmin-hoe*) was established on February 1, 1909, in San Francisco. In the meantime, the *Sinhan Min-po*, or *New Korea*, a weekly Korean language newspaper, began to publish.

According to its original constitution, the Korean National Association had the following objectives: to promote educational and business development in the Korean community, to advocate freedom and equality among the Korean people, to look after the welfare of the Koreans in America, and to work for the restoration of national independence.[8] The leaders of the Association were moderate intellectuals and patriots who came to the United States as political refugees or as immigrants in the early part of this century. The Association acted as the "official agent" of the Korean community in dealing with American authorities. For example, the Association sponsored Korean political student refugees who came to America by way of China or Europe without passports. The refugees were allowed to enter the country because the Association was sponsoring them. The Association also acted as an employment agency for Koreans who were seeking jobs, and it arbitrated any disputes that took place between employers and employees. The Association collected annual dues from its members in order to support its activities and to pay the salaries of staff members. The Association gave financial support to the Korean provisional government after it was established in 1919 in Shanghai.

In 1937, the Association adopted a new constitution, which consisted of fifteen chapters with fifty-four articles. Chapter 1 contained its principles and a platform, which read: "The purpose of the Association shall be to promote the common well-being of Koreans and to push forward the independence movement to restore our fatherland, while respecting freedom and equality" (article 2). It set forth five methods of achieving the objectives of the Association: (1) rendering social services; (2) promoting education; (3) promoting economic development; (4) assisting the Korean provisional government in exile; and (5) encouraging a patriotic spirit among Koreans.[9]

Membership in the Association was never more than one thousand even during its most successful period, but many Korean nonmembers supported the Association because its ultimate objective was to obtain national independence. Therefore the Association was a very active political organization until the end of the Second World War. Today it has become an inactive body, although it still retains headquarters in Los Angeles and publishes *New Korea*.

Ahn Cha'ng-ho believed that attaining Korean independence would be a long process. He rejected the idea of military adventurism advocated by Park Yong-man, and he also disagreed with Syngman Rhee's plan of getting Western powers to put diplomatic pressure on Japan. Instead, he advocated a long-term program and, on May 13, 1913, established the *Hung Sa Dan* (Young Korean Academy) in San Francisco. The name had been suggested originally by Yu Kil-jun, the first Korean student in America, in 1884.[10]

In order to understand Ahn's organization a few words about the social and political conditions prevailing at that time are necessary. The Korean people in general, and the ruling circle in particular, were losing self-respect and self-reliance. Corruption and factionalism were rampant in the public institutions, and reliance upon a big power (*sadae sasang*) played a major part in the power struggle within the ruling class. In addition, a handful of traitors were busy selling the Korean peninsula to Japanese imperialists. Thus, the Korean people looked like a "mass of loose sand."

After the Russo-Japanese War, Japan virtually ruled Korea and in 1910 offically annexed it. The Western powers approved of Japanese expansion in the Far East. China and Russia were defeated by Japan on both the military and the diplomatic fronts. Under these circumstances, restoration of Korean independence seemed impossible in the near future. So Ahn worked out a long-term program for the independence of Korea.

Ahn set forth four principles and three disciplinary measures as the basic philosophy of the *Hung Sa Dan*. The four principles were truth-seeking, deeds, loyalty, and courage; the three disciplinary measures were knowledge, virtue, and health (article 3 of the constitution of the *Hung Sa Dan*).[11] The organization was non-political; as article 6 of the constitution stated: "Due to the permanent nature of its movement, the organization shall not be engaged in political activities; however, the members may have freedom of action in politics in accordance with their beliefs and conscience." In order to stamp out the age-old factionalism based on north–south sectional divisions, the *Hung Sa Dan* was formed by eight delegates, each of whom represented one of the eight provinces then existing in Korea. Ahn himself did not represent any province but served as an advisor to the organization. There was a legislative board, an executive board, and a judicial board. Every member was supposed to acquire at least one professional or technical skill. It also should be noted here that the *Hung Sa Dan* had three kinds of memberships: preparatory, regular, and special (article 13). In order to join, a person had to accept the principles and purposes of the organization, pass an oral test given by the selection committee members, and be sworn in at a ceremony before the committee membership chairman.

Membership in the organization came from Korean intellectuals and students as well as from professionals. Such well-known Koreans as writers Yi Kwang-su and Chu Yoo-han; Yi Yong-sull, one of the best surgeons; Dr. Chang Lee-wook, Dr. Paik Nak-joon, and Dr. Oh Chun-sok, respected educators; and Dr. Chough Pyong-ok, who ran against Syngman Rhee as a candidate for president, have belonged to the *Hung Sa Dan*. During the Japanese domination, members of the organization (which used the name *Suyang Dongwu-hoe* in Korea) were arrested on charges of anti-Japanese activities, and most of them received jail sentences.

It was a well-known fact in the Korean community in America that members of the *Hung Sa Dan* became predominant in the Korean National Association. Today the *Hung Sa Dan* exists both in Los Angeles and in South Korea. Some of its members are very active in social and political matters as individuals but not as members of the *Hung Sa Dan*.

Park Yong-man believed that direct military action was the best way to achieve independence for Korea, because Japan would give Korea up only if defeated militarily. Therefore, he organized a military corps (*kundan*) and recruited more than three hundred trainees among the Korean immigrants. Park and Rhee were unable to work together within the Korean National Association because of their different opinions as to what methods to use in achieving Korea's independence. Accordingly, each organized his own group of supporters in Hawaii and on the mainland.

On March 3, 1919, Park established the League of Korean Independence (*Toknip-dan*) with 350 members. The constitution of the League contained seven articles.[12] Its main purpose was to support the national independence movement of Korea both financially and morally. The immediate duties of the members were to collect funds to organize and train an army, and to publish the *Pacific Times* (*Taepyongyang Si-sa*), a weekly newspaper in the Korean language.

In May 1919, Park went to Manchuria to organize a military training institution there. He returned to Hawaii in July and proposed the following plan at a meeting of the League: (1) The actual campaign of independence should be in the hands of the Korean residents in the Far East. The Koreans in America should provide financial support to the independence movement in the Far East. In the meantime, they should concentrate on educational work for the Korean children in America and continue the weekly newspaper. (2) The League should purchase land in Manchuria to lay a foundation for establishing Korean military bases in the Far East.

These proposals were adopted by the members of the League, and Park departed for China in order to carry out the military training and land-purchase plan. Some of the League members sent Park money for that project. For unknown reasons, Park was assassinated in China by a fellow Korean on October 17, 1928. After his death, the League ceased to exist, and some of its members joined the Korean National Association.

Dr. Syngman Rhee also formed his own political group, called *Tongji-hoe* (The Comrade Society). There are two dates for the establishment of the group. Kingsley K. Lyu said it was formed sometime in November 1920, when Rhee was on his way to Shanghai to take over as president of the Korean provisional government. When Rhee arrived in Honolulu, a number of his supporters persuaded him to organize his own political party, and Rhee did so before leaving for Shanghai.[13] However, both Kim Won-yong and Noh Chae-yon stated that the party was officially established by Rhee on July 7, 1921, after he returned to Hawaii from Shanghai.[14]

One of the reasons for the formation of the *Tongji-hoe* was Rhee's belief that the ultimate objective of the Korean National Association had been fulfilled by the establishment of the Korean provisional government in Shanghai. From then on, Rhee felt, independence activities should be carried out by the government-in-exile. Then Rhee suggested that the name of the Korean National Association be changed to the Korean Residents Association (*Kyomin Dan*). Rhee's views were disputed between members of the Korean National Association and the League of Korean Independence on the one hand, and followers of Rhee on the other. This was the beginning of a factional struggle between anti and pro-Rhee groups that continued for two decades, as will be described in detail later in this book.

The constitution of the *Tongji-hoe* contained four articles. The basic purpose of the organization was to support the provisional government of Korea in Shanghai financially and to follow the policy of the provisional president. Rhee issued a proclamation in which he emphasized that every member of the *Tongji-hoe* should consider himself a self-appointed law enforcement agent and that those who were against the provisional government should be punished. Rhee was elected *ch'ong-che*, or executive-general, of the party. He began to publish the *Pacific Weekly*, a Korean language pamphlet financed by members of the *Tongji-hoe*. Branches of the party were established in major cities on the mainland: Los Angeles, Chicago, and New York. A headquarters building was built on North King Street, Honolulu, and another building on Ellendale Place in Los Angeles. Both buildings still stand.

On November 2, 1924, a general conference of the party was held in Honolulu. It elected Rhee as its lifetime chairman. The conference also adopted the following three principles:

1. The three pledges proclaimed in the 1919 Declaration of Indepen-

dence shall be observed. Let us carry out our great mission in a spirit of non-violence and self-sacrifice.

2. Systematic action is the mother of success. We shall therefore forsake acts of individualism, respect order within the organization, and obey the leadership.

3. Economic freedom is the life of a nation. Let us promote self-reliance together.[15]

The total membership of this party never equalled the membership of the Korean National Association; it never went over one thousand at the most. Some of Rhee's ardent followers have been constant contributors of money. After Rhee returned to Korea in 1945 and became president of the Republic of Korea in 1948, the party concentrated on supporting Rhee's policies. A few of its members served as cabinet members in the Rhee government. As soon as Rhee was dethroned from power by the student revolution in 1960, his party became virtually defunct. It still maintains offices in Honolulu and Los Angeles, but its membership has declined drastically. The building in Los Angeles has been used as a Korean language school (*Mukunghwa Hakwon*) for Korean immigrants' children as well as American-born Koreans.

Yet another organization of the early Korean immigrants is the Korean Women's Patriotic League (*Taehan Yoja Aekook-dan*), which was formed in August 1919 in Dinuba, California. It was a combination of several existing women's organizations.

The Korean Women's Society came into being on May 23, 1908, in San Francisco. Its main purpose was to provide educational and social services to Korean immigrants' children and Korean residents. It was more or less a friendship society among Korean women. On March 29, 1917, a group of Korean women in the Sacramento area formed the Korean Women's Association. Its purpose was to aid the Korean National Association and to boycott Japanese goods. A group of Korean women in Los Angeles organized a Women's Friendship Association on March 28, 1919. The objectives of this organization were to promote friendship among Korean women and to support social and cultural activities as well as church work. Members also pledged themselves to refuse to buy Japanese goods, and they raised money for the Korean independence movement.

On May 18, 1919, all the Korean women's organizations in California decided to merge into one organization. On August 2, delegates gathered in Dinuba and on August 5, the Korean Women's Patriotic League was officially established. The constitution of the League consisted of three articles.[16] The main purposes of the organization were to support the Korean independence movement in cooperation with the Korean National Association; to raise an independence fund; to boycott Japanese goods; and to promote educational and relief work for needy Koreans in America and Korea. Most of their activities were fund-raising, relief, and scholarship funding for Korean students. In 1946 alone, the League sent over one thousand tons of relief goods to South Korea. The League never had its own building; its meetings were held at the meeting hall of the Korean National Association in Los Angeles. Today, fewer than half a dozen of the original members survive, and their ages are well over eighty. Although the League still exists, in reality it is defunct.

Two left-wing political groups existed in America: the Sino-Korean People's League in Hawaii and the Korean People's Revolutionary Party in Los Angeles.[17] The People's League was formed in December 1938 and was dissolved in 1945. Its objectives were twofold: to promote anti-Japanese activities and also to help the Chinese people who were fighting against Japanese aggression in China. Haan Kil-soo, who acted as spokesman of the League, made anti-Japanese speeches prior to 1941 warning Americans that Japan was preparing to attack the United States in the near future and that the Japanese in America were prepared to assist Japan in case of war.

The League participated in the United Korean Committee during the Second World War, and Haan was appointed to a position in the public relations section. He resigned from the position because of a dispute with Syngman Rhee over propaganda policy.

The origin of the Korean National Revolutionary Party goes back to October 1939. Korean progressive leaders in America organized the China-Aid Society to help Chinese refugees after the Japanese invasion of China in 1937. At the same time, the China-Aid Society supported Korean guerrilla activities against the Japanese in China. In February 1941, the China-Aid Society changed its name to the Korean Volunteers Corps Aid Society in China. The Volunteers Corps was organized by Kim Won-bong, a left-wing military officer who became one of the founders of the Korean National Revolutionary Party in Chungking. General Kim served as minister of defense in the Korean provisional government when a coalition cabinet of right wing and left wing parties was formed. In January 1943, the Korean Volunteers Corps Aid Society changed its name again and became the American chapter of the Korean People's Revolutionary Party. It had close contact with party headquarters in Chungking.

The members of the Korean National Revolutionary Party in America were people from all walks of life: intellectuals, Christian ministers, newspaper editors, businessmen, housewives, manual laborers, and students. Their early activities in America had been scattered. They picketed the Japanese consulate in Los Angeles when Japan attacked China in 1937. They also picketed the piers whenever Japanese cargo-ships loaded scrap iron from America. They raised funds to help Korean guerrilla fighters in the

Japanese occupied areas in China. The party joined the United Korean Committee in order to support the war effort of the Allied powers in general and the United States in particular. But the party later withdrew from the Committee because of differences of policy in achieving Korean independence. The conservative Korean organizations, including the Korean National Association and the *Tongji-hoe*, accused the members of the Korean National Revolutionary Party of being leftists and supporters of the North Korean regime. The party published a weekly newspaper, *Independence*, in Los Angeles. The paper reported extensively on North Korean affairs. Some party leaders were investigated by American authorities, and a few were ordered to leave the United States. The Korean National Revolutionary Party was disbanded in 1955.

7.

The Economic Life of Koreans in the United States

LIVING CONDITIONS

Economic improvement for the early Korean immigrants was at first impossible, because they were used as a means of production by the plantation owners, whose main concern was obtaining profit by exploiting labor. Although the Korean immigrants were not contract laborers, like the early Chinese and Japanese immigrants, the language barrier, racial discrimination, and cultural conflicts hampered them from obtaining more gainful employment in accordance with their individual abilities and skills.

To even think of going into business was next to impossible, since most Korean immigrants had no business experience. The traditional Confucian social setting—the scholar on top and the merchant on the bottom—had failed to produce a business class in Korea. In addition, after Korea lost its independence, no official financial aid or protection could be expected from the homeland if the immigrants were mistreated by the plantation owners. As mentioned previously, the average daily wage of a Korean plantation worker was sixty-five cents, just enough to keep him from starving. A single plantation worker's monthly income was about $18; a two-worker family's income was $33. A single man's expenses per month including room and board and other absolutely necessary items such as working uniform, shoes, socks, and bedding were about equal to his income. Families with children often ran into debt.

Until the First World War, the economic status of all Koreans in Hawaii was about the same: immigrants and political refugees alike engaged in hard physical labor for absurdly low wages. They worked with their hands in the fields. Some intellectuals worked as dishwashers, busboys, kitchen helpers, house-boys, and janitors in urban areas.

During the First World War, some Koreans leased farm lands and cultivated them with members of their families. A few Koreans opened small family-operated shops—laundries, shoe repair shops, and used furniture

123

stores—in the cities. The war years were economic "boom" years for the Koreans in Hawaii. Korean economic and social patterns developed a diversity. Koreans became carpenters, tailors, store operators, and laundrymen at Hawaiian military bases. Oahu in particular offered Koreans many business opportunities. The Korean community as a whole was able to stand on its own feet economically. The average daily wage was $1.20; the monthly salary was $30.00. Living costs in rural areas ran about $25.00 for a single person and $38.00 for a married couple per month, not including such miscellaneous expenses as transportation, drinking, and entertainment.

The *Korean National Herald* in Honolulu reported that the total Korean population in the Hawaiian islands, including the second generation, was 5,550, of whom 3,550 were employed. The occupational classification ran as follows: 2,275 worked on the sugar plantations; 750 worked on pineapple plantations; land-owning farmers totaled 75; 150 were engaged in construction work on the military bases; 80 ran their own business establishments; and the rest were engaged in church, school, and community services.

The non-plantation worker's average salary ran from $60 to $100 per month.[1] It was during this period that most of the Korean immigrants were able to save money and pay transportation expenses for picture brides. About eight hundred brides came to Hawaii to marry early Korean immigrant bachelors.

After the immigration of the picture brides, the Korean community began to change from a stagnant society to a more progressive and prosperous one. Most of the old bachelors became family men. They felt they had responsibilities for supporting their families, and some gave up their drinking and gambling habits. Most of the families had American-born children, and Korean community activities increased with the establishment of more churches and language schools for the children.

In addition, many Korean immigrants began seeking a new life away from the plantations. They moved into the urban areas, particularly Honolulu. With their small accumulated capital, some of them bought farms, established family-operated businesses, or invested in real estate. In many cases, the Korean women had a better education and a better sense of business than the Korean men did. So they ran the stores with the help of their husbands. General living conditions greatly improved.

During the depression years of the 1930s, most Koreans in Hawaii did not suffer much, partly because their business establishments were not affected and partly because their jobs were not lost because they were not of a competitive nature. During the depression, many Koreans who worked on plantations moved into urban areas. On Oahu, they were well received by the United States Army, and many became civilian employees at the army camps. Some opened small shops for uniform alterations, laundry, and shoe repair.

During the Second World War, the Koreans had great opportunities for improving their economic state, since they were not treated as enemy aliens. Koreans in Hawaii dominated the apartment and rooming-house business. In Honolulu alone, the value of real estate owned by Koreans was estimated at $4 million soon after World War II.[2] Many Koreans also worked in army barracks, shipyards, and construction worksites, where the average wage ran from $10 to $15 per day. According to a 1973 report, ten Koreans, including second and third generations, became millionaires. Some of the older generation (only twenty-eight of the original immigrants survived) drew income from rental properties.[3]

While building up their financial equity, the Korean immigrants did not neglect their children's education. Today the educational level of Koreans is one of the highest among the ethnic groups in Hawaii. The second and third generations rank proportionately higher than other Asian groups in professions and business, especially in the legal, medical, and law-enforcement fields. In the real estate business, Koreans have done extremely well, but in businesses like the import–export trade, they have done poorly.

Koreans used their hard-earned money to maintain Korean traditions by establishing language schools and social groups, and by publishing newspapers, magazines, and books about Korea for their children. Furthermore, all Koreans in Hawaii participated in the national independence movement in one way or another. Apart from immediate economic needs, national independence was the one critical and predominant issue for the whole Korean community. Until 1945, most of their intellectual and financial resources were invested in this cause.

The living conditions of the early Koreans on the mainland were the same as those of Koreans in Hawaii. From 1903 to 1911, a few Koreans engaged in the ginseng trade in San Francisco. The great majority of Koreans became farm workers in California and Oregon. Some worked in railroad construction, mining, and fishing. Their wages were varied: a farm worker was paid fifteen cents per hour, a railroad construction worker, twenty-five cents, a fisherman's wage was $37 per month; he generally worked five to seven months a year. Most Korean fishermen worked out of San Francisco, Seattle, and Alaska during the fishing season. In the cities, Koreans worked as waiters, kitchen helpers, janitors, and house-cleaning boys. The average wage ran from $20 to $30 per month.

From 1911 to 1920, the general wage scale slowly increased both in urban and rural areas. Some Koreans started small family-operated businesses: barber shops, grocery stores, laundry shops, and vegetable shops.

During the war years, a few Korean farm workers pooled whatever financial resources were available among themselves and rented farm land. They planted seeds, harvested the crops, and then shared the profits.

The average wages of Koreans during this period were as follows:[4] mining workers received $6 and railroad construction workers $4 for eight hours of extremely tiring work. Agricultural workers were paid $3 per day and piece-work laborers made $6. In the cities, the average wage of a cook was $100 per month; a kitchen helper, $75; and a houseboy, $50. A single man's living costs ran from $35 to $40 per month, while a married couple's expenses ran from $55 to $65. Therefore, some Koreans were able to save money.

As in the case of Koreans in Hawaii, the majority of Koreans on the mainland participated in Korean community activities. They established Korean language schools for their children, churches, and political and social organizations for the cause of national independence. Most Koreans spent 5 to 7 percent of their total income on community affairs.

From 1916 onward, some large-scale farming was begun by Koreans. In Nevada, eighteen Korean families owned 290 acres of land on a cooperative basis. In Willows, California, Korean farmers cultivated 43,000 acres, and the total income for one year was estimated at $1.3 million.[5] A Korean farmer named Kim Jong-lim became a successful rice producer, and his nickname in the Korean community was "rice king." In the San Joaquin Valley of central California, a few Koreans began developing their own orchards, vineyards, nurseries, and fruit-packing plants. These became very successful because there was an available wholesale market for these products run by Koreans in Los Angeles. In the 1920s, agricultural production was high, but the price of rice went down sharply during the depression and most of the Korean farmers lost money. Some went into bankruptcy. American banks and loan companies could not lend money to the needy Korean farmers while the Korean community was not ready to rescue them from their financial troubles.

During the depression years, most Koreans continued working. Farmers cultivated their lands. The main products were rice, grapes, melons, and vegetables. In the cities, business establishments included restaurants, laundry shops, barber shops, produce and grocery stores, and variety or ten-cent stores. Some Koreans were also engaged in the wholesale produce-market. General manual jobs were scarce, but backbreaking non-union jobs, such as potato or fruit-packing jobs, were not difficult to find, since whites were not interested in such hard work at low pay in rural areas.

Here is an account of life on a farm by a Korean who worked for the Kim brothers in Reedley, California. As will be seen later, the Kim establishment became one of the most successful in the Korean community in America.

> If you picked grapes you had to be careful where you put your hand in the vines because black widow spiders and yellow-jacket hornets were all over the grapevines. Yellow-jackets built their nests so that they were difficult to find and black widows wove their spider webs all over the vine. As soon as I was stung by yellow-jackets I used to make mud-packs and place them on the wound to prevent the bite from swelling. . . . My mother and my brothers and sisters worked in the fields packing peaches, plums, nectarines, and grapes. Each of us made sixty-five cents an hour and we worked eight hours a day, six days a week. Saturday was a day off. The fruit had to be shipped into the market early Monday morning so we worked on Sundays. . . .
>
> On the days we worked my family rose at five o'clock in the morning and then we ate breakfast. At six o'clock all the workers met at Kim's house where the owners delegated the work. They told you where to go and who to work with in the fields.
>
> Some of the fields had peaches, others had plum trees, and some had grape vines. We followed the leaders of the group to the correct field and then the men did the picking if trees were too tall for the women. Meanwhile, the women, boys, and girls waited on the ground to pack the fruit. The men picked the fruit and put them in large buckets and we packed peaches in lug boxes that were placed on the stands. If we picked peaches we had to dust each one with a feather brush to knock off the bugs that caught on the peach fuzz. All the peaches were sized as we picked them and we checked each fruit for holes or big marks and if they were good we packed them. The fruits were checked carefully so that they would not be dumped by the fruit inspectors. . . .
>
> We packed until twelve o'clock and then we took an hour for lunch. Most of us took our lunch which consisted of rice, kimchi, and maybe some beef or chicken. Each of us picked our own tree and ate under the shade and after we finished we usually took a short nap.
>
> About one o'clock, we began working again until five o'clock. At five, we gathered everything and loaded it into a truck which returned to the owner's place.
>
> We got home around six o'clock and everybody fought to take a bath because if you work in the fields your wholy body gets covered with dirt from head to toe, especially if you pick grapes. When you packed peaches, the peach fuzz made you itchy.
>
> It is very hot and dry in the fields of the San Joaquin Valley. The day starts out around seventy to eighty degrees and by noon time the temperature reaches a hundred and five and a hundred and ten degrees. In the Valley there is no breeze whatsoever. The heat makes that job difficult because you have to lift heavy things in the hot sun. By the end of the day your arms and legs feel very heavy and your back really aches . . . working on the farm has never been easy. Farm labor demands endurance and strength from all workers. I remember the long hours and back-breaking work in the hot farm field.[6]

The unemployment rate was very high in the cities, because no jobs were available for minority groups. During the depression, most Korean students were forced to stop their studies and were not able to obtain even part-time jobs. Many went back to Korea without completing their studies.

From 1931 to 1942, no substantial economic changes took place in the Korean community in the United States. But once again, a wartime economic boom influenced Korean economic life. General wages started to rise, and many Koreans went into business and undertook various economic ventures. Farmers increased their production and made a profit as farm prices went up. Capital savings increased. From 1943 to 1954, the boom produced some wealthy families. The living standards of Koreans in America improved. According to the 1954 report of the Korean National Association, Koreans owned home properties valued at $3 million, while Korean farmers in California and Oregon owned land, farm implements, and facilities worth about $4 million.[7]

Prior to the end of the Second World War, more than fifty small and medium-sized businesses were set up on the mainland. Of the total Korean population of ten thousand, fewer than 5 percent were engaged in business, individually or on a partnership or corporate basis.

The most common businesses were the family-operated small stores, such as produce stores, corner groceries, laundries, rooming-houses, hotels, and restaurants. The capital investment in such small stores ran from $100 to $1,000. There were two medium-sized produce markets in Los Angeles, where about five hundred Koreans resided.[8] Chung Jung-yup and Paul Lim (second generation) established two partnership produce markets as retail stores. They employed five or six people (this author worked there during two summer vacations). Daily income ran from $100 during most of the week to $200 on Fridays and Saturdays. A small store's business volume was $15 to $25 per day. The weekly wage was $15 to $20 for sixty hours. There was no overtime pay, and a work week of six days was common.

The average annual income of Koreans during this period ranged from $800 to $1,000. Few Koreans owned homes. Rent ran between $25 and $50 a month. A few Korean businessmen owned cars or trucks. The monthly wage of the average manual worker was $75 to $85.

According to this author's experiences, the monthly living expenses of a student were as follows. Rent ran from $6 to $7 depending on the location and type of living quarters (usually one room or an apartment with a roommate), food costs ran from $8 to $10 (self-cooking), and miscellaneous expenses, $5. Tuition was usually $150 for two semesters at a private school; city or state colleges were free. Books cost about $30 a year. Clothinging, including shoes and other items, cost between $30 and $35 per year. A total budget for one year ran between $400 and $500.

Therefore, an average Korean family of five (with three children) had to have at least $500 to $1,000 a year. This meant that both husband and wife had to work in order to survive. In general, Koreans have been among the poorest of minority groups in the United States.

KOREAN BUSINESS ESTABLISHMENTS

The first Korean immigrant corporation was established in February 1910 under the leadership of Ahn Sok-jung. Ahn and other Korean residents in Redlands, California, formed the *Hungop Jusik Hoesa* (Business Promotion Corporation) with a total capital of $3,000.[9] Each share was to be sold at a price of $50. The main purpose of the business was to buy or lease farm land in order to produce rice. There is no record as to how long they were in business or how well they did. In the same month, the Korean Trading Company was established in San Francisco by Choi Yong-man. Total capital was set at $20,000. The company was forced to dissolve after Korea was annexed by Japan because the Japanese did not allow Koreans to import and export goods. In March 1910, the *T'aedong Silop Jusik Hoesa* (Great Eastern Business Corporation) was created with a total capital of $50,000 and a price per share of $50. The objective of the company was to create an economic base for the Korean independence army under the supervision of the Korean National Association. The members of the Association wanted to buy land in Manchuria to train a Korean independence army, but they were forced to give up the plan because of frequent attacks by Chinese bandits.

In March and April 1911, the Korean National Association of Hawaii organized the *Hanin Nongsang Jusik Hoesa* (Korean Agricultural and Commercial Corporation) in order to promote agriculture and commerce among the Korean immigrants who desired to engage in private farming. The total capital was set at $100,000 and the price of each share was set at $10. The primary objective of the corporation was to use its profits for training a Korean army, but because of the factionalism between Syngman Rhee's supporters and the Park Yong-man group, the business declined. Finally, the remaining funds were donated to the army training project.

In October 1911, Hu Seung-won and Yi Soon-ki established a variety department store in Stockton, California. They distributed agricultural supplies to the Korean farmers in that area. This was the first Korean department store in America. No record is available as to how long it lasted.

In December, under the initiative of Ahn Chae-chang, Im Jong-soon, Choi Kyung-o, and Yi Myung-sop organized the *Hanin Nongop Jusik Hoesa* (Korean Agricultural Corporation) in Nebraska. The total capital was set at $10,000 and the price of each share was set at $10. The group cultivated vegetables in Nebraska for four years with the invested capital. No information is available as to what happened after the four years.

A sketch of the "big" Korean business establishments might be appropriate here. As early as 1921, a partnership was formed between Charles Kim and Harry Kim (in the Korean community their names were Kim Ho and Kim Hyung-soon) in Reedley, California.[10] The business began as a trucking wholesaler of fruit. As the years went by, it expanded into large orchards, fruit-packing sheds, and nurseries. It was called the Kim Brothers Company. The Kim brothers tried to develop new varieties of fruit trees, working mainly with peaches and nectarines. Eventually, they developed a "fuzzless peach." Today, it is sold on the market as "Le Grand" and "Sun Grand," and saplings from the orchards are shipped throughout the United States. The Kim brothers developed more than a dozen other hybrid fruits for which they obtained patents from the government. They continued their business for thirty years, retiring in 1965. They owned six farms containing five hundred acres. The farms, packing plants, and nursery facilities were worth about $1.5 million. Every year they grossed more than $1 million. The Kim Brothers Company was one of the largest business establishments in the Korean community.

Many nationalities including Koreans, Mexicans, and white Americans worked for the Kim Brothers Company. The average number of employees was two hundred, but the figure doubled at harvest time. Many Korean students worked there during summer vacation. The company provided living quarters for the employees as the Hawaiian plantation owners did. The average wage was low: fifty to seventy-five cents per hour. During the war, it rose as high as $1.25 an hour.

Both Kims were very active in Korean community affairs. They were leaders of the Korean National Association for many years until they split in 1960 over the issue of reorganization. They also established the Korean Foundation, a non-profit organization that provided scholarship funds for needy Korean students. It is interesting to note that Warren Y. Kim (Kim Won-yong), the author of *A Fifty Year History of the Koreans in America (Chaemi Hanin Osipnyong-Sa)*, was associated with the Kim Brothers Company for many years as a top supervisory employee.

The Hanka Enterprise Company was formed by Hahn Shi-dae and members of his family in Delano in the 1920s.[11] Hahn came to Hawaii as an immigrant in 1905. He finished high school and then went to the mainland in order to become an independent farmer. He began by leasing land on which his whole family worked. During the First World War, he was able to save money and buy agricultural land. His company owned about four hundred acres, which was worth half a million dollars by the end of 1945. The company also went into the apartment-construction business in Inglewood, California. Many Koreans, including students, worked for the Hanka Company. Hahn joined the Korean National Association and the *Hung Sa Dan*, and emerged as one of the leaders of both organizations. After the liberation of Korea from Japanese domination in 1945, he sold all his business establishments in California and returned to his homeland.

The K. & S. Company was established in 1928 in Los Angeles as a wholesale company.[12] Its origin goes back to 1922 when two Korean students, Kim Yong-jeung and Song Chull (Leo Song), gave up their studies because of lack of funds and went into business as wholesale agents for the Kim Brothers Company. After a few years, they formed the K. & S. Company, which became one of the most successful wholesaling operations in Los Angeles' Korean community. Most of the Orientals who had retail vegetable stores became customers of the K. & S. Company. Its total assets were estimated at about three hundred thousand dollars at the end of 1945.

Kim and Song have also been active in Korean community affairs, although they belonged to different political groups. Kim belonged to the Korean National Association. For more than thirteen years he published the *Voice of Korea*, a monthly newsletter that provided information about Korea to the American public. The *Voice of Korea* had an anti-Syngman Rhee tone since it advocated neutralization of Korea as a way of unifying the divided country and maintaining national independence. The expenses of the *Voice of Korea* were met by the Kim Brothers Company (Kim Yong-jeung is a son-in-law of Kim Hyung-soon, a partner in the Kim Brothers Company).

Song was a constant supporter of Syngman Rhee from his student days. He joined Rhee's political organization, *Tongji-hoe*. Today he is regarded as a successor to Rhee. He has attempted to reorganize the *Tongji-hoe* under new guidelines based on the principles of "living right and living better than the other minority ethnic groups" in the United States.

The Yu & Han Corporation was formed in 1925 by several intellectual Koreans: Philip Jaisohn, political reformist and physician; Chung Han-kyung (Henry Chung), the author of *The Case of Korea*; and Yu Il-han, a graduate of the University of Southern California.[13] The total capital was set at $50,000 and the price of each share was $10. The corporation was to engage in the import and export of Oriental goods. It had its headquarters in Detroit. However, the venture lost money and lasted only three years.

One of the members of the corporation, Yu Il-han, then went into the pharmacy business. He imported ginseng and Chinese herbs into the United States and exported American drugs to Korea. Yu established his corporation's headquarters in Seoul and later opened branch offices in P'yongyang and in Hong Kong. Within the next ten years, Yu became one of the most successful businessmen in the Korean community. His business prospered during the postwar period under the Rhee administration and emerged as one of the most powerful business establishments in South Korea. It monopolized the trade of pharmaceuticals between the United States and South Korea. After Yu's death, his brother succeeded to the presidency of the corporation.

Peter Hyun established the *Dongyang Sikmul Jusik Hoesa* (Oriental Food Product Corporation) in 1926 in Los Angeles.[14] This corporation engaged in producing bean sprouts, canned mushrooms, soy sauce, and canned chop suey and chow mein. Its products have been widely distributed throughout the United States. It is now called the *Jan-U-Wine Food Corporation*. Total assets were estimated at two million dollars in 1958.

The Korean political and social organizations also started businesses. In 1917, members of the *Hung Sa Dan* (Young Korean Academy) established the *Puk-mi Silrop Jusik Hoesa* (North American Commercial Corporation).[15] The total capital was set at $95,000 and the price of each share was $100. Forty-five hundred shares were sold during the first period; the rest were sold during the second period. Most members of the *Hung Sa Dan* became stock holders. All the capital was invested in rice cultivation, and the corporation continued for a few years without losing any money. In the 1920s, however, it took a loss because of a poor harvest and the low price of rice on the market. The corporation was finally forced out of business in 1927, and only fifteen cents a share was allocated to each of the stockholders.

In 1938, the members of the *Hung Sa Dan* established another business corporation, *Dae-dong Sirop Jusik Hoesa* (Great Eastern Commercial Corporation), in Los Angeles.[16] The total capital was $10,000 which was collected from the members of the *Hung Sa Dan*. It started out as a chop suey wholesale business. Chun Kyung-moo, who came to Hawaii as a child with his parents and graduated college with an M.A., became the business manager and worked as a salesman. Because of a lack of business experience and capital, the firm went out of business within a few years.

The *Tongji-hoe*, Rhee's group, formed its own business corporation in 1925 in Hawaii.[17] Rhee called a *Tongji-hoe* conference at which he emphasized the importance of the *Tonji-hoe's* being self-supporting. The group thereupon agreed to set up the *Tong Ji Siksan Hoesa* (Comrades' Investment Corporation). The capital stock was set at $70,000 and the price of one share of the stock was $100. The corporation was incorporated for twenty-five years in February 1926. The corporation bought 910 acres of land at Olaa, Hawaii, near Hilo. It also constructed the *Tong ji chon* ("comrades village") as a model village for *Tongji-hoe* members, who engaged in the production of such items as vegetables and trees. The business was very poor, however, and the corporation lost money every year. According to a 1931 report, sales totaled $40,000 while debts were estimated at $55,000. The corporation went out of business that same year.

During the postwar period, the Korean National Association in Los Angeles bought a thirty-unit apartment building. The price was $250,000 but the down payment was only $20,000, the total assets of the Association. Within a few years, the Association was forced to declare bankruptcy because of its inability to make monthly payments. Thus, none of the business establishments formed by Korean political and social organizations survived.

RECENT TRENDS IN BUSINESS

A comprehensive presentation of Korean business establishments in the United States is difficult because of the lack of materials on the subject. The influx of a large number of Korean immigrants, an average of twenty thousand per year since 1972, makes it almost impossible to know their occupations and skills. The frequent job changes create further complications. At the present time over three hundred thousand Koreans are scattered over the United States, and the absence of a centralized organization responsible for gathering and disseminating information on business establishments, occupational patterns, and employment situations, makes it difficult to obtain accurate data.

However, there are some general trends to be seen. The new immigrants are better educated and more skilled than their predecessors were. Many are professionals, such as medical doctors, scientists, and teachers. An overwhelming majority of the newcomers have settled in highly urbanized and industrialized areas; fewer than 5 percent of the newcomers are engaged in farming. This is, of course, a reversal of the situation of the early immigrants. This means, among other things, that the economic life of Koreans in the United States has become diversified. Their occupations range from janitorial work to the legal and medical professions, and their business establishments include wig shops, real estate firms, and used-car dealerships.

The postwar Korean businessmen in the United States appears more aggressive and adventurous as well as more profit-oriented than the early immigrants. Some businessmen profited from dubious political connections within South Korean ruling circles. A few wealthy Korean residents in Japan also entered the United States in recent years to avoid unfavorable pressures from the Japanese government and business world since the oil crises. Such businessmen are often referred to as "money refugees." After making money in South Korea and Japan, they came to the United States because they felt it was a safe place in which to enjoy a luxurious life. Some of them have bought extravagant mansions: for example, one Korean, a former resident of Tokyo, purchased Elizabeth Taylor's mansion for $2 million in cash. Most such Korean businessmen have isolated themselves from the Korean community and do not act as Koreans at all. They usually make a few business trips to Korea, Japan, and Hong Kong every year.

On the other hand, many small establishments in the Korean community have come into being all over the country like mushrooms after a rain. Nearly 10 percent of the total Korean population in America is engaged in business. The rest includes manual workers, skilled workers, and professionals.

According to the report of the U.S. Department of Commerce, the total number of large Korean business establishments in America was 1,201. Their total trade amounted to $65 million a year. California had 540 different business establishments with a volume of $32 million a year; Hawaii had 165 business establishments with a volume of more than $15 million a year; and New York had 93 establishments that did $3.5 million a year.[18] This report, of course, does not reveal the real picture of Korean business in America, since it does not include small and medium-sized business establishments.

As I mentioned at the outset, since comprehensive presentation of the postwar economic life of Koreans in America is almost impossible, this study will attempt to analyze two selected areas of Korean business establishments: Los Angeles and Washington, D.C. Then a rough picture of the living conditions of the average Korean family in America will be presented.

Although no systematic and continuous documentation of the activities of Korean-operated businesses in these areas exists, there are some reports in Korean language newspapers on this subject. This author has also made use of personal observations and has consulted a directory of the Korean community published by the Korean Association of Southern California, as well as several unpublished manuscripts.

The interim report on the Korean population in Los Angeles indicated that between 1974 and 1975 there were at least 1,322 Korean-operated businesses in Los Angeles, where seventy thousand Koreans live. The classification was as follows:[19]

Wig shops	140
Services (gas filling stations)	137
Trading companies	110
Groceries	101
Restaurants	56
Maintenance agencies	54
Oriental physical training centers	26
Dressmakers	25
Insurance agencies	23
Shoe repair shops	22
Painting (house painting)	22
Travel-service agents	17
Oriental herb doctors	16

Licensed doctors' offices (private practices) 15
Used-car dealers 15
Income tax services 15
T.V. and radio shops 14
Real estate brokers 13
Law firms 12
Sewing factories 12
Hotels and motels 12
Dentists 12
Gift shops 10

In addition, there were about two hundred other kinds of enterprises, each numbering fewer than ten. These included architects's offices, flower shops, laundry shops, barber shops, driving schools, book stores and theatres. There were eight different Korean language newspapers (both local and national, daily and weekly), five radio and television stations, two Korean-operated hospitals (community type of clinics), three banks, and one Korean language school. Ninety-eight non-profit organizations existed, including student alumni associations, professional clubs like those of doctors and nurses, and scholarship foundations. There were more than one hundred and twenty religious organizations, including Catholic, Protestant, and Buddhist groups.

The Korean Business Association of Washington, D. C., released statistics in 1975 which stated that there were one hundred and seventy-five Korean businesses there, and more than ninety thousand Koreans in residence. The classification was as follows:[20]

Type of Business	Number in 1975	Comparison with 1974
Restaurants	29	Increased from 19
Groceries	23	Increased from 12
Beauty shops	20	Increased from 2
Wig shops	16	Decreased from 19
Trading companies	8	Increased from 6
Service stations	6	Decreased from 7
Physical training centers	6	Increased from 4
Accountants	5	Increased from 4
T.V. and radio shops	5	Remained the same
Travel services	4	Increased from 1
Real estate brokers	4	Increased from 2
Emigration service agents	4	Decreased from 10
House renovating	3	Increased from 1
Farmers	3	Increased from 2
Ice cream shops	3	Remained the same
Oriental herb stores	3	Increased from 2
Flower shops	2	Remained the same
Dressmaking shops	2	Remained the same
Driving schools	2	Remained the same

In addition, there were fifteen other enterprises, including insurance agencies, legal offices, and laundry shops.

A few observations can be made on the above. The wig shop business used to be the top money-making business in the Korean community but today the situation is different. Since European countries began exporting wigs to the United States, the business has become very competitive, and Koreans are not in a predominant position. However, wig shops are still on the top of the list of business classifications in many cities.

Food-related retail shops (groceries selling both Oriental and American food, and restaurants with predominantly Korean menus) have risen to the top of the list of businesses in the Korean community in major cities. For example, according to a recent report, at least one or two new Korean restaurants come into being every month in Los Angeles and competition is severe. In some cases, price wars designed to attract customers have caused some restaurant owners to go out of business.

Many Koreans are now operating liquor stores and service stations, which also have risen to the top of the list of Korean business establishments along with groceries and restaurants.[21]

Since the South Korean government encourages export trade in order to balance its trade deficit, many Koreans have ventured into the trading business.[22] On the other hand, the prospects for professional and semi-professional businesses have also improved. This is partly because the Korean population in America has increased rapidly. It is also partly because most Koreans go to Korean lawyers, doctors, insurance agents and accountants where there are few language barriers or cultural conflicts.

A rapid increase in Oriental physical-training institutes (*tang-soo* in Korean, *karate* in Japanese, and *kung-fu* in Chinese) is an interesting recent phenomenon. A majority of the trainees are Caucasians: learning the art of Oriental physical training seems to have become a fashion trend among the American younger generation. It remains to be seen how long this trend will continue.

In general, the Korean business establishment in America is still in a beginning stage in terms of capital investment, of business experience, of management, and of marketing. Usually the capital investment is small, between $25,000 and $50,000. Most of the businesses are family-operated and most, especially the food-retail businesses, draw their customers from the Korean population. Caucasian customers are limited because of unawareness on the part of Americans of the existence of Korean merchandise. Many Koreans open businesses without much knowledge of business management or marketing research.

A CASE STUDY OF KOREAN BUSINESS IN LOS ANGELES

A recent study of Korean businesses in the Olympic area of Los Angeles reveals some general aspects of Korean-operated enterprises.[23] The Olympic area, which includes Washington Blvd., Beverly Blvd., Hoover Blvd., and Crenshaw Blvd., is a Korean-dominated section and is called "Koreantown."

The study found that there are more than two hundred and fifty Korean business establishments in the area. The largest number are the eighty-two food-related retail and service stores; the next largest are the professional and semi-professional services, of which there are sixty-one; and the smallest number are the twenty-four wholesale and trading businesses. The first two categories of businesses dominate with 52 percent of all businesses in the Korean community. Furthermore, the small-scale service businesses constitute 70 percent of all the category. This means that small-scale business establishments are predominant in the Korean community.

Tables 1 and 2 below show the number of employees and total assets of one hundred and fifty-one business establishments out of two hundred and eighty-seven (136 establishments refused to supply any information). Table 3 shows the source of capital loans from the Small Business Administration (S.B.A.).[24]

TABLE 1: NUMBER OF EMPLOYEES

Number of Employees	Food-related Retail	Services	Wholesale & Trading	Total
1 — 5	24	11	75	110
6 — 10	2	8	23	33
11 — 15	2	1	2	5
16 — 20	0	1	0	1
21 — 25	1	0	0	1
26 — 30	0	0	0	0
31 — 40	0	0	0	0
41 — 50	0	1	0	1
Total	29	22	100	151

TABLE 2: ASSETS

Total Assests	Food-related Retail	Services	Wholesale & Trading	Total
Under $20,000	17	12	10	39
$20,000 $50,000	6	7	16	29
$50,000 $100,000	5	2	17	24
$100,000 $200,000	0	1	14	15
$200,000 $300,000	1	0	17	18
$300,000 $400,000	0	0	11	11
$400,000 $500,000	0	0	7	7
$500,000 $750,000	0	0	4	4
$750,000 $1,000,000	0	0	2	2
$1,000,000 $2,500,000	0	0	2	2
Total	29	22	100	151

TABLE 3: NUMBER AND AMOUNT OF KOREAN LOANS FROM S.B.A., 1971-1974

Business Category	Number of Each Category	Amount of Loans
1. Liquor stores	33	$2,850,550
2. Markets	18	$1,713,400
3. Restaurants (including coffee shops)	15	$1,542,600
4. Grament manufacturers	5	$2,260,600
5. Trading companies	4	$ 660,000
6. Other services	14	$ 346,000
7. Other retail shops	12	$ 995,600
Total	101	$10,368,750

The study found that 93 percent of all businesses have ten or less employees and 54 percent have five or less employees. It also reveals that 68 percent of all businesses, including wholesale and trading companies, have assets of less than $50,000 and 47 percent of all businesses have assets of less than $20,000. The annual sales volume is between $250,000 and $500,000. This annual sales volume looks large but it is a gross receipt, not profit. This sales volume constitutes 41 percent of the total Korean business in the Olympic area.

As for sources of capital, the study findings are as follows. The total number of Korean business establishments that received loans between 1971 and 1974 from the Small Business Administration (S.B.A.) was one hundred and one. The amount they received was $10,368,750. About two-thirds of the loans totaling more than $6.1 million, went to liquor stores (thirty-three), markets (eighteen), and restaurants (fifteen). Garment manufacturers (five) received more than $2.2 million, which represented the largest amount per loan. This figure indicates that the S.B.A. was the major source of capital for food-related retail businesses.

The study also noted that some small Korean businesses have been successful despite their owners' lack of previous business experience. In addition to S.B.A. loans, many Koreans started out with capital of their own, either brought from Korea or built up from savings in this country. A majority of Korean businesses are of the self-employed, family-centered type. And the family members are hard workers. They work from ten to twelve hours a day, seven days a week.

The study found that the food-related businesses which are most often bought and sold are the markets or grocery stores, liquor stores, and restaurants. The most profitable are liquor stores and groceries. Most of these businesses can be run with a capital of twenty to fifty thousand dollars. These businesses are highly competitive, however, and can fail within a short period unless they are well advertised or have reserve capital.[25]

For example, there are about sixty Korean restaurants in Los Angeles. Within a one-mile area centered between Olympic and Vermont Avenues, sixteen Korean restaurants were established in three years.[26] In order to draw customers, the new restaurants started out with lower prices than those at existing restaurants. Soon, the old restaurants began to lower their prices to compete with the new ones. Then the new ones again started lowering their prices even more to prevent their customers from going to the old ones. The price war between the old and new restaurant owners continued until one side or the other went out of business. Many restaurant owners were either forced to declare bankruptcy or had to look for another type of business.

A major contributing factor to such fierce competition has been the inability of Korean businessmen to penetrate the American business world. Most Korean businessmen are afraid of going into business with non-Koreans or non-Orientals because they lack experience in dealing with Americans and also because of language difficulties. Thus, the small Korean businesses are ethnically oriented: that is, the businesses are directed toward serving the Korean community rather than the American community. Most Korean-owned grocery markets, restaurants, night clubs, travel services, and other professional and semi-professional businesses are specifically geared to a Korean clientele. The trouble with this is that the Korean clientele is limited, that is to say, there are too many Korean businesses for the number of Koreans. This means that Korean businesses must expand from being ethnically oriented to being American oriented so that trade can be drawn from the American people at large.

8.

The Korean Independence Movement in America: 1905-1930

THE INITIAL PERIOD

In 1905, a Korean national independence movement was established in the United States under the leadership of Korean patriots, intellectuals, and students. Its activities can be divided into two periods: The period of anti-Japanese activities in Hawaii and on the mainland from 1905 to 1930 and the period of the united front against Japanese military expansion in Asia from 1930 to 1945.

During the initial period of the movement in America, Koreans concentrated on individual action against pro-Japanese persons, both Koreans and members of other nationalities. The Koreans in America also sent delegates to the world peace conferences and petitioned Western powers in general and the United States in particular.

Nearly all of the seven thousand Koreans in the United States were concerned about events in their homeland. The immigrants, political refugees and students alike, had dreams of returning to Korea as soon as they made enough money or the political situation improved. The early Koreans in America always thought of themselves as temporary sojourners, and they all participated in the national independence movement.

On August 7, 1903, the first political organization, called *sinmin-hoe* (New People's Association) was formed in Hawaii under the leadership of Ahn Jong-su and Yun Pyong-ku. The main purpose of this association was to unite the Korean residents of Hawaii in working for the maintenance of Korean independence without interference by foreign powers. On September 22, 1903, the first social organization, named *Chi'nmok-hoe* (Friendship Association), was organized by Ahn Ch'ang-ho in San Francisco. It had nine members, and Ahn was elected chairman.[1]

More social and political organizations were established both in Hawaii and on the mainland. On May 3, 1905, the *Ewha Chi'nmok-hoe* (Friendship Society of Ewha Plantation) on Oahu was organized. Its purpose was to launch a movement to boycott Japanese goods. On August 24, 1905, Korea's Mutual Aid Society was organized in Hawaii, and Song Hyun-joo was elected chairman. On September 22, 1905, the Mutual Assistance Association (*Kongnip Hyop-hoe*) was established in San Francisco by members of the Friendship Association. The headquarters of the Association was located at 938 Pacific Street, and a ceremony dedicating the building was held on November 14.[2] This was the first political organization of Koreans on the mainland, and its main purpose was to work for the restoration of Korea's national independence. Ahn Cha'ng-ho was again elected president of the Association, and on November 22, 1905, the first Korean language bulletin, the *Kongnip Sinpo* (News of the *Kongnip*) was published and distributed to Korean residents in the United States. The ultimate objective of the Korean social and political organizations was the same: the restoration of national independence.

The first political action by Koreans in America was the unsuccessful attempt to send Korean delegates to the peace conference held to end the Russo-Japanese War of 1904-1905. Through the diplomatic initiative of President Theodore Roosevelt, the conference was held in Portsmouth, New Hampshire. On July 9, 1905, the two political organizations, the *Ewha Chi'nmok-hoe* in Hawaii and the *Kongnip Hyop-hoe* in San Francisco, jointly decided to send two delegates to the conference to present the Korean case. The Koreans in Hawaii, after consulting with the Reverend John Wadman, who had helped to establish the Korean Methodist Church in Honolulu, selected the Reverend Yun Pyon-kua to represent all Koreans in America. The Reverend Mr. Wadman introduced the Reverend Mr. Yun to Secretary of War William Taft, who had stopped in Hawaii on his way to Tokyo for a secret meeting with the Japanese prime minister, Katsura Taro. The Reverend Mr. Yun obtained a letter of introduction from Taft to President Roosevelt; no reason has been found as to why Taft wrote the letter. Mr. Yun arrived in San Francisco and had a meeting with Korean residents. Then he and Syngman Rhee, who was then a student at George Washington University, went to New York to see Roosevelt.[3] They asked the president for permission to attend the conference. Roosevelt told them that such an important official matter should be presented through official channels. So Mr. Yun and Rhee called upon Kim Yun-jong, the Korean minister in Washington, D.C., and asked him to intercede on their behalf. Kim refused, saying that he had received no instructions from the Korean government on the matter and had no authority to do anything about it. The minister's refusal led to furious arguments between him and the two delegates, and Rhee even threatened to burn down the minister's home. Kim responded by threatening to call the police if they did not get out of the building.

Rhee and Mr. Yun gave up and returned to their hotel.[4] Since they had failed to receive help from either the United States government or the Korean minister, they were forced to abandon their hopes of attending the peace conference.

The Portsmouth Treaty of September 5, 1905, approved the gradual Japanese domination of Korea. The Korean people felt their country had been betrayed by the big powers. The news of the treaty and the subsequent Japanese Protectorate Treaty over Korea caused Koreans in America to think about anti-Japanese activities in a more militant way.

The renewal of the Anglo-Japanese Alliance Treaty stated that "Great Britain recognizes the rights of Japan to take such measures of guidance, control and protection in Korea, as she may deem proper and necessary to safeguard and advance their interests."[5]

In a secret agreement between Roosevelt and Katsura, the United States endorsed Japanese domination over Korea in exchange for a pledge that "Japan does not harbor any aggressive design whatever against the Philippines." The defeated Russian government recognized Japan's "paramount political, military, and economic interests" in the Korean peninsula. Later the Korean people learned that George Kennan, a well-known writer and an influential friend of Theodore Roosevelt, had played an important role in formulating the Roosevelt-Katsura secret agreement on Korea.

On November 17, 1905, the Japanese Protectorate Treaty over Korea was signed. It was made public on November 29. Its main points were that Japan, through its foreign ministry, was to have control over Korea's foreign relations, and that the Korean government hereafter was not allowed to make any international agreement without prior approval by the Japanese government. A Japanese resident-general was to be stationed in Seoul. His main responsibilities were taking charge "of and directing matters relating to diplomatic affairs." At the same time, he was to "have the right of private and personal audience with His Majesty, the Emperor of Korea." Japan was to station residents at various other cities in Korea.

At once the Japanese government ordered the Korean government to close down all Korean legations and consulates abroad. On February 5, 1906, the Japanese government advised all Koreans abroad to place themselves under the jurisdiction of Japanese consulates. Koreans in Hawaii and on the mainland of the United States jointly called a protest rally and passed a resolution condemning Japan's aggressive policy in Korea and pledging themselves never to recognize Japanese authorities either in Korea or abroad. The resolution also stated that the Koreans in America would fight against the Japanese until they stopped their aggressive actions in Korea.[6] A copy of the resolution was sent to the Japanese government as well as to the Korean government.

Korean residents in San Francisco were determined to oppose any interference by the Japanese in Korean community affairs. At the same time, they refused any help from the Japanese consulate in the United States. For example, during the San Francisco earthquake in 1906, a few Koreans were injured and the Korean church and the Mutual Assistance Association building were destroyed. One of the Korean newspapers in Seoul published an inaccurate report, supplied by the Japanese consul-general in San Francisco that twenty-four Koreans had died and eighty-seven had been wounded during the earthquake. The same newspaper also said that the Korean king was about to send 10,000 won (Korean currency) in relief funds to the Japanese consul-general, authorizing him to distribute the money to Korean residents. The members of the Mutual Assistance Association investigated the matter and made a strong protest against the Japanese consul-general, stating that Koreans in San Francisco would not tolerate any further false information about their affairs. On June 24, 1906, the Association sent an announcement to all Koreans in America which read in part: "We are calling your attention to the fact that we are anti-Japanese, so we shall not accept any relief fund from the Japanese consulate. We shall reject interference of Japanese authorities in our community affairs in any manner. No matter how great a plight we are in, we must always refuse Japanese help."[7]

The announcement was published in the *Tae-han Daily News* in Seoul, and the Korean king sent $2,000 in relief funds to the American Foreign Mission in New York, asking them to distribute it to the Koreans in San Francisco. Korean newspapers in Korea launched a relief fund campaign and sent money to Mr. Drew and the Reverend Mr. Moffett, American missionaries to Korea who were then in the United States. The missionaries turned the money over to the Mutual Assistance Association to help needy Koreans.

TAKING DIRECT ACTION

A brief summary of some important events may be necessary in order to understand the violent activities of Koreans in America against pro-Japanese persons. In May, 1907, the Korean king sent a secret mission to the Second Hague Peace Conference. Although Korea had not been invited to the conference, the Korean secret mission presented its credentials and asked for recognition. The Korean mission was headed by Homer B. Hulbert, a trusted adviser of the Korean king, and included Yi Sang-sul, Yi Chun, and Yi Wi-jong. At this time, Korea was a Japanese protectorate. So the peace conference refused to recognize the credentials of the Korean delegates and even refused to receive their petition. The petition pointed out that the

Japanese had acted without the consent of the Korean king on the protectorate treaty; that in order to attain their aims, the Japanese had resorted to armed force against the Korean government; and that the Japanese had acted without any regard for the laws and customs of the Korean people. Therefore, the so-called protectorate treaty was illegal and invalid.[8]

When the peace conference turned down the Korean petition, one of the delegates, Yi Chun, committed suicide in protest. Hulbert and the two remaining delegates came to the United States to ask President Roosevelt for his aid in conformity with the Korean-American Treaty on 1882. Article I reads: "If other powers act unjustly or oppressively with either government, the other will exert their good offices, on being informed of the case, to bring about an amicable arrangement, thus showing their friendly feelings."

But President Roosevelt did not even grant them an interview. Thus the mission failed completely. Yi Wi-jong returned to Korea, while Yi Sang-sul remained in the United States and worked with the leaders of the Korean community. Later he was sent to Manchuria as a representative of the Korean National Association to form anti-Japanese Korean organizations in that part of the world.

The general feeling of the Korean people against Japanese domination was expressed as follows: "Let us strike against Japan, and then, if must be, all die together with our country and with our Emperor, for there is no other course open to us. . . . Mr. Yi Chun went to foreign lands to plead for our country, and his plans did not carry well, so he cut his stomach asunder with a sword and poured out his blood among the foreign nations to proclaim his patriotism to the world. . . . Those of our twenty million people who do not unite offend against the memory of Mr. Yi Chun. We must choose between destruction or the maintenance of our country. Whether we live or die is a small thing, the great thing is that we make up our minds at once whether we work for or against our country."[9]

The Korean king had to pay a price for his secret mission. On July 19, 1907, he was forced to give up his throne in favor of his son, who was still a minor. The abdication plan was devised by two pro-Japanese Koreans, Yi Wan-yong and Song Byong-jun, with the approval of the Japanese resident-general Ito Hirobumi. The new terms of the Japanese Korean agreement were signed by pro-Japanese Korean cabinet members. The new agreement stated that the Korean government agreed to act under the guidance of the resident-general in all administrative matters—all reforms, laws, ordinances, and regulations—and to appoint as high officials Japanese subjects or other foreigners recommended by the resident-general. Thus, the resident-general became the virtual dictator of Korea.

Hereafter each department of the Korean government had a Japanese vice-minister who became the actual head of the department. The national police, courts, and even prisons were taken over by the Japanese. On August 1, 1907, the Korean national army was disbanded.

Koreans in America heard the news with indignation. They considered it a national humiliation. The Koreans in San Francisco called a mass meeting and discussed ways and means of stamping out pro-Japanese Korean quislings. One of the members of the Mutual Assistance Association volunteered to go to Korea to kill the quislings. He was twenty-year-old Yi Chae-myung, who had come to Hawaii as an immigrant in 1905 and landed in San Francisco the following year. On October 9, he went to Korea on the S.S. *Siberia*. He had to wait for two years before taking action. Finally, his opportunity came when the pro-Japanese Korean prime minister, Yi Wan-yong, attended memorial services for the king of Belgium at the Catholic Church on Jong-hyun Street, Seoul. Yi Chae-myung attacked the prime minister with a knife as he was returning from the church. The prime minister was seriously wounded but his life was saved by immediate medical treatment. Yi was arrested and charged with murder. He was executed on September 10, 1910, in Seoul.[10]

The Stevens assassination was the second direct action taken by Koreans in America against pro-Japanese persons. The Japanese government recommended that the Korean government appoint Durham White Stevens, who had been in the diplomatic service of the Japanese government since 1885, as adviser to its Foreign Affairs Department. The Korean government did so. In the meantime, under the Japanese domination of Korea, Western business enterprises, including American interests, suffered. Naturally, American businessmen, as well as the government authorities, were concerned about the Japanese monopolization of the Korean economy, which was contrary to the Open-Door policy America advocated in the Far East. At this juncture, Japanese authorities thought that it might be a good idea to send Stevens to Washington to explain the Japanese position and to seek some kind of compromise between the United States and Japan on the economic problems of Korea. At the same time, Stevens wanted to present to the American public the view that the Japanese administration in Korea was working for the benefit of the Korean people, that the Koreans were happy and welcomed Japanese rule.

On March 20, 1908, Stevens arrived in San Francisco aboard the ship *Nippon Maru*. He made a public statement on Japanese policy in Korea, which was printed in the *San Francisco Chronicle*. The statement made four points. First, Korean government officials had corrupted and exploited the people, so that the Koreans had no confidence in their own government. Second, the Korean people were illiterate and backward, and were unable to govern themselves. Third, if Korea were not under Japanese protection, it might now be under Russian domination. Fourth, the present Japanese resident-general was acting in the interests of the Korean people, who were very happy and enjoyed a better life in every aspect.[11]

The Koreans in San Francisco were outraged by Steven's remarks. On March 22, they called a mass meeting and decided to send representatives to protest his statement. The four delegates chosen were Choy Chung-ik, Chung Chae-Kwan, Moon Yang-mok, and Yi Hak-hyun. According to an eyewitness, Yang Choo-en, the only original Korean immigrant still living, the meeting with Stevens took place in the following fashion.[12]

The four delegates met Stevens in the lobby of the Fairmont Hotel. The spokesman of the delegation asked Stevens whether the *Chronicle's* article about Korea was his own and whether it gave a true picture of the Korean situation. Stevens replied that the article *was* his own and that it was factual. The delegates then told Stevens that his views were totally wrong and demanded a public retraction. He refused. At this juncture, one of the delegates, Chung Chae-Kwan, knocked Stevens down with a chair. The other delegates hit him with their fists and bruised his face. The fight was stopped by guests at the hotel. But the guests were angry at the Koreans because, as Yang remembers the incident, "the yellow people insulted the white people." At this point, Yi Hak-hyun explained to the angry crowd the reason for the attack, saying that Koreans were indignant at Stevens' views justifying the Japanese domination of Korea. During Yi's speech, Stevens rushed into his room. The crowd calmed down, and the Korean delegates left the hotel.

The delegates reported the result of the confrontation with Stevens to a meeting of Korean residents. They could not decide what their next action should be. During the meeting Chun Myung-woon, a member of the Mutual Assistance Association, said: "I will volunteer for taking care of that pro-Japanese Stevens in my own way." Chang In-hwan, a member of the Great Eastern Protection Association (*Taedong Pokook-hoe*), was also present at this meeting but, as Yang recalls, he was very quiet and did not say anything about his plans.

According to Yang, Orientals were not able to buy guns at that time, and Chun brought a toy gun to attack Stevens.[13] However, Chang In-hwan secured a real gun from his roommate and took it with him. In the meantime, the Koreans watched Stevens' movements closely, and a Japanese-speaking Korean found out by phoning the Japanese consulate the exact time of Stevens' departure from the San Francisco Ferry Building for Washington, D.C.

At 9:30 AM on March 23, Stevens stepped out from his limousine with the Japanese consul, Shoji Koike. A waiting Chun attacked Stevens with his toy gun, and the two men engaged in a fist fight. At this moment, Chang fired three shots. The first one hit Chun's chest. The other two hit Stevens, who fell to the ground. The crowd shouted "lynch the yellow devils."[14] Chang was apprehended by the police, and Chun and Stevens were rushed to the hospital by ambulance. Two days later Stevens died at St. Francis Hospital.

Chang was charged with murder, while Chun was charged with attempted assassination. Chang's trial lasted several months. During the course of the trial, Chang testified in court as follows:

> I was born on March 30, 1875, in a northern Korean province and became a baptized Christian in my early age. When I saw my country fall into the hands of the Japanese, I was filled with sorrow, but I was unable to do much to help. I came to Hawaii as an immigrant to learn something in order to help my country. . . . While hundreds of thousands of Koreans are dying at the hands of the Japanese invaders, Stevens has the effrontery to invent the lie that the Koreans are welcoming their Japanese aggressors. . . .
>
> When Stevens was in Korea, he claimed to be working in the interest of Korea, but when he came to the United States, he made a complete about-face in attempting to cheat the public and in creating public opinion by means of dishonest propaganda, such as what he published in the *San Francisco Chronicle*. If Stevens ever got back to Korea, he would have done more to advance the interests of the Japanese.
>
> As a traitor to Korea, Stevens. . .made the Japanese occupation of Korea possible. . . . To die for having shot a traitor is a glory, because I did it for my people.[15]

The Koreans in America rallied, and formed a committee for the defense of Chang. They raised funds for attorneys and other expenses. Three attorneys were hired, but one of them volunteered his services. The committee needed a good interpreter for Chang. They asked Syngman Rhee, who was then a graduate student, for his services. But he refused because he was busy with his studies and did not want to be an interpreter for a man who had killed another human being. Finally Shin Hung-woo, a graduate student at the University of Southern California, Los Angeles, was hired as an interpreter.

The defense attorneys argued in court that "passion of patriotism" had forced Chang In-hwan to take his action, and that he should not be considered a murderer. On December 22, 1908, after nine ballots, the jury reached its verdict that Chang was guilty of murder in the second degree. Chun Myung-woon was acquitted on the grounds of insufficient evidence.

On January 2, 1909, Judge Cook sentenced Chang to serve twenty-five years in San Quentin. Chang said to the judge through his interpreter that he "preferred martyrdom by death rather than by imprisonment."[16] He served ten years and was released from San Quentin on January 17, 1919. He died on May 22, 1930, at the age of fifty-five and was buried in the Cypress Cemetery in San Francisco. Koreans consider Chang In-hwan a patriot, and many

Koreans have visited his grave to pay their respects. On August 3, 1975, Chang's corpse was flown to Seoul on Korean Air Lines and was buried in the National Cemetery.[17]

THE MILITARY TRAINING PROGRAM

On August 22, 1910, the Treaty of Annexation was signed by Governor-General Terauchi and the Korean puppet prime-minister, Yi Wan-yong. The formal announcement was made on August 29, and Korea became a colony of Japan under the rule of a military dictator. The annexation document included a proclamation as well as a treaty. The proclamation explained the so-called reforms in the Korean administration. Reforms here, of course, did not mean the needed socio-economic improvements for the benefit of the Korean people. Reforms meant the complete reorganization of the native political structure to resemble Japan's centralized political structure. The governor-general became an absolute dictator, and complete Japanization of the Korean economy, cultural life, and educational system emerged in Korea.

The Treaty of Annexation contained seven articles. Article I read: "His Majesty the Emperor of Korea completely and permanently cedes to his Majesty the Emperor of Japan all rights of Sovereignty over the whole Korea."

When Koreans in America heard the news of annexation, they held mass protest meetings everywhere. They declared that the annexation was outrageous and null and void because it was the act of a few national traitors and not the will of the Korean people. They also pledged never to accept Japanese rule under any circumstances, and they determined to fight for the restoration of national independence.

On September 1, 1910, the Korean National Association in America held an all-out rally. Representatives of every political, social, and religious organization adopted a resolution that read in part:

> Japan's annexation of Korea was forced by the Japanese agents in Korea with a few traitors of the Korean puppet government and was carried out without consent of the people. Therefore, we Koreans in America oppose it in the name of justice and humanity. . . . All Koreans in America regard Japan as an enemy nation and we shall sever all contacts with the Japanese government and its agents abroad. Those Koreans who make contact with and do business with Japanese authorities and the Japanese people in America shall be subject to punishment by the proper authorities of the Korean community. Hereafter, the Korean National Association both in Hawaii and on the mainland of the United States shall become the only legitimate official agent of all Korean residents. In every public event the Korean national flag shall be displayed and the national anthem shall be sung in order to demonstrate that we Koreans are an independent nation, and not a colony of Japan.[18]

The resolution also stated that military-training programs should be encouraged both in America and in Manchuria. August 29 was designated as a day of national humiliation, and Koreans were asked to observe it every year in order to renew and refresh their determination to oppose the annexation and restore Korea's independence. The resolution concluded by stating: "We are now resolved to oppose the Japanese annexation, and we call for the united efforts of all Koreans to put this movement into effect."

A copy of the resolution was sent to every head of government throughout the world, including the Japanese government and the governor-general in Korea. Since then, most Korean residents in America boycotted Japanese goods and refrained from any private or public contacts with Japanese people or Japanese authorities in the United States until the end of World War II.

After annexation, Korean leaders in the United States were divided on a policy for achieving independence. One group advocated militant action, including military-training programs among Koreans in America and Manchuria. The other group was for limited educational and diplomatic activities, on the basis that the restoration of independence was not possible in the near future. The militant group, headed by Park Yong-man, seized leadership and put the military programs into practice.[19]

There were about seven hundred ex-soldiers in America who had served in the old Korean army before annexation. Park became leader of this ex-soldier group. He had been a political prisonmate of Syngman Rhee, who opposed his approach. Park came to the United States as a student in 1904. He majored in political science and minored in military science at the University of Nebraska. He believed that Korean independence could never be possible except through a military revolt against Japan. Upon his graduation in 1910, he established a Korean Youth Military Academy in Hastings, Nebraska, with twenty-seven cadets. This military training program was endorsed by the president of Nebraska University, and university classrooms and playgrounds were used for military training. The Korean cadets worked on farms during the day and received military training in the evening: three nights of drill with wooden guns (aliens were not permitted real rifles) and two nights of class work (lectures) per week. In 1912, thirteen cadets completed training at the Korean Youth Military Academy.

In the meantime, military-minded Koreans established other military training camps: The Claremont and Lompoc Training Center in California; Kansas Camp in Kansas City; and the Superior Training Center in Wyoming, and later in the Hawaiian islands. Each center had about twenty cadets, some old and some young. A pilot-training center was established at Willows, California, under the leadership of Roh Paik-lin and Kim Jong-lim, who financed the project. The center bought two airplanes and trained nineteen pilots in two years under one American technician and six Korean instructors.

In the latter part of 1910, the Korean National Association in Hawaii set up military training centers and recruited about two hundred cadets. Realizing the necessity of consolidating the different centers, Korean military leaders agreed to set up a Korean National Brigade Center on Ahumanu Plantation, located on Oahu Island. Park Yong-man was elected head. More than fifty staff members, including five full-time instructors, worked on this project. The main financial support came from Korean plantation workers and the cadets themselves. The latter erected their billets and training camps and obtained use permits from the plantation owners. They worked on the plantations during the day and attended military training at night.

The brigade's organization and drill exercises were modeled after American ones, but the cadets had to use wooden rifles. Although private military training programs were illegal, the commanding officer gave tacit approval as long as real rifles were not used. In the beginning, more than three hundred Korean cadets enrolled for military training, and in August 1914, more than six hundred Korean residents of Hawaii attended the opening ceremony of the Brigade Center. It was equipped with more than three hundred wooden rifles, a few dozen pistols, a half dozen drums, ten sabers, and assorted military textbooks in both English and Korean. All the cadets worked two days a week on plantations and received three days of military training.

The military program continued for three years and trained more than two hundred cadets. Then it was forced to close, in part because the work contract with the Libby Pineapple Company was terminated, the Brigade Center had to move, and no other plantation owner offered grounds for military training. In addition, some of the Korean leaders were not in favor of continuing the military program, and financial support had declined.

As will be treated later in more detail, the ideological struggle between the Syngman Rhee faction and the Park Yong-man group intensified. Rhee had from the beginning rejected Park's military training plan on the grounds that it was not a realistic approach. Instead, Rhee stressed educational and diplomatic means as the surest and most reasonable avenue for achieving independence. These two approaches proved to be irreconcilable, and the factionalism seeded within the Korean community lasted for many years.

The military-training program came to an end when Park left Hawaii for China, where he wanted to establish a Korean military-training headquarters. The Korean military training program in Mexico, established by the Korean National Association, was also closed, because the Mexican

Revolution broke out and most of the Korean cadets joined the revolutionary forces. The total number of cadets in Mexico was 118. The name of the military school was Soong-mu Academy.

When the Brigade Center in Hawaii closed, it had a balance of approximately twenty thousand dollars. This money was kept for the establishment of military programs in China.[20]

ACTIVITIES BEFORE AND AFTER
THE MARCH FIRST INDEPENDENCE UPRISING

Koreans in America began to take an active role against Japan when President Woodrow Wilson announced his famous Fourteen Points, including the "self-determination" of small nations. As early as December 1918, the Korean National Association (hereinafter to be referred to as KNA) of America sent an open letter to all Koreans in the United States and Mexico. The letter appealed for unity and asked all Koreans to be ready to fight for the cause of national independence when the proper time arrived. The letter also proposed a unity conference with representatives from all existing social, cultural, religious, and political organizations in the two countries.

At this unity conference, it was decided to send a delegation to the forthcoming Paris conference. A three-man team, consisting of Syngman Rhee, Chung Han-kyung (Henry Chung), and Min Chan-ho was elected. In January 1919, the three delegates applied to the State Department for travel permits. Their applications were turned down on the grounds that Korea was under Japanese rule and the United States government was not in a position to issue exit permits to Korean nationals, although American authorities personally sympathized with the cause of Korean national independence.

The frustrated Korean delegates remained in Washington, D.C. and attempted to obtain visas from other countries, including Britain and Canada, but without success. It was at this time, perhaps in desperation, that Syngman Rhee submitted a proposal for Korean trusteeship which later became a political controversy within the Korean community. According to the *New York Times*: "On February 16, 1919, the delegate Syngman Rhee proposed a trusteeship for Korea under the League of Nations supervision until such time as Korea may be able to establish an independent government. It was signed by those three delegates and sent to President Wilson."[21]

The *New York Times* commented as follows: "President Wilson has been asked by the Korean National Association to initiate action at the Peace Conference looking to independence for Korea, with the country to be guided by a mandate until such time as the League of Nations shall decide that it is fit for full self-government. . . . The copy of the letter to the President was made public here today by Syngman Rhee, who, with Henry Chung, is an authorized delegate of the Association in the United States."[22]

In contrast to the situation in the United States, Korean nationalistic leaders in China were successful in sending a Korean delegate to the peace conference. Dr. Kim Kiusic (Kim Kyu-sik)[23] was sent to Paris in January 1919 by the New Korean Young Men's Association of Shanghai. On May 12, 1919, Dr. Kim submitted the "petition of Korean people and Nation for liberation from Japan and for Reconstruction of Korea as an Independent state, and the claims of the Korean people and nations to the peace conference."[24] The petition insisted that "the treaty of annexation of August 22, 1910 should be declared null and void or otherwise abrogated by the peace conference."[25]

The Paris peace conference never considered the Korean issue because of strong objections by Japan, one of the victors in the war. The Japanese delegates argued that the Korean issue was a domestic problem, just like the American administration of the Philippines. In addition, the Allied powers, including the United States, refused to give any support to the Korean people against Japanese rule.

Nevertheless, when news of the March First independence uprising reached the United States, Koreans in America called a mass meeting under the leadership of the KNA and decided to carry out independence activities regardless of the outcome. On March 15, 1919, the mass meeting passed a thirteen-point resolution as a guideline for the independence movement in the United States. Some of the main points were[26]:

1. The executive authority of the independence movement in America shall be granted to the Central headquarters of the Korean National Association of America; however, the regional headquarters of the Hawaiian Korean National Association will exercise its own autonomic power in conducting independence movements.

2. All expenses of the independence movement in America and [the] Far East (China) shall be met by the patriotic contribution funds collected from the Korean residents in the United States, Hawaii and Mexico.

3. Dr. So Chae-p'il (Philip Jaisohn) shall be appointed advisor to the KNA for diplomatic and propaganda activities, and a Korean Information Office will be established in Philadelphia under his chairmanship; the KNA will provide $800 per month for such activities.

4. The KNA will send its representatives to China to participate in the establishment of the expected Korean Provisional Government. (Ahn Ch'ang-ho was sent to China as representative of the KNA.)

At the same time, Ahn Ch'ang-ho issued a statement on behalf of the KNA, which read in part:

Remember the past; during the day we did our back-breaking physical work with our sweat and blood and we spent restless nights. Why
was it? Because we felt that we lost our liberty as human beings and our
country as an independent nation. Our earnest desires have been the restoration of national independence and our human rights, and now we
saw the birth of the March First uprising, which is the revival of our national spirit and this uprising will become an eternal foundation for our
Korean people's independence movement. . . .

As the world history teaches us, national independence has seldom
been obtained by passionate behavior alone and no people achieved
their independence without paying its price. There will be no exception
in our case: therefore, we must be ready to sacrifice ourselves for the
cause of national independence. We should remember that this struggle
is going to be a long and hard one.[27]

The statement concluded by suggesting three things that every Korean
in America should pledge himself to do. First, since developing unity was absolutely essential, Koreans should be honest with one another. Second,
Koreans should appeal their case to the American public in general, and to
Christian friends in particular, through the mass media. Third, Koreans in
America should carry the main responsibility for the independence movement's fund-raising campaign because they were in a better economic position than other overseas Koreans.

Koreans in America united under the banner of the KNA and concentrated on three things: diplomatic and propaganda activities, participation
in the establishment of the Korean provisional government in Shanghai, and
the launching of a fund-raising campaign. On March 17, 1919, the KNA set
up a Korean Information Office headed by Dr. So Chae-p'il in Philadelphia. Three representatives of KNA—Kim Ho, Kang Yung-so, and the
Reverend Whang Sa-yong—were sent to the Korean community to raise
funds. On April 4, a three-man delegation headed by Ahn Cha'ng-ho left the
United States for Shanghai to join the Korean provisional government.

On April 14, 1919, full propaganda activities began. The first Korean
Liberty Congress was called in Philadelphia under the leadership of Philip
Jaisohn and Syngman Rhee. Twenty-seven organizations from the United
States and Mexico sent representatives. The objectives of the Congress were
made public by Philip Jaisohn: "We called the Korean Congress because we
want America to realize that Korea is a victim of Japan. Korea's wrongs
have been insidiously covered up by Japan, and we believe that America will
champion the cause of Korea as she has that of other oppressed people, once
she knows the facts."

During the three-day session, a series of speeches from various delegates and lectures by Korean and American leaders in the fields of education, religion, politics, and business were delivered to the American public

through the mass media. Our case, the Korean leaders asserted, is "a just one before the laws of God and man. Our aim is nothing but freedom from the Japanese military rule, hence our objective is democracy for Asia. Our ultimate hope is universal Christianity."[28]

The Congress passed a ten-point resolution entitled "Aims and Aspirations of the Korean People." It can be summed up as follows[29]:

1. To accept the concept of the People's sovereignty.

2. To organize a Korean government based on the separation of powers.

3. To guarantee basic human freedom and civil rights.

4. To support the Korean provisional government in Shanghai as a legitimate government of the Korean people.

5. To support the Korean Liberty Congress in its representations to the United States government and the League of Nations to recognize the Korean provisional government in Shanghai.

The resolution obviously reflected Western democratic political ideology. On the last day of the Congress, the participants, including Koreans and American friends, staged a mass street parade headed by a platoon of reserves and a band, with each individual carrying Korean and American flags. The march ended at Independence Hall, where Syngman Rhee read the Proclamation of Independence of Korea. C. W. Kendall described the event as follows:

> In Philadelphia, the Cradle of American Liberty, a Congress of Koreans and sympathetic Americans convened. . . . Just before it broke up, the delegates adjourned to the Declaration Room in Independence Hall. Here, after reading the Korean Proclamation of Independence, they approached the old, cracked Liberty Bell. Amid profound silence, they placed their hands upon it, and, closing their eyes, prayed for the freedom of Korea and the success of the new movement. Those who saw it say it was the most impressive ceremony the city of Philadelphia has ever witnessed.[30]

Philip Jaisohn's views on the status of the Korean provisional government should be noted here. He said:

> It does not make any difference whether the President of the Korean government is in prison or whether he is in France; he may be in America; that does not make any difference. . . . It does not make the government non-existent, because it is not generally known where it is located. It is the will of the people that makes the government. . . . If you read the history of this country when the Revolutionary War broke out, you will recall that the Government was not established in any one place, they were forced to move around. . . . They had a capital in Yorktown, and then came to Philadelphia. That does not make the government illegal. . . . As somebody has well expressed it in Korean, the new provisional government of Korea is a personification of the will

of the people of Korea. . . . There is a will manifested by these Korean revolutionists and they should be the government of Korea. Now we want to recognize them. Whether or not we believe in the cause that these Koreans are fighting for today, that is the question that is before us, and the question as to where they are located will be developed in good time.[31]

The Korean people accepted Jaisohn's arguments justifying the provisional government installed by the Korean revolutionalists. But the cold fact was that none of the foreign powers were willing to recognize the Korean provisional government, although some of them expressed their sympathy.

Subsequently, the Liberty Congress changed its name to the Bureau of Korean Information and engaged in propaganda and information activities on behalf of the Korean provisional government. Jaisohn also organized the Korean Friends Society with more than one hundred prominent Americans who sympathized with the cause of Korean independence. The Bureau of Korean Information published various pamphlets, reporting Japanese atrocities and suppression of the demonstrators of the Korean independence movement. A monthly magazine called *Korea Review* was issued regularly from April 1919 until 1922. The Bureau's activities, however, ceased when elected president Rhee established the Korean Commission by executive order in September 1919. Rhee appointed Dr. Kim Kuisic, who came to the United States from Paris, to be chairman of the Commission.

Before discussing the activities of the Commission, it is necessary to say a few words about the Korean provisional government. Three different governments were established soon after the March First uprising in Korea: the Manchuria group, which was installed by left-wing leaders; the Shanghai group, which was a pro-American coalition of nationalist leaders; and the Seoul (*Hansung*) group, which was dominated by conservative leaders. None of the provisional governments was presidential like that of the United States. Instead, the head of the government was called the Chief of Executive (*chip-chung-gwan*). The Seoul and Shanghai groups elected Rhee as the Chief of Executive, while the Manchuria group elected Son Pyong-hi. Rhee opened an office in Washington, D.C. and began acting as president of the Korean provisional government. The title of "president" became a controversial issue between Rhee and the members of the cabinet, who were in Shanghai. For example, Ahn Ch'ang-ho, who then presided over cabinet meetings in Rhee's absence, sent the following cablegram to Rhee dated August 25, 1919: "Since neither government (Seoul and Shanghai group) uses the presidential designation, you are not a president. At present you must use the title of Chief of Executive to represent the government. If you act as president without amending the constitution, you are violating the constitution and opposing the principle of unity. Please do not act as president."

To this Rhee replied on August 26: "In order to obtain recognition of the provisional government, I used the title of president to communicate with other governments. I announced the conditions in Korea under the presidential designation. Therefore, I cannot alter it now. If the news of conflict among ourselves is known to the world, it will create a great obstacle to the independence movement. If so, the responsibility will rest with you."[32]

After much debate among the members of the cabinet in Shanghai, the Legislative Assembly finally adopted a presidential form of government, with a cabinet under the president responsible to the legislative branch.

The Korean Commission consisted of three commissioners who were appointed by the president. Their main responsibilities were to carry out the diplomatic and propaganda activities which were formulated by the provisional government. The Commission was also given the right to appropriate all the funds raised in the United States for the provisional government. Activities of the Commission were subject to constant supervision by the president.

The Commission concentrated on propaganda activities aimed at influencing members of the United States Congress, and it received some responses.[33] For example, on September 19, 1919, Senator Spencer read into the Congressional Record a statement submitted by the Commission that summed up the Korean claims for independence and attacked Japan's unjust rule. On October 9, Senator James D. Phelan of California introduced a resolution expressing the sympathy of the United States government with the aspirations of the Korean people for liberty and national independence. On October 24, Representative William F. Mason of Illinois made a similar speech about Korea in the House of Representatives.

Encouraged by the sympathetic attitudes of American and English official and unofficial friends, the commission undertook publications on the subject. Two books were sponsored by the Commission: *Korea's Fight for Freedom* by Frederick A. MacKenzie, and *The Case of Korea* by Henry Chung, who was one of the members of the Commission. MacKenzie's book produced some results in England. It was read by many people, and favorable reviews were printed in the English press and magazines. Influenced by this book, the League of the Friends of Korea was organized on October 26, 1920. The opening meeting was presided over by Sir Robert Newman. MacKenzie attended the meeting and introduced a Korean speaker, Earl K. Whang, a representative of the Korean Commission. The introduction stated: "He came to Europe as a soldier in the American army during the war, and after the armistice, hearing of the great needs of his people, induced the American authorities to give him his discharge in France and since then he worked mainly in Paris for Korea. . . . . His services have been of the most varied kind and of the utmost value. . . . He looks after the interests of his fellow Koreans of all classes who come to Europe."[34]

The Commission's activities were also rewarded by an expression of sympathy from the American ambassador in Tokyo. He told the Japanese minister of the army that he received "appeals from all directions regarding the wretched conditions in Korea and that reform in Korea would be most welcome to the United States."

The Commission's activities extended to a fund-raising campaign within the Korean communities in the United States and Mexico. At this writing, there are no reliable sources of comprehensive information on contributions by Korean residents in America, However, the following information is a matter of record.[35] On December 29, 1919, the central headquarters of the KNA reported that their total revenue was $88,030.50. Expenditures were: $32,600 for the Korean provisional government and the Korean Commission in Washington, D.C.; $14,000 for diplomatic and publication expenses; $13,500 for travel expenses in the United States; $8,500 for dispatching representatives to the Far East and Europe; $2,600 for communications; and $500 for relief.

The Korean Commission made a financial report for the fiscal year December 1919 to November 1920. A total of $70,190 was collected, as against expenditures of $75,230. The Commission also reported that Koreans in the United States and Mexico bought government bonds issued in the names of Syngman Rhee and Dr. Kim Kiusic in the amount of $46,404, while Chinese residents in America bought bonds worth $15,987.

Among the Korean contributors, rice farmers gave a total of $42,955. Four farmers (Kim Jong-lim, Kim Sung-sil, Sin Kwang-hi, and Im Jun-ki) donated more than $1,000 apiece, and each received a citation from the minister of finance of the Korean provisional government.

Between March 1919 and December 1920, patriotic fund contributions including government bonds amounted to well over $200,000, not including Chinese contributions. During the same period the total Korean population in the United States and Mexico was estimated at a little over 7,000. The average monthly income of a Korean laborer was about $30. Living costs for a single person ran about $20; for a married couple, $30. This meant that every Korean resident made an average contribution of $30, or one month's income, to the cause of national independence.

During the two years the Korean Commission was in existence one of the disputed issues was the right of the government to issue bonds. Rhee issued $250,000 worth of bonds in the name of the Korean provisional government without consulting either the National Assembly or the Korean National Association. The expected total amount of the bonds was to be $5 million, in denominations of $10, $25, $50, and $100. The bonds, paying an annual interest of 6 percent, were redeemable within one year after the recognition of the Korean provisional government by the United States government.[36] The certification of the bonds was signed by Rhee as president of the Korean provisional government and by Dr. Kim Kiusic as chairman of the Korean Commission.

Rhee was not satisfied with the budget provided by the KNA for the Korean Commission's expenses. He wanted to control all the funds raised by the Korean communities in the United States and Mexico. He also thought that the Commission needed money to carry out its extensive diplomatic and propaganda activities in America and in Europe. Accordingly, he circulated a presidential directive to all Korean residents in America urging them to buy the bonds and send all contributions to the Korean Commission directly, not to the KNA or Korean provisional government in Shanghai as originally planned.

The bond issue was resented by the KNA, but it was approved by the National Assembly of the Korean provisional government. The KNA opposed Rhee's financial policy for the following reasons. First, the Korean commission was an agent of the government and had no authority to issue bonds or to collect patriotic contributions from Koreans. Second, the bonds were issued without the approval of the National Assembly, which had the sole authority to deal with financial matters. Third, the KNA had the authority to handle its own budget, and it intended to continue sending money to the provisional government without the approval of the Korean Commission. Accordingly, Rhee's directive in the name of the president was not in conformity with the existing constitution of the Korean provisional government.[37]

As was to be expected, the bond-selling campaign directed by Rhee was not successful because the KNA opposed it. Also, many Koreans had no confidence in redemption inasmuch as no Western powers recognized the government in Shanghai as the government of Korea. As the bond-selling campaign failed, the chairman of the commission, Dr. Kim Kiusic, submitted his resignation and left for Shanghai. In the meantime, Rhee also had to go to Shanghai in order to assume presidential duties there.

After the two leaders had gone to Shanghai, Dr. Philip Jaisohn took on the public relations and diplomatic work. KNA members and other Korean residents raised more than twenty thousand dollars for that purpose. One of Jaisohn's immediate tasks was to submit a petition to the Washington Conference (November 12, 1921-February 2, 1922). The petition was drafted by prominent Korean leaders and signed by the representatives of the 13 provinces, 260 counties, and 52 social, economic, and religious organizations in Korea. The petition was sent to Jaisohn and he, in turn, presented it to the

secretary of state, asking him to submit it for consideration. The petition
contained the following points:[38]

1. Korea has been an independent nation with its own history and
civilization for more than forty centuries.

2. The Japanese authorities have been suppressing and exploiting the
people and natural resources of Korea for the interests of the Japanese
Empire ever since the annexation of Korea by force.

3. As a result, today the twenty-million Korean people face virtual ex-
tinction as an independent race.

4. As history proves, whenever Korea has been controlled by a foreign
power, there has been no real peace in the Far East: therefore Korea
should be preserved as an independent buffer state in East Asia.

5. If the Conference could achieve the restoration of Korean independence, then a disarmament agreement would be more possible and practical, because the suspicions of conflicting powers would be reduced and
the peace of the world would be preserved.

6. The Korean provisional government in Shanghai is the government
of the Korean people. Koreans have pledged their allegiance to it and
urge the five powers to accept the representatives sent by the Korean
provisional government and to hear the Korean appeal.

However, the petition never reached the conference table because of strong
objections by the Japanese delegates, and the Korean problem was not discussed at the conference at all.

Thereafter, Korean diplomatic and propaganda activities gradually decreased, coming to an end in 1922. During the three-year period from 1919
to 1922, overseas Koreans, especially those in the United States, did their
best for the cause of national independence. They tried to obtain recognition of the Korean provisional government from European governments in
general and the United States in particular. However, their efforts were rewarded only by a token expression of sympathy from a few American
congressmen, as well as from religious and publishing circles in America and
Europe. According to the report of the *Korean National Herald* in
Honolulu, between 1919 and 1921 a total of 9,702 editorials in favor of
Korea were published in newspapers and weekly magazines in America,
while only 52 pro-Japanese articles appeared. Over sixty pages of the United
States Congressional Record covered resolutions, proposals, and speeches
made about Korea by American lawmakers.[39] The League of the Friends of
Korea was organized in England. Dr. Kim Kuisic published various pam-
phlets and gave numerous speeches in Paris, and French newspapers carried
many articles about Korean affairs during the peace conference of the

League of Nations. Thus at least the aspirations of the Korean people for the restoration of their national independence became known to the world.

FACTIONALISM WITHIN THE KOREAN COMMUNITY

Factionalism within the Korean community in America goes back to 1913.[40] The Korean National Association in Hawaii invited Park Yong-man, who had just completed his studies at the University of Nebraska, to become the editor of the Korean weekly newspaper, then called the *United Korean News*. Park arrived in Hawaii on December 6, 1912, and immediately devoted all his time and energy to the improvement of Korean community affairs. His interests extended from the newspaper to the military training program and the educational field, and he gained confidence from the Korean residents in Hawaii. Thus, Park emerged as a young, dynamic leader.

In 1913, Syngman Rhee, who had attended a conference of the Methodist Mission in Minneapolis, expressed to Park his desire to remain in the United States rather than go back to Seoul to his old job at the YMCA. Park approved Rhee's decision and recommended him to the Korean National Association in Hawaii. The KNA then appointed Rhee as principal of the Korean Language School. For a short period Rhee worked without salary; his expenses were financed by Korean residents and the Korean Methodist Church. Rhee gradually expanded his teaching curriculum from Korean language and history to English and Western civilization. Thus, the school became more or less a junior high school. It also provided a dormitory for children who came from outside Honolulu. The Korean Language School changed its name to Korean Compound.

The Koreans in Hawaii were impressed by Rhee's efforts to educate Korean children and his hard work. The Korean residents collected $1.25 from each parent per month. Twenty-five cents went for school expenses and the remaining $1.00 for Rhee's living expenses. It is said that a few hundred Koreans thus became supporters of Rhee.

On July 29, 1914, Rhee established a Girls' Residential School with a fund allocated under the educational budget of the Korean National Association. On October 24, the girls' dormitory building was completed, as were some classrooms. This new school was located on a three-acre lot in the Puunui district of Honolulu. All these educational projects were achieved under the supervision of the Korean Methodist Church of Honolulu.

Quite unexpectedly, Rhee proposed a new school-management plan to the Korean National Association. The proposal contained two main points: first, that school management should be under the authority of the principal; and second, that the ownership of the school properties should be changed so that the principal (Rhee) would become the legal owner with the right to sell. Naturally, the KNA rejected Rhee's proposal on the ground that the school properties belonged to the Korean community and could not be transferred to an individual. This was the beginning of a power struggle between Rhee and Park.

The direct cause of confrontation between the Rhee group and Park's followers was the problem of misuse of public funds. On December 9, 1914, the KNA constructed its new building at 1306 Miller Street, Honolulu. The total amount donated by Koreans was $7,404.50, while the actual cost of the construction was $4,040.65. Thus, the balance should have been $3,363.85. Instead, it was only $984.53. This meant that the sum of $2,379.32 had been misused by two individuals who handled the money on behalf of the Association. When this news was revealed to the public, Rhee launched a general criticism of the KNA as well as a personal attack on Park through his monthly publication *Pacific Magazine*. Rhee wrote: "Can the construction of the Korean National Association building provide the Korean people the knowledge they need? As a matter of fact, it would be much better to give money to Syngman Rhee and let him use it, instead of giving money to the Korean National Association, which has been the bottomless pit."[41] He suggested that from then on, all fund raising for the purpose of education should be conducted under his personal supervision since the members of the KNA were not to be trusted.

The Korean community was faced with turmoil when Rhee called a mass meeting and demanded the resignation of all committee members of the KNA. The KNA refused to participate in the meeting. So Rhee's followers held the meeting alone and passed a resolution of nonconfidence in the committee members of the KNA. They also elected a new chairman of the KNA from the pro-Rhee group. In the meantime, Rhee's followers filed a law suit against the former KNA chairman, Kim Jong-hak, on the grounds that he should be responsible for the mishandling of the KNA building construction fund. Anti-Rhee Kim Jong-hak was brought to the court but he was cleared, because there was no evidence against him. But Kim felt so badly humiliated that he attempted suicide, leaving a note in which he accused Rhee of being a traitor to the Korean community.[42] The suit was withdrawn when the two individuals involved repaid the missing funds in full.

Park and his followers were ousted from power and Rhee's group took over the leadership of the KNA. But the bitterness and hostility remained, and the unity of the Korean community was broken. Park left Hawaii for San Francisco on June 6, 1915. Thus, the Hawaiian Korean community appeared to be under the complete control of Rhee. Ahn Cha'ng-ho was sent to Hawaii by the mainland KNA in order to mediate between the Rhee and Park factions. His four-month effort, however, did not produce any results, and he returned to San Francisco disappointed.

The second factional fight between Rhee and Park occurred soon after Rhee returned to Hawaii from Shanghai on July 1, 1921. To understand the fight, it may be necessary to review the historical background. Park Yong-man, having lost the leadership of the Korean National Association of Hawaii to Syngman Rhee, organized his own political group, the Korean Independence League (*Choson Toknip-dan*) on March 3, 1919. Some of the main purposes of the League were: to support the Korean national independence movement; to train soldiers in Hawaii and Manchuria; to promote unity among the different organizations; to collect patriotic funds to support the above programs; and to carry out diplomatic and propaganda activities on behalf of the independence movement.[43] The League had a membership of 350. On March 10, 1919, it set up its headquarters on Kukui Street, Honolulu and started to issue *Pacific Times*, a weekly newspaper in Korean. During the absence of Rhee, who went to Shanghai to take over as provisional president, the League provided financial support to Park, who concentrated on the establishment of military training programs in Manchuria, after closing the one in Hawaii.

When Rhee returned to Hawaii, the newly organized Korean Resident Association (*Kyomin Dan*) gave him a welcome party. Rhee made a speech of almost two hours telling about his experiences in Shanghai and the political situation within the provisional government. His main points were: (1) the main reason he had visited Shanghai was to bring about cooperation between the members of the different factions within the provisional government; (2) the provisional government faced a financial crisis and expected Rhee to provide some kind of magic formula to solve its problems, but when it realized that such an expectation was impossible, it began to attack him and to raise irrelevant issues; (3) when he opposed a communist-type reorganization of the governmental structure, some of the cabinet members resigned, including Yi Tong-whi, Ahn Cha'ng-ho, and Dr. Kim Kiusic; (4) the Park Yong-man group in Manchuria had been advocating anarchism as a means of destroying the Korean provisional government, while the Ahn Cha'ng-ho group had called for a so-called Peoples' Representative Conference in order to hinder reform of the independence movement.[44]

Then Rhee submitted his own plan to protect the Korean provisional government as well as to maintain law and order in the Korean community in Hawaii. He said: "If people do not support their government, the government cannot exist and we cannot be an independent nation without the government. Therefore, all of us should be ready to fight to preserve the provisional government in Shanghai . . . we do not have at the present time law enforcement officers to punish the law breakers in our community, and therefore, you yourself should become policemen and soldiers to maintain law and order in our community."[45]

As a counterpart to the Korean Independence League, Rhee organized the *Tongji-hoe* (Comrade Society) on July 7, 1921. The main purposes of the *Tongji-hoe* was to support the provisional government of Korea and to give absolute obedience to the head of the organization. On Inauguration Day, Rhee issued a statement that "this organization would enforce severe punishment on those who worked against the provisional government . . . the members of the Tongji-hoe should consider themselves self-appointed law-enforcement agencies to keep peace in the Korean community." A few hundred Koreans, including many women, joined the *Tongji-hoe*. Later, the party elected Rhee its lifetime chairman and adopted three new principles: non-violence, self-sacrifice, and self-reliant economic independence.

Thus, both leaders now possessed their own organized groups and supporters. Park had the Korean Independence League, the Korean National Association, and a few hundred military cadets, whereas Rhee had the *Tongji-hoe*, the Korean Resident Association, and the Korean Christian Church, which he had established in 1918.

The immediate cause of the second confrontation between Rhee and Park was an article about Rhee that appeared in Park's publication *Pacific Times*. Under the title "Missing Syngman Rhee," the article said: "Rhee went to Shanghai in order to take over the presidential office of the Korean provisional government, but he brought internal disputes and divisions within the cabinet members. Because he could not control the political and financial situation of the government, he was forced to leave Shanghai in great secrecy."[46]

When this was released to the public on August 2, 1921, six members of the *Tongji-hoe* went to the office of the *Pacific Times* and demanded correction of the article on the grounds that it was completely false. But the editor refused, saying that the information in the article was factual and came from a highly reliable source in Shanghai. That same evening, more than thirty members of the *Tongji-hoe*, including women, invaded the newspaper building and destroyed the inter-type machine; they also physically attacked several members of the Korean Independence League. At this juncture, the police were called in, and some of the *Tongji-hoe* members were arrested and charged with illegal entry and destruction of property. The Park group filed a law suit against the *Tongji-hoe*, and the court battle lasted several years. Both sides spent time, energy, and money for this fight, and both groups were exhausted in terms of financial resources as well as the will to carry the case any longer. As a result, both sides became the losers.

It was during this period that Rhee faced trouble with the cabinet members of the Korean provisional government in Shanghai. On January 17, 1922, the National Assembly of the Korean provisional government passed a non-confidence resolution against Rhee (who was then living in Hawaii) on the grounds that he had completely failed to carry out his duty and had left the government in a confused state. Rhee was informed of the resolution, but he refused to resign from the presidency. He argued that he had been elected by the representatives of the thirteen provinces in Korea, and that the National Assembly had no authority to make him resign from office. Finally, on March 13, 1925, after three years of bitter arguments and debates between pro- and anti-Rhee factions in the government, the Judiciary Committee of the National Assembly recommended impeachment procedures against Rhee based on Chapter IV, Article 21 of the Constitution of the Provisional Government. Then the National Assembly passed the impeachment recommendation with a 75 percent majority.

The legal grounds for specific charges against Rhee were: first, that he failed to perform the duties provided by the constitution; second, that he usurped power by selling government bonds and using the money raised by Korean residents in the United States without authorization from the National Assembly; and third, that he had been absent from the office for more than three years to carry out diplomatic activities in Washington but had failed to do so.[47] Rhee ignored the impeachment resolution, and in reality he now became a frustrated factional boss within the American Korean community. Thereafter, he lived quietly in Hawaii and devoted his time to religious and educational work. He also concentrated on development of the *Tongji-hoe*, establishing branches on the mainland of the United States.

Rhee's rival, Park, also became a frustrated man. His military training programs in Manchuria were forced to close altogether because of the lack of funds and support from the Korean community. His publication, *Pacific Times*, also closed after the legal battle with the *Tongji-hoe*. Park went to Manchuria and was assassinated in Peking on October 10, 1928. Factional fighting within the Korean community diminished for the next few years, but it revived during the Second World War.

To sum up: during the initial period of the Korean national independence movement in the United States, Koreans concentrated on individual action against pro-Japanese persons, Americans and Koreans alike. The Koreans appealed to the Second Hague Peace conference of 1907 by sending delegates and making petitions. They failed because of strong objections from the Japanese government as well as a lack of sympathy from Western powers.

The Korean leaders in the United States were divided on the policies for achieving independence for Korea. One group advocated militant action, including military training of Koreans in America. The other group favored educational and diplomatic activities. However, when the March First uprising took place in Korea in 1919, Koreans in the United States united under the name of the Korean National Association and launched an all-out effort to obtain help and sympathy from Western democratic countries in general and the United States in particular. Many Korean community leaders in the United States, such as Syngman Rhee, Ahn Ch'ang-ho, Park Yong-man, and No Paik-lim, participated in the establishment in 1919 of the Korean provisional government, which lasted until 1945.

The realization of Korean independence failed because Japanese military power suppressed the movement and the Western powers paid no attention to the Korean issue at the Paris Peace Conference of 1919. Japan was one of the victorious powers and was determined not to leave Korea. After 1919, the Korean independence movement began to decline. Koreans in the United States, who had devoted their time and energy to the cause of independence, were mentally and physically exhausted and financially bankrupt. Frustrated, they turned against each other, forming factions within the Korean community.

9.

The Korean Independence Movement
in America Since 1930

A Period of Stagnation

The March First uprising in 1919 was the peak of the drive for national independence. Thereafter, Korean political activities in both America and China stagnated. Internationally the political climate was dark: Hitler and Mussolini rose to power; Chiang Kai-shek set himself up as a fascist dictator in his fight against the Chinese Communists; and the Japanese invaded Manchuria and established the puppet state of Manchukuo in 1932. The Western democratic powers faced economic depression and were not prepared to meet the challenge of the rising Axis powers (Germany, Italy, and Japan). Historically, it was a time when human nature showed its lowest depths.

During this period an unexpected incident took place. It is known as the student uprising of 1929–1930. One of the main causes of the incident was the Japanese discriminatory educational system which was based on the supposed racial superiority of the Japanese over the Koreans.[1] The Japanese police suppressed the peaceful student demonstrators with the same ruthless methods used in dealing with the 1919 demonstrators. Overseas Koreans, including Koreans in the United States, gave their moral and financial support to the striking students, and protested against the Japanese military suppression of the peaceful demonstrators. After the student uprising, the Korean liberation movement was gradually driven underground. There formed a united front of left-wing and progressive nationalists on the one hand, and conservative nationalists on the other. The front began to take direct terrorist actions against the Japanese.

Right-wing nationalist leader Kim Koo trained a special young action group. It was funded by Korean residents in Hawaii, who sent Kim a thousand dollars.[2] In January 1932, Lee Bong-chan made an unsuccessful attack on the life of the Japanese emperor in Tokyo. Three months later, Yun Bong-gil made an attack on the life of General Shirakawa, the conqueror of

Manchuria, when the Japanese celebrated their victory with a parade in Shanghai. At this bombing incident, Admiral Nomura, later a special envoy to the United States on the eve of the Pearl Harbor attack, lost his left eye, and Foreign Minister Shigemura, who later signed the surrender terms with the Allied Powers on the battleship U.S.S. *Missouri*, was also injured.

In the United States, Korean diplomatic agitation against Japanese military expansion in Manchuria was launched once again under the leadership of Syngman Rhee. Members of the *Tongji-hoe* in Hawaii decided to set up a Korean Commission in Washington, D.C., headed by Rhee. Rhee was sent to Geneva and Vienna in 1932 to present the Korean case to the League of Nations, which was discussing Japanese aggression in Manchuria on the basis of the report of the Lytton Commission.[3] However, Rhee never succeeded in stating his case to the League of Nations because the majority of the great powers did not pay attention to the Korean issue, although they disapproved of Japanese military expansion in the Far East.

Two unexpected things happened in Rhee's personal life during this period. First, he met Francesca Donner in Geneva; they were later married in the United States. Second, he had an opportunity to visit Moscow on his return trip to the United States. Rhee's impression of the Soviet Union was that "the Russian farmers were extremely poor-looking."[4] Rhee was told that no Russian authorities would talk with him about the Korean problem, and he left Moscow after one night.

During the next few years, Koreans in America remained inactive. Most of the leaders were conservatives and had little contact with Koreans in Korea. However, many of the left-wing Korean revolutionists in China, such as Kim San (whose real name may have been Chang Ch'i-rak),[5] Kim Il-sung (the present ruler of North Korea), Yi Tong-hwi (the first organizer of the Korean Community Party), Kim Chaek, and Choe Yong-gun, advocated direct action against the Japanese authorities. The conservative faction proposed diplomatic pleading with the democratic nations to pressure Japan to give up Korea.

A few partisan movements were created by the left-wing leaders. Kim Il-sung organized a Korean partisan group in Manchuria and cooperated closely with the Chinese Communists. Choe Yong-gun and Kim Chaek organized the Choson People's Revolutionary Army, which was later renamed the Fourth Army. Kim San established a Korean United Front of Communists and Nationalists and fought with the Chinese Red Army against the Japanese. Kim Won-bong, a moderate leftist within the Korean provisional government, organized a Korean Volunteer Corps that fought with the Chinese Nationalist army against the Japanese invaders.[6]

In 1936, liberal and left-wing political groups in China formed the National Revolutionary Party, headed by Dr. Kim Kiusic, a liberal, and Kim

Won-bong, representing moderate left-wing political forces. The most significant achievements of the National Revolutionary Party were the organization of the Korean Volunteer Corps under Kim Won-bong, and its participation after the Pearl Harbor attack in the conservative-dominated provisional government.[7]

When Japan invaded China in 1937, progressive Koreans in the United States formed a China Aid Society in Los Angeles and protested the Japanese military expansion. Later this group was renamed the Society for Aid to the Korean Volunteer Corps in China. It advocated anti-Japanese political actions in the United States. It urged all Koreans to cooperate with American as well as Chinese progressive social forces in the United States. Its political activities included boycotting Japanese goods, protesting American sales of scrap iron to Japan, picketing Japanese consulate buildings, and picketing the shipyards where Japanese ships loaded the scrap iron, which was used to manufacture weapons to kill Chinese.

At this time, Korean traditional nationalists in the United States rejected such anti-Japanese measures. They felt these actions were not realistic and might offend American authorities and businessmen. They also thought that such anti-Japanese activities were Communist-inspired tactics. This division of opinion on the anti-Japanese struggle was the first real ideological difference between the old guard of the Korean nationalist leaders and the progressive young liberals in the Korean community in the United States. The former insisted on their traditional line of politics, namely, continuation of financial aid to the Korean provisional government and cooperation with American government authorities to obtain sympathy for the restoration of national independence. The latter advocated a united front with the liberal social forces in America and in China as a means of opposing Japanese imperialism in the Far East. Naturally, the former groups had close relations with the conservative leaders within the Korean provisional government in China, while the latter group supported the liberal and left-wing political forces within and without the factionalistic government circles in China. Nevertheless, as we will see later, the Korean community in the United States was completely dominated by the traditional nationalistic leaders, members of the Korean National Association and the *Tongji-hoe*.

THE UNIFICATION EFFORT

As early as September 2, 1940, about fifteen months before the Japanese attack on Pearl Harbor, Koreans in America launched a unification movement. The leaders of the Korean National Association (KNA) on the mainland proposed a joint meeting of representatives of all existing political and social organizations of Koreans from the mainland and Hawaii. One of the main reasons for such a meeting was the pressure of rapidly changing events: the aggressive actions of Hitler and Mussolini in Europe, and the constant Japanese military expansion in the Far East. Koreans in America were keenly aware of the absolute necessity of unity in order to accelerate the drive for national independence.

It should be noted here that Syngman Rhee wrote a book in 1941 entitled *Japan Inside Out* in which he suggested that "the United States should employ all her power, economical, moral, and military, now to check Japan in order to prevent an ultimate conflict with her." He further advocated preventive war, saying: " Is it not equally clear, then, that your true policy should be to act quickly and keep him down by force before he grows too big, so that he can never get out of hand?"[8]

About the same time, another Korean, named Haan Kil-soo, warned the American public that Japan was preparing to attack the United States soon and that thirty-five to fifty thousand Japanese on the Hawaiian Islands, who were either citizens of Japan or held dual citizenship, were prepared to assist Japan in the event of war with the United States.[9] Haan also pointed out that members of certain Japanese secret societies such as the Black Dragon Society had engaged in spying and sabotage activities for the Japanese government. The leaders of the Korean community urged Koreans to register as Koreans and not as Japanese subjects under the Alien Registration Act of 1940. Subsequently, Earl G. Harrison, Washington director of the Alien Registration office, ruled that Koreans had the right to register as Koreans, not as Japanese subjects.

An all-Korean representative convention was held on April 20, 1941, at 1306 Miller Street, Honolulu, the headquarters of the Korean National Association of Hawaii. Fourteen representatives from nine social and political organizations attended. The representatives organized the United Korean Committee and decided to support the Korean provisional government-in-exile in China. They proclaimed what is called the Declaration of the All-Korean Convention and adopted a nine-point program. The declaration stated: "How pathetic it was! Hundreds and thousands of our brothers and sisters have died in the past on the battle fronts for the cause of national independence, and their sacrifices have become a living symbol for our guidance today and it stimulates us to create a new era. . . . We Koreans in America are proud of ourselves for what we have done in helping this great task of national independence through financial and spiritual support of the Korean provisional government." The declaration concluded by saying: "We Koreans in America should unite together as one body and should support the Allied Powers until they bring a final victory of the present war against the Axis powers."[10]

The nine-point program can be summed up as follows. The United Korean Committee was to consist of a policy-making board of directors and

an administrative executive board. All Korean organizations were to maintain their status quo, but they were to entrust the United Korean Committee
with all diplomatic and political activities. All contributions were to be
called independence contributions and were to be forwarded to the United
Korean Committee. The United Korean Committee was to be the only diplomatic agent of the Korean provisional government in China, and Dr.
Syngman Rhee was to be appointed chairman of the committee. Haan Kil-
soo was to be appointed liaison man between the Committee and the United
States government. The Committee was to appropriate two-thirds of the
contributions for the Korean provisional government and use the remaining
one-third for administrative expenses, including diplomatic activities and
liaison services. All Koreans in America were to pledge themselves to unite
under the Committee's leadership in support of the Korean provisional
government-in-exile.

The declaration and the nine-point program were signed on April 28,
1941, by the representatives of nine organizations:[11] Korean National Association of North America (Han Shi-dae, Kim Ho, and Song Jong-ik),
Tongji-hoe of Hawaii (Ahn Hyung-kyong, Lee Won-soon, and No Chin-
ho), Korean National Association of Hawaii (Ahn Woon-kyo, Kim Hyun-
ku, and Kim Won-yong), Sino-Korean People's League of Hawaii (Cha
Shin-ho), Korean Independence Party of Hawaii (Kang Sang-ho), Society
for Aid to Korean Volunteer Corps (Kwan Do-in), Korean Women's Relief
Society of Hawaii (Shin Yong-shin and Min Han-na), Great Korean
Independence Party (Kang Sang-ho), and Korean Women's Patriotic So-
ciety of Los Angeles (Lee Sung-nae and Park Kyung-shin). A majority of the
Korean organizations, six out of nine, were conservative traditional groups.
Two of them, the Sino-Korean People's League and the Great Korean Inde-
pendence Party, were middle-of-the-road groups. The Korean National
Revolutionary Party was a left-wing group.[12] Hence, the leadership of the
United Korean Committee was dominated by conservative nationalists, es-
pecially leaders of the Korean National Association and the *Tongji-hoe*.

The unification effort within the Korean community in America was
credited to the leaders of the conservative nationalists; unity was achieved
about eight months before the Japanese surprise attack on Pearl Harbor.
The Korean leaders believed that conflict between the United States and
Japan was inevitable. They also believed that such a war would mean the
end of the Japanese Empire and that emancipation of the Korean people at
long last was near. However, the conservative nationalists and the progressives held markedly different views about the war and the postwar outlook.
The conservative nationalists insisted upon unconditional support of the
Korean provisional government in China and upon cooperation with the
Chinese Nationalists. The progressives advocated a united front supporting

left-wing Korean partisan forces in China and the establishment of a people's democracy as the postwar Korean government.

WARTIME ACTIVITIES

As we have seen, Koreans in the United States had been active in the anti-Japanese movement. In Los Angeles, the Society for Aid to the Korean Volunteer Corps in China sponsored a Korean Night program on December 7, 1941, the day of the Japanese surprise attack on Pearl Harbor. One of the main purposes of the program was to raise funds for the relief of more than two hundred thousand refugee Korean families in China and also for Korean volunteers who had been fighting against the Japanese in China. At the same time, the Society wanted to let the American public know that Koreans in America had been taking an active part against the Axis powers. The Korean Night program included a performance of the Korean traditional marriage ceremony. American-born Koreans acted the parts of the bride and bridegroom, and a student from Korea performed the marriage ceremony. An American friend, who worked in Hollywood, directed the play.[13] During the rehearsal, someone shouted, "The Japanese have attacked Pearl Harbor; let us go to war against Japan." Simultaneously, everybody in the play shouted "*Teahan Toknip Mansee* (Long Live Korean Independence)." No Korean, old and young alike, could control his emotions of joy. Some old Korean immigrants had tears in their eyes and kept silent. Every Korean felt that the long dream for national independence would soon become a reality.

The play started at seven o'clock, and the auditorium was packed with enthusiastic and happy Koreans, Chinese, and Americans. It was a great success and a timely program for the cause of national independence. It was for this author an unforgettable experience.

When war broke out, there were about two hundred Korean students in the United States. The great majority of them went to work for the American government; they knew Japanese, and not many Japanese speaking Americans existed at that time. There were many *kibei nisei* (born in America, educated in Japan, and returned to America) who spoke Japanese and English, but they were sent to the Japanese relocation camps. Japanese-speaking Koreans were employed in various branches of the United States government as interpreters, translators of Japanese secret documents, and teachers at the Japanese language training school. Some joined the army and received special training as underground agents to be sent to Korea and Japanese-occupied areas in China and Southeast Asia.

The following incident might be worth mentioning. Many Japanese residents in Los Angeles were picked up by the American authorities and put in temporary prison compounds. Some did not speak English, and Korean students in the Los Angeles area were hired by the federal government to act as interpreters.

The American authorities were concerned about Japanese secret organizations and their activities on behalf of the Japanese government. One of the dangerous secret organizations was the Black Dragon Society (*Kokuryu Kai*), an ultra-nationalistic organization originally established by Toyama Mitsura, a chauvinist who advocated military expansion of Japan into Korea and Manchuria at the beginning of this century. American authorities knew about the existence of a branch of this society in Los Angeles. After intensive investigation, the head of the branch was arrested and interrogated. The man was a graduate of Tokyo Imperial University and had served in the Japanese army for many years. He was a retired major-general and had lived in Los Angeles for more than six years. But he wanted an interpreter because he did not understand English well. A Korean student acted as his interpreter. At first the man denied that he belonged to the Black Dragon Society but finally he admitted that he had been its head. To no one's surprise he committed suicide at his temporary prison compound, perhaps so as not to reveal his secret activities in the United States. Later, other members of the society were also interrogated. But all of them said they did not know anything about the activities of the society. Only the dead man knew; he was responsible for everything.

It should be pointed out here that anti-Japanese feelings became acute among the general public. Several Japanese were attacked by white Americans in daylight on the streets and on public transportation. Chinese and Koreans were also insulted by white Americans because their physical appearance resembled that of the Japanese. Subsequently, all Japanese, including American-born citizens, were removed from West Coast states and placed in relocation camps.

It was at this time that the United Korean Committee sent representatives to the American authorities and convinced them that Koreans should not be treated as enemy aliens. As a result, the State and Treasury departments of the United States issued a special order stating that Koreans in the United States were not citizens of Japan and should enjoy the same treatment accorded to citizens of other allied nations. The United Korean Committee issued identification badges with the Korean flag, and urged all Koreans to carry the badges at all times as protection from the hysterical anti-Japanese public. Special automobile stickers were also issued as a safety measure.[14]

Korean wartime activities were varied. Men of military age served in the American armed forces. Older men volunteered as emergency fire wardens and worked in military construction. Elderly women served in the Red Cross and in the USO; they also launched a war-bond selling campaign. As mentioned previously, Japanese-speaking Koreans worked in various government agencies and in the front lines of the Pacific war areas as interpreters, translators, intelligence officers, and propaganda broadcasters.

Perhaps one of the most noticeable wartime activities of Korean residents on the mainland was the establishment of a Korean brigade incorporated into the California National Guard under the command of Colonel Hughes. The Korean unit was named the Tiger Brigade (*Manghokun*), and it began training on December 29, 1941, in Los Angeles.[15] At first 50 Koreans, whose ages ranged from eighteen to sixty-five, were enrolled; the number increased to one hundred and nine in the Los Angeles area alone. At this time, the total Korean population in Los Angeles was about five hundred. Many of the men were past the age of military duty, but they volunteered to receive military drills as a sign of patriotism. The military instructor was Lieutenant Sherry of the United States Army. Because of a legal technicality that prohibited inclusion of a foreign unit in the United States armed forces, the Tiger Brigade was detached from the regular National Guard and was attached to the civilian militia.

Every Saturday and Sunday afternoon, the Korean unit exercised for three to four hours in Exposition Park, Los Angeles. A similar unit was established in San Francisco and drilled at the War Memorial Auditorium every Sunday afternoon.

On April 26, 1942, the Tiger Brigade had its first gala review in Los Angeles. Official representatives of various organizations from both the Korean and American communities were invited. The mayor of the city of Los Angeles, a representative from the California State Guard, United States Army officials, and delegates from the United Korean Committee were present at the review ceremony. It was a holiday for the entire Korean community in Los Angeles, and almost all Koreans attended the military drill celebration. For many Koreans it was their first opportunity to see their countrymen in army uniforms since the Korean national armed forces had been forced to disband by the Japanese authorities in 1907.

Another celebration was held on Korean National Flag Day, August 29, 1943. This was the thirty-third memorial day of Korea's annexation by Japan, and the United Korean Committee decided to have a rededication of Korea's national flag. A colorful ceremony took place in front of the Los Angeles City Hall. The ceremony started at 2:00 P.M. with a colorful parade from Pershing Square to City Hall. The Tiger Brigade marched first, followed by a band and a group of Korean girls wearing native dresses and waving Korean flags. The climax came when Mayor Fletcher Brown raised the Korean flag, while the U.S. Army and Tiger Brigade bands played the national anthems of both countries. The Korean representative read a resolution of the Korean people that said in part: "We pledge ourselves to fight until ultimate victory of the war against the Axis powers and eventual liberation of the Korean people from the Japanese domination." This resolution was translated into twelve different languages and broadcast throughout the Far East and Europe.

The United Korean Committee also sent an official letter to governors and mayors throughout the United States requesting that the Korean national flag be displayed with flags of the Allied Nations at public buildings. Many governors and mayors responded to the request. Cited here is one letter, which came from the mayor of Chicago.[16]

> Mr. C. Ho Kim, Executive Chairman   June 29, 1943
> United Korean Committee in America
> 1326 West Jefferson Boulevard
> Los Angeles, California
>
> Dear Mr. Kim:
>
> This is to thank you for your letter of June 4 and to let you know of my appreciation for bringing to my attention the attitude toward and the participation in the present war of the Korean people.
> You may be sure that we in Chicago shall be glad to display the Korean emblem at municipal and government functions.
> With kind wishes, I am
>
> Sincerely yours,
>
> Edward Kelly
> Mayor

In Hawaii, the United Korean Committee launched an extensive fund drive on August 29, 1943. More than $26,000 was sent to the president and more than $400 to the American Red Cross as a token expression of Korean participation in the war against the common enemy, Japan. Between 1942 and 1943, Koreans in America bought defense bonds worth more than $239,000.

RIVALRY BETWEEN THE SYNGMAN RHEE GROUP AND THE UNITED KOREAN COMMITTEE

The Korean Commission was created by the United Korean Committee in America in conformity with Article 6 of the Committee's nine-point program, which was adopted on April 20, 1941, by the representatives of the All-Korean Convention in Honolulu. The Commission was the only diplomatic agent of the Korean provisional government in China. Syngman Rhee was appointed as Chairman, and Haan Kil-soo was appointed as liaison officer between the United Korean Committee and the United States government. However, the Commission was to be under the supervision of the board of directors and executive board of the United Korean Committee. This meant that, technically, the diplomatic activities of Rhee were subject to the guidance of the United Korean Committee and were not under the supervision of the Korean provisional government, because the United Korean Committee was given the authority to collect funds from Korean residents in the United States.

One of the main objectives of Korean diplomatic activities was to secure recognition of the provisional government from the Allied powers in general and from the United States government in particular. Rhee met many American officials and presented his views on this matter. First, he had a conference with Dr. Stanley Hornbeck, who was in charge of Far Eastern Affairs in the State Department. Dr. Hornbeck treated Rhee "merely as an individual who walked into the State Department to present his own personal viewpoint." Then Rhee got in touch with Senator Guy Gillette, who replied: "I have discussed the recognition of Korea as an independent political entity with the State Department. I found them sympathetic but no action can be taken until the exchange of diplomatic representatives and attaches between the Japanese Empire and the United States Government have been effected. You can readily see that we could not and should not take any steps to arouse resentment which might find expression in abuse or misuse of Americans still resident in the Japanese Empire."[17]

However, Rhee received some encouragement from the Army Intelligence Service of the War Department. Major Wallace H. Moore expressed the opinion that "he would do all that he could to secure aid for the Koreans fighting in China."

At this juncture, the Korean provisional government in Chung-king formally declared war against Japan and asked for aid. Rhee again called the State Department and had a conference with Alger Hiss. Rhee pointed out that Koreans could develop their potentialities for sabotage and guerilla activities only if their government were recognized and given economic and military aid. To this Hiss said that "since Rhee's proposals involved a recognition of the Korean government in Chungking, there was little or nothing the United States could do." He further stated that "to recognize an independent Korean government at this stage was premature since the Soviet Union could not take a part in such discussion—not being at war with Japan."[18]

On March 14, 1941, Rhee wrote the following letter to Secretary Cordell Hull:

The government of the Republic of Korea is the sole representative of the Korean people, whether they are residents in Korea proper, Manchuria, Siberia, China, or elsewhere, and regards itself, on the basis of the treaty of 1882, negotiated between the Government of Korea and the Government of the United States, not as a free movement in any sense whatever of that phrase, but as the only government agency of Korea that is in existence.

It is the desire of my Government to be advised how the Government of the United States regards the aforementioned treaty between the two countries. It is the plea of my Government that the existence of this treaty be noted by the Government of the United States, for anything to the contrary would seem to further countenance the act of wanton aggression perpetrated by the Japanese Government upon the people of Korea.[19]

As part of the effort for recognition of the Korean provisional government a Liberty Conference was held in Washington, D.C. Unfortunately, this effort again did not elicit more than expression of sympathy and encouragement from various government officials of the United States. As for recognition of the provisional government, there was unanimous opinion among American authorities that such "action would be premature and unwise."[20] The official view on recognition of the Korean provisional government was, at long last, expressed clearly by Acting Secretary of State Joseph Grew in reference to Korean participation in the United Nations Conference in San Francisco:

The United Nations which are represented at the United Nations Conference on International Organization all have legally constituted governing authorities whereas the 'Korean Provisional Government' and other Korean organizations do not possess at the present time the qualifications requisite for obtaining recognition by the United States as a government authority. The 'Korean Provisional Government' has never exercised administrative authority over any part of Korea, nor can it be regarded as representative of the Korean people of today. Due to geographical and other factors its following even among exiled Koreans is inevitably limited. It is the policy of this Government in dealing with groups such as the 'Korean Provisional Government' to avoid taking action which might, when the victory of the United Nations is achieved, tend to compromise the right of the Korean people to choose the ultimate form and personnel of the government which they may wish to establish.[21]

This official statement sorely disappointed Koreans in America and indicated the failure of Korean diplomatic activities in Washington.

Because of frustration on the diplomatic front and policy differences between Rhee and other leaders within the United Korean Committee, factional struggle once again appeared within the Korean community.

Personal rivalry between Rhee and Haan Kil-soo was the first cause of division within the United Korean Committee.[22] As mentioned previously, Rhee was chairman of the Korean Commission, the official diplomatic agency of the Korean provisional government, while Haan was liaison officer between the United Korean Committee and the United States government. Haan had been very critical of Rhee's policy of giving priority to diplomatic activities. Haan came to Washington and won the sympathetic interest of several congressmen as well some officials in the State and War departments. He stressed propaganda activities and secret intelligence work. By his own admission, he had worked as an anti-Japanese underground agent for many years in Hawaii and obtained much secret information. Long before the Pearl Harbor attack, he testified, at the request of Senator Gillette, before the United States Senate Foreign Relations Sub-committee about the Japanese plan for war against the United States. Haan made many speeches to the American public warning about Japan's aggressive policy. A few American organizations supported his activities, and some Korean organizations, such as the Sino-Korean People's League in Hawaii and the Society for Aid to Korean Volunteers Corps in Los Angeles, also supported his efforts. Haan, naturally, became a more active anti-Japanese propagandist than Rhee and wanted more funds for his activities. Rhee, on the other hand, totally ignored Haan's work and argued that concentrating on recognition of the Korean provisional government should be the first task. According to Oliver's book, Haan won a certain degree of influence in the lower echelons of the State and War departments, which he used to undermine Rhee and the provisional government. He stated that Rhee and his associates had been out of Korea so long (Haan himself had not been in Korea since he was nine years old) that they no longer represented the people there and were, in fact, unknown to them. Because of the personal antagonism and policy differences between Rhee and Haan, there was no cooperation, and each claimed to be the representative of Koreans in the United States.

The second cause of division within the United Korean Committee was the problem of sending a fact-finding mission to the Korean provisional government in Chungking. In 1942, factionalism took place within the provisional government between the conservative right wing nationalists and the left-wing progressive group. The former group was headed by Kim Koo, chairman of the Korean provisional government and founder of the Korean Independence Party. The latter group was led by Kim Won-bong, then minister of defense and organizer of the Korean Volunteer Corps (this group later established the Korean National Revolutionary Party headed by Dr. Kim Kiusic). The primary issue between these two groups was the question of military cooperation with the Chinese armed forces. The Kim Won-bong group wanted a close tie with the Chinese Communist forces in fighting the

Japanese war, while Kim Koo's group desired close cooperation with the Chinese Nationalists. Politically, the progressives advocated unity with Chinese liberal and left-wing political groups, whereas the conservative nationalists emphasized close ties with the Kuomintang headed by Chiang Kai-shek.

The disunity between Rhee and Haan in Washington, and disputes between conservatives and progressives within the Korean provisional government in Chungking, became acute. The independence movement overseas came to a standstill. At this critical juncture, the United Korean Committee decided to send representatives to Washington, D.C., and to Chungking in order to mediate the disputes. The Committee selected four delegates for two missions: Cho Pyong-yo and Lee Won-soon were to go to Washington, and Kim Ho and Chun Kyung-moo to Chungking.

However, Rhee rejected the plan to send a mission to Chungking on the ground that disputes within the Korean provisional government should be ironed out internally and the United Korean Committee in America had no authority to interfere. Kim Koo, the chairman of the provisional government, sided with Rhee. This was a reversal of the original agreement between the provisional government and the United Korean Committee. The provisional government had stated that it would obtain entry permits from the Chinese Nationalist government for the mediation mission and that it welcomes the idea of a mission from the United Korean Committee. But Rhee persuaded Kim Koo not to receive the mission. Thus, although the mission delegates obtained exit permits from the United States government, they could not get entry permits from the Chinese government, apparently because Kim Koo took no action on the matter. Kim Ho and Chun Kyung-moo attempted to persuade Rhee to be conciliatory, but he flatly refused. It is reported that in the midst of their hot argument in Rhee's office, Rhee told the two men to "get out of my office" with anger.

Reconciliation between Rhee and Haan was also impossible, because Rhee wanted everything concerning diplomatic matters run his own way, while Haan was irritated by Rhee's dictatorial manner in handling diplomatic activities. Rhee told the two mediators, Cho Pyong-yo and Lee Won-soon, that "the United Korean Committee in America should not interfere with diplomatic policies of the Korean Commission since diplomatic affairs are under the jurisdiction of the Korean Commission as official representatives of the Korean provisional government."[23] But the United Korean Committee members argued that the Korean Commission was created by the United Korean Committee in conformity with Article 6 of the Committee's nine-point program adopted by the All-Korean Convention on April 20, 1941. They further pointed out that all the expenses of the diplomatic activities had been met by the United Korean Committee and that the Korean

Commission's chairman was appointed by the Committee. Therefore, the Commission was to be under the supervision of the United Korean Committee. Rhee refused to discuss the matter any further.

The delegates returned to Los Angeles and made a public statement of the reasons for their failure in the *New Korea*, a weekly newspaper of the Korean National Association. The anti-Rhee report of the mission irritated Rhee and his followers, and a countering statement was issued by the *Tongji-hoe*. In the meantime, the *Tongji-hoe* called a membership meeting and decided to withdraw from the United Korean Committee. Members once again pledged to support the Korean provisional government in Chungking and to continue to support the Korean Commission in Washington, D.C. headed by Rhee.[24]

In order to avoid a complete breakdown of unity among the Koreans in America, the United Korean Committee once again made an attempt to patch up differences between itself and Rhee. This time, Kim Won-yong, leader of the Korean National Association and Lee Won-soon, leader of the *Tongji-hoe*, were sent to Washington to represent the United Korean Committee. On March 28, 1943, a compromise was reached. Rhee accepted Lee Won-soon as a new member of the Korean Commission to assist him in making diplomatic policies. Rhee also expressed his desire to cooperate with the United Korean Committee's decisions on questions of diplomatic policies. Thus, on the surface, unity was achieved.

A few months later, however, Rhee took a unilateral action urging every Korean in America to send his contribution directly to the Korean Commission instead of the United Korean Committee. This action was a direct violation of Article 5 of the United Korean Committee's nine-point program regulation, which stated that "all the member organizations shall be responsible for the collections and for forwarding them to the United Korean Committee."[25] Finally, on September 27, 1943, the *Tongji-hoe* officially withdrew from the United Korean Committee upon the advice of Rhee. This was the end of the unity of the Korean community in America.

The United Korean Committee called a conference and adopted the following resolutions[26]:

1. The withdrawal of the Tongji-hoe is highly regretted, but there was no recourse, so the Committee has resolved to regroup its remaining member organizations and to carry out its task.

2. The Committee shall recall Syngman Rhee from the chairmanship of the Korean Commission and the detailed proposals for the reorganization of a new Commission shall be submitted to the Korean provisional government.

3. The Committee shall establish a new diplomatic office in Washington, D.C., at such time as it deems necessary.

In October 1944, the United Korean Committee in America held a conference in Los Angeles. They ousted Rhee from the chairmanship of the Korean Commission and replaced him with Kim Won-yong. They also set up a diplomatic office headed by Kim Won-yong, with Chun Kyung-moo as a staff member. Now there were two Korean diplomatic offices in Washington, D.C. Rhee maintained his position as chairman of the Korean Commission and claimed that he was the official representative of the Korean provisional government in Chungking, while Kim Won-yong acted as the representative of the Koreans in America who had established the United Korean Committee. However, neither of them was recognized by the United States government, and neither was allowed to participate in the United Nations Conference held in San Francisco in 1945.

Thus, on the eve of the collapse of the Axis powers, the Korean community in America was in a stage of confusion and division. Nobody knew who or what group would lead the Korean independence movement. The Korean community called for new leadership with new guidelines, but the tragedy was that new leadership had not emerged from the new generation. The voices of the left-wing Korean intellectuals, who advocated a united front and a coalition government based on people's democracy as the postwar Korean settlement, were rejected by the conservative Korean community in America.

Nobody could predict the future. The international political climate was not clear on the Korean issue. The Cairo Declaration only promised Korean independence "in due course". The unexpected division of the Korean peninsula into two military-occupation zones by the Allied powers and the subsequent announcement of a five-year trusteeship system were sad news to the Korean people, who had been hoping for the restoration of national independence soon after an Allied victory. During this period, even Rhee did not know what he should do. He said to his friends that he and his wife "can always retire to a farm and raise chickens."[27]

POSTWAR ACTIVITIES

When Japan accepted the unconditional surrender terms of the Allied powers on August 15, 1945, many Koreans in America wanted to return to their homeland to participate in the reconstruction of the war-torn country. On October 25, 1945, the United Korean Committee called a conference in Honolulu and decided to send delegates to South Korea to help the postwar reconstruction. The delegation team was called the Korean Delegation of America. It was composed of five delegates from the mainland and nine from Hawaii. Because of difficulties in obtaining transportation permits from U.S. Army authorities, the first group of delegates left on December 27, while the second group left about a month later.

Prior to the arrival in Seoul of the Korean Delegation of America, Rhee arrived there with the title of Korean Commissioner. Some State Department officials were not happy about permitting Rhee to go back to Korea because of his stubbornness and ultra-conservative political views. But the influence of the War Department, especially of General MacArthur, Supreme Commander of S.C.A.P., and General John Hilldring, Assistant Secretary of State for Occupied Countries, overrode their objections. General MacArthur suggested to General John R. Hodge, commanding general of American armed forces in South Korea, the "wisdom of greeting Rhee as a homecoming national hero."[28]

The United States military authorities supported Rhee for two reasons. First, he had been conservative and would emerge as a leader of the traditional conservative nationalist political forces in South Korea. Second, he had been a militant anti-Communist and would cooperate with American foreign policy. Thus, Rhee was to be considered as a counterpart to Kim Il-sung, the North Korean pro-Russian Communist dictator, who by October had become an unchallengeable ruler under the sponsorship of Soviet military authority.

Rhee served as a political adviser to General Hodge in South Korea, but because of personal ill feelings between the two as well as American support of the middle-of-the-road group headed by Kim Kiusic, Rhee came back to the United States to launch an anti-USAMGIK campaign. He appealed the Korean issue to the United Nations.

However, when the United States adopted its cold war policy against the Soviet expansionism, Rhee's political fortunes rose again. He supported the U.N.-supervised election in South Korea, and he opposed the Korean political leaders conference for unification. Rhee was elected president of the Republic of Korea (South) in 1948 and ruled the country for twelve years until he was ousted in 1960.

In addition to Rhee, two Koreans, Kim Ho and Kim Won-yong, who returned to Korea as members of the Korean Delegation of America, also participated in the American military government. They were appointed as South Korean assemblymen by General Hodge when the American military government changed its structure into the South Korean interim government. Many Koreans who had finished their studies in America and worked with the United States government during the war returned to South Korea as civilian employees of the War Department. However, many of them later returned to the United States after Rhee became the ruler of South Korea.

President Rhee took a passionate interest in all Koreans in America, even those who were naturalized citizens. They were subject to punishment unless they supported his policies. Rhee and his diplomatic representatives in the United States attacked anti-Rhee intellectuals, who were critical of his dictatorial power, as "Communists or Communist sympathizers." Rhee used McCarthy-type tactics against his political opponents. He branded even the members of the Korean National Association as pro-Communists and urged his followers to refrain from seeing or talking to them. Many Koreans who held different views from those of Rhee were unable to visit South Korea because the Korean consulate refused to issue visas for them. Korean students in America who expressed anti-Rhee views were denied extensions of their student passports and were forced to return to South Korea before finishing their studies. Some anti-Rhee Koreans were helped to remain in the United States by sympathetic and knowledgeable American friends and by organizations like the American Civil Liberties Union. A few were forced to leave. For example, one young Korean writer fled to Europe and returned to America after Rhee was ousted from power. During Rhee's rule, the most democratic Koreans became militantly anti-Rhee. Nevertheless, some of them were suspected and even rejected as undesirable aliens by the American authorities when the Korean War broke out.

During the Korean War, most of the twelve thousand Koreans in the United States had mixed feelings, partly because it was a war in which Koreans were killing Koreans, and partly because the war could not settle the problem of reunification of the country. In general, there were three different groups of Koreans who voiced their views on the Korean War. Some Koreans believed that the war was a civil war between northerners and southerners for unification of the divided country by military power. Some thought it was a war of ideologies, democracy versus communism. Some regarded it as American imperialism against Asian peoples' nationalism. The first group did not take sides, hoping that reunification would be achieved after the war ended. The second group supported the Rhee government because victory of the north would mean communization of the Korean peninsula. The third group sided with the northern regime because they thought that American imperialists wanted not only to exploit Korea but also the whole of Asia. Most members of the Korean National Association and the *Hung Sa Dan* (Young Korean Academy) belonged to the first group, while members of the *Tongji-hoe* belonged to the second group. A handful, mostly members of the Korean National Revolutionary Party in Los Angeles, belonged to the third group and opposed American intervention in the Korean War in the name of the United Nations. Some of the left-wing Koreans were under constant surveillance by American authorities. A few received deportation orders from the Immigration and Naturalization Service and went to North Korea by way of European Communist countries. One changed his mind while in Europe and returned to the United States, where he cooperated with American authorities.[29]

During the Korean War, some Korean intellectuals in the United States organized the Korean Preparatory Committee for the Neutralization of Korea. The Committee drafted the following proposal and submitted it to the United Nations and to the heads of the major powers, including India and the People's Republic of China. In part, the proposal read:

> Independence is a nation's birthright, and liberty is a God-given right of the people. The Korean people are entitled to have these rights without any conditions or intervention from foreign powers. Nevertheless, because of the geographical location of Korea, surrounded by Japan, China, and Russia, she became many times a battleground in the struggle for power: the Sino-Japanese War, 1894-1895; the Russo-Japanese War, 1904-1905; and the present Korean War, 1950-1953. It is a historically proven fact that as long as Korea has been dominated by any foreign powers, there has been no real peace in the Far East, and there can be no durable world peace, if Korea is to be dominated by any big power.
>
> Therefore, it seems that the only practical and far-sighted political technique for the solution of the Korean problem is to agree on PERMANENT NEUTRALITY OF KOREA (like that of Austria and Switzerland) by the concerned powers, including the Soviet Union, the People's Republic of China, Japan, the United States and Great Britain. The neutrality of Korea means: to guarantee independence and neutrality of Korea by the above mentioned powers and that Korea would not be involved either militarily or politically in the game of power politics; absolutely no foreign countries establish military bases on the territory of Korea; and Korea will maintain and defend the neutrality with all means at her disposal. This formula conforms with the National interests of the Korean people and would pave the way for a rapid peaceful unification of the country based on the self-determination principle, and for the future protection of national independence and territorial integrity. It would also reduce tension in the Far East generally and would contribute a durable peace in that part of the world.[30]

This statement was the only constructive effort made by Koreans for the solution of the Korean problem. No action on this proposal has been taken by the major powers.

THE STUDENT REVOLUTION AND KOREANS IN AMERICA

The student revolution of April 19, 1960, that ended Syngman Rhee's twelve-year iron-fisted rule in South Korea is a highlight in the struggle for human liberty. Rhee's police state fell because of official corruption, favoritism, political oppression, and fraudulent elections. All of these were practiced in the name of patriotism and in the guise of anti-communism.

The student uprising first took the form of protest against government interference in academic freedom during the presidential campaign. Then it developed into mass street demonstrations in major cities. The uprising against the Rhee regime was touched off by the finding of a student's dead body in the bay. Sixteen-year-old Kim Chu-yul was missing, but the police claimed they knew nothing about him. Eventually his body was found floating near the beach of Chungan-dong in the southern part of Masan. The corpse's head contained a fragment of one of the tear gas shells that police had used to put down the demonstrators. The police had stuffed a fake Communist leaflet in the corpse's pocket. During the student demonstration more than nine hundred casualties were counted. Many persons died or became permanently disabled. Koreans in America, especially students and intellectuals, called for mass meetings and decided to launch an anti-Rhee movement throughout the United States. But opinions were divided. Some of the conservative leaders thought that the student demonstrations were a Communist-inspired plot as the Rhee government claimed; they took the attitude of wait and see. The students and anti-Rhee intellectuals, on the other hand, issued statements condemning Rhee's rigged elections and police brutality. A statement issued by Koreans in the Bay Area read:

> We herewith declare that the spontaneous mass anti-Rhee demonstration of the Korean people in south Korea is the clear evidence for opposition of Syngman Rhee administration on the one hand and their desire for protection of their democratic rights and freedom on the other; therefore, their demonstrations are the expression of human liberty against tyranny. We demand that: (1) Immediate withdrawal of the martial law and immediate end put to the brutal police suppression against the peaceful demonstrators; (2) Immediate release of all arrested students and civilians; (3) The government should pay adequate compensations to the victims and families who suffered during the demonstrations; (4) To punish the policemen and soldiers who committed brutal actions against the peaceful demonstrators; (5) Tyrant Syngman Rhee should resign from the presidency at once and he should be tried in court, charged as a traitor; (6) All overseas high government officials should resign from their present posts, because they have been acting as Rhee's private agents rather than representatives of the Korean people; and (7) The presidential election of March 15 was rigged and a new election should be held within three months.[31]

Many Korean residents in the United States were under the eyes of Rhee's agents, diplomats and paid undercover informers in the guise of students or merchants. Some of the high officials, including consuls, often exceeded their official authority and abused public funds for their own personal interests. For example, one of the main duties of a consul-general was to collect information through his informers about the activities of every Korean resident in his jurisdictional area. He also attempted to control the Korean student organizations, Korean churches, and other social or political organizations by means of bribery or intimidation. Korean students and residents were told whom they should and should not see, and which church they should and should not attend. The consul-general falsely identified

individuals or organizations that had opposite views from the Rhee government as "communists or communist-front organizations." When an anti-
Rhee Korean professor was invited as a speaker by an American university a
member of the Korean legation from Washington (a former foreign minister) flew to the university to try to get the speech canceled. His efforts were
not successful.

After April 23, Korean students in the United States began staging
peaceful demonstrations in front of the Korean consulate buildings in Los
Angeles. Leaders of the Korean National Association of North America held
a mass meeting in Los Angeles and issued a protest statement against the repressive measures of the Rhee government against the student demonstrators. At this juncture, the United States government issued its strongest
statement yet to Rhee's government, denouncing "repressive measures un-
suited to a free democracy" and demanded that "the Korean government
. . . take necessary and effective action aimed at protecting democratic
rights of freedom of speech, of assembly, of press, as well as preserving the
secrecy of the ballot and preventing unfair discrimination against political
opponents of a party in power."[32] The representatives of the sixteen nations
which had fought for South Korea in the Korean War issued a joint statement urging "an early resolution of the situation in a manner which would
permit the orderly functioning of democratic government."

Knowing that Rhee's fall from power was a matter of time, Koreans in
San Francisco, for the first time, also staged a mass demonstration in front
of the consul-general's office. They demanded the resignation of Rhee from
the presidential office, the immediate end of repressive measures against
peaceful demonstrators, the release of all arrested students, and a summary
dismissal of the consul-general in San Francisco. On April 27, Rhee was
ousted from power, and a few days later he was forced to flee the country.
He returned to Hawaii. Thus, the oppression of a native tyrant was temporarily alleviated in South Korea, but not in the north.

After Rhee was out of power, some timid Korean intellectuals in America who had been silent during the Rhee rule came out of hiding to seek high
public positions in Korea. They claimed that they had been fighting against
the anti-democratic Rhee administration all along. Thus a few opportunistic intellectuals secured government positions when the Second Republic of Korea was established under a democratic party—the Chang
Myon administration—in August of 1960.

On the other hand, some Koreans in America devoted their time and
energy to helping those families who suffered during the student uprising.
The following incident is worth citing. Chin Yong-sook, a fifteen-year-old
high-school girl, died from a police bullet during the Seoul demonstration.

She died shouting "Long live democracy," and left a note to her mother, which read:

> Dear Mother,
>
> I am sorry that I, without saying goodbye, have left you to join the demonstration. I will fight to the last against the fraudulent election. All my high school friends, together with the students of the Republic of Korea, are participating in the bloody street demonstration for the cause of democracy.
>
> Mother, please do not scold me for taking part in the demonstration: who should demonstrate if we don't? I know I am still an unthinking child, but I also know how to show my love for my country and my people. All my school mates are ready to lay down their lives for our country and so am I. I do not mind even if I should die during the demonstrations.
>
> Mother, I know you will feel grieved about my decision because you love me so much, but you should be cheerful when you think of freedom for the people and a bright future for our country. It would seem that in my mind I have already joined the demonstrating crowd.
>
> Since I am writing this note very hurriedly my hand is shaking. I pray that you should be in good health. Let me say again, I made up my mind to lay down my life for the cause of democracy. I have to close, time is short.[33]

Miss Chin's mother was a widow with two children of school age. One was forced to quit school because she could not afford the expenses. Concerned Koreans in the San Francisco Bay Area collected money for the Chin family and sent it to Mrs. Chin for her children's schooling.

After Rhee's fall from power, the Korean community in America began to change. Many pro-Rhee leaders, including ministers of the Christian churches, retired from community activities. Undercover informers disappeared from student and social organizations. As expected, the *Tongji-hoe*, Rhee's private organization, was no longer considered an effective political organization, although it still maintains offices in Honolulu and Los Angeles.

Within the Korean National Association, two factions formed. Ahn Cha'ng-ho's group, known as the *Hung Sa Dan* members, who had dominated the Association for many years, wanted to continue its name and called for unity under the Association. The non-*Hung Sa Dan* group, headed by Kim Ho, Kim Won-yong, and Kim Hyung-soon (The Reedley group), advocated a new organization in order to meet the demands of the postwar period. The latter group argued that the mission of the Korean National Association ended when national independence was restored in 1945, and that it was time to establish a new organization based on new guidelines.

On May 1, 1960, a mass meeting was held at the Danish Hall in Los Angeles to discuss the possibility of a new organization. Most of the *Hung Sa Dan* members, however, did not attend. In reality, the meeting was sponsored by the Reedley group and Song Chul, a leader of the *Tongji-hoe*. Three resolutions were passed at the meeting: establishment of a committee to promote unity among the Koreans in America; establishment of a Korean Center; and the recruitment of young members with high academic training as potential leaders of the new organization. In 1962, a preparatory committee for the establishment of the Korean Center was formed, headed by Kim Ho, Kim Won-yong, Kim Hyung-soon, and Song Chul. The Korean ambassador to the United States, Chung Il-kwan, and Ahn Kwang-soo, the consul-general in Los Angeles, were elected as advisers. In February 1963, the group bought the Korean Center building (the Danish Hall) with funds raised mostly from among its members. Kim Ho and Kim Hyung-soon donated ten thousand dollars each; the South Korean government, fifteen thousand dollars; and Song Chul and Yim Il-yang, five thousand dollars each. The organization was named the Korean Center; Kim Ho was elected chairman and Song Chul, vice-chairman.

Because of the large influx of new Korean immigrants into the Los Angeles area after 1965 following the American government's change in immigration policy, many new community organizations developed. In the meantime, differences of management as well as policy-making procedures became a controversy between the old guard headed by the Kim Ho group and the younger and newer members of the Korean Center. Finally, the traditional old leaders retired from the Center and the newcomers took over leadership. They formed a new organization, now known as the Korean Association of Southern California. Dr. Cho Yong-sam was elected the first president, and a board of directors was chosen to act as a policy-making body.[34] The organization has attempted to consolidate various community groups under its leadership but, as will be seen later, it is still in a formative stage in terms of structure and purpose.

To sum up: hope for restoration of national independence revived when Japan attacked Pearl Harbor. The Korean independence movement developed from individual terrorist activities against the Japanese in China into an organized front combining both conservative and progressive leaders in the United States and China.

Most Koreans in the United States rendered service in the war against the Axis powers. Military-age Koreans served in the American armed forces. Older men worked in military construction. Elderly women served in the Red Cross. Japanese-speaking Koreans worked as interpreters in the intelligence service. And, in 1943, a Korean military unit was formed in cooperation with the California National Guard.

Koreans in the United States established the United Korean Committee and launched diplomatic activities to obtain official recognition of the Korean provisional government from the Allied powers. Nevertheless, Korean diplomatic efforts ended in complete failure. Unfortunately, the United Korean Committee split into two factions. One was headed by Syngman Rhee and members of the *Tongji-hoe*; the other was led by the Korean National Association. Both groups set up diplomatic offices in Washington, D.C., and each claimed to represent all Koreans in the United States.

In 1945, the United States established military government in Korea below the 38th parallel. Rhee and other Korean leaders were repatriated from the United States. Rhee emerged as the leader of the Korean conservative forces and was elected first president of the Republic of Korea in 1948. He ruled South Korea for twelve years as a one-man dictator until he was ousted by the student revolution in 1960.

A left-wing Korean political organization was established in the Korean community before the Second World War broke out. They advocated a united front and supported left-wing groups in the Korean provisional government. During the Korean War, they took a sympathetic attitude toward the Communist regime of North Korea. This group became defunct soon after the war ended.

During the Rhee regime, anti-Rhee Korean intellectuals in the United States had a tough time, because Rhee and his official agents identified them as Communists or Communist sympathizers. Most Koreans in the United States took no sides in the Korean War, because "Koreans killed Koreans." Gradually Koreans became less active in politics, and many postwar Korean organizations emerged as non-political groups.

3

Postwar Korea and Koreans in America

10.

Divided Korea

The Division of the Country

South Korea comprises primarily the agricultural zone of the peninsula. It covers 37,000 square miles and has a population of thirty-four million. North Korea, the industrial zone, has 48,000 square miles with a population of fifteen million. Although the cultivated areas in each zone are about equal (6 million acres), the mountainous north has rich mineral resources and hydroelectric power. The southern zone is blessed with rich soil and a mild climate. The peninsula has about 5,400 miles of coastline, with many good harbors on the south and west coasts but few on the east coast. Korea has a variety of mineral deposits, including gold, coal, and copper. Korean economists believe that the natural resources of the peninsula could be developed so as to make the country self-sufficient.

The artificial division of the country by the Allied powers extends through all phases of Korean life—economic, political, and social.[1] The division at the 38th parallel destroyed national unity, led to war, and produced many other human tragedies. One of the most serious results of the division has been the crippling of the economy, because neither zone can establish economic independence in a real sense. For example, before the division, northern Korea produced about 86 percent of the heavy industry, while southern Korea produced 75 percent of the light industry. The south had almost three times as large an area of irrigated rice land as the north. The consumer-goods industry of the south depended upon northern electrical power and their semi-finished materials. In return, the south depended on the chemical fertilizers produced in the north, while the north needed rice from the south. Since the Korean War, both the northern and southern governments have launched development plans year after year and have made impressive progress. But so far, neither side has been able to establish a self-sufficient economy. This means, then, that as long as the peninsula remains divided, it will be difficult, if not impossible, for Korean people to attain a reasonable standard of living.

Opposing political ideologies in each zone brought antagonistic feelings between northern and southern Koreans. The northern Communist leaders have denounced the southern political leaders as agents of American imperialism, while the southern politicians have condemned the northern Communists as traitors or puppets of the Russian and Chinese governments. The Soviet bloc was determined to install a Communist-dominated Korean government, whereas the United States government insisted on a pro-American government. As a result militant Communists monopolized power in the north while pro-American Koreans, civilians and military personnel alike, succeeded in establishing themselves as the ruling class in the south.

In the early 1960s, northern Communist leaders advocated the idea of *juche* ("self-reliance") as the guideline of the Democratic People's Republic. Southern Korean leaders formulated the concept of Korean indigenous democracy as the principle of the Republic of Korea.

Because of the atmosphere of international détente, both Korean governments agreed to a peaceful unification of the country, stating that national unity "shall be sought above all, transcending differences in idea, ideologies, and system."[2] Nevertheless, subsequent evidence leads one to believe that a peaceful unification is still remote, because neither side seems likely to abandon its own terms for national unification. Thus, political uncertainty exists now in Korea, and many Korean people live in fear of war or the communization of the country.

In the postwar period, the North Korean regime adopted a modified communal social structure in rural areas. People work and live together as one economic unit. The children stay in nurseries while their parents work in the fields. In addition, the life-style of industrial workers in urban areas has slowly been changed to resemble the life-style of people in the country. Individual rights are restricted, and worship of Kim Il-sung as the most "respected and beloved national hero" has been taught to the people. Thus, the traditional family-centered feudal society has been completely transformed into a regimented socialistic society under state control.

In contrast, in South Korea, the family-centered feudal society has been in transition toward a Western-oriented individual society. The American way of life has influenced South Korea, especially the new-rich middle class that became wealthy through American aid during the Rhee administration. The members of this class, as well as the younger generation, go to American movies, dance to American music, read American books, and receive an American-oriented education. They also build Western-style houses and drive American cars.

Since General Park Chung-hee seized power in 1961, South Korean authorities have emphasized Korean nationalism. They have appealed to the people to learn more native history and culture and to preserve traditional values. Despite such efforts, the yearning for an American way of thinking, "liberty, equality, and abundance of material wealth," by Koreans have caused many to leave their native land. The large influx of new Korean immigrants into the United States began after 1964 when the American government changed its immigration policy and repealed the national-origin quota system that had been in effect for forty years. Therefore, this study will concentrate on an analysis of recent South Korean internal political, economic, and social development as a background for the influx of new Koreans into the United States.

THE POLITICAL SITUATION

A Korean saying goes: "No flower can remain in full bloom for more than ten days: no man alive can last longer than ten years in power."

Since the liberation of Korea from Japanese rule in 1945, the South Korean regime became a militantly anti-Communist one, both under civilian and military rule. American-educated Syngman Rhee ruled South Korea for twelve years in the name of patriotism, anti-Communism, and democracy. His corrupt one-man tyranny was overthrown by a student revolution in April 1960. The incompetent Second Republic, headed by John Chang, also educated in America, came to an end when a military coup took place in May 1961. General Park Chung-hee, a Japanese-trained samurai-type military officer and an admirer of Japan's Meiji Restoration of 1869, has been governing South Korea ever since. Both Rhee and Park have done their best to disprove the Korean adage, primarily by applying the principle that the end justifies the means.

President Park wrote three books in which he expressed his political ideology.[3] He advocated three types of democracy: administrative democracy, national democracy, and Korean or indigenous democracy. To put it briefly, the concept of an administrative democracy is as follows. "The military revolution was absolutely necessary to save the nation from complete destruction just as the physician had to perform a surgical operation to save the patient's life. During the process of revolution, democratic procedures had to be suspended temporarily in order to remove all social, political, and economic evils on the one hand and to lay a foundation for the reconstruction of a new society, the true democracy, on the other." According to Park, an administrative democracy was to exist during the revolutionary period as a transitional state. The military elite appointed him the exponent of democracy and educator of the masses.[4]

A national democracy means "national self-dependence in terms of economic independence." Park argued that "self-dependence is the foundation on which national democracy is to be established, and it furnishes an environment where democracy can prosper." Therefore, he advocated a policy of "economic development first and political democracy second."[5]

In 1972, Park announced his principle of Korean democracy. His statement read: "Just as we make our clothes to fit our own measurements . . . we will creatively have to develop a democratic political system of our own, commensurate with our historical and cultural tradition and present reality, and operate it with self-confidence."[6] Then he proclaimed the October Reformation Program, which he explained as follows: "The Reformation means an expression of national will in order to create a new national history, namely, reunification of the country and establishment of a stable and prosperous political system based on self-reliance principles of our great people. . . . The Reformation social order will be a new social ethic which everybody should follow, and the ethic principles contain the concept of one nation, prosperity, cooperation, efficiency, and productivity."[7] Park believed that this was his mission on behalf of the Korean people.

During the period from 1961 to 1963, General Park removed all rivals from the power structure. Then he "retired" from the army, ran for the presidency three times, and won three times by revising the two-term limitation in the constitution through undemocratic procedures in the National Assembly in 1969. In 1972, he pushed through another constitutional change enabling him to remain in office for life.

Under the new constitution, Park can run for an unlimited number of six-year terms as president. Election is by the National Conference for Unification, which consists of 2,359 members elected by the voters.[8] The constitution also empowers the president to hand-pick one-third (73 members) of the National Assembly; the rest are elected by popular vote. The president can assume dictatorial power whenever he decides there is a national emergency. Furthermore, he can dissolve the National Assembly whenever he wants. The constitution also reduces the power of the supreme court by setting up a constitutional committee that "empowers the constitutionality of a law at the request of the court, impeachment and dissolution of a political party." Thus, the legislative body has been turned into a rubber-stamp debating club, and the judicial branch has been reduced to a puppet of the executive branch.

The constitution does not guarantee basic rights, such as freedom of residence, speech, press, assembly, and association. Nor is there a provision against ex-post-facto warrants. Every article contains the catch-all disclaimer "except provided by law." This means that these democratic rights of the people can be voided at any time by the government authorities.

This new constitution is the product of Park's political thinking. He is a Japanese-trained military man. His early education, including normal school (elementary teacher's institute) and the Japanese Imperial Military

Academy, as well as his experiences in Manchuria as a second lieutenant in the Japanese Kwantung Army during the Second World War, became predominant factors in his political outlook. Park is a man of Eastern traditions: Confucianism and Buddhism. He is a self-confident individual who sees himself, rightly or wrongly, as a man of virtue, governing his people with paternal good will and benevolence, but whose word must not be questioned. Although he is a soldier from a rural background, the son of a poor peasant, he understands the value of modern technology, science, and a scientific Western education.[9]

As a revolutionary leader, Park was determined to achieve his ideological commitment, which he describes as Korean democracy and a unified Korean nation. The meaning of Park's democracy is, at best, ambiguous, but his ultimate goal is to establish a welfare state that will benefit the Korean people.

As a politician, he believes in strong leadership and favors a centralized political structure rather than a representative democratic form of government. He calls such an authoritarian political system a "Koreanized democratic structure." He is concerned mainly with administrative efficiency, and puts political and social stability before individual freedom.

There are three factors in Park's justification of his authoritarian system. First, South Korea was born in the midst of the cold war, with implacable enemies to the north: Communists who were determined to destroy the southern government. They might have succeeded during the Korean War, had the United States not intervened in the name of the United Nations. Even today, Kim Il-sung's goal has not been abandoned. Only his tactics have changed. Park is fully aware of Kim's tactics, and South Korea has lived under a constant threat. Thus, Park feels that South Korea cannot afford to be divided politically internally.

Second, most political leaders in South Korea do not have confidence in Western democracy. They are strong nationalists and disciplined military officials whose primary aim is economic modernization in order to compete with the Communists. Maintenance of political and social stability, even at the expense of individual freedom, has had top priority.

Finally, the withdrawal of United States troops from Vietman led Park and his colleagues to believe that, in the forseeable future, South Korea will be essentially on its own to face the threat from North Korea and its allies.[10] Thus, the Park government has followed a policy of national security first and democracy second.

Since Park came into power, his regime has disregarded or totally denied basic human rights. For example, the Korean Central Intelligence Agency has unlimited authority to investigate and detain any person accused or suspected of aiding the enemy. The right to dissent and criticize

Park's administration has been sharply restricted. Among the many incidents that have occurred, the following are typical. In 1967, the CIA and the national police searched the New Democratic Party's headquarters and seized their account books because Kim Chae-hwan, a candidate for the National Assembly, was arrested for allegedly receiving campaign funds from a Communist-front organization in Japan. In 1968, more than thirty Korean students and professors from abroad, mainly from Western Europe, were brought back forceably and charged with espionage for the North Korean regime. The South Korean court found them guilty and then announced mild sentences. Someone who enjoyed legal immunity sent out anonymous threatening letters to the judges who handled the case and to the press covering the case.[11]

Perhaps the most outrageous and shocking incident was the kidnapping of Kim Dae-jung by South Korean government officials from the Grand Palace Hotel in Tokyo on August 8, 1973. Kim was the New Democratic Party's candidate for the presidency in the 1971 election, in which he received 46 percent of the popular vote. While he was in the United States and Japan, he criticized the Park administration. Five days after the kidnapping, Kim was released near his home in Seoul. He was told by the kidnappers that "they are the members of the Save-the-Nation Federation. . . . Korean overseas activities should not harm the prestige of fatherland and Koreans should fight each other within the Korean territory and not outside of the country."[12]

At first the South Korean government repeatedly denied involvement by any government officials in the kidnapping. However, because of evidence produced by the Japanese government, the South Korean prime minister, Kim Jong-p'il, walked into the office of Premier Kakuei Tanaka of Japan on November 2, 1973, and offered his government's apology for the abduction of Kim Dae-jung. The South Korean prime minister further promised that such incidents would never happen again.[13]

On December 16, 1975, Kim Dae-jung was sentenced to one year's imprisonment for election violations in the 1967 and 1971 elections. The major charges were that Kim allegedly spent too much money, and that he had also illegally started his presidential campaign as early as 1969 by saying that Park's political ambition, if elected in 1971, was to install a dictatorship or, in Kim's phraseology, a "generalissimo system" patterned after that of Chiang Kai-shek on Taiwan. The Seoul District Criminal Court also leveled a $300 fine. However, it suspended the fine and did not order Kim's arrest. But his lawyers said that the ruling technically made Kim a prisoner and that he would be treated as one while confined to his home. After the trial, he commented that "the verdict was influenced by outside pressures."[14]

The case of Kim Chi-ha, an internationally known poet, is another ex-

ample. He had been one of Park's most vociferous critics and admitted giving money to help the student movement against the Park administration.
The government ruled that the anti-Park student movement was a Com-
munist-directed conspiracy to overthrow the South Korean government. A
military court martial sentenced Kim Chi-ha to death. But international protests began to rise, and the death sentence was reduced to life imprisonment.
In February 1975, the poet, as well as 160 other political prisoners jailed under an April 1974 special decree, were released.

But the poet attacked the Park administration again by writing a newspaper article in the *Tong-A Ilbo* entitled "Asceticism—1974." In this article
Kim Chi-ha not only described his own experiences in prison but also said
that the government case against alleged members of a so-called "People's
Revolutionary Party" had been fabricated upon confessions extracted by
torture. Kim was re-arrested on March 13, 1975. Subsequently, the government announced that he had confessed in a handwritten statement that he
was a Communist. In September, a military court martial reinstated the life-
imprisonment sentence against him.

No one has been allowed to visit the poet in jail, and it is said that he is
not even permitted to read a Bible. But somehow he was able to write a
twelve-thousand-word memorandum entitled "Declaration of Conscience."
It was smuggled out of the prison and handed to Father Yun Hyung-jung,
the past representative of the National Association of Catholic Priests for
the Realization of Justice, who in turn sent it overseas (to Father James
Sinnot). According to the memorandum, the confession Kim made was
false. He had been forced to write it after five days of torture.

> I have never thought of myself as a Communist. . . . I see myself as
> a man able to think independently and free from the limitations of any
> one thought system. I sincerely desire for my thought to be neither influ-
> enced by personal ambition of any kind nor subject to coercion of any
> kind, but rather, completely independent from any dogmatic position.
> Therefore, I have not once in my whole life identified myself with any
> particular 'ism.' My present position is to strive to reach an awareness of
> truth by constantly throwing myself into a situation of creative tension
> which is formed in the confusion of freedom. . . . I hope to be a man
> able to love compassionately, concretely and with all of myself, my flesh
> and blood neighbors who are suffering from oppression and exploita-
> tion and who are painfully and contemptuously denied their basic
> human rights. This is for myself, the whole task of human integrity. This
> is the beginning point for all of my groping thought, and at the same
> time its final destination. I want the whole process of my intellectual
> struggle to be interpreted from the perspective of love for people. . . .
> In being raised as one of the people, as one of those who are oppressed
> . . . my confidence grew firm that all the questions we have will find
> their right answers only when the people have in their own hands the key
> to unlock their own destiny.[15]

He then pledged himself to continue opposing Park's government, and to fight for the restoration of democracy and a better deal for the nation's poor.

More recently, a female member of the National Assembly, Kim Ok-sun, who belonged to the opposition New Democratic Party, was forced to resign under implied threats of physical attack. The law-maker made a speech in the National Assembly—where an unqualified right of immunity is guaranteed by the constitution—saying that "today's parliamentary system is nothing but a decoration to fortify a one-man dictatorship. . . . Recent so-called security rallies being staged by the government, the inauguration of a student-defense corps and a civil-defense corps, and the airing of military songs on the radio . . . are nothing but means designed to perpetuate the regime."[16]

The ruling Democratic Republican Party at once launched a move to expel Kim from membership in the National Assembly and even called seven of its members to return from overseas trips to participate in the vote. In the meantime, veterans organizations and anti-Communist groups marched in a demonstration against the anti-Park law-maker and hinted at possible physical attack.

Under these circumstances, Kim submitted her resignation before the issue came to a vote. Thus, her party was saved from the trouble of defending her. This incident served to underscore not only how feeble the opposition party had become, but just how insecure any person in South Korea can be, regardless of what the laws state.

On August 17, 1975, Chang Jun-ha, a 1962 winner of the Philippines' Magsaysay Award for contributions to journalism and a constant critic of the Park administration, died in a mountain-climbing incident. The widow of Chang was reportedly afraid to demand an autopsy. The only witness to Chang's accident had contradicted himself in his account of how Chang allegedly fell to his death. But "even if the doctors were honest, they would not be allowed to announce anything that might contradict the police conclusion that it was an accident."[17]

The press has also been under complete control of the government. The *Tong-A Ilbo*, Korea's leading national newspaper, was critical of the present administration policies. Because of pressure from agents of the Korean Central Intelligence Agency, Korean businessmen began to cancel their advertisements in the *Tong-A Ilbo*. The government-inspired boycott of advertising continued until the *Tong-A Ilbo* agreed to cease criticizing government policies. Two staff members who supported freedom of the press were fired.

Even the overseas Korean newspapers that have been critical of the Park administration are now under close surveillance by Korean government agents. The *New Korea* in Los Angeles, which dedicated its past seventy years to the cause of national independence and the promotion of democratic principles in the Korean community in the United States, has faced financial difficulties. According to reports, "Korean Consulate General and KCIA (Korean Central Intelligence Agency) forced Koreans to cancel advertising in the *New Korea*" because "often the *New Korea* expressed anti-Park views."[18]

Freedom of religion is theoretically guaranteed by the constitution, but dissident sermons and prayer meetings are not allowed. Only prayer meetings supporting government policies are encouraged. Former critics of government policies, such as Cardinal Steven Kim and Bishop Daniel Chi, have been freed from jail but remain silent. Other critics like the Rev. Park Hyong-ku are still in jail, charged with misappropriating church funds. A few anti-government Christian leaders, including the Rev. Kim Chai-choon, are in exile in the United States and Canada.

The South Korean government also expelled two American missionaries from South Korea because they took part in anti-government activities.[19] Two Japanese nationals, convicted by a South Korean court, were charged with anti-government activities, and one Japanese newspaper office was forced to close in Seoul. One American newspaper correspondent had his visa revoked because of anti-government reports.

College and university professors, who once enjoyed tenure, have to take periodic examinations for continued employment and have been given responsibility for checking up on the activities of specific students.

The anti-government movement, touched off by Kim Dae-jung's abduction, was first led by university students and then by discontented intellectuals, including civic and religious leaders. They condemned Park's dictatorial measures on the one hand, and also called for unity of the people to restore a democratic government in South Korea, on the other. The opposition parties, the New Democratic Party and Unification Party, also joined the anti-Park movement. Under these circumstances, the Park government became somewhat conciliatory. The president made a cabinet change by removing the chief of the CIA, Lee Hu-rak. Anti-government demonstrations have been mushrooming, supported by people of all walks of life. At this juncture, the North Korean Communist regime resumed its propaganda against Park's administration. In his New Year message, the North Korean dictator, Kim Il-sung, praised South Korea's anti-government movement and expressed North Korea's complete support for restoration of democracy in South Korea. The Park government was under attack from all directions and its fall seemed possible.

On January 8, 1974, Park issued another dramatic emergency measure, stating that "It is imperative for us, first of all, to firmly maintain political and social stability and to solidly foster and organize our national strength, in view of the rapidly changing international political and economic situation and of various acts of the provocation perpetuated by the North Korean Communists." He went on to say that he was compelled to act because "some impure elements with delusions, taking no heed of the reality confronting us, were attempting to create social unrest and confusion by agitating the general public and spreading malicious rumors."[20]

There were two emergency measures. The first prohibited the following acts: (1) denial of, opposition to, and misrepresentation or defamation of the constitution, and any effort to revise or repeal it; (2) advocation or instigation of any action prohibited by the emergency measure, or communication about such action by any means; and (3) criticism of the emergency measure itself. Violators may be arrested without warrant for trial by court-martial.

The second emergency measure created an emergency court-martial. General Lee Sea-ho, Commander of the Third Army and former top commander of troops in Vietnam, was appointed president of the Appellate Court-Martial, and the KCIA was given the power to investigate cases.

Since the two emergency measures went into effect, unknown numbers of students, civic leaders, Christian ministers, and newspaper editors have been arrested and sentenced to fifteen-year prison terms for defying a presidential ban against calling for changes in the constitution.

After the fall of Vietnam and Kim Il-sung's trip to Peking in April 1975, Park issued the May Thirteenth Edict banning all forms of political criticism. Park also called for unconditional unity to meet the threat from North Korea.

According to the May Thirteenth Edict, each of the following acts were prohibited: (1) an act fabricating or disseminating false rumors or misrepresenting facts; (2) an act denying, opposing, misrepresenting, or defaming the constitution, or asserting, petitioning, instigating, or propagandizing revision or repeal of the constitution by means of assembly, demonstration, or through public media such as newspapers, broadcasts, or press services, or by such other means of expression as writings, books, or recordings; (3) an assembly, demonstration, or political activity except for classes or research programs under the supervision of school authorities, or except when authorized by the school principal in advance, or for routine activities; and (4) an act openly defaming this decree. Violators are subject to one year's imprisonment.[21]

A different opinion was expressed by opposition leader Kim Dae-jung on the political outlook of Korea after the collapse of Vietnam and Kim Il-sung's visit to Peking. Kim said, "I don't believe that our present situation is the same as the Vietnamese situation. But if we don't change the suppressions and corruptions early, we can't avoid the fate of another Vietnam." He further stated that most Korean people "are becoming skeptical about fighting against Communism under the present dictatorial rule, disappointed with the big gap between the haves and the have-nots and angry with the extent of corruption and the luxurious life of the privileged class." He also does not believe that Kim Il-sung will take military action to take over South Korea. Instead, "he will try to organize a fifth column to infiltrate among a people dissatisfied with suppression, poverty and corruption in the South."[22] Therefore, Kim Dae-jung believes that restoration of democracy in South Korea is the first order in politics and the surest way to defeat Communism. This statement was made by Kim before he was sentenced on political charges for breaking the presidential and parliamentary election laws.

THREE VIEWS ON PARK'S POLITICS

In general, there have been three views on Park's politics. Some Koreans admire him as a great political leader. For example, Yun Chi-yong, former acting chairman of the Democratic Republican Party, praised him as the most respected hero since Tan'gun, the legendary first ruler of the Korean peninsula about twenty centuries before the birth of Christ.[23] The South Korean official publication *Minjok Ui Dungbul* (Limelight of the Nation) stated: "In the process of Korean National history, Park Chung-hee has emerged as a symbolic leader who redefined a new direction of national destiny, which otherwise would have faced total destruction." He also laid the foundation for "political independence, economic self-sufficiency, and a national reunification policy based on the self-determination principle," which can be characterized as "self-reliant power." The statement went on to say that, above all, "Park has been a people's leader who understands the aspirations, desires, and needs of the common people through his own experiences as the son of a poor village peasant."[24]

On the other hand, some observers think that Park's basic mentality in politics emerged from his profession as a career soldier in the Japanese Imperial Army and later as an officer of the Republic of Korea. Park came to power through a military coup in 1961. Thus, his military experiences were "to remain a dominant factor in his political thinking." Park said, "Human life is sacred and respectable, and everyone has the right to live happily and successfully. But in order to protect the right to live, it is necessary to sacrifice individual rights for the sake of national life. The path of a soldier should be identical to this idea of sacrifice of his own life for the nation. Therefore, the soldier's death is a glorious and sacred one, because small I, my life, sacrifices for big I, the nation."[25]

As a politician, Park favors a traditional authoritarian government. He emphasizes administrative efficiency and demands absolute obedience and personal loyalty from public officials. Thus, to him, obedience and loyalty have more value than individual rights. Often Park attaches himself to Korean tradition or native culture; he prefers native folk songs and rice wine to Western music or liquor. He used to say that he likes to live in rural areas rather than in urban areas, which he often referred to as a "rotten and filthy" life.[26] In this sense, he is almost a cultural chauvinist. Yet he sees the value of modern science and technology. In short, according to these observers, Park is a combination of old and new, a Japanese samurai or a Prussian type of strong administrator who is equipped with zeal for the modernization of Korea. He will not allow anybody to challenge his leadership until South Korea has been modernized and the country reunified.

Finally, some observers, including ex-president Yun Po-sun, questioned Park's political beliefs, saying that he is "a man of heterogeneous ideology, or a Red." Sometimes he is referred to as "a man involved in the Army mutiny (revolt) at Yosu by Communist infiltrators in 1948." Yun stated in his book *Thorny Road of Country and My Memo* (*Kukook ui kasibal-kil: Na ui Foiko*): "Park Chung-hee once became a Japanese military man by profession; he pledged himself to sacrifice his life for [the] glory of the Japanese Emperor. . . . After [the] liberation of Korea, he returned to Korea and participated in Communist activities in order to overthrow this government (Republic of Korea in South). Thus, he attempted twice to harm the motherland."[27] Many Koreans have known that sooner or later Park would turn out to be a dictator. Ever since his takeover of the government by a military coup, he has been moving toward one-man rule. These observers believe that the Republic of Korea is at present an authoritarian state in which political repression has grown steadily more severe. Freedom of speech and press as well as assembly are now strictly limited. Opponents of government policies, no matter how strongly anti-Communist, run increasing risks. The government has set up a secret police force, the Korean Central Intelligence Agency, to silence dissenters. Church services and prayer meetings are under the surveillance of government agents. Thus, the Korean people feel that they are sitting on "needle cushions", to use a Korean metaphor. Many Koreans are overwhelmed by a sense of hopelessness, because any criticism of the government is equivalent to asking for a prison sentence.

One Korean anti-Communist in the United States wrote an article in the *Christian Century*. It said in part: "Twenty-five years ago I escaped from the Communist dictatorship of North Korea to the democracy of South Korea. Several months ago I had to escape again, this time from a democratic dictatorship, in South Korea. . . . One asks, what is the difference between Park and Kim Il-sung, the brutal Stalinist dictator of North Korea? Park has taken Kim as a model; he has practically succeeded in establishing over South Korea a control as absolute as that Kim exercises over the North."[28]

THE SOUTH KOREAN ECONOMY

The Park government's first order of business has been economic reconstruction, because Park believes that "modernization of the country through economic reconstruction is a basic prerequisite for a genuine free democracy which guarantees man's freedom and dignity." He promised to build "a welfare state for the greatest benefits to the greatest number possible."[29] Thus, national resources and energy have been concentrated on increasing gross national production and expanding exports through industrialization and the modernization of agriculture.

The Park administration has made rapid economic progress since 1961. Three five-year economic plans were launched, designed to achieve a self-sufficient economy by the end of 1976. During the past decade, South Korea has maintained an average growth rate in the gross national product of 10 percent per year, one of the world's highest. Official figures indicate an 8.3 percent increase during the first five-year plan and a 12.6 percent increase during the second five-year plan.[30] The growth rate was around 9 percent between 1970 and 1971, but jumped to 17 percent in 1973. Because of the oil crisis, the 1974 and 1975 growth rates were about 8 percent. This growth has been called "an economic miracle" by the Park government. Under Rhee, the growth rate averaged only 3.5 percent. The value of the gross national product grew about four times from 1960 to 1973, from $2.3 billion to $9.5 billion. The per capita national income rose more slowly, but by an impressive multiple of 3.5 percent, from $90 to $320.[31]

Exports also rose spectacularly from $175 million in 1965 to $4.5 billion in 1974.[32] The major items of export have been clothing, textiles, electrical goods, and wood products. These are all products of light industry which require a heavy input of labor. Because South Korea lacks natural resources, raw materials must be imported from abroad.

A few years ago, South Korea seemed on the verge of achieving its goal of economic self-sufficiency, and the government claimed that South Korea was about to join the ranks of semi-industrialized or middle-income countries, with a per capita GNP of $380. Hopefully, Park projected another blueprint for expansion. Per capita income is expected to increase to $1,000 by the year 1980, up 320 percent over 1972. Annual trade will reach $10 billion, up 1,000 percent, and the GNP will be over $36 billion, up 370 percent. This project set goals of "transforming Korea from a borrowing to a lending country by 1981" and financing Korean industry "with continued increases in domestic savings without relying on foreign sources."[33]

Park also launched the New Community Movement, based on a combined economic and spiritual scheme to raise living standards and to improve the appearance of South Korea's thirty-three thousand villages. A total of $5 billion has been allocated to encourage deserving farmers and fishermen to "learn the wisdom to help themselves and cooperate with each other to create a self-sufficient community."[34] This project is also aimed partially at reversing the population flow to the cities. During the last decade, the rural population has declined from 56 percent to 46 percent of the total population.

It should be pointed out here that one of the basic agrarian problems in South Korea has been the shortage of arable land. Out of a population of thirty-four million in 1975, over fifteen million were crowded onto six million acres of land. The average farm contains two and one-half acres, while one-third of all farm families depend on one acre of land or even less. There is little possibility of reclaiming land in South Korea. Moreover, the soil has suffered a depletion of plant nutrients after centuries of intensive use without planned rotation. Consequently, good yields are possible only with adequate supplies of commercial fertilizers, which are very expensive. Good yields also depend on the weather. Floods sometimes wipe out a peasant village or villages. Because of the lack of an adequate farm credit system, and the government's do-nothing policy on the low price of agricultural products (sometimes the rice price in the market is below the cost of production), there has been a considerable turnover of land. Many peasants have not been able to meet their payments and have been forced to leave their farms.

Although the third five-year plan emphasized improvement of agricultural products, South Korea still has to import foodstuffs from abroad to meet domestic needs. Naturally the living standard of the peasants, who still constitute nearly 50 percent of the total population, has not been improved much, and many of them live in poverty. The past decade's unbalanced economic growth will have to be overcome if the farmers are to take part in the benefits of economic modernization. Rural income has been well below that in urban areas, and the gap continues to widen. It remains to be seen whether Park's New Community Movement will close this gap.[35]

PROBLEMS OF THE SOUTH KOREAN ECONOMY

Perhaps the most important and simultaneously the most difficult problem for the South Korean government is the economy's almost total dependence on foreign countries in terms of its exports, raw materials, and capital investments. The basic feature of its export-oriented industry is its concentration in the light-manufacturing sector. A high dependence on imported raw materials, and energy leaves it relatively limited room to maneuver when terms of trade deteriorate. South Korea's textile industry spins and weaves imported cotton; its electronic industry assembles imported components; its steel industry works with imported ore and scrap iron; and its sawmills process imported lumber. All South Korea's industries depend on imported energy.

A similar situation exists with regard to capital. Under the 1972 Foreign Capital Inducement Law, the Park government is responsible for guaranteeing payment of all previously approved foreign loans and investments. Foreign capital accounted for 45 percent of investments under the first two five-year plans, and it probably rose to 60 percent under the third five-year plan, which ended in 1976. Long-term foreign debt shot up from $3.3 billion in 1973 to $5.9 billion in 1975. Thus, payments of principal and interest on short and long-term debts ran over $1 billion in 1975 alone.[36] This means that every South Korean already owes more than $200 to foreign countries. And every South Korean also has to pay annually more than $30 in principal and interest on these debts.

The United States and Japan have been the main investors in South Korea. Official U.S. expenditures in South Korea from 1946 to 1976 was a little more than $189 billion. This figure includes payments for the Korean War, the cost of stationing U.S. troops in Korea, payments to Korean troops in the Vietman War, military assistance and credit sales, and economic assistance in loans and grants. Only $6.5 billion, including the 1976 proposed estimate, are attributed to economic assistance. Since the conclusion of the normalization treaty between Korea and Japan in 1965, Japanese investments in South Korea have already amounted to more than $1 billion, and Japan's investments will exceed those of the United States.[37] Japanese capital has penetrated into almost every industry: power, railways, telecommunication, iron and steel, oil refineries, mining, machines, shipping, and hotels. The only major industries left for Korean businessmen are textiles and construction.

The South Korean balance of payments in international trade suffered the impact of the twin shocks of sharply increasing world prices for fuel, food, and raw material, and the recession in Japanese and American markets. The current account deficit increased from $309 million in 1973 to $1.8 billion in 1974. The 1975 deficit was estimated at $2.2 billion by foreign economists, but South Korean government officials said it would not exceed $1.4 billion, since the country had a record rice crop and was able to eliminate most rice imports.[38] During the oil crisis, South Korea's trade dropped 18.5 percent from 1973 to 1974. Although no sharp deterioration is expected in following years, external borrowing increased in 1975 by 96 percent over 1974. South Korean exports grew only 6 percent in 1975, compared with an average expansion rate of 35 percent during the previous ten years. According to International Monetary Fund statistics, all non-oil developing nations dropped about 4 percent in their trade in 1974, compared to Korea's 18.5 percent drop.

Some United States government analysts project that "even assuming future real export growth of 15 percent a year, South Korea will require a gross capital inflow of $14 billion over the period 1976–1980," because of Korea's growing deficit and debt service.[39] If this is the case, the South Korean government will soon face a real financial crisis. No foreign governments will extend any more credit, and private direct investment in South Korea will be out of the question since no improvement in its trade balance will be possible.

Many foreign economists, including the staff of the Institute for International Policy, expressed pessimistic views about South Korea's pattern of export-oriented growth fueled by foreign capital. One economist commented: "There is still overinvestment, especially by the Japanese, who have put well over a billion dollars into South Korean factories and firms, which could lead to bankruptcies, with the Japanese picking up the pieces. A sort of re-colonization of Korea could thereby occur."[40] The Institute states: "As the situation escapes the South Korean government's control, Koreans may well recall an old Chinese saying: 'He has so many lice that he doesn't itch anymore.' [Thus] the Republic of Korea is headed for default on her debts abroad and economic chaos at home."[41]

To this, South Korean authorities reply that the report of the Institute for International Policy "is based on false assumptions" and that it "would vanish if South Korea's present economic situation were better understood." Nam Duck-woo, the deputy prime minister and head of South Korea's economic planning board, said that "many persons don't realize that South Korea's revenues from exports have been growing about as fast as its long-term debt obligations." He further stated that "everybody knows the non-oil producing countries are having balance-of-payment problems and that is not new. The real issue now is that we have managed our debt, and we have gotten through the oil crises."[42]

Phillip Sherman, head of the First National City Bank in Seoul, expressed the same view as Nam. He said: "There is always vulnerability when a nation has a high debt, but that debt can also be a sign of dynamism. Korea's debt is related to development and it is making good use of the funds brought in. In that respect, the situation is somewhat similar to what Japan went through several years ago."[43]

Strong government action also has helped to turn the economy around. The reestablishment of strict import and export controls led to a small trade surplus as of May 1975. As a result the government predicted that the 1975 deficit would not exceed $1.4 billion, well below the foreign economists' projection of $2.5 billion.

The political calm on the Korean peninsula after the United States renewed its commitment to defend South Korea and after North Korea's Kim Il-sung returned from a trip to Peking without a public promise of Chinese support for war is another hopeful sign for the economy. Many foreign banks are now willing to lend to South Korea.

Inflation and unemployment problems also cannot be overlooked. The government achieved economic progress, but it did not curb inflation. General prices began to rise as a result of high export prices and a sharp increase in the money supply. Since the oil crisis, general prices began to rise again. Wholesale prices, which rose about 45 percent in 1974, rose another 20 percent in 1975. Inflation is not only a source of hardship for the public but reduces South Korea's trade benefits, too. Even before the oil crises, export prices rose 30 percent in 1973 while import prices rose 50 percent. Rates in 1974 and 1975 almost doubled.[44]

Unemployment has been 10 percent in urban areas but much less in rural areas. The country as a whole has an average rate of a little over 5 percent. In order to keep the present level of unemployment from increasing, an additional 3.8 million jobs will have to be created by 1980. Any slowdown of economic progress, with increasing unemployment combined with runaway inflation, would certainly cause social unrest. Also, the past decade's unbalanced growth will have to be overcome if the farmers are to take part in the benefits of economic modernization. The average rural income is well below that in urban areas, and the gap continues to widen.

The concentration of national wealth in the cities, especially in Seoul, is another problem. Almost all the wealthy families of South Korea live in Seoul, where over 80 percent of the business capital is concentrated. Sections of downtown Seoul have become showcases of the South Korean economy and give an inaccurate picture of the country. The phenomenal development of modern Seoul, now the eleventh largest city in the world, inhabitated by over seven million people, has not only brought comfortable living benefits to the privileged upper class, but has also brought human poverty and misery. At present, Seoul has ten golf courses, modern freeways, newly completed subway lines, modern office buildings, banks, and apartments, as well as factories, stores, and hotels with shopping arcades. At the same time, approximately one-sixth of the population finds shelter in shacks and slums. This means that nearly one million people do not have decent homes to live in, and many have to sleep at night in the dry open sewers or in pedestrial tunnels.

In addition to slum conditions for the urban working class, there is also the poverty of the peasants, who comprise almost a majority of the population.[45] The gap between the haves and have-nots has widened.

The government faces some difficulty in obtaining future American aid because of the human rights amendment (the Abourezk amendment) passed by the U.S. Senate on November 4, 1975. The operative section is as follows:

No assistance may be provided under this part to the government of any country which engages in a consistent pattern of gross violations of internationally recognized human rights, including torture or cruel, inhuman, or degrading treatment or punishment, prolonged detention without charges, or other flagrant denial of the right to life, liberty, and the security of person, unless such assistance will directly benefit the needy people in such country.[46]

Section 617 provides that Congress may terminate any assistance program by concurrent resolution, which cannot be vetoed. In 1974, Congress, in light of oppressive measures taken by the South Korean government, placed a ceiling of $145 million on all forms of military aid. An additional $20 million could have been expended provided the president determined that the government was making substantial progress toward observing human rights standards.

Many observers believe that an American president will have trouble persuading Congress that the South Korean government qualifies for continued American aid. The Park government issued an emergency decree banning assembly and all forms of criticism as of May 13, 1975. Many congressmen, such as Edward Koch and Don Fraser, expressed their concern about human rights violations in South Korea. Representative Koch stated in a colloquy with Assistant Secretary of State Philip Habib on June 19, 1975:

> If we do not get the South Korean government to end repressive policies, which you have conceded exist, that people are in jail, that universities and newspapers are not free and that parliamentary immunity is the only safeguard that keeps its opposition members from going to jail, I foresee the same kind of pressures building up in this country that built up to get us out of South Vietnam and Southeast Asia. Only it won't take that long in terms of years.[47]

South Korean authorities denied the existence of political prisoners. At the same time, they claimed that freedom of speech, of press, and of assembly exist in the context of the South Korean political climate, which has faced constant threat from northern Communists.

SOCIAL CONDITIONS

South Korean society can be divided into two classes: the small group of privileged "haves" and the majority of "have nots." The former group includes big businessmen, political opportunists, top public officials both military and civilian, and top political leaders, including members of the National Assembly of the party in power. The latter group is composed of peasants, industrial workers, white-collar workers, and intellectuals and embraces more than 75 percent of the population. An overwhelming majority of the people are poor, with a per capita income of a little more than $500 in 1976.

Constant foreign aid (estimated as well over $5.9 billion in 1975), coming mainly from the United States, has created a handful of Korean million-aires and has sustained many corrupt practices. The great portion of foreign aid, as well as Japanese reparation payments, went to political funds of the ruling party during the elections. Meanwhile, some specially privileged indi-viduals were able to create their own community in Seoul called by the peo-ple a "thief village."[48]

Following the military coup in 1961, a new social class has gradually emerged as an unchallengeable ruling clique in place of the old ruling class, commonly referred to as the old politicians or old guards. Most of the old guards, who had been freedom fighters against Japanese rule and became dominant political leaders during the Rhee and Chang administrations, have departed from the political scene. Some leaders, such as Chough Pyong-ok, Shin Ik-ki, and Chang Myon, died of old age, while others were forced to re-tire. The same thing happened in the business field: the old landlord class gradually disappeared as land reform measures were put into practice after the liberation of the country from Japanese domination. The Japanese-oriented business class has also retired, and a new and young business elite, cooperating with and rewarded by the ruling Park administration, has emerged.

The political ruling class is composed almost entirely of former mili-tary men. Only a few old politicians like Paik Tu-jin, Yun Chi-yong, and Chang Ki-yong joined in the new group, and as of 1976 only one of them, Chang Ki-yong, was still active. Since the installation of Park's civilian government in 1963, more than half the cabinet posts have been held by for-mer highranking military officials. Ten out of eleven directorships of inde-pendent regulatory commissions and thirty-two out of fifty-nine ambas-sadorial posts were rewarded to inactive military officers. In the legislative body, nearly 25 percent of the seats have been held by retired military men. In addition, about 14 percent of high-ranking public posts as well as poli-tical appointees have some military background.

Military penetration into key positions of the economic field has also been noticeable. Retired generals and admirals loyal to Park were ap-pointed as heads of the multimillion-dollar government corporations that came into existence after the military coup. For example, in 1969, thirty-three out of forty-two government industrial corporations were headed by retired generals. Generals Song Yo-chan, Ahn Ki-song, and Park Jin-soh, to name just a few, became chairmen or presidents of government-owned corporations.

It is estimated that well over another two thousand retired military per-sons with the rank of major or colonel were placed in both central and local key government positions. Retired military officers also have been in con-trol of the ruling Democratic Republican Party, which was created by Col.

Kim Jong-p'il, then the CIA director. Park Chung-hee has headed the party since its establishment in 1962. As of 1969, the fifteen key heads of administration, including the prime minister, were former high-ranking military officials.[49]

Another ruling group is the South Korean Central Intelligence Agency (CIA), which can be characterized as the "omnipotent power source" in South Korean society.[50] No reliable data about the structure and operation of the CIA are available today, but the following outline was pieced together from newspapers and other sources. The CIA was formed at the time of the military revolution in 1961 under the leadership of Colonel Kim Jong-p'il, nephew of General Park Chung-hee. From the beginning, the CIA was immersed in politics. The first director, Kim Jong-p'il, an ex-prime minister, utilized the CIA to organize the Democratic Republican Party. He was provided with almost unlimited funds and man power during his directorship. Kim persuaded Park Chung-hee to run for the presidency as a "civilian" party candidate in 1963. All the directors of the CIA, including the present ones, have been former high-ranking military officials, and they have been Park's closest, most trusted, and most loyal supporters. Perhaps one of the most powerful directors in CIA history was Lee Hu-rak, who was removed recently from the directorship because of the CIA's involvement in the kidnapping of Kim Dae-jung. Lee helped to push through the constitutional revisions of 1969 and 1972 by which Park assumed absolute power for his lifetime should he desire it. Lee was the person who suggested negotiations between South Korea and North Korea, and it was he who was sent to P'yongyang, capital of North Korea, as Park's personal secret representative. As a result, the July 4, 1972, peace accord was announced. Subsequently, Lee was appointed chairman of the South-North Coordination Committee, representing the South Korean government, but he later resigned this position.

Neither the budget nor the size of the CIA has been made known to the public. At present, its personnel is estimated to number from one hundred thousand to three hundred thousand persons, including undercover agents, businessmen, students, retired military men, and faculty members at the universities. It is said that there are two types of agents. Some are well-educated, intelligent, and capable of acquiring and analyzing information. Others are action men who do rough jobs without question.[51]

A *New York Times* correspondent wrote: "The agents watch everything and everyone everywhere. . . . The network is so extensive that the agency once put a telephone call through from Seoul to a noodle restaurant in the remote countryside where a foreign visitor had wandered on a holiday without telling anyone. . . . South Koreans believe that the best way is not to talk about anything at all to anybody, even his own members of family."[52]

Korean residents overseas have also been under constant surveillance of the CIA. Most Koreans in this country hesitate to express their views on the Park administration, because they will be charged with anti-government opinions or intimidated by undercover agents, who have been placed in every Korean social, religious, cultural, and student organization. Many Koreans here have relatives in South Korea, and they do not want to jeopardize their relatives.

The CIA is active in all Korean communities in America. The following incidents represent their tactics. Kang Yong-chee, editor of *Free Republic*, received a letter from his ailing mother in Seoul, accusing him of collaboration with Kim Dae-jung. The letter went on to say if he continued to do so, her life and the lives of his sisters and two brothers would be in jeopardy.[53] On April 14, 1973, when Kim Dae-jung made a speech before the annual conference of the Association of Korean Christian Scholars at St. Louis, the head of the Eighth Department of the CIA in Seoul telephoned the presiding chairman of the meeting and warned that "Mr. Kim should restrain himself from attack on the Park government." About a month later, Kim made another speech in San Francisco. This time several pro-Park youths headed by a *taekwon-do* instructor attempted to disrupt the meeting by shouting at Kim: "Why do you criticize the head of our nation . . . you should fight in Korea."[54] It should be noted that the Save the Nation Federation, which kidnapped Kim in Tokyo, publically declared: "We will bring home in the same manner anyone who betrays his country while overseas as Kim Dae-jung did."[55]

The ruled class consists of students, intellectuals, peasants, and industrial workers. They have been the discontented and rebellious anti-government forces. Although Korea has had six political revolutions within the past one hundred and sixty years, all indications today lead to the conclusion that genuine democratic revolution has not ended but has just begun. This is because age-old social injustices have not been removed and the people have not obtained their basic rights. The main social injustices have been the wide gap between the privileged few and underprivileged majority, the chronic official corruption, the moral degradation of opportunistic intellectuals, and the factional fights for power within the ruling class.

In spite of the present government's arbitrary measures, such as suppression, intimidation, and sometimes bribery through the CIA, police and other agents, the discontented intellectuals and students seem determined to continue to fight for rights on behalf of the underprivileged majority. Rebellious students want a new democratic constitution in place of the present one. They also want the CIA abolished so that the surveillance of students and faculty ceases to exist. Other demands include the doing away of dependence on foreigners and foreign investments, especially those of the Japanese; the making public of the true story of Kim Dae-jung's kidnapping; and the release of all arrested students and political prisoners.[56]

Striking journalists issued a statement that "we are keenly aware that the Korean press has failed in its mission to report truth and facts and criticism." The statement called for "restoration of a free press so that journalists could report domestic and foreign events objectively."[57] Leading intellectuals and Christian leaders also issued an anti-government declaration. In part it reads: "The dictatorial regime and its reign of terror had shaken off freedom of assembly, freedom of speech, freedom of religion, and academy." It called for a unified struggle for "the complete restoration of democracy."[58] Then they launched a campaign to collect one million signatures on a petition to Park "for a restoration of a democratic constitution." Despite Park's constant warnings, the campaign has been supported by the South Korean public, and two opposition political parties joined the one million signatures' movement. Within a short period more than half a million people signed the petition. At this juncture, Park issued an emergency decree on January 8, 1974, and branded the discontented Koreans as "impure elements" who "were attempting to create social unrest and confusion by agitating the general public and spreading malicious false rumor." A few hundred anti-government leaders were arrested by the Korean Central Intelligency Agency. Many of them received prison sentences.

As mentioned before, following the fall of South Vietman to the Communists, Park established a semi-totalitarian state and emerged as a one-man ruler under the May 13, 1975, presidential edict. Thus, today the people live in fear and keep silent like those in North Korea. Some observers believe that the majority of South Koreans support the Park government, because they still prefer to live under the Park administration rather than under the Communist tyrant Kim Il-sung. On the other hand, some observers interpret the uneasy silence as a sign of passive resistance, like the calm before a storm.

THE ATTITUDE OF KOREANS IN AMERICA

It should be noted that discontented Koreans abroad, including those in Japan and in the United States, have formed various organizations such as the Korean Congress for Democracy and Unification, Korean-American Citizens Committee for the Protection of Kim Dae-jung, Scholars for Democracy, American Scholars for a Democratic Korea, and Council for Restoration of Democracy in the Motherland. These organizations condemn Park's dictatorial, oppressive measures on the one hand and urge a united struggle for the restoration of democracy in South Korea on the other.[59] Semi-monthly newspapers like *New Korea*, *Free Republic* (defunct), *Korean Journal*, and *Hanmin Shinbo* have been published by anti-Park Koreans. Christian intellectuals as well as students in the United States have also expressed their disapproval of Park's authoritarian tactics and called for the restoration of democracy.[60] However, a great majority of Korean residents in the United States are silent and hesitate to speak out.

More recently, eight publishers—owners of independent Korean language media in the United States and Canada—held a two-day conference at Stoneypoint, New York, and formed a United Front to restore Democracy in South Korea. They issued a statement saying that "the realization of individual freedom and social justice embodied in the democratic spirit is a precious human ideal that could only be attained through constant struggle."[61]

On March 17, 1976, the Subcommittee on International Organization of the House Committee on Foreign Affairs held a hearing on the activities of the Korean Central Intelligence Agency in the Korean community in the United States. Two Korean community leaders and two American experts on Korea testified before the Subcommittee, which was chaired by Representative Donald M. Fraser (Democrat from Minnesota). Kim Woon-ha, editor of *New Korea* in Los Angeles, told the members of the subcommittee that the Korean CIA "tried for months to close this paper or end his criticism of the Park government by pressing businessmen to cancel advertisements, offering him money, free tickets to Korea or a government job, and spreading rumors he was a Communist." In contrast to this, Professor Kim Hyung-il, president of the Korean Association of Southern California, said that "he knew of no case of KCIA intimidation in his community."

However, Donald L. Ranard, the former director of Korean affairs of the State Department, testified that "he knew, based on U.S. Intelligence reports, that the KCIA has organized demonstrations in support of the president Park Chung Hee government, and at other times attempted to break up demonstrations against that government." Professor Gregory Henderson, author of *Korea: The Politics of the Vortex*, said among other things that the CIA is "a vast, shadowy world of an estimated one hundred thousand to three hundred thousand bureaucrats, intellectuals, agents and thugs." He further stated that "he knew at least eighteen agents were stationed in the United States." A spokesman for the Korean embassy in Washington, D.C. said that "he did not believe the allegations and he had no knowledge of any KCIA harassment activities in the United States."[62]

11.

Postwar Korean Emigration

THE GENERAL PATTERN

The postwar pattern of Korean emigration to the United States is complex in quality, quantity, and motivation. The occupational pattern in America today is drastically different from that of the early immigrants. The early immigrants did monotonous, manual work, mostly in agriculture, mining, and railroad construction. The new immigrants' occupations are heterogeneous; and many are in professional fields, and many are engaged in business. The nature of the Korean community has also changed, from being country-centered to being city-centered. The purposes of community organizations are also markedly different, having changed from a support of national independence to the protection of the welfare of fellow countrymen, the promotion of economic development, and participation in the minority ethnic rights issue of American politics. At the same time, the motivation, or mentality, of the early immigrants and the new immigrants is different. Early residents thought of themselves as temporary sojourners who would return to their homeland when they made enough money or the political situation permitted their return. The new immigrants are here to stay and to start a new life for themselves and their children. A recent study reveals that most Koreans have emigrated to educate their children, to join family members, to improve their standard of living, or to obtain better jobs.[1]

Newcomers are literate. Eighty percent of the immigrants between 1965 and 1972 were high school graduates: 50 percent were college graduates and classified professionals. This picture has changed recently: the professional-preference immigrants have decreased from 25 percent in 1972 to 19 percent in 1974, while the non-preference immigrants increased from 1 percent in 1968 to 28 percent in 1974.

Another change has taken place. Between 1959 and 1971, an overwhelming majority of Korean immigrants were female. A majority of them were wives and children of American citizens, and they did not need gainful employment. Since 1971, male immigrants have exceeded female immigrants, and their percentage of the total has increased steadily. Statistics show that between 1961 and 1965, male immigrants numbered 29 out of 100; between 1969 and 1972, 55 out of 100; and between 1973 and 1974, 65 out of 100.

A change in age composition is also noticeable among the male immigrants. During the above-mentioned periods, males over twenty years of age entered at the rates of 41 percent, 64 percent, and 55 percent, respectively. One study reveals that the combined number of males and females of the two age groups, namely, twenty to twenty-nine and thirty to thirty-nine, constituted nearly 61 percent of the total Korean immigration. This means that the postwar Korean community in the United States is a community of young people.

The rate of naturalization has also increased rapidly in recent years. For example, in 1971, about two thousand Koreans were naturalized, while in 1974 the number doubled to more than four thousand.[2] One of the reasons for such an increase was the change of political climate in Korea after the failure of the American policy in Vietnam.

As noted above, a large influx of new Korean immigrants to the United States began after the American government eliminated the national-origin quota system that discriminated against Asian immigrants. There is no exact count as to how many Koreans came to the United States between 1945 and 1950, but an unofficial estimate puts the number at close to a hundred. The number of Korean immigrants between 1950 and 1975 are reported by the U.S. Naturalization and Immigration Service as follows:[3]

Year	Immigrants		
1950	10	1966	2,492
1951	32	1967	3,395
1952	127	1968	3,811
1953	115	1969	6,045
1954	254	1970	9,314
1955	315	1971	14,297
1956	703	1972	18,876
1957	648	1973	22,930
1958	1,604	1974	28,028
1959	1,720	1975	32,158
1960	1,507	Total	173,418
1961	1,534		
1962	1,538		
1963	2,580		
1964	2,362		
1965	2,165		

A few comments are necessary here to clarify the meaning of these statistics. The updated figure system used by the NIS is the annual alien registration taken every January 31. The above figures do not, of course, include the 13,000 American-born Koreans, nor do they include the 28,618 Korean residents who have been naturalized since their arrival.[4] Korean students who came to America for their studies are also omitted from this figure. There are about 5,000 Korean students in America today. Another factor is that many Koreans entered the United States by way of Canada, Germany, South America, and South Vietnam. They are therefore not included in the report from the NIS. The last consideration on the NIS statistics is that the non-quota immigrants, wives, children, and other close relatives of U.S. citizens were not included.

On the other hand, the statistics of the U.S. Bureau of the Census are also far from accurate. Until 1958, Koreans were not listed as Koreans but were identified as "Chinese," "Japanese," or "other Asians." According to the 1970 Census report, only 8,881 Koreans lived in the whole of Los Angeles County. Yet at the same time the NIS reported more than 20,000 Koreans.[5]

Reports from the Korean government are also not accurate, because the Korean foreign office does not change the status of Koreans who first emigrated to South America or Canada and then entered the United States. Many Koreans who came to the United States did not report or register with Korean official representatives. This means that, at present, figures on the Korean population in American are only guesses. It is estimated (1976) that there are over 200,000 Koreans here, including immigrants, American-born Koreans, and wives, children, and other relatives of United States citizens.

In the course of one year alone, 1975, a total of 32,158 Koreans emigrated to the United States. This constituted the second largest national group, next to that from the Republic of the Philippines. There are several reasons for this. When the United States finally repealed the national-quota system in 1965 and gave Asians an equal chance to immigrate, the South Korean government encouraged their people to leave the country because of the acute pressure of population increase. South Korea's population density is the third highest in the world, 782 per square mile. Each farming family has less than one acre of cultivated land. In addition, because of the division of the Korean peninsula, political uncertainty still exists, and many South Koreans live in fear of another war. Furthermore, when President Park Chung-hee installed a totalitarian political structure in 1972, he did not allow South Koreans to exercise basic human rights. Therefore, many discontented Koreans, especially intellectuals and professionals, have left the country.

The majority of the new Korean immigrants were told in Korea that the United States was a land of opportunity and happiness, in terms of economic betterment and political freedom. But as soon as they landed in America, they found that this image was exaggerated. They all faced many problems. Most of the newcomers, including intellectuals, professionals and skilled workers, found that they were unable to find meaningful employment in their own fields because of the language barriers, cultural conflicts, and lack of training.

Traditionally, Korean women do not work outside the home. Today this has changed, but upon entering the United States, wives have had to change their roles and take outside employment in order to supplement the family income, just as the early immigrants did. If there are grandparents or older children in the family, they take over the chores in the home and care for the younger children. Thus the new immigrants of today face problems similar to those that troubled their forebears, though in a much less stressful environment. Each successive wave of immigrants who uproot themselves from their homeland to set down roots in a foreign country are faced with problems of racial hostility, poor housing, and unemployment.

Today, the areas of heavy concentration of Korean immigrants are Los Angeles, San Francisco, New York, Chicago, Washington, D.C., and Honolulu. Of the two hundred thousand Koreans in America, approximately half settled in these six areas.[6] Los Angeles alone has seventy thousand Korean residents, who have formed more than two hundred and fifty different social, cultural, economic, academic, and political organizations with various principles and objectives.

Of the many new organizations in the major cities where Korean immigrants concentrated, the Korean Residence Association (in Los Angeles and some other cities, it is called the Korean Association) is the largest and strongest. The professed goals of all the organizations are about the same: protection of the well-being of Korean immigrants; promotion of living standards through economic development of Korean communities; participation in such social issues as minority ethnic rights; and social services to the Korean community. The new organizations, however, have many problems in terms of purpose and principle, leadership, factional struggles, and coordination with other ethnic groups.

Since the Koreans in America have not yet developed a united national organization comparable to the Japanese-American Citizens League or the National Association for the Advancement of Colored People, no single Korean organization can claim to be representative of Koreans in the United States. Consequently, Koreans in America do not receive their share of local and federal government aid as do other ethnic groups, nor are their hardships and problems heard by the proper American authorities. On this matter, the California Advisory Committee to the U.S. Commission on Civil Rights stated that in spite of the rapid increase of Korean immigrants since

1969—in 1971 alone, 23,473 Korean immigrants entered the United States—the American government has failed to provide them with any aid: "Korean-American professionals trained in Korea had extensive problems in obtaining states licenses; . . . social services had not been provided for the needs of Korean-American immigrants whose knowledge of and facility in English was limited; and . . . the public school system had not responded with programming for the increasing enrollment of Korean-American students."[7] Thus, Koreans in America face many problems, some of which will have to be solved by the Korean community as an independent ethnic group and some of which will have to be solved by individuals themselves. (These subjects will be treated in Chapter 12 of this book.)

THE INTELLECTUAL CLASS

The postwar Korean community in the United States is composed of three groups: professional intellectuals such as physicians, lawyers, scientists, teachers, and engineers; businessmen; and laborers, including farmers.

At present, professional intellectuals number about ten thousand. In general, this group can be subdivided into two categories: the successful and the frustrated. The former are in the minority and belong to the upper social class of the Korean community. The latter are in the majority and belong to the lower-middle class in terms of annual income. On the whole, those Korean scientists and engineers who were educated in American institutions are well established and live in comfort. About one hundred top scientists, including college and university professors and researchers, also belong to this social group. Among the Korean professionals, Korean-educated medical doctors, pharmacists, and nurses who failed to pass State Board Examinations because of the language barriers, belong to the frustrated group. They are forced to find jobs as clerks, technicians, or nurse's aids, sometimes at minimum wages, in order to support their families. In addition, most of the Korean-educated intellectuals such as high-school teachers, college professors, and skilled workers also belong to the frustrated group. Because of language difficulties and cultural conflicts, most find themselves in jobs that are inconsistent with their qualifications and experience and that pay low wages. The average annual income of the top Korean professionals is $20,000 to $25,000, while the displaced professionals' annual income is between $8,000 and $10,000.

According to a study made by one Korean sociologist, the following are some of the major findings.[8] He interviewed one hundred Korean immigrant families out of a total of four hundred households. The average age is thirty-five years; the average number of children is 2.5; the average period of residence in the U.S. is three years. Fifty-six percent are college graduates, 15 percent with higher degrees, and the rest are high-school graduates. Their occupational status before entering America is as follows: 18 percent worked in professional fields, and 64 percent worked in government and business establishments as specialists. But after entering the United States, 63 percent are working in fields for which they were not trained, and they are unhappy with their jobs. The ratio of the intellectual's participation in the Korean community affairs is very low. "The more you become intellectualized, the less you participate in Korean community issues," it appears.

This study confirms the negative attitude of Korean intellectuals toward the Korean community in the United States. Most Korean-American intellectuals isolate themselves from the community and live by themselves, looking only after their own interests. Their ambition is to be a part of an American establishment, to secure their position first and then to advance into the American elite circles. Some even forget that they are descendants of Koreans. In this respect, the Korean-American intellectuals follow the same path as their Korean contemporaries; that is, they stay away from political and social issues and become only spectators of events in their communities. It is unfortunate that there are not many Korean-American intellectuals who stand up for protection of the long forgotten Korean minority ethnic group in white-dominated American society. It is truly a tragedy that no constructive criticism, debate, or discussion for improvement of the existing Korean community has taken place among the Korean-American intellectuals. Today, Koreans everywhere in the United States look for new intellectual leaders who can lead the community into a new and better era.

According to reports of the 13,401 medical doctors licensed to practice in South Korea since 1948, only 8,700 remained in Korea by 1973. Between 45 and 60 percent of the graduates of the eleven medical schools of South Korea found employment abroad. There were about 3,000 Korean doctors in the United States in 1975. This means that far more Korean physicians are working in the United States today than are serving the 15 million people in South Korea's rural areas. Since the change in the immigration law of the United States, the Korean physician has the freedom to leave his country for money and a better living standard, while "the South Korean farmers have the freedom to die of preventable causes."

The South Korean government reported that in 1968, only 64 out of 325 Koreans who received doctoral degrees in the United States returned to Korea. Over a fourteen-year period, only about 6 percent of the Korean students who finished their advanced studies in America returned to South Korea. Most Korean Ph.D.s are employed either at colleges and universities or in American corporations. This fact indicates that higher education of Koreans in the United States has benefited individual Koreans and the United States far more than it has benefited Korea and the Korean community in the United States. Thus, the Korean intellectuals in America can be characterized as a "do-nothing class" within the Korean community.

THE BUSINESS CLASS

An analysis of the postwar business class of Koreans in the United States is only exploratory, for a number of reasons. First, the large number of immigrants (averaging twenty thousand per year since 1972) makes it difficult to obtain accurate information on their occupations, skills, and business establishments. Second, their frequent changes of jobs and businesses add complications. Third, the absence of a centralized organization such as a Korean National Chamber of Commerce makes it difficult to get data. Fourth, official United States data are behind the times because they are based on Bureau of the Census information of 1972. Therefore, the data for this study were based on reports from Korean language newspapers, a directory of the Korean community, and personal observations, as well as studies available in unpublished manuscripts.[10]

General trends within the postwar Korean business community can be summed up as follows. The rapid increase of Korean enterprises began after the United States changed its immigration law in 1965. The new Korean immigrants wanted to make America their home and their children's home. Hence, most of them planned long-term projects for their livelihood. A majority of them had never engaged in manual labor in Korea and had high educational standards but their knowledge of English was limited. Therefore their job opportunities in an English-speaking world were not bright. As a result, they chose to live in urban areas and to open family-operated businesses. Most started with an average capital of ten thousand dollars and opened ethnic-oriented consumer stores, such as food-related businesses, restaurants, and grocery stores. However, recently Korean businessmen have extended their activities into other fields, from wig shops to dressmaking stores. In Los Angeles, there are twenty-three different types of Korean business establishments, including massage studios, and in Washington, D.C., nineteen different types of businesses.

In general, present-day Korean businessmen in the United States appear more adventurous and profit-motivated than their predecessors. The business class can be divided into three groups: big, medium, and small. The meaning of "big business" here, by the Korean community standard, is having more than twenty paid employees; "medium" means the firm has eight to ten paid employees; "small" businesses are operated either exclusively by members of a family or by four to six paid employees. No data are available about big and medium-sized Korean business establishments, but these two groups are in the minority. Some of the big businessmen are often referred to as "money refugees." They made money in South Korea and Japan, and came over to the United States as already established businessmen. Most engage in the export and import trade, and usually make a few business trips to Korea, Japan, and Hong Kong every year. Such businessmen form a privileged group that has isolated itself from the Korean community in general. They live luxuriously in mansions in exclusive areas, and tend to be selfish and greedy individuals. Some of them made money from dubious political connections within South Korean ruling circles.

A few sewing factories, wig shops, the Korean Food Corporation, and some restaurants can be considered medium businesses. Their annual volume runs from $250,000 to more than $1 million. Their pay scales and working conditions are bad. They usually pay no more than the minimum wage, and in many cases even less than the minimum. Overtime pay is rare. Sanitary facilities are poor, with no separate washrooms, and working areas are without sunlight. In short, these businesses have not been Westernized, and their owners are not a respected group in the Korean community. The rapid growth and general characteristics of small Korean businesses were reported by the U.S. Bureau of the Census in 1971.[11]

In the United States, there are 1,201 commercial firms, with a total trade amounting to $65 million a year. California led all other states with 540 Korean firms having a business volume of $32 million. Hawaii had 165 firms doing a little over $15 million of trade, and New York had 93 firms doing over $94 million worth of business. Out of the total of 1,201 firms, only 249 have paid employees. The average number of employees per firm is six. Of the 540 firms in California, only 141 have six paid employees. Their business volume amounts to $21 million, or approximately 49 percent of the total gross volume. The 399 firms that have no paid workers make about $10 million. The 249 firms with paid employees made about $41 million, while the 952 firms with no paid employees brought in about $21 million worth of business a year. But the average receipt per firm with paid employees was $17,500, whereas the average receipt per firm with no paid employees was $22,000. Although it is assumed that these receipt figures are net profits, the income of these small Korean businesses is low relative to their hard work and the demands of taking care of their families. One interesting fact should be pointed out here. The 399 firms with no paid employees in California, which make up 41 percent of the total of 952 firms in the United States with no paid employees, did 49 percent of the total business transactions.[12]

A few characteristics of the Korean small businessman should be noted. First, his most distinctive characteristic is his high educational background. Nearly 70 percent of the Korean businessmen in the United States have college degrees. The age structure reveals a middle-aged group; about 62 percent are around the average age of forty. It is estimated that nearly 10 percent of the total Korean population in the United States is engaged in business. According to Professor Kim Hyung-Chan's findings, there are only nine businesswomen, of whom six have a college education. For the first time in the United States, a Korean Woman's Business Association was formed in Los Angeles, headed by Sonia Sook, the first Korean real estate broker.

Next is the matter of the sources of capital. Many Korean businessmen have received loans from the Small Business Administration (S.B.A.). For example, in the Olympic area of Los Angeles, 101 out of 250 Korean businessmen received a total of $10 million between 1971 and 1974. About two-thirds of the loans went to food-related retail stores, including markets, restaurants, and liquor stores. On the other hand, quite a few Koreans began with a small investment of their own. The initial capital investment of a family-operated business ran from $10,000 to $15,000.

Third, a great majority of the Koreans started their business ventures after fewer than three years of residence in the United States. A large number were high school teachers and college instructors before entering the United States. Since they did not have business experience or formal training in business, they faced problems of management, marketing, and finding proper locations as well as difficulties of communication with non-Korean customers.

Fourth, most of the small businesses are food-related retail stores and are concentrated in one area, the Korean or Oriental residential area. Naturally, competition is acute, and many firms go out of business within a short period.

Fifth, Korean businessmen hesitate to venture into non-ethnic business fields, that is, to penetrate into the American business world. This is because in addition to the language barrier they lack business experience with American customers and lack capital as well.

There are many stories about Korean businessmen. Some are success stories,[13] while others are the opposite. The following two are typical.

A Korean couple with no previous business experience bought a coffee shop in an American business section. The first day, the cook (husband) wasted a dozen eggs when a customer ordered a sunny-side-up fried egg, because he did not understand the order and did not know how to make it. He also wasted more than half a dozen pancakes before making and serving them to a customer. When a customer asked for a beef sandwich, he served him just two pieces of bread without beef, because he was so busy. After two months in business, the couple sold the coffee shop at a loss, because no customers came there to eat.[14]

On the other hand, another couple developed one of the most successful businesses in the Korean community in Los Angeles. Mr. and Mrs. Lee

Hi-duk arrived in Los Angeles seven years ago from West Germany, where Lee had worked as a miner. The couple was almost penniless when they reached Los Angeles. Both were college graduates. Lee worked in Los Angeles first as a can inspector, then as a welder. His wife was employed as a nurse. During their first three years, they saved about eight thousand dollars and decided to venture into business. First, they bought the Olympic Market (a Korean and American combined grocery store) at 3122 W. Olympic Blvd., the center of Koreatown today. They paid sixteen thousand dollars, of which half was borrowed. They worked from twelve to fourteen hours a day, seven days a week. Business volume increased over the next few years, and today the store does twenty times more business than when they took over. In 1974, they purchased property and built one of the most expensive Korean-style restaurants, the VIP Palace Restaurant and Nightclub on Olympic Blvd. The *Los Angeles Times* reported that "nowadays, he (Mr. Lee) drives a new black Mercedes and spends more time on his second business, a restaurant. Lee's rise epitomizes the remarkable growth and organization of immigrants from South Korea.[15]

Such success and failure stories of Korean immigrant businessmen stem in part from the inability of many educated Koreans to find jobs in their professions. Many were granted entry on preferential visas to alleviate the American shortage in certain professional fields. However, many—especially in the medical field—find their native degrees and training are not recognized by state agencies, although Korean education has been patterned after American curricula. As a result, many professionals have been forced to venture into business.

THE WORKING CLASS

About 85 percent of the Koreans in the United States belong to the working class, while 5 percent belong to the professional class and 10 percent to the business class. The average annual income of a manual laborer is between six and nine thousand dollars. A survey of the Korean-English Language and Job Training Program (now called the Multi-Service Center for Koreans) in San Francisco confirms this estimate.[16] The Center provides language and job training to Korean immigrants under a contract with San Francisco under the federal Comprehensive Employment Training Act of 1973. In 1975, the Center trained about eighty Korean immigrants and placed them in various business establishments, including hospitals and banks, in the Bay Area. Their average monthly salary was five hundred dollars; few earned as much as eight hundred dollars. All of the enrollees were at least high-school graduates in Korea, and many were college graduates who had worked as professionals, technicians, or teachers before entering the United States. Because of the language barrier and cultural conflicts, they had to go through a retraining program. This means that the low-income group of Koreans in the United States is not necessarily illiterate or unskilled. On the contrary, most are highly educated people, because more than 50 percent of all immigrants were college graduates.

Many Korean-educated professionals belonged to this group until they passed required examinations. For example, in 1973 there were about six hundred Korean-educated nurses in the Los Angeles Area. Of these, only two hundred had been able to obtain state licenses as registered nurses. The other four hundred worked as manual laborers or were employed as nurses's aides at minimum wages of $1.85 an hour.[17] Many of the Korean physicians and pharmacists were forced to work as clerks and technicians or sometimes gas-station attendants. Korean immigrant high-school teachers and college professors were forced to find jobs as restaurant busboys, janitors, or gardeners' assistants at starvation wages.

The average Korean family consists of four members: husband, wife, and two children of school age. In many cases, both parents have to work because one paycheck is not enough to cover expenses. Therefore the majority of manual laborers in the United States do not have time to enjoy family life, and most of the children stay home by themselves after school lets out.

A few words should be said here about the lives of Korean women in America. It is said in Korea that children have a school life, fathers have a job life, and mothers have a domestic life. Many Korean women in Korea have the misconception that women in America live in a worldly heaven. To be sure, it is good for a wife to be out of the house of the in-laws, to be free of their domination, and to assert herself as a woman as well as a wife and a mother. However, Korean women would be surprised to know the hardships and difficulties that the immigrant women in America have to go through. First, because of their severely limited outside contacts in American society, they suffer from the language barrier. There are many Korean mothers who do not speak English and who have a hard time communicating with their own children, who either forget or have no chance to learn their native language. Second, very often the mothers have to work in order to supplement the family budget, since the father's income alone does not cover the needs of the family. Thus, the Korean mother in America carries a double responsibility.

The following life story of a Korean working woman is typical of the general living conditions of Korean women in this country.[18] Mrs. Park Jong-eun, who was forty-eight years old in 1975, came to the United States three-and-one-half years ago. She had a reputation as an excellent cook and was hired by a Korean restaurant owner in Los Angeles. Her work starts at ten o'clock in the morning and ends at seven o'clock in the evening. She works nine hours a day, six days a week. Tuesday is her day off. Therefore, Mrs. Park works an average of 234 hours for a monthly wage of $700. But after deductions for taxes, social security, and other needs, she takes home only $600.

Mrs. Park's living expenses are minimal compared to others. She pays $100 a month for her studio apartment. She walks to work in the morning (about a thirty-minute walk), and a co-worker takes her home in the evening. After returning home, she usually reads and watches television. She does not have any time left for a social life, because she is tired after her nine-hour day.

Mrs. Park describes her work in the following fashion: "Once I have started my work my hands are moving constantly to prepare meals for lunch and dinner customers. I cook for an average of two hundred people every day. I usually eat my meal, which is breakfast and lunch together, at three in the afternoon, and this is the only break I can have during my work. Then I start again my work, chopping, cutting, and washing the vegetables and marinating the meats. When dinner time comes, my hands are moving like automatic machines since I am the only cook and sometimes ten or twenty customers are waiting for their dinners for serving at the same time." She continued, "When I face such a situation, I do not have time even to catch my breath. When my quitting time comes, I am so exhausted and I don't feel like eating supper and return home with my friend."

Mrs. Park's ambition is to save enough money to bring her son from Seoul in order to give him an opportunity to attend an American college. In her opinion, America is not for older people, because after a certain age one becomes much less adept at learning a new language and a new way of life. She wants to go back to Korea to live when she becomes older.

A COMPARISON OF OLD AND NEW COMMUNITY ORGANIZATIONS

The early Korean immigrants in the United States organized many social, cultural, and political groups. These traditional organizations, almost without exception, were established for one purpose, namely, the fight for restoration of national independence. The founders of these organizations were patriotic political exiles, and many young intellectuals became the core of the organizations. Many Korean immigrants belonged to several organizations. Koreans were an invisible minority ethnic group who did not have any political force to influence American foreign policy in favor of the Korean community or Korean national independence. Nor did they directly participate in American politics because they did not have voting rights. Therefore, any improvement in individual living conditions as well as community improvements were entirely in the hands of the Korean people themselves.

Whenever the national issue of freedom from Japanese domination rose, all Koreans in America worked together. The Korean National Association acted as a representative body of all Korean community organizations during the First World War. When the Second World War broke out, the United Korean Committee became the official representative of Koreans in America dealing with the American government. In short, in the past, a single issue—national independence—made it possible to unite Koreans under one representative body that could speak to American authorities on behalf of all Koreans. In the meantime, the organizational leaders were patriotic intellectuals who dedicated their time, energy, and financial resources to the improvement of the Korean community as well as to the national independence movement.

Nevertheless, there were many faults within the traditional organizations. Factionalism was a bad example. When one leader was more successful than another, there soon developed jealous feelings, followed by attacks on integrity and reputation that were often based on false rumors. The traditional Korean leaders were silent on the issue of racial discrimination in American society. They thought that, as far as Koreans in America were concerned, the national independence issue took top priority. Another serious fault was that they failed to develop a democratic community organization. Most of the leaders as well as their followers were not familiar with democratic group processes. Many community organizations were authoritarian in terms of their structure and decision-making procedures. A classical example of this was the *Tongji-hoe*. Dr. Syngman Rhee was elected a lifetime chairman, and every member of the group pledged himself to respect the order of the organization and to "obey the leadership". The concept of individual rights was absent in the traditional organizations.

New Korean community organizations began to increase with the large influx of new Korean immigrants into the United States after 1965. Today there are hundreds, if not thousands, of Korean community groups in this country. In Los Angeles alone, more than two hundred and fifty different organizations came into being, not counting religious and student groups. The community organizations can be classified in the following five categories:[19]

1. Political organizations: Korean-American Political Association; National Council for Restoration of Democracy for the Motherland; Korean Congress for Democracy and Unification; United Front to Restore Democracy in South Korea; and so on.

2. Professional and academic organizations: Korean Medical Association in America; Korean Scientists and Engineers Association in America; Association of Professional Korean-Americans of Northern California; Society for Korean Academic Studies; Korean Political Scientist Association in America; and so on.

3. Economic organizations: Korean Chamber of Commerce in Los Angeles, San Francisco, and other places; Korean Food Association in Southern California; Korean Commonwealth Credit Union of California; Korean Businessmen's Association; Korean Women's Business Association; Korean Christian Businessmen's Association; Korean Trade Association; and so on.

4. Cultural and educational associations: Korean Artist Association of Southern California; Korean Musician Association of California; Korean Youth Academy; Korean Language Schools in Los Angeles and San Francisco; and so on.

5. Social service organizations: Korean Ministers' Association of Los Angeles; Youth Guidance Center in Los Angeles; Korean Women's Society in Los Angeles, San Francisco, and other places; Korean Planned Parenthood Association of California; Hot-Line in Los Angeles; Korean-American Social Health Science Center in Los Angeles; Korean Methodist Center; Korean Youth Community Service Center in San Jose; Multi-Service Center for Koreans in San Francisco; and Korean Residents' Association, which exists in major Korean communities in America (called Korean Association of Southern California by Koreans in Los Angeles).

The name of each organization speaks for itself, and all of them claim to be nonprofit.

In general, many of these organizations are still in the formative stage; their organizational objectives and structures are not clear. As in the case of traditional Korean organizations, the new community organizations have not yet demonstrated their ability to develop a coalition with other ethnic groups. Nor have they established close contacts with American government authorities at either local or federal levels, so that they are not able to present the Korean community's needs. Furthermore, no organization has attempted to research population data in each Korean community, the sole basis for securing funds and services from local and state governments.

Unfortunately, many leaders of community organizations today, like their predecessors, are not experienced democratic leaders. Some are title and position seekers rather than servants of community development. As a result, most Korean community organizations suffer from a lack of participation by Korean residents. Most have faced financial difficulties, too. For example, in the Los Angeles area where seventy thousand Koreans reside, the Korean Association of Southern California (KASC) is lacking in funds. Its annual expenditures run about fifty thousand dollars, of which thirty thousand comes from generous Korean businessmen. It is reported that the elected staff of the Association has to beg for contributions from various business establishments in the Los Angeles area. In fact none of the Korean organizations, including professional and academic groups, are self-supporting bodies.[20]

A detailed analysis of the financial situation of the KASC is a case in point.[21] The KASC was established in 1968 as a successor to the Korean Center in Los Angeles, and many young intellectuals joined it. Gradually, the young generation took over the leadership from the traditional leaders, who retired from social activities. Today, the total membership is reported to be from three to six thousand. Membership dues are two dollars a year, and members may vote at the Association's annual election.

During the 1974 election, the Association received $8,790 in membership dues. This meant that 4,245 members paid their dues. Contributions made by the president, three vice-presidents, and nine members of the Board of the Association amounted to $4,504. Registration fees from candidates who ran for KASC offices accounted for $7,600. Thus, the total revenue of the Association was $20,549. As mentioned above, the total annual expenditures of the Association ran to $50,000, and the deficit of $30,000 had to come from outside contributors.

During the 1975 election, the revenues of the Association were less than in 1974, although membership dues were increased. The total membership dues were $11,906 from 5,998 members. Candidates' registration fees were $5,200 from two presidential candidates, two vice-presidential candidates, and six Board candidates. The total revenues were $17,106. Against this, election expenses ran more than $8,000 and the debt from the previous year was $7,000. It was reported that the Association has only a little over $1,000 in cash in its treasury.[22]

As a main source of revenue, the Association purchased a community building for $300,000. There were many disputes on the issue of ownership of the property and other related matters.[23] One member of the Community Building Trust Committee even filed a lawsuit against KASC for breach of charter and alleged abuse of authority by some KASC officials, although he later withdrew it. The South Korean Government donated $100,000 and expects to donate an additional $50,000. Local Koreans pledged $90,000 in donations. The down payment was $200,000; the balance of $100,000 is to be paid in monthly installments. The building is located at 981 South Western Ave., Los Angeles, and is expected to receive about $50,000 annually from office rental. Hopefully, this income will cover the monthly payments for the building and maintenance expenditures, including the salaries of the Association's staff. Many Korean observers believe that the financial resources of the Association are shaky, and an increase in membership dues is not the answer unless the Association demonstrates that its activities are of interest to all Korean residents.

The lack of democratic leadership and insufficient funds are not the only problems of Korean community organizations. Repeated irregularities in elections have long been an evil. The 1975 election of the KASC was a case in point. Briefly, the annual election for officers—president, vice-president, and board members—was scheduled to be held on December 6, 1975. The deadline for candidates' registration was November 19, but only one presidential candidate was registered with his vice-presidential running mate by November 18. Because of the lack of candidates for the presidency, election management committee members talked about the possibility of a one-week extension of the deadline. However, just one hour before the deadline, Dr. Kim Hyung-il and two vice-presidential running mates registered as candidates. At this time, only forty members of the Association had paid their dues. Accordingly, they were the only qualified voters.[24]

The deadline for voting registration of members of the Association was December 1. Between November 19 and December 1, 500 members came to the KASC office and paid their annual dues. By noon of December 1, the number of voters, including those who registered by mail, had increased to 1,600. Between 3:00 P.M. and 5:00 P.M., more than 4,300 people registered by mail or by acting procedures, that is, someone paying dues and registering in the name of another. The total number of "qualified voters" now amounted to 5,998. In short, an overwhelming majority of the voters' dues were paid by others on behalf of the real voters, presumably by staff members and supporters of the candidates. For example, one unnamed staff member of a candidate brought 500 names in and paid their dues with a $1,000 check. Two unknown young people brought in 500 names each and paid their dues with two $1,000 checks.[25]

The voting result spoke for itself. Only 2,338 out of 5,998 "qualified" voters cast their votes. This means 44.4 percent voted and 55.6 percent did not vote.[26] This fact alone clearly indicates that the majority of "qualified" voters either had chosen not to vote or were not aware of the fact that somebody else had paid their dues and registered them for election purposes. After the election, the chairman of the election management committee said that the mail and registration procedures were regrettable.

Dr. Kim Hyung-il, professor of legal philosophy at the State University of Long Beach, was elected president of KASC by 1,495 votes, or 56.7 percent, out of 2,638 cast. His opponent, Kim Ki-sung, a Los Angeles businessman, received 1,123 votes, or 43.3 percent. The voting percentage indicates that the elected president received 25.1 percent of the total qualified votes, while the defeated candidate received 18.9 percent. In other words, the elected president was chosen by a minority of the Korean residents.

A few observations can be made here. The election campaign was not conducted on community issues, policies, and problems. No campaign speeches or public debates between candidates took place. Each candidate's views were expressed through newspaper advertisements and hand bills. Both candidates promised almost everything, including the promotion of welfare and protection of the rights of Korean residents. The only difference between the two candidates was that Dr. Kim asserted that "gradual progress" should be applied in improving the Korean community, while Kim Ki-sung urged immediate wholesale reform measures.[27] However, both candidates failed to spell out detailed guidelines of how to implement their ideas. As election day came closer, both candidates engaged in personal attacks. Kim Ki-sung charged that the South Korean government had been interfering in Korean community affairs through its agents and that Dr. Kim was "the puppet" of the government. Dr. Kim denied the charge and stated that the accusations were completely false.[28]

Some observers think it is questionable whether the KASC can be considered a legitimate representative body of the seventy thousand Korean residents because of the lack of support from the people. These same observers believe that once again the officials of an Association will fail to articulate the legitimate interests of the Korean community. This would mean that there would be no organization by which Koreans can effectively voice demands to government policy-makers on local or state levels. Nor are there channels by which they can convert their demands into authoritative alternative policy measures.

The new president stated that he would "exert every effort to promote the welfare of the Korean residents in the area in a concerted effort with state and local officials and civic groups."[29] But it remains to be seen how much the new president can do since he is not a full-time paid administrator and much of the work will depend on inexperienced staff members. In addition, the problem of a power-struggle between two rival factions within the KASC will have to be resolved in order to carry out even the routine functions of the Association.

Some Koreans, including old traditional leaders who worked in the early immigrant Korean community, condemned the election, blaming the corrupt practices on newcomers from South Korea. These observers call for a community clean-up first, and then the establishment of a new organization "of the people, by the people and for the people."

AN IRREGULAR ELECTION OF THE KOREAN-AMERICAN ASSOCIATION OF SAN FRANCISCO AND THE BAY AREA.

The election of directors and officers (president and vice-president) of the Korean-American Association of San Francisco and the Bay Area, Inc. was held on March 6, 1976. The election was the most fraudulent election in the history of the Bay Area Korean community.[30] A neck-and-neck race between two rival candidates, it was also the most expensive election, with a campaign that cost one hundred thousand dollars.

Here are a few facts about the irregularities of the election. An overwhelming majority of the voters' dues were paid by others on behalf of the real voters, presumably by staff members or candidates. The deadline for voting registration of the members of the Association was February 6, 1976. Until noon, only 168 members had paid dues. This meant that only 168 members were qualified to vote (this author was one of them). However, at 11:45 P.M., fifteen minutes before the deadline, the two candidates bought 5,298 "voters." Kim Kyong-ha (Kenneth Kim) submitted 3,039 names and paid their dues of $18,234, while Kim Yong-baik bought 2,259 names and paid their dues of $13,554. The election committee discovered that eleven hundred names were double registered, that is, they had paid their dues twice. This meant that each candidate paid voters' dues without the voters' knowledge. The election committee also found that more than a hundred people who live outside the Bay Area had registered to vote. The committee asked the Board of Directors of the Association if this were legal. A majority of the directors present at the meeting, although not a quorum, authorized voting by persons living outside the San Francisco Bay Area.

The election results were as follows: Kim Kyong-ha was elected by 799 votes—only 32 votes more than his opponent, Kim Yong-baik. Thirty-two percent of the total registered voters, or 1,603 voters, took part. The losing team found out that 89 people who do not live in the San Francisco Bay Area cast their votes for the winner. Therefore the Kim Yong-baik team filed suit against the Association and Kim Kyong-ha on the ground that the 89 voters who came from outside the Bay Area were not qualified to vote within the meaning of the Association's geographical limit.

On April 23, 1976, the Superior Court of the State of California for the City and County of San Francisco declared that the election was "irregular and had no effect, and set aside said election." The court issued a temporary restraining order based on Sections 2236 and 2238 of the California Corporations Code, which apply to nonprofit corporations like the Korean-American Association of San Francisco and the Bay Area, Inc. According to the court's findings, the Association had violated its own rules, which restricted voting to Korean residents of the nine counties. The evidence showed that 89 people who cast their votes in the election were outside residents.

According to the temporary restraining order, the Association should not engage in or perform, directly or indirectly, any and all of the following acts for two weeks (April 24 to May 7):

1. Assuming, receiving, or exercising any power, duty, benefits, or emolument of said Association.
2. Acting in the name of or on behalf of the Association.

3. Using corporate funds to defend this action.
4. Appropriating the corporate name in any action taken by them.
5. Appropriating the corporate name in any advertising or publication.
6. Wasting of the corporate assets.
7. Conducting any meeting of the Board of Directors or of the officers of Korean-American Association of San Francisco and the Bay Area, Inc.

This order was signed by Judge Robert J. Drews of the Superior Court on April 23, 1976. On May 5 and 7, 1976, the court held a hearing on the matter and heard testimony from the plaintiffs and defendants. Judge Byron Arnold was on the bench. Robert Sheridan represented the plaintiffs, while Thomas H. Bomar was legal counsel for the defendants. At the end of the hearing, Judge Arnold expressed his personal views by suggesting that "for the best interests of the Korean community harmonious and amicable solution between the disputing parties is desirable. This problem could be settled outside of the Court by agreeing to have a new election."

Nevertheless, both sides failed to reach any workable solution. The plaintiffs insisted that the defendants should declare the March 6 election illegal and agree to have a new election, whereas the defendants requested that the plaintiffs withdraw the suit.

On May 14, Judge Arnold ruled that a new election should be held on June 20, 1976, and the result of the election should be reported to the court on June 21. The court also stated that eligible voters were to be limited to Korean residents of the nine counties.

The text of the court's findings of fact and conclusions of law can be summarized as follows:

First, based on the evidence of custom and usage within the Association (Korean-American Association of San Francisco and the Bay Area, Inc.), the court finds that the term "area" in the by-laws is limited to mean the San Francisco area . . . and it includes, at most, the nine counties fronting on San Francisco Bay, to wit: San Francisco, San Mateo, Santa Clara, Alameda, Contra Costa, Solano, Sonoma, Napa, and Marin. Further, that said terms do not include Monterey, Marina Township, Sacramento, Fort Ord, Salinas, Pacific Grove, Fresno, and Davis.

Second, persons residing in said areas were erroneously permitted to vote in violation of the by-laws of the Association, and the number of such persons illegally determined as eligible to vote was substantially greater than the margin of the election. As a result, the number of such persons illegally permitted to actually cast a ballot in the election was also substantially greater than the margin of the election.

Third, the plaintiffs, Kim Young Baik and Kim Tong Ok, filed a written protest concerning voters from outside the San Francisco Bay Area with the board of directors on February 17, 1976. The meeting of the board on

February 29, 1976, was invalid, lacking a quorum. Further, the resolution purportedly enacted on the same day, authorizing voter eligibility outside the San Francisco Bay Area as defined herein, was in excess of the jurisdiction of the board and was an abuse of discretion. The said resolution is therefore void and of no effect.

From the foregoing facts, the court concludes: (1) That the election of March 6, 1976, is hereby declared illegal and invalid, and is hereby set aside, and all vacancies filled in said election for officers and directors positions are hereby declared vacant as of the date of said election. Furthermore, all acts done in the name of the Association by persons claiming title of office to said Association as a result of said election are hereby declared to be void and of no effect as of the date of the said election. (2) For purposes of the court-ordered election, and for all future elections whose voting membership is territorially limited by the terms "San Francisco Area" or "San Francisco Bay Area" or "San Francisco and the Bay Area" said term(s) shall be defined to mean the nine counties fronting on the San Francisco Bay. (3) A new election shall be held under the authority, supervision, and review of this court on June 20. . . . Cost of the election is to be borne by the Association; offices to be filled in said election are those of president and vice-president and nine directors, and candidate eligibility shall be open only to those persons who qualified as candidates in the election of March 6, 1976. (4) Voter eligibility shall be open to those persons whose names appear on the voting list which was closed on February 6, 1976, excepting those whose address is not indicated and those whose address indicates residence outside the nine San Francisco Bay Area counties. (5) A new election list shall be prepared by a representative of plaintiffs and defendants, and submitted to the court for approval at least five court days prior to the date selected for election. The results of election shall be certified to this court for review and official announcement at 9:30 A.M. of the first court date following the election. (6) The Association is ordered to reimburse plaintiffs and plaintiffs' counsel for costs, expenses, and attorney's fees in the amount of $3,633 payable through the attorney, Robert Sheridan.

It would seem that four things are clear as a result of the court decision. First, a new election is to be held under the close supervision of the court, and the election result is to be reviewed by the court. Second, the Korean-American Association of San Francisco and the Bay Area lost the confidence of Korean residents, and it is doubtful whether it can claim to be the representative body of Koreans in the San Francisco Bay Area. It is a general view that the great majority of Korean residents will not participate in the new election. Third, Koreans in general and their leaders in particular have learned that they are under the jurisdiction of United States law. They have to give up the idea that the end justifies the means, an idea common in South Korean elections. Fourth, many concerned Koreans in America believe that it is time to start fresh community organizations with new guidelines and principles.

On June 29, Judge Arnold ordered a new election to be held on August 15 under the supervision of a new election committee. The committee he appointed included Robert Sheridan (representing the plaintiffs), Thomas H. Bomar (representing the defendants), and Park Sang-yul, representing the Korean community at large. The result of the election is to be reported to the court on August 16 for its approval. Thus the 1976 election of the Korean-American Association of San Francisco and the Bay Area became the first election within the Korean community to be held under the direction of an American court.

12.

Characteristics and Problems
of the Korean Immigrants

CHARACTERISTICS OF THE EARLY IMMIGRANTS.

Until the end of World War II, three groups had been the pioneers of the Korean community in the United States. The first group was composed of political and social reformers who went into exile after the unsuccessful coup d'etat of 1884, known as *Kapshin Chongpyon,* and the failure of the Reform movement of 1896-1898, led by the members of the Independence Club (*Tongnip Hyop-hoe*) under the leadership of So Chae-p'il. Dr. So later became a naturalized American citizen, taking the Anglicized name of Philip Jaisohn.[1] Other Reform movement leaders such as Syngman Rhee, Ahn Ch'ang-ho, and Park Yong-man came to the United States between 1884 and 1905 to pursue advanced studies in American universities.

The second group of pioneers consisted of seven thousand laborers who came to work on Hawaiian plantations between 1903 and 1905, plus a few hundred picture brides who came to marry the early male immigrants. This second group was the largest of the three.

The third group comprised several hundred political refugee "students", intellectuals and patriots who came to the United States by way of China and Europe between 1910 and 1920. They had special permission to enter from the secretary of state. In addition, during the period of Japanese rule over Korea (1910-1945), two hundred and fifty Korean students came to the United States for advanced study at American universities. They had Japanese-government-issued student passports, and most of them returned to Korea after finishing their studies. A few remained in the United States.

The leadership of the Korean community in the United States emerged from the first and third groups. Some of the leaders were Ahn Ch'ang-ho, Syngman Rhee, Park Yong-man, So Chae-pi'l, Lee Dae-wii, and Kim Won-yong (Warren Y. Kim). The early Korean leaders were inspired by two principles proclaimed in the American Declaration of Independence: independence is a nation's birth right; and life, liberty, and the pursuit of happiness

239

are the inalienable rights of all the people. They believed that the Korean people, too, were entitled to these rights. However, the Korean people had either been totally denied these rights or had not fully enjoyed them. The leaders believed there were two reasons for this: the domination of foreign powers as a result of Korea's location in the midst of three aggressive, powerful nations—Japan, China, and Russia; and the rule of the native Confucian authoritarian regime under an absolute monarch. Thus the Korean intellectuals and reformists came to the United States in search of political freedom, like the Puritans who crossed the Atlantic to find religious freedom. The early Korean leaders in the United States were convinced they could make a contribution toward the eventual liberation of their homeland by working with the Koreans in the United States, although the numbers were small. They urged every Korean in the United States to consider himself a freedom fighter and to work toward the common goal of restoration of independence from Japan. This ideology dominated the Korean community in the United States until the emancipation of Korea in 1945.

The Korean leaders organized social, religious, cultural, and political organizations in every Korean community. These organizations had one or more of the following purposes: (1) nationalism, which meant restoration of national independence and anti-Japanese activities; (2) financial support of the Korean provisional government in China, which came into being after the March First uprising of 1919; (3) restoration of Korean traditional values by the teaching of history, language, and culture to immigrants and their children in Korean community schools; (4) reform measures concerning aspects of daily life in order to build a healthy democratic community; and (5) the development of educational and religious (Christian) work.

The Koreans in the United States—fewer than ten thousand before the end of the Second World War—were a minority among the minority ethnic groups. They were "invisible" Americans. They faced an identity problem: they were (and still are) mistaken for Chinese because both groups have many of the same last names (Lee, Chang, Wong, and Lim, for example). Sometimes they were mistaken for Japanese because of their similar physical appearance. In the academic world, Korean studies suffered from a lack of scholarly interest. Also, the early Koreans in the United States had to depend on individual strength because no official protection was possible after the loss of national independence.

Because of the language barrier, cultural conflicts, and racial discrimination, many Korean intellectuals became laborers and earned a living as hotel, restaurant, farm, factory, and house-cleaning workers. They used their spare time for national independence activities with their fellow countrymen. They formed political and social organizations, such as the Korean

National Association in 1909 and the Young Korean Academy in 1913 in San Francisco, the Korean Women's Patriotic Association in 1919 in Danuba, California, and the Friend's Society in 1921 in Hawaii. These four organizations still exist and are somewhat active in Korean community affairs. Christian churches were established wherever Koreans lived, and became the centers of religious and social life. Various weekly newspaper and magazines were published: *New Korea* (still published in Los Angeles), *Pacific Times*, *National Korean Herald*, *Independence*, and *Pacific Magazine*.

To sum up: the early Korean immigrants struggled for survival, earning their living by physical labor. They were active in efforts to restore national independence. And they educated their children so as to preserve their Korean heritage. They never considered the United States their permanent home, and they dreamed of going back to their homeland as soon as the Japanese domination was terminated. They felt racially discriminated against, a helpless minority in a white people's society. Most Koreans isolated themselves from American society and hardly participated in general social or political issues. Thus they stood aside from the mainstream of American life.

The dream of independence came true in August 1945, when Japan unconditionally surrendered to the Allied powers. The early political refugees, including Syngman Rhee, So Chae-p'il, and others, returned to South Korea. Many Koreans who were educated in the United States also went back as civilian employees of the American military government. During American military rule, Rhee and So served as political advisers to General John R. Hodge. In 1948 Rhee became president of the First Republic of Korea (South). During American military rule and the subsequent First and Second Republics of Korea, many high government positions were occupied by American-educated Koreans. A pro-American Korean government was established in South Korea as a counterpart to the pro-Russian regime in North Korea.

CHARACTERISTICS OF THE POSTWAR IMMIGRANTS

After World War II, Koreans in the United States became "visible" because: (1) the United States ruled South Korea from 1945 to 1948 through a military government; (2) the United States became involved in the Korean War from 1950 to 1953, and after the war spent $3.5 billion for the economic reconstruction of South Korea; and (3) there has been a substantial influx of Korean immigrants into the United States between 1965 and 1976.[2] It is clear that the new wave of Korean immigrants will have a socioeconomic and political impact on American society in general and on the Korean-American community in particular.

More than 30 percent of the recent Korean immigrants to the United States are college or university graduates. Many held high social positions in both private and public establishments before they came here. About three thousand are professionals in the medical field, and a similar number are scientists. About two thousand college professors and high-school teachers, including those educated in this country, joined American educational institutions. Most are dissatisfied with the present political and economic situation in Korea.

The Korean people lived for centuries in fear of foreign domination. Today, Japanese and American economic intervention have penetrated into all phases of the South Korean economy. The economy depends on foreign aid and loans. Thus, it can be characterized as a "foreign-loan-initiated-and-dominated economy."[3]

In addition, Korea's two giant Communist neighbors, the Soviet Union and the People's Republic of China, have been competing with each other in attempting to dominate the peninsula by aiding the North Korean Communist regime. America's so-called détente policy has not increased the feeling of security of the Korean people. The recent failure of American policy in Indo-China is interpreted by many Koreans as a prelude to the total withdrawal of American forces from South Korea, although Washington authorities have denied this supposition. The South Korean government, under a strong military ruler, has been taking increasingly dictatorial measures since the announcement of the détente policy. Basic human rights have been restricted, and no dissident political views are allowed. Thus South Korea has duplicated many of the political methods of North Korea.

This political climate moved many intellectuals to look for another place to live. In South Korea, the more advanced the education, the greater the frustration. The American-type educational system has produced Western-oriented intellectuals. But social positions and jobs are limited. Not all intellectuals can stand the restrictions or fight the system. And so, many chose to come to America as immigrants.

The early immigrants came as temporary residents. They intended to return to their homeland when they had made enough money or when the political situation in Korea changed. The postwar immigrants, on the other hand, came here to live permanently and to make a home for their children.

It is characteristic of the new Korean immigrants that a high percentage are females. Among the early immigrants only 15 percent were women. The reason for this high percentage is that most immigrants are wives or children of American citizens. Also, adult males are not allowed to leave Korea until they complete their military service. The educational standard of the women is much higher than that of the early immigrants. Nurses, pharmacists, and other professionals came as preferential immigrants.

A further characteristic of the new Korean immigrants is that they have a tendency to settle in urbanized and industrialized areas, especially in Hawaii, California, New Jersey, New York, Michigan, Pennsylvania, and Illinois. This is, of course, the reverse of the practice of the early immigrants, 90 percent of whom were farmers, who settled in agricultural areas. Professionals, skilled workers, and technicians constitute 22 percent of the new immigrants, farm workers only 4 percent. The rest consists of housewives, children, and small businessmen. The unemployment rate of the new Korean immigrants is high, more than 20 percent. The early immigrants had hardly any unemployment problems.

Another characteristic of the new Korean immigrants is their age composition. The combined number of males and females in two age classifications, females in the twenty to twenty-nine category and males in the thirty to thirty-nine category, constitutes 61 percent of the immigration total since the end of the war.[4] Thus most Koreans come to the United States during their most productive years. In these two age groups, skilled workers and professionals predominate. This represents a serious drain on Korea's professional personnel, especially doctors, scientists, and nurses.

It is also characteristic of the new Korean immigrants that many are wealthy, although no exact figures are available. Wealthy Koreans and former government officials took up residence in major cities in the United States as import and export businessmen or as visitors and then changed their status to that of immigrant. Most of them isolated themselves from the Korean community and live in exclusive Caucasian residential areas. Many established dual residences in South Korea and the United States to evade taxation.

Both the early immigrants and the postwar immigrants came to this country for economic betterment and political freedom, but whereas the early immigrants wanted freedom from Japanese domination, the postwar immigrants wanted freedom from the oppression of their own native government.

COMMUNITY ISSUES

Today many issues affect the Korean community in the United States, but only some of the main ones will be discussed here. Paramount among them is the political division of Korea. Koreans, no matter where they live, are keenly conscious of the 38th parallel, the artificial division created by the Allied powers at the end of the Second World War. As long as this tragic division remains, there will be no real peace in Korea.

Peaceful reunification of the country is one of the main aspirations of the Korean people. There seems to be little hope that Korea will be unified either by the big powers or by the two native governments. This means that the Korean people themselves will have to solve the problem.[5] Koreans in the United States, whether we like it or not, cannot be indifferent toward reunification, because our individual fates are affected by relations between the United States and the land of our ancestors.

Neither of the two present Korean governments allows its people to enjoy basic human rights. The reunification issue has been used as an excuse for increasing governmental power. During the postwar period the national interests of the United States, the Soviet Union, and later Communist China clashed and became the major obstacle to reunification.[6]

Through free discussion and seminars on the reunification issue in the United States, constructive proposals and recommendations could be submitted to the two native governments and to the concerned powers, including the United Nations. Koreans in the United States could take more positive action for bringing about reunification, just as the early Korean immigrants fought for independence.

The next important issue within the Korean community in the United States is democratization of the community. There are various political, social, religious, cultural, and academic organizations in the Korean community. But most of them are not democratic groups in terms of their principles, structures, and election procedures. None of the organizations can be considered as representing "the Koreans in the United States." The largest Korean group of seventy thousand resides in Los Angeles, called "Small Seoul" because its politics, business establishments, and social patterns are similar to those of Seoul. Many newcomers retain the traditional authoritarian family system in which the father acts as dictator in family affairs. Election procedures have been undemocratic; bribes, frauds, and threats have occasionally been used. Some candidates for offices of the Korean Residence Association spent between thirty and fifty thousand dollars in a recent election; these candidates paid the membership dues of voters to get their votes just a few hours before the election. Many leaders of Korean organizations have become spokesmen for the South Korean government.

In the early period, Christian churches played an important role in the development of Korean society.[7] Since the new influx of Korean immigrants, the number of church goers has increased. Today there are 293 Korean churches in the United States.[8] But these churches have failed to provide democratic leadership to the Koreans. Most church leaders are indifferent to social issues such as racial discrimination, minority protection, and human rights. Many ministers are engaged in petty denominational disputes. Most churches concentrate their energy, funds, and time on traditional evangelistic services.

The democratization of Korean organizations, including the Christian churches, is an important issue among Koreans. Therefore, this study suggests that all Koreans in the United States must unite and make an effort to establish a democratic community so that the Korean community may become a community "of the people, by the people and for the people."

Another issue is the gap between the earlier immigrant Koreans and the new generation of American-Koreans. There are several reasons for this gap. First, the language barrier prevents full communication between these different groups. Most members of the second and third generations do not speak their ancestral tongue, while many of the first generation do not speak English.

Second, the different cultural background causes difficulties. The first generation holds traditional Eastern cultural values. The father, as the head of the family, decides his children's future in terms of a school major, specialization of study, and even a marriage partner. Parents tend to disregard their children's rights. The American-born children, in turn, tend to ignore their parents' authoritarianism. Hence, a lack of mutual respect between parents and children is widespread.

Third, life perspective and philosophy differ. The primary objective of the first generation was to survive by hard labor, and then to save money for future security. In contrast, the main concern of American-born Koreans has been to secure a blue-collar job, and then to spend the earned money, usually for pleasure. The older generation's first concern was to buy a house; the younger generation's first desire is to buy a car.

In recent years, the third generation American-born Koreans have begun to realize some of the value of Korean traditions. It is also true that many first-generation Koreans have begun to accept some Western values and have tried to understand the younger generation's mentality.

It must be added here that American-born Koreans have their own problems. Their number is estimated at thirteen thousand (four thousand in Hawaii, three thousand in California, and the rest throughout the country). They are indeed the "forgotten citizens" in this democratic society. Many have received a good education and are able and qualified professionals, but they cannot find jobs in accordance with their ability because of racial discrimination.

In the past, many of the second generation were not willing to get a college or university education, because after graduation they had to work as grocery checkers, truck drivers, or in similar occupations. Today the situation has changed, yet American-Koreans have a hard time securing challenging jobs. Virtually no Korean-American holds a position as a business executive in a big American corporation. No Korean lawyers work in big American law firms.

Unlike Japanese-Americans or Chinese-Americans, Korean-Americans do not have social or political organizations in the real sense. Although they tried to form a national organization in 1974 at a meeting in Los Angeles, they failed because of opposing views as to its nature and purposes. There are some local organizations, such as the East Bay Coalition Korea in the San Francisco Bay Area and others in Hawaii and New York, but they are still in a formative stage. Besides, Korean-Americans do not participate as an ethnic group in local, state, or federal political and social concerns. They do not even have a means of communicating with one another. There was a Korean-American newsletter, *Insight*, but it no longer exists. Therefore the first order of business for Korean-Americans would seem to be to form a national organization to protect their rights.

THE QUESTION OF BILINGUAL EDUCATION

Another problem confronting Korean-Americans is the education of the new immigrants' children. Korean children suffer from the lack of bilingual teachers. For example, there are six hundred Korean students in the San Francisco Unified School District but only one qualified bilingual teacher. Korean children who cannot speak English are sometimes taken to the nearest Chinese person, because the teacher or other school authority thinks that person can interpret Korean.[9]

But bilingual education for Korean-American children in the United States faces many problems. Chang Byoung-hye, the coordinator of the Korean component of the Asian-American Bilingual Center, pointed out four major problems after she visited various Korean communities. (1) There are no sequential textbooks for Korean children anywhere in the United States. (2) There are not enough bilingual teachers who possess the credentials to teach in school districts. (3) There is a desperate need to inform the community about the goals of bilingual education and its progress. (4) In most parts of the United States, state laws prohibit the holding of a class without a minimum number of thirty students; hence, many Korean-American children have had to enroll in Chinese bilingual classes. It is Chang's opinion that the Korean component of the Asian-American Bilingual Center "can provide needed bilingual curriculum materials and systematic guidance, bridging the gap between community support and education institutions for a quality bilingual education."

The basic philosophy of the Asian-American Bilingual Center was defined as follows: "It is the right of Asian children in the United States to enter an educational system which both recognizes and reflects the diverse histories and dynamic linguistic and cultural environments of their homes and communities. The Asian-American Bilingual Center is thus committed to the development of materials that provide a comprehensive academic program which furthers the conceptual growth, content mastery, and affective development of Asian-American youngsters by maintaining their native languages and reinforcing the abilities and self-esteem that stem from the children's ethnic backgrounds. By so doing, the Center's efforts contribute to the realization of an equal, quality education for all children."[10]

Most school teachers, as well as the general public, have little knowledge of Korea. The *Seattle Times* of September 19, 1949, said: "A Korean boy, David Choy, could not speak English or Chinese when he was enrolled at the School." The American newspaper writer was not aware that Koreans have their own language. According to a recent survey of fifty school teachers in San Francisco, most of them had first heard about Korea during the Korean War. A California social studies textbook contains just a few pages about Korea, mainly describing the Korean War.[11] Thus, school teachers lack English materials on Korea. No Korean wants to be known only in terms of the Korean War.

Korean immigrant children usually take from six months to one year to adjust to the American school system. During this period, many suffer mentally and physically because they do not speak English and do not play with their American "friends" who sit next to them. Immigrant children keep silent during class hours and the recess period, and feel isolated and rejected by both teachers and peers.

The Bilingual Education Act of 1972 of California provides that "it is the policy of the State to insure the mastery of English by all pupils in the schools."[12] But it is the responsibility of each local school board to initiate English as a second language and institute bilingual education. However, as in the case of Koreans, the school boards, with the exception of six cities including Los Angeles and San Francisco, do not realize the need for bilingual education programs for Korean children. Many local school boards have been conducting bilingual education classes in Spanish, Chinese, and Japanese. One reason for the bypassing of Koreans has been the lack of statistics about the Korean population in the major cities. This deficiency is the fault of both the Korean community and the local school authorities, who have neglected research on Korean population.

At present, there are some hopeful signs concerning bilingual education programs for minority groups. The California state legislature passed a million dollar bilingual education program for non-English speaking students, and the money will be distributed to each local school district for implementation. Also, the Berkeley Unified School District was recently funded by the federal government to develop a bilingual curriculum, and a Korean component was included.

It is the desire of the Korean community that a competent staff for bilingual education be selected, qualified by experience and academic background rather than by politics. In addition, the local school districts need quality bilingual materials.

INDIVIDUAL PROBLEMS

In addition to community problems, Koreans in America have to cope with individual problems. Most newcomers believe that the United States is the land of opportunity and happiness in terms of economic betterment and political freedom. But they soon find that their hopes were exaggerated and they become frustrated.

First, cultural differences make it difficult for newcomers to adjust to American society. The family-centered, traditional Korean immigrant finds the free-style, aggressive, individualistic American way of life incompatible with what he was accustomed to in his homeland. The discovery of a communal life style is a shock to many. Some have attempted to imitate the free American style rather hastily, only to be rejected by Americans who expected them to be docile.

Second, the language barrier is a hurdle even for those who learned some English before leaving their homeland. They find themselves unable to communicate adequately with American employers and friends. Here is a moving example of a Korean high-school teacher who, because of language difficulties, could find employment only as a high-school janitor. He wrote the following poem in Korean:

> I do not see, although I have eyes. Then, have I become blind? No, I have not. I do not hear, although I have ears. Then, I have become deaf? No, I have not. I do not speak, although I have a mouth. Then, have I lost my speech? No, I have not. I have become an old stranger who wants to raise a young tree (to educate his child) in this wealthy land.[13]

Most newcomers do not have the time and energy to learn English even if there are adult evening classes, because they have to work to survive. Because of the cultural and language barriers, too many immigrants feel helpless and inferior. Thus they have a tendency to isolate themselves from American society and stay within the Korean community, where they have no chance to learn about the American way of life.

According to one Korean community study report on the age group over twenty-three, only 10 percent have no difficulty with English, 25 percent barely speak the language, 25 percent have previously studied English but cannot understand it well, and 40 percent do not speak English at all.[14] A command of English is the most important factor in determining one's opportunity for employment. It is also a necessary tool for the pursuit of higher education, social adjustment, and economic betterment.

In Los Angeles, where seventy thousand Koreans reside, they have established a Korean-town on Olympic Boulevard and Hoover Street as one attempt to solve the language problem. In this area the newcomers feel comfortable, because they do not need to speak English in the Korean-operated grocery stores, churches, barber shops, book stores, insurance companies, real estate offices, civic and social organizations, restaurants, and night clubs. The newcomers there have isolated themselves in the island of the Korean community. As one old lady said, "One does not feel that one lives in America when one lives on Olympic Boulevard."

Views about the benefits of a Korean-centered community town are divided. Some favor it on the grounds that the Japanese and Chinese have their own towns, so why not the Koreans too? Then the Koreans can retain their traditional values. Proponents of this view feel that Koreans should combine their financial strengths to build a Korean-town. The opposing view holds that Koreans will never learn and understand the American way of life if they remain isolated. The United States should be considered their permanent home, and Koreans should not be just spectators of American society but should become a part of the mainstream by participating in local, state, and federal institutions.

A third serious problem is that of getting meaningful jobs or setting up profitable businesses. There are many small and medium-sized Korean business establishments in the United States.[15] These businesses (such as restaurants, grocery stores, service stations, and wig stores) are very competitive, and frequently their owners do not have enough capital to survive. Many who do manage to stay in business work hard and are barely able to sustain their livelihood. Only a handful of Korean businessmen have been able to live comfortably. Most businesses are family-operated; even school-aged children work there after school.

It is difficult for Korean immigrants to secure employment in American firms, factories, and public or private institutions because of racial discrimination, lack of training and skill, and the language barrier. Many American business firms require permanent resident status by their employees, and many government jobs require citizenship. It is estimated that 20 percent of the Koreans in Los Angeles are unemployed.

According to Henry Yum, the only Korean in the California Employment Development Department in Los Angeles, between thirty and fifty Koreans file job applications daily. Unfortunately, the job placement rate is less than 1 percent. Yum says that a Korean, regardless of his educational background and experience, must accept a low paying job such as janitor, warehouseman, or nurse's aid. "The irony of this is," he says, "that 70 percent of the Korean immigrants are professionals."[16]

If skilled workers find employment, they are usually underpaid because their skills are not good enough for jobs in American firms. The most conspicuous cases of underemployment are medical doctors, dentists, nurses, architects, and pharmacists. Only 5 percent are doing what they were trained for. A physician may be working as a medical social worker, if he is lucky. In this connection, a serious deficiency in the American immigration law should be pointed out. The United States government gives preferential admission to persons of select professional classes, including doctors, nurses, and pharmacists. However, licensing institutions are independent of the federal government. Each state has its own regulations, and foreign professionals often find state board examinations difficult to pass.

In Southern California alone, there are some six hundred immigrant Korean physicians who have no license to practice medicine. Dr. Park Hakto, spokesman of the Korean-educated physicians in Los Angeles, says that "the average Korean immigrant physician is over 40 years of age and has at least 10 years of practical medical experience,"[17] but he is forced to find a job as a clerk or technician to support his family. This leaves him little time to prepare for license examinations. One example is Dr. Choi Chin, who served in the Korean army as chief surgeon and was decorated in 1952 by President Truman for his services to the American army. He was promoted to the rank of full colonel. He returned to Kyoto University in Japan for further studies and received a doctorate in biological medicine. In 1972, Dr. Choi immigrated to the United States, but he cannot practice medicine in California because he did not take the state examination and has no license.

Korean-trained nurses are exploited by hospitals and medical clinics who classify them as nurse's aides at $1.85 an hour and have them perform tasks usually assigned to registered nurses.

Lee Kong-mook, a Korean-educated pharmacist and vice-president of the Korean Pharmacist Association of California, says: "We never expected to lose our profession when we immigrated to this beautiful and wealthy country. Today, most of us find ourselves in a job which is inconsistent with our qualifications and experience. We are living on starvation wages." He adds: "The American Immigration and Naturalization Service gave high priority to Koreans with pharmaceutical training, implying that persons of this training and experience would be welcome additions to the United States. Yet, when we landed in California, we were denied the opportunity to take the examinations."[18]

According to California regulations, a candidate for the licensure examination must have graduated from a school on the board's accredited lists. No foreign school has ever been included on this list. Even though the state law was amended in March 1972 to allow foreign-trained pharmacists to take the examination upon certification by the Board of Pharmacy, none have been permitted by the board to do so to this day.

Some of the problems faced by Korean immigrants in America must be solved by efforts of the Korean immigrants themselves. They have to give up some of their traditional concepts, such as considering manual labor inferior to white-collar work. They must make a determined effort to learn English.

They must cultivate their skills, resources, and self-confidence by attending evening schools.

Korean community organizations can help by acting as employment referral centers, conducting English language classes, teaching driver education, and helping to set up small family-operated businesses. Korean churches could set up orientation programs, and pastors could render counseling services in welfare affairs, domestic problems, and educational programs. The Christian Women's Society could provide free meals for senior citizens or sponsor programs for isolated newcomers. The Christian youth organization could sponsor sports, games, or tours. In this connection, it could be pointed out that the Korean Youth Community Service Center of San Jose, funded by the University of California Student Association, was established by American-born Koreans and has been working for immigrants, rendering services in such areas as transportation, interpreting, and welfare guidance. Every Korean community needs this kind of organization.

Finally, it is incumbent on American society to abolish discrimination against minorities in general and Koreans in particular. High public and private positions should be opened to minority members according to their abilities. Equal opportunities with equal rights for minorities are essential in a democratic society. American-born Koreans, on the other hand, could involve themselves more in public issues. They have a moral obligation to help improve the economic and social status of the newcomers.

The American government, on local, state, and federal levels, has a responsibility to provide needed services to Korean immigrants and to guide and assist them. Koreans often do not get their share of assistance as do the Japanese, Chinese, and Filipinos.

Vocational education is needed for training or retraining Korean immigrants. English-language and job-training program centers should be established in cities where Korean immigrants are concentrated. In San Francisco, such a center was funded by the city government and has been very successful under the leadership of Hannah Surh as head of the Korean Advisory Committee (KAC) and Dr. Kim O-dong as program coordinator.[19] During the first year of operation, the center performed language and job training for Korean immigrants as a contractor to San Francisco under the Federal Comprehensive Employment Training Act of 1973. The training program was operated as the Korean Unit of the Chinatown Resources Development Center, and has now become an independent Korean service center called the Multi-Service Center for Koreans. Between 1974 and 1975, the Center trained ninety Korean immigrants, sixty of whom were placed in permanent jobs. Another successful service program was started in Tacoma, Washington, under the guidance of Sil D. Kim. It is a demonstration project for Asian-Americans funded partly by the Department of Health, Education, and Welfare.[20] Other programs were established in some cities, but all these facilities are insufficient for the needs of Korean immigrants today.

13.

Korean Religious and Cultural Activities in the United States

American envoys as well as American missionaries played an important role in persuading Koreans to emigrate to Hawaii. The American minister in Seoul, Dr. Horace N. Allen, the first physician-missionary sent by the Presbyterian Board of Foreign Missions of the United States, became one of the most trusted of the Korean king's advisers. After his successful treatment of the queen's nephew, who was wounded during a political coup d'etat in 1884, he became the royal family's personal physician. Thus he was able to persuade the king to permit his subjects to emigrate to Hawaii. In the meantime, American missionaries such as Mr. H.G. Underwood, Mr. Henry G. Appenzeller, and Mr. George Heber Jones encouraged Korean Christians to go to Hawaii because they saw "an opportunity for Koreans to improve their conditions and to acquire useful knowledge and better themselves financially."[1]

The Reverend Mr. Jones in particular was greatly interested in Korean emigration to Hawaii. On the departure date of the first group of emigrants (December 22, 1902), he went to the seaport, then called Chemulpo (now Inchon), and offered his prayers for the safety of the emigrants in the strange land. He also handed a few of the leaders among them letters of introduction to the superintendent of the Methodist mission in Hawaii.[2] Therefore, there were already Christians among the first Korean immigrants to Hawaii, and a few of them had engaged in church work as preachers.

THE ESTABLISHMENT OF THE EARLY KOREAN CHURCHES

According to one source, one-third of all Koreans in Hawaii were professing Christians. They dominated life in the early plantation camps, and soon Korean "churches" (meeting places for worship) were established wherever Koreans lived in Hawaii and on the mainland. It is difficult, if not impossible, to collect the stories of the origin of each Korean church in the Korean communities, so the following examples will have to serve our purpose.

The first worship service was held at the plantation camp in Molokai, on July 4, 1903, under the leadership of Kim I-che.[3] The place of worship may have been the living quarters of the camp. These services among the Korean immigrants, without contact with the American mission churches, continued for three months. On November 3, 1903, a group of Koreans in Hawaii elected Ahn Chung-su and Woo Byong-kil as representatives to consult with the Methodist Superintendent, the Reverend Mr. Pearson, on the possibility of establishing a Korean Methodist Church in Hawaii. As a result, on November 10, the Korean Evangelical Society was formed and church services started at a rented house on River Street, Honolulu. This was the actual beginning of the Korean Methodist Church in Hawaii, but official church status was not approved until April 1, 1905, when the Reverend Mr. John W. Wadman became superintendent.[4] For nearly ten years Mr. Wadman and his wife did their best to develop the Korean Methodist Church, as well as to establish a Korean school for the immigrants and their children. The Reverend Hong Sung-ha became the first minister of the Korean Methodist Church, and more than a dozen Korean ministers have served there. It is the oldest church in the Korean community of Hawaii.

The second Korean church movement was started under the leadership of Chung Hyun-ku and Kim Ik-sung. On February 10, 1905, a formal service dedicating the Korean Episcopal Church was conducted at Saint Andrews Church in Honolulu by Bishop Henry B. Restarichs. Because no Korean-owned worship-service area was available at that time, a classroom in Iolani Elementary School was rented as a place for services. Later, Koreans were permitted to use the sanctuary of the Chinese-owned Saint Elizabeth Church in Honolulu. Much later, in 1925, members of the Korean Episcopal Church purchased a small building of their own.

On the mainland, a group of Koreans in San Francisco started a church movement on October 8, 1905. Moon Kyung-ho[5] and others organized the Korean Evangelical Society, and Moon conducted services every Sunday at a private home on Ellis Street. During this period, fewer than fifty Koreans lived in the Bay Area. When Moon left San Francisco, Bang Wha-jung served as preacher until a young evangelist student, Ryang Ju-sam, landed in San Francisco in 1906 on his way to attend divinity school at Vanderbilt University in Nashville, Tennessee. According to the eyewitness story of ninety-six-year-old Yang Choo-en, the only survivor of the first immigrants to Hawaii in 1902, Ryang, who came from Shanghai, was very concerned about prevailing conditions within the Korean community. Following the big April earthquake in San Francisco, Koreans were in deep trouble, because they did not have jobs or places to live. Everywhere, the life of the Korean people was sad and poverty-stricken. Ryang was so moved emotionally by what he saw with his own eyes and also heard that he decided to postpone his studies in order to render his services to his countrymen, who needed spiritual and material improvement. He succeeded Bang as preacher and worked about three years until resuming his studies. The Reverend Mr. Ryang later became the first Korean bishop of the Korean Methodist Church in Korea.

Ryang first contacted the Board of Missions of the Southern Methodist Church and organized the Korean Evangelical Society. Then, with the help of the Board, the Society rented a three-story building on California Street. The third floor was used as a rooming house for Korean bachelors. The second floor was used for church services on Sundays and as a meeting hall for Korean social and political groups. And the first floor served as a dining and social room for Korean residents. It was at this time that Ryang began publishing the *Korean United Church News* (*Hanin Yonhap Kyobo*). The name was later changed to *Daido-bo* (*Great Guidance News*). It contained both world and Korean community news, and was distributed to Korean residents throughout the United States.[6]

The church officially became the Korean Methodist Church on August 5, 1911; the Reverend Lee Dae-wii was appointed pastor. The present church building, located at 1123 Powell Street, was built in 1928 when the Reverend Whang Sa-sun was minister. It was the first Korean church building constructed with funds provided by both the American mission and the local Korean residents. As will be seen later, this church became the center of Korean community activities in San Francisco.

The origin of the Korean Methodist Church in Los Angeles was unique. Mrs. Sherman, a retired American missionary from Korea, opened a residential mission school on March 11, 1904. It was financed by the Board of Missions of the Southern Methodist Church. The school had a Bible-study class and an English-language class for Korean immigrants in the evening.[7] On Sundays, the school building was used for church services. Shin Hung-woo, a graduate student of the University of Southern California, conducted the services until returning to Korea after obtaining his doctoral degree. Then the Reverend Min Chan-ho served as minister for a while. After Mr. Min left Los Angeles, the church became inactive for many years.

There existed another Korean church at that time called the Free Christian Church, headed by Kang Young-sung. Several individuals, including Kim Sung-kwan, Kim Kwan-oo, and Whang Sung-taik, were dissatisfied with the Korean Presbyterian Church, and they joined with members of the Free Christian Church in order to revive the Korean Methodist Church. However, it took a long time—until October 16, 1931—before the group was officially recognized as the Korean Methodist Church in Los Angeles by the Board of Missions of the Southern Methodist Church. The Reverend Whang Sa-yong was appointed minister.

The first Korean Presbyterian Church was formed in Los Angeles by a group of Korean residents on May 10, 1906. The Korean group sent its representatives to negotiate with the members of the Board of the Presbyterian Extension for a place to hold services. The Board authorized the Reverend Richard to help find a proper place for worship. With his assistance, the Koreans rented a house on Bunker Hill Street and started holding services. However, the Korean Presbyterian Church was under the supervision of the Board of the Presbyterian Missionary Extension for many years before becoming independent. Officially, the Board appointed an American pastor as minister of the Korean Presbyterian Church, but the sermons were given by a Korean preacher in the Korean language since all of the congregation were Korean and most of them did not understand English. A few Korean preachers such as Cho Sung-whan, Chang Woon-kyun and Lim Jun-ki carried on the church work and preached sermons. Finally, on April 9, 1921, the Board recognized the Korean Presbyterian Church as an independent self-governing church. The Reverend Kim Jung-soo became the first Korean "independent" minister and conducted the church work without supervision by the Board of the Presbyterian Ministry Extension.

Within the next two decades, almost every Korean community in the United States established churches. Koreans in Oakland formed the Methodist Church on June 5, 1914, under the leadership of Cho Sung-hak, Moon Won-chil and others. The Reverend Whang Sa-yong was its first minister, and Yim Chung-ku, who was then a student at the Pacific School of Religion, served as preacher. The Korean Christian Church of Hawaii was begun by Syngman Rhee on July 29, 1918. A group of Koreans headed by Kim Hyung-soon and Kim Ho organized the Korean Presbyterian Church in Reedley, California, in February 1919. In New York City, the Reverend Lim Jong-soon established a Methodist church whose status was recognized by the American Methodist Mission Board on February 10, 1923. Korean residents in Chicago started their church movement on August 30, 1919, and the Chicago Korean Methodist Church was formally established on July 27, 1924, by such Korean community leaders as Kang Yung-so, Yum Kwang-sup, and Kim Won-yong. In addition to these churches, many small church groups were formed. Some of them disappeared, whereas some survived.[8]

THE CHURCH AS THE CENTER OF THE KOREAN COMMUNITY

Of the nearly seven thousand early immigrants, more than four hundred were professed Christians. Thirty had engaged in church work as local preachers or pastors prior to their coming to the Hawaiian islands. Within the next two decades, the number of Korean churches and the Korean Christian population increased rapidly. During the first decade, it is reported that twenty-eight hundred Koreans in the Hawaiian Islands were converted to

Christianity and thirty-nine churches were established.[9] This meant that 40 percent of the total Korean population in Hawaii were Christian and almost every Korean community had at least one church. Korean residents on the mainland followed a similar pattern. In both rural and urban areas, wherever Koreans lived, there was a Korean church.

At the beginning, there were five different denominations among the Korean Christians, namely, Methodist, Presbyterian, Episcopalian, Baptist, and Catholic. Later the denominational number increased to twelve. However, Methodists, Presbyterians, and Episcopalians were predominant in the Korean community. Among the original Korean immigrants there were a few Buddhists and some Confucian scholars but they also gradually converted to Christianity. Therefore, the Christian religion was really the only religion practiced by the Korean community in the United States until the end of the Second World War.

There were reasons why the early Korean Christian churches became centers of the Korean community. First, the leaders of the Korean churches were dedicated Christian servants, and they had a strong sense of responsibility for the improvement of the Korean community. They always looked after the welfare and interests of the Korean immigrants who lived alone and in poverty in a strange land. An overwhelming majority of the immigrants were bachelors, isolated from the outside world by a language barrier and cultural conflicts. They were also discriminated against for racial reasons. Their life was confined to plantation work camps. They had to work ten hours a day, six days per week, and many of them spent sleepless nights because of the pain they suffered from the hot sun. When Sunday came, they were exhausted both physically and mentally. Therefore, the Korean immigrants needed someone who cared for them and gave them some hope for bettering their lives in the future.

Most of the church leaders understood the emotional and physical problems of the immigrants and had a sympathetic attitude toward them. The Korean immigrants, whether Christian or non-Christian, felt that they could talk their problems over with the pastors. On Sundays, they worshipped together and had social gatherings after the services. They enjoyed meeting friends and talking to each other in their native language. They shared their problems and helped each other whenever someone was in trouble. Thus, the churches emerged as the center of hope and social life for the early Koreans in the United States. It was true that there were various social and political groups, such as *Dong-hoe* (village council) and New People's Society, but these organizations failed to provide what the Korean immigrants wanted.

Second, almost the entire leadership of the Korean churches emerged from the young intellectual patriots who had been fighting for national independence from the Japanese. Most of them were unable to find employment even with their educational accomplishment because of racial discrimination. They had only three alternatives: to go back to Korea where they would be subject to Japanese persecution; to find jobs in American establishments, even if they were menial; or to stay within the Korean community and work for community organizations. But positions in community organizations were limited. Very few social and political organizations could afford to pay for such services. The churches were the only established institutions which could give employment, although the monthly salary of the pastors was incredibly low. So, many young Korean intellectuals took over church work. It was also true that all the well-known political exiles were Christians: So Chae-p'il, Ahn Ch'ang-ho, Syngman Rhee, and Park Yong-man.

Because of the patriots who became ministers, the Korean churches became institutions for perpetuating Korean aspirations for independence. Korean ministers considered themselves freedom fighters for the cause of national liberation on the one hand, and spiritual leaders of the Koreans in America on the other. During the first two decades, therefore, the Korean churches became headquarters for the national independence movement. Policies and activities were debated, and national celebrations and protest meetings were held at the church buildings. The San Francisco Korean Methodist Church was used for these purposes for many years until the Korean National Association building was constructed in Los Angeles in 1937.

Third, the Korean churches became educational and social-service centers for Koreans in America. Most of the early immigrants had had no opportunities for education in Korea and about 65 percent were illiterate. Therefore the church leaders felt that the first order of Korean community projects was the establishment of evening schools. Immigrants and their children were encouraged to learn how to read and speak Korean. They were also encouraged to study history, culture, and geography. As a result, within a ten-year period, illiteracy among Korean immigrants was wiped out, while Korean children were able to read and speak their ancestral language and to have some background of Korean history and culture. Korean parents and American-born children were able to communicate with each other, family life became happier, and Korean traditional values were retained in the Korean community.

In addition to evening schools, in 1906 the Korean Compound School (a residential school for boys) was established by the Korean Methodist Church in Honolulu. In 1914, a girls' seminary was also established with funds provided by the Korean National Association in Hawaii. In 1918, these two schools merged into one[10] named the Korean Christian Institute; it was headed by Syngman Rhee.

The Korean National Association has been the principal financial resource for education ever since it was organized in 1909. Its education department conducted afternoon and summer schools. At first church leaders published mimeographed textbooks, but later the Korean National Association turned out printed textbooks, which have been used by all Korean language schools in America.

The Korean churches performed various cultural and social services. Korean classical music, folk songs, dances, and arts were introduced to the young generation and to the Korean community at large. Newspapers and magazines were published in both Korean and English. In San Francisco, the first Korean weekly newspaper, *New Korea*, established in 1909, began to print with the metal type machine invented by the Reverend Lee Dae-wii, who also served as editor for many years. *New Korea* still survives. The *Korean National Herald* (now defunct) was published in Honolulu. Within the decade, five weekly newspapers and four monthly magazines, as well as such books as *The Case of Korea* and *Truth About Korea,* were published jointly by the Korean churches and political organizations such as the Korean National Association.

Whenever Koreans were in trouble with domestic affairs or job matters, they first visited their pastors for help. When Korean students came to the United States for advanced studies, they usually called on Korean ministers for advice about their studies as well as for financial aid. Sometimes Korean students ran into trouble with immigration authorities over visa extensions or violation of immigration rules. Then the Korean minister often got them out of trouble by talking to the concerned authorities. Between 1910 and 1918, a few hundred Korean political refugee "students" were able to land in the United States without passports because the ministers of the Korean churches, together with the Korean National Association, became sponsors for them.

The church buildings in the Korean community were open to needy Koreans. Persons who lost their jobs or students who were short of money were welcome to stay in the church, where they could have free room and board. It should be pointed out that in those days a minister's monthly income ran from seventy-five to one hundred dollars. Because few Korean churches were self-supporting, most ministers received their pay from the American denominations, whose average financial help ran from twenty-five to fifty dollars per month. Therefore, Korean ministers and their wives either had to find other jobs or had to run small businesses such as laundry shops or corner grocery stores. Most ministers shared their incomes with their needy fellow countrymen.

As mentioned before, the Reverend Mr. Lee Dae-wii (David Lee) was a devoted minister and a dedicated patriot. He served as minister of the

Korean Methodist Church from 1910 to 1928 and also worked as editor of *New Korea* for many years. He was a leader of the Korean National Association until his death. Most of Mr. Lee's work was, of course, free service in the interests of the Korean community and members of the church. Because of the pressures of community work, he often missed meals and worked twenty-four hours without a rest. As a result, his health deteriorated; he contracted pneumonia and died in 1928. The ninety-six-year-old Yang Choo-en, a good friend of the Reverend Lee told this author that "Reverend Lee was a real Christian minister who followed the foot steps of Jesus Christ. I do not know any minister who is harder working than Reverend Lee in the Korean community today."

In the early days, the Korean churches were the communication channel between the Korean community and American society. American Christian denominations wished to set up their denominations in the Korean community in order to demonstrate their goodwill toward poor Koreans in America. On the other hand, the Korean church leaders wanted American Christians to understand the Korean national issue—restoration of independence from Japan—and Korean community problems. That is to say, the Korean church leaders felt that they were the representatives of the Korean nation and that the Korean church in America was a Korean national body.

CHURCH DISPUTES

The rapid growth of the Korean church during the first decade led to internal and external problems that plunged the entire Korean community in America into a confused state. The major disputes were set off by Japanese interference in Korean internal affairs, disagreement as to the general policy guidelines of the Korean church operation, and questions about management of the Korean school.

The first controversial incident occurred outside the Korean community. On October 5, 1912, a Japanese newspaper in Honolulu reported that the Japanese consul in Hawaii had donated $750 to the Reverend John Wadman, who was then superintendent of the Hawaiian Mission of the Methodist Episcopal Church, for the ostensible purpose of helping needy Koreans. When angry Koreans, who hated any interference by the Japanese in Korean affairs, asked about the donation, Mr. Wadman acknowledged the receipt of money. But he explained that the donation was not for relief but for maintenance of the Korean boarding school. He further stated that "since the Korean boarding school has been under the management of the Hawaiian Mission of the Methodist Episcopal Church, Koreans had no authority to interfere on this matter."[11] Koreans resented Mr. Wadman's view and stated that they did not want any help from the government that had destroyed Korean independence in 1910. When this issue could not be resolved, the students of the boarding school went on strike and refused to attend school. Thus, Mr. Wadman was in an embarrassing position. At this time, Dr. Syngman Rhee came to Hawaii, at the invitation of the Korean National Association of Hawaii, to work for the Korean community. Rhee was asked by Mr. Wadman to intervene in the dispute. He agreed, and worked out a solution by persuading the Koreans to accept the donation. Mr. Wadman was able to avoid a collision with the Koreans, and Rhee was appointed principal of the boarding school.

But disputes over the school did not end with this incident.[12] In 1913, the school expanded and changed its name to the Central Institute. Rhee wanted to construct a dormitory for the students on a lot that had been purchased by the Korean National Association for $1,500. His proposal, however, was rejected at the annual convention of the Association. Rhee did not give up his plan and decided to use direct threats against the leaders of the Association. He learned that members had misused public funds that were to be used for the construction of the Association building. Rhee demanded that he be given the authority to supervise the treasury of the Association. He also demanded that the lot be turned over to him for the construction of a dormitory. In the meantime, a group of Rhee's supporters attacked some of the Association's leaders and beat them up. The local police force was called in to stop the fight. The controversial issue was brought into court in July 1915. Finally, the issue was settled out of court in favor of Rhee, who now emerged as a strong leader within the Korean community in Hawaii.

Rhee faced another dispute. In 1914, Mr. Wadman was replaced as superintendent of the Hawaiian Methodist Mission by William H. Fry. Mr. Fry set forth new policies on the operation of the Korean church and the school. He noticed that both the church and the school were being used as centers of political activities by the Korean residents. He also learned that the church's finances had not been handled in a businesslike manner. The Reverend Mr. Fry opposed the idea of using the church and school for political purposes. Instead, he felt that the church should be only a religious center, and the school only an educational institution. Rhee and his followers, on the other hand, wanted to continue the old policies, namely, to use both the church and school to teach Korean nationalism and to train political leaders along with teaching the Christian faith. Rhee was also of the opinion that he did not have to take orders from Mr. Fry since the Koreans in Hawaii might be able to support the church and school by themselves. He advocated complete autonomy and self-determination of the Korean church and school without depending upon other American missions.

Nevertheless, there were many within the Korean Methodist Church who disagreed with Rhee's view. The two groups opposed each other, and separation finally took place in the fall of 1916 when more than seventy members left the Methodist Church to establish a new church under Rhee's leadership. At first, services were held at the residence of Park Nae-soo. Later, they were held in the Korean school building located at Wailaie Street and Seventh Avenue, Honolulu. In 1917, the new church was named the Korean Christian Church. It was the first independent, self-governing Korean church in America.

The new movement spread to various places throughout Hawaii. It is reported that within a few years there were as many as fifteen churches that held an annual conference under the name of the Central Korean Christian Church. Its leaders emphasized the idea of independence and self-government without help from outside. On this matter Rhee stated: "When I founded the Korean Christian Church with you people, I was sure I would lose my Korean and American friends in the Methodist Church. But I was resolved that we Koreans should control our own church administration without depending upon foreign missions; that we should govern our own affairs.[13]

When the Korean churches were established throughout Hawaii, they had a difficult time finding trained and qualified pastors who could take care of church administration as well as the complex problems of church members. In addition, the pastors had to be politically motivated and yes-men to Rhee in order to keep their jobs. For example, in 1919, the Reverend Min Chan-ho, an ordained minister from an American theological school, was appointed minister at the church that Rhee attended. From the beginning, most of his sermons were of a political nature, emphasizing the activities of the *Tongi-hoe*, Rhee's political organization. During the sermon, Mr. Min always praised Rhee as the founder of the Korean Christian Church and the patriotic leader of the Korean people. He also mentioned Rhee in his prayers without fail. Thus, the church was converted into Rhee's political clubhouse rather than being a place of worship of God.

As time went by, internal division within the Korean Christian Church grew. In 1929, the Rev. Mr. Min was forced to resign after being charged with misappropriating some fifteen thousand dollars of church funds. The Reverend Yi Yong-chik became the new pastor. He was determined to restore the church as a place of worship rather than an institution for political activities. Soon the congregation was divided into two groups: one group supported the new pastor's policy, the other followed Rhee. The latter group wanted to oust Mr. Yi at all costs. Both sides made false charges and countercharges against each other, and every Sunday each group tried to occupy the church sanctuary first. Sometimes violence was used and the local police had to be called in to stop the fights. A great amount of money was wasted by each side in legal fees in order to establish the legitimate ownership of the

Korean Christian Church and its property. The legal battle continued for many years; the final court decision was that "both groups must be united."[14]

The church disputes in Hawaii spread to the mainland. The first incident took place within the Korean Presbyterian Church in Los Angeles.

Kim Won-yong stated in his book that there were two groups in the church, as was the case in Honolulu. One group was pro-Rhee, the other anti-Rhee. On October 14, 1924, the pro-Rhee group occupied the church building by force and expelled anti-Rhee members from the congregation. The latter group thereupon formed a new church and began holding services at a rented home located on Hill Street. On October 3, 1926, the new church adopted the name of the Free Church. However, on October 16, 1930, the congregation decided to dissolve and merged with the Korean Methodist Church in Los Angeles.[15]

Disputes within the Korean Presbyterian Church did not end with the separation of the anti-Rhee group. Soon, a factional struggle erupted within the pro-Rhee group itself and the pastor, Kim Jung-soo, was ousted. Mr. Kim then organized the Korean Christian Church of Los Angeles, modeled after the one in Hawaii. Later, the Korean Christian Church again split into two groups. Again, each group established its own church in Los Angeles, and claimed to be the orthodox congregation of the Korean Christian Church which adhered to Rhee's philosophy of nationalism and self-government without depending upon outside help.

In summary, today all the old church leaders have gone. Most of them came to the United States when the Korean nation was being swallowed by the Japanese Empire. After they landed here, they kept their patriotism burning and regarded the national liberation movement as an imperative duty in their lives. The Korean churches became places of political activity as well as sanctuaries of worship. No church leader believed that such dual activities would produce conflicts within his congregation, but gradually some of the church leaders questioned whether the church should be a political clubhouse. Disputes arose; the churches divided and subdivided; and no solution seemed in sight.

However, the Korean church in America made several important contributions during the early period. First, it was a social center and a means of cultural identification for Koreans in America. At the church, they spoke the same language and retained the same traditional value. Second, the church served an educational function by teaching American-born Koreans the Korean language, history, and culture. Thus they became heirs of the Korean ethnic group. Third, the church kept Korean nationalism alive, although some of the churches were swept into a vortex of political activities by nationalist leaders.

POSTWAR KOREAN CHURCHES IN AMERICA

An increase in the number of Korean ethnic churches began almost simultaneously with the large influx of Korean immigrants into the United States after 1965. Today, it is estimated that there are more than three hundred Korean churches and more than five hundred clergymen throughout the United States, most of them in large metropolitan areas.

Los Angeles, the city with the largest Korean population, provides a good case study of the postwar Korean church. According to the *Hankook Ilbo* report, there are now 121 Korean Christian churches there, 5 Buddhist temples, and 250 clergymen. The number of professed Christians is estimated at 15,000.[16] This means that more than 20 percent of the Koreans in the Los Angeles area are churchgoers; this is 10 percent higher than the Christian population of South Korea, which is the largest Christian nation in Asia except for the Philippines. Clergymen form the largest occupational group in the Korean community of Los Angeles. One out of every 240 Koreans is a clergyman.

Three major Korean daily newspapers provide church information once a week. They list the names, addresses, and telephone numbers of churches and pastors; sermon topics; and times of services. However, only 78 churches out of 121 are listed. The breakdown of the churches according to denomination is as follows: Presbyterian churches, 22; Methodist and Baptist churches, 3 each; and the rest belong to other denominations. This indicates that the Korean churches either joined established American denominations or created their own sectarian churches.

Church attendance varies from 20 to 50 at small churches, 60 to 100 at medium churches, and 150 to 600 at the largest churches. The first two groups of churches are predominant; fewer than ten churches have an average attendance of more than 200 at a Sunday service.

The rate of increase of converts to Christianity among the newcomers ran from 20 to 50 percent during the past few years. One of the main reasons for such an increase was the fact that many of the newcomers felt lonely and insecure. They hoped that the church would provide psychological comfort and material aid through employment services. However, as will be discussed later, most of the clergymen have not been trained as professional ministers, and very few churches are self-supporting.

San Francisco furnishes another case study of the post-war Korean church. Until 1966, there was only one Korean church, the Korean Unified Methodist Church, located at 1123 Powell Street. This was the first church established by the early Korean immigrants on the mainland of the United States. In 1976 there were twelve Korean churches affiliated with many different denominations, from the Korean Assembly of God to the Unification Church founded by the Reverend Sun Myung Moon.

There are a number of reasons for the emergence of many denominational churches within the Korean community. First, the new immigrants came to the United States with their own religious preferences. When they arrived here, they wanted to attend the same denominational church or to establish their own church with similar-minded fellow countrymen sharing the same religious faith and outlook. The establishment of the Korean Presbyterian Church (now called San Francisco Korean United Presbyterian Church) is an example. In 1966, the Korean United Methodist Church had some internal disputes over petty individual likes and dislikes among members as well as over the leadership of the pastor. Congregational members who had been affiliated with the Presbyterian Church prior to coming to the United States, left the Methodist Church and established the Korean Presbyterian Church. This was the first separated church in San Francisco's sixty-year Korean church history.

Second, a clear difference of faith played a major role in the establishment of new churches. For instance, the Unification Church was established upon the basis of faith in the Reverend Sun Myung Moon, who claims to be a second Messiah, told by God "to go to America and speak to the American people about hope and unification, in order to save the world from Communism."[17]

Third, the Christian churches in South Korea produced too many clergymen in too many different denominational theological seminaries. As a result, those who could not find ministerial jobs in Korea emigrated to the United States. As soon as they arrived here, many started holding services with a small group either in private homes or in rent-free American churches. Soon they affiliated with American denominational churches and established Korean churches. Furthermore, under the new immigration law, the ministerial occupation has been an easy way to change from non-immigrant status to permanent residency.

As far as religious preference is concerned, an overwhelming majority of Koreans in America are Protestant; Roman Catholics are second, and Buddhists are third. However, improvement of the quality of Korean churches in terms of the content of sermons and theological interpretations of the Bible, as well as the teaching in the Sunday schools, has not reached a point where the average intellectual can be satisfied. Many ministers belong to orthodox evangelical groups and emphasize disciplined Christian asceticism. Thus, they focus on personal faith in Christ and have little sensitivity to the social witness of the gospel. They believe that social and political issues within their community are secular interests.

On the other hand, a small group of theologians, both Protestant and Roman Catholic, contend that the responsibility of the Christian church is to carry the message of Jesus to the poor masses, because Jesus was a poor man who lived and died for the salvation of man's soul and society. They further note that while clergymen have no political or social ambitions, they do have a responsibility to preach Christ's message of salvation, freedom, and justice, and to serve those who are suffering.

CURRENT CHRISTIAN RESISTANCE AGAINST OPPRESSION

For background, it is necessary to sketch the beginning of the resistance movement of the South Korean Christians. On April 22, 1973, Easter Sunday, a group of Korean Christians, including the Reverend Park Hyong-kyu, minister of the Seoul First Presbyterian Church, held a peaceful mass demonstration against the oppressive measures of the South Korean government. They distributed more than twenty thousand leaflets to the public. The Reverend Park and five other leaders (four Christian students) were arrested by the Seoul police. Their leaflet was brought out of Korea secretly and printed in America.

This Korean Christian Manifesto contained the following points:

1. The present regime in Korea is a one-man dictatorship, and it rules the people by force. Such arbitrary rule is contrary to the will of God. Korean society has become a jungle where the weak are eaten by the strong.

2. The present regime is destroying freedom of conscience and freedom of religious belief. The Korean Christian Church must defend the God-given individual basic rights of the Korean people.

3. The present regime is using systematic deception, manipulation, and indoctrination to control the people. Korean Christians are witnesses to the truth, because we believe in the ultimate power that sets men free for the Kingdom of God.

4. The present regime has been employing inhuman and ruthless methods to destroy political opponents, intellectual critics, and innocent people. People are physically and mentally tortured by the agents of the Korean Central Intelligence Agency, which is similar to the Nazis' Gestapo or Stalin's KGB. Once the suspected person is seized by an agent, he disappears completely. We Korean Christians condemn such acts as murderous.

5. The present regime has been the government of the privileged few, for that class and by that class. The so-called economic development or modernization of the fatherland has widened the gaps between haves and have-nots. We Christians believe in the principle of equal economic well-being of the people and oppose economic exploitation.

6. The present regimes of South Korea and North Korea are using the unification dialogue only to prolong their own powers. They betray the true aspiration of the people for the unification of the country. We Christians believe tolerance and forgiveness and Christian love will bring peace and reunification to our land.

Then the Manifesto urged Koreans as well as Christians throughout the world to undertake three specific actions. First, we should withdraw any form of recognition of the laws, orders, policies, and other political processes of dictatorship that have been wrought since October 17, 1972, and we should develop solidarity among the people to struggle for the restoration of democracy in South Korea. Second, as a preparation for the above struggle, we Christians should renew our churches by deepening our religious thinking, by our clear stance and solidarity with the oppressed and the poor, by the relevant proclamation of the gospel of the Kingdom of God, and by praying for our nation. We should prepare ourselves for martyrdom, if necessary, as our forefathers did. Third, most of all we Korean Christians need the prayers of the churches of the world, and we ask your encouragement and support until the final victory of our struggle.[18]

The first protest statement of Korean Christians in the United States against the interference of South Korea's Central Intelligence Agency (KCIA) was issued in the name of the executive committee of the Association of Korean Christian Scholars on April 15, 1973. While the Association was holding its seventh annual conference at St. Louis, Missouri, a KCIA overseas agent called Dr. Dong Won-mo out while he was presiding over the meeting. The agent asked Dr. Dong to persuade Kim Dae-jung, the keynote speaker, who had been the presidential candidate of the opposition party in 1972, to restrain his attack on the Park administration. When Dr. Dong disclosed the nature of the request to the meeting, the people present were so offended at such undue meddling by the KCIA that they issued the following statement:

> During the three-day conference, members of the Association of the Korean Christian Scholars in the United States reaffirmed their Christian faith of love and peace among their fellow men. The 120 Korean Christian Scholars expressed their concern for freedom of speech, association, religion, and worship of all Koreans. . . .
>
> The intimidation by the Korean CIA in Seoul, when they placed a call to the program chairman of the 1973 conference while he was serving as Master of Ceremonies for the evening meeting of April 14, was a most blatant interference of our freedom of religion and assembly. We feel such uncalled for interference to our organization is both deplorable and intolerable. . . .
>
> We frown upon any further Korean government's attempt to influence our members through unfair pressure and harassment as experienced on the night of April 14, 1973, in St. Louis, Missouri.[19]

The United States government was concerned about political repression in South Korea, and on July 30, 1974, a sub-committee of the House Committee on Foreign Affairs, under the chairmanship of Rep. Donald M. Fraser, held a hearing on the situation in South Korea. Among the witnesses was the Reverend W. Sterling Cary, president of the National Council of Churches of Christ in the United States of America, an ecumenical instrument of thirty-two major Protestant and Orthodox denominations. Mr. Cary stated the Council's position on human rights as follows:

> Christians believe that man is made in the image of God, that every person is of intrinsic worth before God, and that every individual has a right to the fullest possible opportunities for the development of life abundant and eternal. Denials of rights and freedom that are inherent in man, under God, are not simply a crime against humanity, they are sins against God. . . .
>
> There is repression of human rights in the Republic of Korea; such violation of human rights anywhere must be a concern of Americans—especially those in the Judeo-Christian heritage—and because the United States Government participates in this repression through its aid, it has both the responsibility and the means to effect a change in the Korean situation.[20]

He also pointed out that American Protestants and Catholics are increasingly concerned about the excessively repressive conduct of the Park government since the declaration of martial law in October 1972. Thus, all Christians throughout the world reaffirm that fundamental human rights are God's gift to *all people*, and that no person or government has the right to deprive people of these human rights.

In October 1974, nine Korean ministers in the Los Angeles area, including Mr. Kye Dong-choon, Mr. Kim Dae-sun, and Mr. Cho Nam-eun, held a save-the-nation prayer meeting at the First United Methodist Church. More than a hundred Christians attended the meeting and prayed for the immediate release of their imprisoned fellow countrymen and for a restoration of democracy in Korea. They also prayed to "make the Korean leaders repent for what they have done to their people, help them put democratic principles into practice, and help the Christians die as martyrs for their noble Christian teachings."[21]

On July 24, 1975, forty Korean clergymen representing the Korean Presbyterian Church Association in America attended the annual conference of the Asian Presbyterian Church Association at Mills Women's College, Oakland, California. The Korean delegates drafted an eleven-point human rights resolution, similar to that of the Korean Christian Manifesto. The resolution was unanimously adopted by the conference members, all of whom pledged themselves to work together for the restoration of human rights in Korea and to pray for the oppressed, imprisoned, and condemned victims of the South Korean government.[22]

On May 10, 1975, a group of Korean American Christians headed by the Reverend Lim Dong-sun held a breakfast prayer-meeting in the Los Angeles Hilton Hotel for the purpose of consolidating the activities of Koreans and Americans on the human rights problem in South Korea. Many American missionaries who had worked in Korea, as well as local government leaders, attended this religious gathering and expressed their concern about the repressive measures of the South Korean regime.

Dissident Christian leaders in South Korea had been holding a prayer meeting every Thursday morning to protest government oppression. The government banned these meetings on the grounds that they did not serve the best interests of national security. In response, the East Asian Section of the National Council of Churches in America called on its membership to hold similar prayer meetings. Korean Christians in eighteen American and two Canadian cities have responded to the call.

One of the participants in these prayer meetings wrote: "We have repeatedly drawn inspiration and courage from these periods of recollection when the profound realities of the revolutionary path have come home to us through our sympathetic entry into the situations of such people as Kim Chi Ha and others."[23]

In January 1976, a group of Korean Christians in the Los Angeles area organized the Christian Society for the Realization of Justice. The founders of this new society are Kim Sang-don, a former mayor of Seoul and member of the South Korean National Assembly, and the Reverend Kim Chai-choon, a well-known theologian, social critic, and author, who was the former president of Han Kuk Theological Seminary in Seoul and is now chairman of the Korean Congress for Democracy and Unification (*Minju Faibok T'ongil Chokjin Kungmin-hoe*). The Society is still in a formative stage but it hopes to launch a new faith-movement among overseas Korean Christians. The Society emphasizes the following points:

1. There must be no one who can deprive people of their God-given human rights. Therefore, it is our duty to oppose all forces that attempt to deprive people of their human rights.

2. We reject one-man totalitarian rule and we also reject the attitude of silence of Christians toward the absolute ruler.

3. We must be ready to sacrifice our lives with our Christian friends in Korea who have been fighting against the Park regime.

4. We must equip ourselves with the spirit of Jesus Christ in order to establish a clean, honest, and peaceful Korean community in the United States.

5. The Christian Church is to be the conscience, critic, and custodian of the Korean nation; therefore, the church cannot be used as a political tool of the dictator and, at the same time, it cannot be a haven of refuge for cowards and hypocritic clergymen.

6. We resolve that we will follow the footsteps of our Lord by launching a new faith-movement in order to create a new history of our nation, a Messianic Society.[24]

As its first social action, some twenty members of the Christian Society for the Realization of Justice in Los Angeles staged a silent prayer gathering to protest the appearance of guest preacher Hahn Kyung-chik at a revival meeting at the Yung Nak Presbyterian Church. The Reverend Mr. Hahn is a nationally prominent clergyman and a founder of the Yung Nak Church in Seoul, the largest church in Korea. According to the spokesman of the Society, the Reverend Mr. Hahn "failed to stand up against the South Korean government's persecution of Christians and suppression of human rights." Thus, "he is betraying the call of Jesus Christ." The spokesman also said that "the pastor from Korea was touring the United States on a mission to preach to the Korean community for the cause of the dictatorial Park regime."[25]

On the other hand, defenders of the Reverend Mr. Hahn, under the leadership of the Reverend Mr. Kim Kye-yong, asserted that the invitation to Mr. Hahn had no political motivation whatever. Mr. Hahn had been invited solely to preach the gospel at the revival meeting. The Reverend Mr. Kim also pointed out that there are many different schools of thought within Christian theology regarding social and political issues. He further asserted that "if you believe in a democratic principle, you should learn to respect other people's opinions too; neglecting others' views leads in a dictatorial direction." It was very unfortunate, Mr. Kim said, that "the opposing side issued the protest statement even without having a personal conversation or interview with Reverend Hahn, so that the statement is to be considered as slander."[26] The New Korea reported that Mr. Hahn rejected a request for an interview. He was quoted by one of his associates as saying that "time will tell."[27]

Today, Korean Christian leaders are divided into three groups on Park's policies: the pro-government group, the anti-government group, and the silent or so-called neutral group. The pro-Park leaders, who are a minority, believe that all we need is a personal faith in Christ; we should stay out of social and political issues. Some quote Romans 13:1: "Let every soul be subject unto the higher powers. For there is no power but of God; the powers that be are ordained of God." They assert that all powers are ordained of God; therefore all Korean Christians must be subject to the powers of the Park government. This group further emphasizes that the Communist regime of North Korea is still attempting to take over South Korea and that Christians should be prepared to sacrifice some personal liberties in order to maintain the security of the South Korean government, which will eventually establish a democratic society.

On the other hand, the anti-Park leaders, also a minority at the present time, believe that the gospel of Jesus Christ, rightly understood, provides not only a personal faith but also the motivation to deal with anything that dehumanizes people, such as poverty, the suppression of human rights, and the threat of war. They point out that Jesus Christ lived among the oppressed and the poor, and spoke about the justice of God before Pontius Pilate, the representative of the Roman Empire. He was crucified in the course of His witness to the truth, and He rose from the dead to release the powers of transformation that set us free. Therefore, it is our duty as Christians to follow in the footsteps of Jesus Christ, living among our brothers and sisters and standing up against political oppression in order to create a new society that will protect God-given human rights. This group believes that the pro-Park leaders are either naive or political opportunists. When you say that God is the source of all power, what is meant is the power of justice and truth, not a tyrannous and oppressive power like the Park government. The anti-Park leaders further assert that opportunistic Christian leaders became pro-Japanese during the period of Japanese domination under the same false argument. And they assert that these opportunistic Christian leaders would support the North Korean Communist regime, should it dominate South Korea, under the same false argument. The anti-Park leaders feel that a one-man dictatorship is neither the people's wish nor God's wish; it is a demonic and destructive power. Under the rule of a dictatorship, people live under police surveillance, enslaved and oppressed by modern weapons.[28]

The vast majority of Korean Christians in the United States are silent. On this matter, one foreign observer said: "I do not know why the United States seems to produce a silent majority among Koreans. . . . It is really not part of the Korean tradition. Korea in her recent history relied greatly upon her sons and daughters abroad to speak up for her when Koreans at home could not speak up fully for themselves, as in the case of the Japanese domination period."[29]

There are two points of view regarding the reasons for silence. One view holds that a majority of Korean Christians in general, and clergymen in particular, are so-called evangelists who believe that the Christian Church should detach itself from Korean internal politics and social issues, because they are secular interests. The main responsibility of the Church is to preach the gospel to the people. A church is a place of worship and not a political clubhouse. The other view holds that the majority of Korean Christians are waiting for the proper time and that they will rise up sooner or later. This view was expressed by the Reverend Kim Chai-choon, leader of social activists abroad, who said: "I think the vast silent majority are in the second line to support us even though they keep quiet."[30] Therefore, it remains to be seen whether the Korean church in America will detach itself from Korean internal politics and social issues or will plunge itself into them.

It would seem that there are too many churches and too many clergymen in the Korean community today. Most of the churches are non self-supporting financially. Only a few clergymen are trained professional ministers. Many lack an academic background and are indifferent to such social questions as racial discrimination, minority rights, youth guidance, education of the new immigrants' children, unemployment problems, and the language barrier.

Sometimes, clergymen waste time and energy in petty denominational disputes and attempts to make their own positions secure. As a result, they have established many different denominational churches with a small membership. Many Korean churches have isolated themselves from the mainstream of Korean community life and have been converted into do-nothing social clubs.

Many observers believe that if the Korean churches want to play a major role in the development of the Korean community, they must start out with an internal house-cleaning.[31] Only then should they involve themselves in community issues. In the meantime, as a long-term project, the Korean churches should prepare themselves to participate in American society on the same basis as other ethnic groups.

EDUCATIONAL AND CULTURAL ACTIVITIES

In the early period, churches and social and political organizations played active roles in the effort to perpetuate Korean traditions in the Korean community. Most of the Korean immigrants sent their children to Korean language schools to learn the Korean language, history, and culture. The churches were centers of educational and cultural activities, because they already had such facilities as classrooms, playgrounds, teachers, and teaching materials. Many churches published bulletins that took the place of newspapers within the Korean community. The Korean National Association also played an important role in maintaining the Korean heritage among American-born Korean children. The KNA's Bureau of Education was established in order to provide funds and teaching materials for Korean language schools. During summer vacations, a full-time Korean language summer-school was operated under the supervision of the Bureau of Education of the Korean National Association.[32]

But postwar Korean educational and cultural activities in the United States have been negligible. In general, the Korean community in America has no meaningful educational and cultural programs for immigrants' children and American-born Koreans. Korean immigrants' children suffer from the lack of a bilingual education. They suffer both mentally and physically during their first six months to one year in school until they understand English and adjust to the American social system. For example, in Los Angeles, there are forty-five hundred Korean children of school age. But there are only two elementary schools—Hovard and Wilton Place—that provide bilingual classes, and only ten qualified bilingual teachers. Another example is San Francisco, where there are more than six hundred Korean children but only three bilingual teachers.[33]

As far as Korean schools are concerned, the Mugunghwa School (now known as the Korean School of Southern California) has been operating since 1973 at the *Tongji-hoe* building. It is open only on Sunday afternoon for three hours. The average attendance is about eighty. The main subjects offered are the Korean language, English, and Korean history, culture, dancing, and singing. The San Francisco Korean school, which is called the Korean-American Education Center, was established in 1973. It rents classrooms from the Madison School at 3950 Sacramento Street. It, too, is open on Sunday afternoons. The average attendance runs from thirty to seventy, and classes go from kindergarten to sixth grade. Teaching materials are prepared by the bilingual staff to meet the needs of non-English speaking children as well as non-Korean-speaking American-born children. Nevertheless, all Korean schools in the major rural areas in the Korean community suffer from a lack of funds, a qualified teaching staff, and teaching materials. The average annual budget of the Korean school system runs between fifteen and twenty thousand dollars. The money comes partly from the South Korean government and partly from Koreans generally, as well as members of the Board of Trustees. In short, the existing Korean school system in America is inadequate for bringing up Korean children, teaching them their traditional values, and helping them improve their studies in American public schools.

No meaningful cultural activities have taken place in the Korean community. Although there are many cultural organizations, it seems that they are still in the formative stage. Perhaps the only noticeable cultural event for the American public is the Korean festival in Los Angeles, which is similar to the Chinese New Year's parade or the Japanese Cherry Blossom Day celebration. The first Korean festival was held in November 1974. A festival committee was organized by the representatives of various social, cultural, and business organizations. The program consisted of street parades with brass bands, folk-dancing performances, the wearing of native clothing, the playing of instruments, and beauty pageants. The program also included singing contests and lectures on Korean culture. The main purpose of the festival was to promote good will and friendship between Koreans and other ethnic groups. The festival was successful. More than thirty thousand people saw the parade, and 120 different ethnic organizations participated in it.

Expenses were $30,000 in 1974 and $50,000 in 1975. The Korean news media reported that, at long last, the American public and other minority ethnic groups had an opportunity to see what the Koreans and their culture were like. Community leaders are now putting the finishing touches on plans for a $50 million Korean plaza in the Wilshire commercial district. The private investment project is "conceptualized to be both a cultural and commercial center for Americans and Koreans."[34] However, many Koreans think that Korean cultural activities should not be used in a commercial manner by businessmen, because the real value of Korean culture cannot be measured in dollars.

14.

Korean Contributions to America

CONTRIBUTIONS TO AGRICULTURE

The importation into Hawaii of Chinese labor, based on contract agreements, came to an end with annexation. In 1902, Japanese workers in Hawaii predominated. They made up 73.5 percent (31,029) of the total sugar plantation working force of 42,242. The Chinese constituted 9.3 percent (3,928).[1] Previously illegal strikes became legal. These two developments set into motion the tendency of the Asian immigrant labor force to shift from one plantation to another in search of higher wages and better working conditions. If the plantation owners refused to accept the demands of their workers, they went on strike or left the plantation. For example, between 1900 and 1905, there were thirty-four strikes by the Japanese. In 1902 alone, more than one thousand Japanese plantation workers quit on the spot and left for urban centers in Hawaii or came to California. Thus, the plantation owners faced a labor shortage. It was at this time that the plantation owners worked out new labor policies. They were careful to avoid dependence upon workers of any one racial group and devised a policy of drawing workers from a number of different racial groups as a means of effective labor control.[2]

Under these circumstances, the five thousand Korean immigrant plantation workers became one of the main productive forces in Hawaii's sugar economy over the next decade. Although they were not composed exclusively of farmers, they were good field workers. A few American businessmen as well as missionaries who had had experience with the Korean labor class said that Koreans were the best workers of all Orientals.[3] During this decade, Koreans ranked second in number on the sugar plantations 9.71 percent. The Japanese averaged 65.8 percent, and the Chinese 9.14 percent.[4]

Between 1920 and 1921, Japanese workers on the sugar plantations went on many strikes and threatened to close down the entire sugar industry. At this critical juncture, Koreans were used as strike-breakers to save the sugar plantations. The reason for their willingness to work as strike-breakers was political. Koreans hated the Japanese as the enemy that had destroyed the Korean nation in 1910.

Between 1905 and 1907, until the anti-Oriental Immigration Law became effective, about one thousand Korean plantation workers from Hawaii came to the mainland, mostly to California and Oregon. There are two main factors that caused this migration. First, treatment by the plantation owners had been bad from the beginning. As noted before, the average monthly wage was eighteen dollars for male workers and fifteen dollars for female workers. Living conditions were poor, and no improvement was in sight. Koreans felt that they were treated almost like slaves by the plantation owners, and they were looking for an opportunity to escape. They had heard that the West Coast states, especially California, offered better economic opportunities for Orientals. Second, the Korean immigrant group was heterogeneous, having come from every province of Korea and from all walks of life. They were farmers, common coolies who worked periodically in port cities and towns, ex-soldiers, household servants, former government officials, Confucian scholars, clergymen, and priests. A few were political exiles, and some were students who wanted to study at American universities. In other words, the early Korean immigrants represented the existing Korean society of that period. This was a unique characteristic of the Korean immigrant group in comparison to other Oriental groups. Immigrants from Japan, China, and the Philippines, for example, were more or less homogeneous, predominantly farmers or coolies. Naturally, many of the Korean immigrants had no intention of staying indefinitely in Hawaii, and some of them ventured into other occupations on the mainland.

Nevertheless, when they landed in California, they faced the same difficulty in finding better occupations as they had in Hawaii. Most Koreans, including intellectuals, became farm workers in California. The hope of every Korean farm worker was to have his own farm. As soon as he saved enough money, he invested it in farmland. Koreans were often forced to buy only the land that was unwanted by white farmers. Korean farmers could not buy good rich land because the owners did not want to sell to Orientals. But with hard work and a lot of patience, the Korean farmers turned poor land into fertile, productive farms. The swampy marshlands of the San Joaquin Valley and Sacramento delta were drained and turned into potato and rice fields. Dry land near Vacaville was changed into fruit orchards. Hot, alkaline fields were converted into vineyards. The sand dunes of Fresno and Reedley became vegetable plantations. And the desert-like land of southern California was converted into orange orchards.

Historically, Korean farmers have been the best rice growers in Asia, and a few Korean immigrant farmers became some of the best rice producers in California. Within a decade, a Korean farmer named Kim Jong-lim emerged with more than two thousand acres of rice fields and the nickname of "rice king" of the Korean community.[5] (He is the man who donated three airplanes to the Korean School of Aviation in Willows, California during the 1920s and contributed $3,000 a month for its operating expenses.) The average Korean farmer in California and Oregon produced more and better rice crops than did the Chinese and Japanese. For example, a few Korean farmers in Willows grew 1.5 million bushels of rice on forty-three hundred acres of land in 1919. Their total revenue amounted to more than $1.3 million.[6]

The Koreans were also good workers in orchards. Mrs. Mary Steward, the owner of an orchard during the period of the "yellow peril," praised the Koreans as "hard working, diligent, honest, and the best orange pickers among the Orientals."[7] She protected the Korean workers from hostile white laborers who attempted to attack them for taking jobs away.

In the 1920s, some of the Korean farmers ventured into truck farming businesses. They loaded their trucks with vegetables and drove them to the markets to sell. One truck-farming business owned by two Koreans was very successful. The men started by trucking wholesale fruit and nursery products, and eventually expanded their enterprise to include orchards, fruit-packing sheds, and nurseries. In 1921, they established a partnership called the Kim Brothers Company in Reedley, California. As stated previously, the Kim brothers developed more than a dozen new fruits and nursery plants on which they obtained patent rights from the government. For example, they invented new varieties of nectarines such as Le Grand and Sun Grand which are sold today throughout the United States. During thirty years of business, the company operated five hundred acres of farmland in six different locations, a $400,000 packing facility, and a $100,000 nursery house. Total assets were estimated at $1.5 million, with an annual business volume running about $1 million.[8] Thus, the two Kims played an important role in the American orchard economy.

CONTRIBUTIONS TO ETHNIC IDENTITY

Until the end of World War II, American institutions, both private and public, advocated the "melting pot theory" as a means of incorporating minorities into the dominant Anglo-Saxon culture. In reality, the melting pot theory turned out to be a policy of cultural assimilation. During this period, Asian ethnic groups suffered not only from cultural pressures but from racism as well.

However, the policy of Anglo-Saxon supremacy is being challenged by the postwar generation. People now argue that American society has always been heterogeneous and that Americans are a mixture of various ethnic groups with different historical and cultural backgrounds. All Americans are immigrants, and American culture contains many strands. The concept of cultural pluralism has more or less replaced the melting pot theory, and ethnic identity has emerged as a major social force in American society.

During the period of Anglo-Saxon cultural supremacy, Koreans in America had a constant struggle to preserve their ethnic identity. Koreans did not use the word "identity." However, they expressed the idea through a nationalist movement in opposition to Japanese domination of Korea; through the establishment of Korean language schools and weekly newspapers; and through the establishment of ethnic enterprises based on family-centered businesses. Some of the typical political activities used to preserve the Korean identity will be described here briefly.

As early as July 22, 1906, Korean residents in Hawaii sent a petition to President Theodore Roosevelt. In part, it said:

> We know that the people of America love fair play and advocate justice toward all men. We also know that your Excellency is an ardent exponent of a square deal between individuals as well as nations, therefore, we come to you with this memorial with the hope that your Excellency may help our country at this critical period of our national life. . . . We earnestly hope that your Excellency will see to it that Korea may preserve her autonomous government and that other powers shall not oppress or maltreat our people. The clause in the treaty between the United States and Korea gives us a claim upon the United States for assistance, and this is the time when we need it most.[9]

This petition was sent as an expression of opposition to the establishment of the Japanese protectorate over Korea after the Russo-Japanese War. At the time of the March First uprising in 1919, the Korean National Association in America issued a statement entitled "A Korean Appeal to America," which read:

> The Japanese Government has not only robbed us of national liberty, but has deprived us of those rights which are the heritage of every human being. It deprived us of justice, of freedom of thought, of our language, of the right to educate our children according to our ideals, imposing upon us a system of education not only destructive of our national ideals, but imperiling the very foundation of the Christian religion. . . .
> At last our race has arisen and proclaimed to the world, in no mistaken terms, its desire for liberty and for freedom from oppression and unbearable tyranny. . . . And surely America will not, cannot, stand by and let us suffer.[10]

On the other hand, some Koreans took direct action against the pro-Japanese and established military training camps both in Hawaii and on the mainland. On March 23, 1908, a pro-Japanese American diplomatic officer, Durham White Stevens, was assassinated in San Francisco by a Korean patriot, Chang In-whan. In July 1909, Park Yong-man, Im Dong-sik, and Chung Han-kyung (Henry Chung) established the Korean Youth Military Academy in Hastings, Nebraska and trained Korean youths in military tactics. In 1914, various Korean military training camps were established both in Hawaii and on the mainland. A Korean National Brigade was established under Park Yong-man and more than two hundred and fifty Koreans received military training. Some were then sent to Korea and China as underground agents to organize an anti-Japanese movement.

Koreans also formed organizations for diplomatic and propaganda activities. On March 17, 1919, they established the Korean Information Bureau headed by So Chae-p'il (Philip Jaisohn) as an official representative body of the Korean provisional government in Shanghai. On April 14-16, it held a mass meeting under the name Liberty Congress. Representatives of all Korean social, political, and religious organizations in America, Mexico, and Cuba, as well as many prominent American civic and government leaders, attended the meeting. Following a street parade, the Declaration of Independence of Korea was read at Independence Hall and a resolution was passed calling for an all-out effort to gain official recognition of the Korean provisional government by the United States.

On September 2, 1940, nearly three months before the Japanese attack on Pearl Harbor, Koreans formed the United Korean Committee in America and launched an independence movement. One of the first activities of the Committee was an effort to persuade American authorities to recognize that Koreans were not Japanese subjects under the Alien Registration Act of 1940. As a result, Earl G. Harrison, head of the alien registration office in Washington, D.C., ruled that Koreans had a right to register as Koreans and not as Japanese subjects. Thereafter, the Committee issued identification badges which every Korean in America carried during the war period. In 1943, the Committee proclaimed August 29 as Korean National Flag Day. Many American mayors and governors responded to the Committee's request and flew a Korean flag on public buildings for the first time since Korea was annexed by Japan in 1910.

Korean political activities between 1905 and 1945 have had a dual purpose. On the one hand, they represent an effort to retain ethnic identity through the rejection of Americanization. On the other hand, they represent a desire for the reestablishment of a Korean nation free from Japanese domination.

WARTIME CONTRIBUTIONS

Koreans in the United States have gone through four wars: the two World Wars, the Korean War, and the Vietnam War. During and after the First World War, the Koreans' main concern was the restoration of national independence. Their activities centered on obtaining sympathy from the United States government for national independence after the March First uprising in Korea in 1919, which was inspired by the Wilsonian principle of the right of self-determination by small nations. Korean residents in America were inactive during the Korean and Vietnam Wars, because Koreans killed Koreans during the former, while the latter had nothing to do with the problem of reunification of Korea.

However, Korean activities during the Second World War were noticeable. Koreans believed that victory against the Axis powers would mean the liberation of Korea from Japanese rule, and they regarded it as a war for independence. Young Koreans, American citizens and noncitizens alike, served in the American armed forces. Older Korean immigrants who had passed the age of military service volunteered as national guardsmen and emergency fire wardens, or worked in naval shipyards and other defense facilities. Elderly Korean women participated in the Red Cross and the USO, and organized groups to sell war bonds. About two hundred and fifty Japanese-speaking Koreans, including students, were called by the United States government to work as interpreters, translators, and intelligence workers with various wartime agencies, such as the Office of War Information, the Army, the Navy, and the Air Force. Some of these Koreans received special military training and were sent out to the Pacific war front as underground agents against the Japanese. Such qualified Japanese-speaking Koreans were a valuable asset to the American government in its struggle against the Japanese.

After the war, many Koreans in America returned to South Korea as civilian employees of the American military government there. The United States government had practically no trained American experts on Korean affairs, and the American military government in South Korea had to depend on English-speaking Koreans. Some observers even characterized the American military government as a "government of interpreters" of English-speaking Koreans.

Perhaps one of the most unusual activities of Koreans in California was the creation of a Korean brigade within the California National Guard. It was named the Tiger Brigade, *Mangho-kun*. It was composed mostly of early Korean immigrants, including women, many of whom were more than sixty years old. One hundred and nine Koreans in Los Angeles received military training every Saturday and Sunday afternoon. In San Francisco, thirty Koreans received similar training.[11] The military drills were practiced under the supervision of U.S. Army officials. All the uniforms and military equipment was supplied by the United States government. The main duty of the Tiger Brigade was to help defend California should an enemy invasion take place. After a few months of military drill, one of the American army officials praised the Korean Tiger Brigade by saying: "I myself have learned the real meaning of patriotism during my participation in this Tiger Brigade, and I cannot find adequate words to describe your contribution in winning this war."[12]

Koreans also launched an American-Korean Victory Fund drive headed by the United Korean Committee. Many Koreans bought defense bonds with their monthly paychecks. Thus, all Koreans, young and old, numbering fewer than ten thousand, made their contribution according to their individual ability. They were bitterly disappointed when the Korean peninsula was divided into military occupational zones by the Allied powers after the war instead of being a unified and independent nation.

INTELLECTUAL AND PROFESSIONAL CONTRIBUTIONS

Among minority ethnic groups in the United States, Koreans rank proportionately high in representation in intellectual and professional brackets. This is a noteworthy accomplishment for those early immigrant families of relatively modest social backgrounds who made their way to a strange country. It is also a remarkable record for Korean-born students who distinguished themselves as competent scholars and intellectuals in the competitive American academic world. Korean contributions in American intellectual and professional fields have been especially noticeable in literature, law, medicine, and music. Here are a few examples of successful people.[13]

David Hsin-Fu Wand said that "at present three well-known names in Asian-American fiction are Korean-born Americans." They are Younghill Kang (1903–1972), Richard E. Kim, and Yong-ik Kim. All came to the United States as students and became naturalized citizens.

The late Professor Kang was the best-known Korean writer. The son of a Confucian scholar, he was born in a northern province of Korea in 1903. He landed in San Francisco just before the Oriental Exclusion Law was passed. He was eighteen years old, and when he reached New York, he had only four dollars in his pocket. But his heart was full of ambition, and he was both dauntless and lyrical, wanting to master Western learning and civilization. His four dollars had already been spent for a hotel room, and he had no money for food. So he went to a Chinese restaurant, as most Oriental newcomers usually did. He introduced himself to the proprietor by writing a poem on the theme of vegetable soup, and was able to arrange for a meal a day on credit until he could find a job. In the same way, he later got a room near Chinatown. He managed to keep going until a Korean friend took him to a Korean rooming house where he stayed until he was able to find work. He did many kinds of odd jobs as a houseboy, restaurant waiter, dishwasher, and grocery worker while attending school to learn English. After attending college in Canada, he went on to Harvard.

Kang was one of the top students in his class in every subject. He was especially gifted in literature and poetry. He distinguished himself by being the first Korean-born scholar to become an assistant professor of comparative literature at New York University. He also became a member of the staff of the Department of Far Eastern Art at the Metropolitan Museum of Art and served on the staff of the Encyclopaedia Britannica. During the last twenty-five years of his life, he lectured in hundreds of cities in America, Europe, and Asia. During the Second World War, he worked for the United States government as a language consultant to the Army Education Division. At the end of the war, he became chief of publications for the American military government in South Korea.

Above all, Professor Kang was gifted as a writer. His first book, *The Grass Roof* (autobiography), brought him fame as a Korean-American writer. This was followed by his second book, *East Goes West*, and then by a third, *The Happy Grove*. Said the U.N. World: "[Professor Kang is] one of the top half-dozen classical Oriental scholars; he is, at the same time, a scholar of major stature, occidental style." The late Pearl S. Buck wrote: "Younghill Kang, distinguished author and lecturer, is one of the most brilliant minds of the East." She went on to say that Professor Kang's "eloquent, provocative platform manner has won him acclaim as a man with poetry in his heart. He presents the enduring aspects of the Orient in impeccable, vigorous English." Thomas Wolfe in the *New York Post* said, "Kang is a born writer, everywhere he is free and vigorous; he has an original and poetic mind, and he loves life; again and again in his books a person, a scene, and an action are described in a few words of rich and vivid brevity." The *Boston Transcript* wrote, "Younghill Kang writes more richly and wisely and delightfully of America than a great majority of writers who are American-born."

Professor Kang was the recipient of a Guggenheim Award in creative literature as well as several European literary prizes. His book *Au Pays Du Matin Cale* received Le Prix Halperine Kamnisty as the best book translated into French in 1937.

He wrote his last poem in memory of his wife, Frances Keely Kang, in 1970:

> Too soft for a grave-digger's tune,
> Bleak for that child Spring's mid-wife;
> Mouldering impassively
> Dearest leaves of life;
> Burying Summer without voicing
> Anguish for any leaf forgotten;
> Neither sorrowing nor rejoicing
> As next summer is begotten.
>   Autumn Rain: Frances Keely Kang.

On January 18, 1971, Professor Kang wrote his last letter to this author, which read:

> Dear Friends—the B.Y. Choy Family;
> Please forgive me for my long silence. We had a wonderful time in Berkeley with you. Many thanks for this. Now I am changing my way of living. I will sell my house and move away—perhaps to California. You may keep this in mind; if you see a small house or any apartment or hotel room near the University library, please let me know. I am alone in this big house. How much does that hotel charge by month where we were last time in Berkeley? If you know of any please, let me know . . .
> With best wishes and warmest regards to you all.
>
> Yours very sincerely,
> Younghill Kang

Professor Kang was actively engaged in opposing racism and other anti-democratic social forces, in fighting against the tactics of Sen. Joseph McCarthy and Syngman Rhee's dictatorial rule. As a member of the American Civil Liberties Union, he worked for the protection of minority rights in America. He sent fifteen thousand books from his own library to the Korea University Library as a donation to Korean students in Seoul.

Richard E. Kim was born on March 13 in Hamhung City in northern Korea. He served in the South Korean army during the Korean War as a liaison officer between the American and Korean armed forces. He came to the United States and studied at Middleburg College, Johns Hopkins, and Harvard. He was appointed an instructor of English at Long Beach State University, California; became an assistant professor of English at the University of Massachusetts; and is presently a professor of English at San Diego State University. He wrote two powerful novels, *The Martyred* (1964) and *The Innocent* (1968), both of which received much critical acclaim. His short stories appeared in a collection entitled *Lost Names* (1970). In all three books, there are references to the Japanese oppression and exploitation of Koreans during the Japanese domination of Korea. The short story *Lost Names* treats specially the incredible humiliation of Koreans who were forced to give up their family names and adopt Japanese surnames.

The Martyred was a final nominee for the National Book Award. For *The Innocent* and *Lost Names*, Prof. Kim received such awards as the University of Iowa Writers' Workshop Fellowship, Mary Roberts Rinehart Foundation Fellowship, Ford Foundation Foreign Area Fellowship, and Guggenheim Foundation Fellowship. The *New York Times* described Kim's novel *The Martyred* as "a magnificent achievement . . . in the great moral and psychological tradition of Dostoyevsky and Albert Camus." The late Pearl S. Buck said that the novel is "a major achievement, in my opinion." Maurice Dolbier, *New York Herald Tribune*, wrote that Kim was "one of the ablest young novelists to appear in any nation, in decades." Robert Kirsch, *Los Angeles Times*, said that "Richard E. Kim's brilliant and powerful novel deserves to be included in the small group of twentieth-century novels which may be called great." His second book, *The Innocent*, "is an equally compelling story which faces up to unavoidable moral issues in the context of violence and duplicity and almost unbearable suspense." S.K. Oberbeck, *Newsweek*, said: "*The Innocent* blends the most formidable human ambiguities into a jetsmooth narrative that bristles with the stuff of today's headlines and news flashes."

Recently, Professor Kim said: "Korea is the foundation of my literature, my eternal pursuit of my literary way and all of my literary resources." He further asserted that "what matters in writing is the viewpoint of a writer. It engulfs all ideas of the novelist. However, what is more important is his inspiration." He also revealed that his future writings would be on the life of "the immigrant third generation."

Yong-ik Kim was born in 1920 in Korea and educated in Korea and Japan as well as in the United States. He is known as an excellent short story writer. His "From Below the Bridge" was cited in Martha Foley's *The Best American Short Stories of 1958*. He is the author of "The Happy Days" (1960), "The Dividing Gourd" (1962), "The Blue in the Seed" (1964), "Love in Winter" (1964), and "The Shoes from Yan San Valley" (1970).

The late Henry Moon was an internationally known hormone researcher. He was chairman of the Department of Pathology at the University of California School of Medicine, San Francisco. He was born on September 28, 1914, as the first son of Mr. and Mrs. Moon Yang-mok, who were early Korean immigrants to the United States. Henry attended elementary school and high school in San Francisco and received his B.A. and M.A. in anatomy from the University of California, Berkeley. After graduating from the University of California School of Medicine, San Francisco, in 1940, he served in the coroner's office in San Francisco for two years. He then entered the army as a first lieutenant in the Medical Corps, where he served as a pathologist, and was discharged with the rank of major in 1947. He then joined the faculty of the University of California School of Medicine, San Francisco, and also worked as chief of the Pathology Service at the Veterans Administration Hospital, San Francisco. He became chairman of the Department of Pathology in 1956.

Dr. Moon was part of a team that first isolated the ACTH hormone. His research reputation was enhanced by his work on arteriosclerosis, or hardening of the arteries. Because of his outstanding record in research, he was awarded a $40,000 research grant from the United States government.

Some of Dr. Moon's major experimental works deal with the following subjects: (1) purification and biologic studies of ACTH; (2) the role of the anterior pituitary gland and growth hormone in experimental carcinogenesis; (3) mechanism of action of growth hormone; (4) arteriosclerosis in man and experimental animals; (5) lysis of homologous cells by sensitized lymphocytes and mechanisms of immune cytolysis; and (6) immunopathologic studies of porcine and human pancreatic elastase.

According to Dr. Moon's curriculum vitae, he wrote ninety-five articles on hormones and related subjects that appeared in medical magazines in the United States. He served as a member of the Scientific Advisory Board and of the National Board of Medical Examiners. He was a visiting professor to the U.S.S.R., worked in Korea for the United States government, and was president of the University of California Alumni-Faculty Association. He also served as a member of the editorial board of Laboratory Investigation, Archives of Pathology, Proceedings of the Society for Experimental Biology and Medicine, and the American Journal of Pathology. He belonged to more than a dozen scientific societies and held such important positions as president of the American Association of Pathologists and Bacteriologists, president of the American Society for Experimental Pathology, and president of the International Academy of Pathology. Dr. Moon distinguished himself as one of the prominent medical scholars in the world. He passed away in 1974 at the age of fifty-nine.

Professor Joseph Park was born the son of a Korean immigrant family in 1906 in Honolulu. He became one of the outstanding organic fluorine chemists in the United States. He studied at Dayton College and received his Ph.D. from Ohio State University in 1937. He engaged in extensive research for various corporations and became research supervisor for I.E. duPont de Nemour and Co., Delaware, in 1944. He served as a consultant to the armed forces during the Second World War. In 1947, he joined the faculty of the University of Colorado, Boulder, where he became a professor of chemistry in 1953.

He was the first American-born Korean to become head of the Institute of National Academic Sciences of the Republic of Korea (South) in 1972. He worked there for more than two years before returning to the United States, where he was elected president of the International Organic Fluorine Chemical Society.

Dr. Park said that he faced an identity problem when he was young because he did not know whether he was a Korean or an American. Because of the influence of his parents, he decided to work for Korea when it was liberated from Japanese rule in 1945. When he was invited to take over the position of head of the Institute of National Academic Science by the South Korean government, he even considered giving up his American citizenship in order to dedicate himself to the cause of development of Korean scientific institutes. During his two years in Korea, he discovered that Korean students still followed traditional methodology in learning—memorization from a teacher's lectures and textbooks—and that they lacked initiative and the experimental spirit. He also noticed that many Korean educators had a bureaucratic and factional mentality. He thought that Korean businessmen have a tendency to accept the advice of foreign scientists without evaluating that advice in the context of the Korean social and economic situation. He has doubts about how successful the Americanization of Korean enterprises may turn out to be.

Dr. Park also observed that Korean scientific institutions suffer from a lack of facilities and research funds. Accordingly, he was critical of the $1.5 million donation made by the Korean Trade Association to Harvard University, because he felt that this money would be more useful to Korean scientists.

Professor Tai-gyu-Ree, one of the Korean pioneers in science, was born in 1902 in Korea, where he graduated from high school. After attending Hiroshima Normal College, he majored in chemistry at Kyoto Imperial University in Kyoto, Japan. He received the degree of Doctor of Science and joined the university's faculty. From 1939 to 1941, Dr. Ree did post-doctoral work at Princeton University. In 1943, he was the first Korean to become a full professor at Kyoto Imperial University. He taught physical chemistry there until 1945.

Professor Ree returned to Korea at the end of the Second World War and became dean of the Faculty of Science and Engineering at Seoul National University. In 1946, he was appointed dean of the College of Liberal Arts and Science. That same year, he established with his fellow scientists the Korean Chemical Society and was elected its first president. In 1948, Dr. Ree came to the United States and became a professor of chemistry at the University of Utah, where he remained until 1970. Upon his retirement, he became a professor emeritus. At present Dr. Ree serves as a distinguished professor of chemistry at the Advanced Institute of Science and an advisor to the Korean Institute of Science and Technology in Seoul.

Professor Ree joined many American and Korean academic societies, including the American Chemical Society, the Pacific Science Association, the National Academy of Science of Korea, and the Korean Chemical Society. He received various awards, including the *Medial Mugunwha* (the highest award of the Republic of Korea) for his scientific contributions. He also received an honorary degree of Doctor of Science from Seoul National University, and served as South Korea's chief delegate to an international conference on atomic energy held in Vienna.

Professor Ree has done most of his research in chemistry. His work can be classified into four categories: chemical kinetics, catalysis and surface chemistry, molecular rheology, and the theory of liquids. The Ree-Eyring theory of non-Newtonian flow is widely known. "This theory explains very well not only the experimental facts but also the flow mechanism from the molecular viewpoint." In this theory Dr. Ree and his associates assumed the existence of various kinds of flow units with different relation times in a liquid; their flow behavior was described by a "theory of rate processes." With slight modification, the theory of non-Newtonian flow is applicable to thixotropy. The Ree theory of thixotropy has been applied in many instances with great success. Dr. Ree is still working to improve and extend his theory.

Professor Ree published more than one hundred and fifty research papers. The Korean Chemistry Society published *The Collected Works of Taikyu Ree* in two volumes, the first in commemoration of his sixtieth birthday (*han kap*), and the second in celebration of his seventieth birthday in 1972. The preface to the second volume states: "Professor Ree is not only one of the Korean pioneers in science, but he is also Korea's most distinguished chemist. His outstanding personality and his impressive research are highly admired by his students and colleagues."

Judge Herbert Y.C. Choy became the first Oriental appointed to a United States federal court. He was born on January 6, 1916, in the sugar plantation village of Makaweli, Kauai, Hawaii. His parents, Mr. and Mrs. Choy Doo-wook, had come to Hawaii as immigrant children with their respective parents. When Choy was five years old, his family moved to Honolulu, where he grew up. He graduated from the University of Hawaii in 1938. He then attended Harvard Law School and obtained his J.D. in 1941. After passing the bar examination, he decided to work as a clerk in the office of the attorney of the City and County of Honolulu. He entered military service during the Second World War and served for five years with the rank of lieutenant-colonel in the Judge Advocate General's Corps.

He joined the law firm of Fong and Miho as a partner on June 10, 1974. On May 16, 1975, he was appointed by President Nixon to the United States Court of Appeals for the Ninth Circuit.

Choy's appointment was recommended by Senator Hiram L. Fong of Hawaii. It was welcomed by the Asian community in Hawaii because Choy was the first Asian-American to be named to the post. The court's jurisdiction covers nine states: Hawaii, California, Washington, Oregon, Nevada, Arizona, Idaho, Montana, and Alaska. It also includes the territory of Guam. The *Pacific Citizen* wrote: "The Japanese-American Citizens League wholeheartedly supported Choy's appointment to the Ninth Circuit Court of Appeals because (1) Two-thirds of the entire Asian-American residents in the U.S. reside in the nine states covered by the Court, and (2) It is most appropriate that a distinguished Asian-American attorney is named to the post."

Judge Choy belongs to several legal organizations: the Bar Association of Hawaii, the American Bar Association, and the World Peace Through Law Center. He was a member of the committee that compiled the revised laws of Hawaii in 1955. He was also a member of the committee that drafted the state's rules of criminal procedure in 1958 and 1959. He is a director of several corporations and non-profit organizations, including the Consolidated Amusement Co., Ltd., the American Security Bank, the Hawaii Medical Service Association (Blue Shield Plan), the Legal Aid Society of Hawaii, and Hawaii Loa College.

A Korean born American, Hark-joon Paik was appointed by California Governor Edmund G. Brown, Jr. to be a judge of the Superior Court of Monterey County in August 1975. Paik was born in Seoul and came to the United States when he was a high school student. He finished high school in Monterey, where he received first prize in a speech contest sponsored by the Lions Club. He received his J.D. from Stanford University at the age of twenty-four.

Paik worked as a deputy public defender in Ventura and Los Angeles counties and was an assistant city attorney in Burbank. He became the public defender in Monterey County prior to his present post. Judge Park is the youngest (thirty-eight years old) superior court judge in California. He is also the first naturalized Korean-American to sit on the California bench. He has taught at the Monterey College of Law since 1973.

Francis (Myung-do) Whang became one of the first American-born pianists in the Korean community. He is the son of the Reverend and Mrs. Whang Sa-sun. His late father fled Korea in 1913 to avoid Japanese persecution; he belonged to an anti-Japanese secret organization called Sinminhoe (New People's Society). He landed in San Francisco as a political refugee ("student without a passport") and worked on a farm. Later he opened a family-operated tailoring and cleaning shop in San Francisco. In the meantime, he served in the Korean Methodist Church as its first local preacher and later became its minister for more than fourteen years. Francis's mother was a high-school teacher in P'yongyang. She served a three-month jail sentence because she participated in the March First national independence uprising in 1919.

Francis was born the youngest son of the Whang family on September 20, 1936. He watched his mother play the piano, and he himself began to play at the age of four. His mother realized his musical gifts but could not afford private lessons for him because of financial difficulties.

Francis's cousin David was working as a houseboy in the family of Mrs. Henriette Lehman (then Mrs. Durham), who had been helping many needy foreign students, especially Koreans and Chinese. One day, David told Mrs. Lehman about Francis's talent. Francis was invited to play the piano at Mrs.

Lehman's home. She was so impressed that since then, she has financially and morally supported his musical studies. He received private piano lessons from Adolph Baller, Hans Neuman, Rosina Lhevinne, Jeaneane Dowis, and other well-known teachers. He also studied theory at the San Francisco Conservatory of Music and obtained an M.S. from the Juilliard School of Music in New York in 1966.

Whang began giving solo recitals when he was six years old at the San Francisco Conservatory of Music (this author attended a recital). He has performed throughout the United States and South Korea. He was the first Korean-American to perform in his parents' native land. His teaching experiences include Juilliard and Yale, and he is now chairman of the Department of Music at the University of North Carolina at Chapel Hill.

As did other Korean Americans, Francis had many difficulties. He helped his parents in their cleaning and laundry shop after school and during summer vacations. One time, he thought about giving up his music lessons because he would have to compete with white American musicians and he feared he might not be able to make a living as a musician. But encouragement from his mother and the constant financial and moral support of Mrs. Lehman made it possible for him to overcome his doubts.

There are many excellent comments on Francis's piano performances. The most recent article appeared in the *Washington Post* on December 4, 1972. "He has mastered the ways of probing the piano's secrets of attack and of its ability to sustain sound. Whang's artistry made itself most evident in two entirely different worlds, those of Haydn and Schumann. In the latter's 'Carnaval,' he preserved the necessary continuity between the extremes of full-throated brilliance and wispishness that oscillate both within individual sections and from one movement to the next." The *Evening Star and Daily News*, Washington, D.C. reported that "Whang's style is classical, poised, controlled, balanced, elegant."

So the Korean-American from San Francisco became a nationally known pianist.

Ernie Kim, an American-born Korean, is a well-known potter. He is the son of the late Mr. and Mrs. Kim Sung-kwon, early Korean immigrants and long-time residents of Los Angeles. He was born on September 2, 1918, in Manteca, California, and graduated from the Ceramics Craft Studio in Mt. View in 1955. He has been head of the Ceramics Department at the San Francisco Art Institute and is presently director of the Richmond (California) Art Center.

Kim's work has been displayed in numerous places throughout the United States, including the Smithsonian Institute and the Emerson Museum of Art in Syracuse, New York. He has also exhibited at the Cannes Festival and in Buenos Aires. His awards include first prize at the Eleventh

·Pacific Coast Ceramic Exhibit held in San Francisco, and first prize at the Sixth International Exhibit of Ceramic Art, Washington, D.C.

Korean-born Ki-suk Han, known professionally as Nong, has distinguished himself as a natural artist. He never received any formal training in art. Beginning in 1965, his one-man exhibitions have been held in the United States, Korea, China (Taiwan), France, India, and Japan. His work is part of the permanent collection of art museums in major cities of the United States as well as in capital cities of Europe and Asia.

Reviews of Nong's work have appeared in many publications. The *Santa Barbara News Press* wrote: "Nong is a unique creative mind devoted expressively to cultural form of Korean background. The relief polyester techniques are most effectively suited to the subjects of his painting." The *Daily News* of Athens, Georgia, said that "Nong's inventiveness and fresh insight in painting and sculpture have won him wide recognition. He has earned much acclaim, as his art works are owned by museums throughout our country." A French publication commented: "Nong, a Korean painter, is the inheritor of an enduring oriental tradition, his art combines his tradition with the technique of modern painting in composition of great originality."

No comprehensive materials are available at this time as to how many other Korean Americans have contributed to American society. But there is some information about the role of the Korean political scientist in America. Up to the present time, it is estimated that there have been about two hundred Korean-born political scientists engaged in teaching, research, or study in the field of Korean politics as well as other subjects in American institutions of higher education.

From an historical point of view, Korean political scientists can be divided into four groups. The first group came to America as political refugees before and after the annexation of Korea by Japan. These political exiles came both to study and to work for the cause of national independence. A few graduated from such first rank universities as Yale, Harvard, Columbia, Princeton, and the University of California. Most attempted to combine political activism with academic contributions. Dr. Syngman Rhee was a typical example of this group.

The second group came to America after World War II. Its members had great expectations, because they saw a chance to do something for their homeland after completing their studies. Many of them, however, eventually stayed in the United States because the newly established Rhee regime was dictatorial. Some have been working in the academic field and have published a few scholarly books. Professor Lee Chong-sik, the author of *The Politics of Korean Nationalism*, is such a one. He is also co-author with

Robert A. Scalapino of *Communism in Korea*, which received the Woodrow Wilson Award. There is Kim Sei-jin's *The Politics of Military Revolution in Korea*, and Han Sung-Joo's *The Failure of Democracy in South Korea*. These are just a few among the many books written by Korean scholars on political subjects.

The third group dates from the close of the Korean War. Its members are acquainted with the American educational system because South Korean education has been influenced by American methods. It is expected that this group will produce a large number of scholars that will make rich academic contributions in the future.

The fourth group consists of American-born Koreans. In due time, this group will be the most promising group, because its members can serve as a bridge between the two cultures—the Korean culture of their ancestors and the Western culture of their country of birth.

At present, few American-born Koreans are taking leading roles in politics on the national level. However, some are interested in local and state politics. For example, in 1962 Alfred Song, an attorney, became the first American-born Korean to be elected as an assemblyman to the California legislature. In 1966, he was elected to the State Senate from the Twenty-eighth District (Los Angeles). He served as chairman of the Senate Committee on Judiciary, and was the author of a bill which protects newsmen from contempt citations for refusing to surrender unpublished notes, photographs, tapes or films obtained in their gathering of news. This bill became law in 1974.

Gene Roh was the first American-born Korean to be elected to the school board in the Unified Berkeley School District in 1973. He is a graduate of the University of California with a B.A. in criminology. He also holds an M.S. in educational psychology from California State, Hayward. He is employed as a juvenile probation officer with Alameda County. He has involved himself in community affairs and has been chairman of the Asian-American Community Alliance, among other activities. During the election for the school board, Roh advocated multicultural understanding by saying that "the existence of cultural diversity in our community should be a source of pride, not hostility. This diversity creates a responsibility to reduce the institutional aspects of racism." He further said that "our differences are our dignity. Respect is learning how to live with our differences. Physical, verbal, and psychological abuse of our children have no place in the Berkeley school." Roh advocated bilingual education for minority ethnic groups in general and for Asian immigrants' children in particular.

Finally, Dr. Sam Lee was the first American-born Korean to twice win the world diving championship in Olympic competition. His father was one of the early Korean immigrants who worked on a Hawaiian plantation and later operated a restaurant in Los Angeles.

Today there are a few thousand Korean scientists, engineers, and physicians engaged in teaching, research, and practice in the United States. They are potential contributors to American society in the coming decades.

15.

Oral History of Early Koreans in America

At the time of this writing, no more than twelve of the original Korean immigrants to America were still alive. This author was privileged to interview five of the twelve and to record the interviews on tape. Most of the tapes run from one to two hours, and many events have been described by several of the people. Such repetitions are omitted here. It should be pointed out that material from one tape recording has already been used in previous chapters.

YANG CHOO-EN[1]

Yang Choo-en was born in Kaesong (Sondo), which was the capital of the old Koryo Kingdom, on May 25, 1879. His father was an *insam* ("ginseng") merchant. *Insam* is a medicinal herb highly valued by the Koreans and the Chinese, and Kaesong produces the best quality *insam* in Korea. Unfortunately, because of droughts and floods in 1902, Yang's father lost money and had to give up the *insam* business.

Yang studied the Chinese classics at the local Confucian school and helped on his father's *insam* farms. In the autumn of 1902, he met a friend in Seoul who told him that some of his friends were planning to go to Hawaii to work on the sugar plantations. Yang, then twenty-four years old, decided to join the first emigration group, primarily because he believed that he would have an opportunity to learn Western civilization in the United States.

So Yang and his friends went to Chemulpo (today called Inchon), submitted the required application forms, and sailed on the first emigration ship. According to Yang, his steamship fare, including meals, was paid by Hawaiian plantation owners with the understanding that the total expense of one hundred dollars would be deducted from his monthly paychecks over a three-year period. He was also told that he was to work at least three years, although he does not recall signing any contract.

The first Korean emigration ship left Inchon on December 22, 1902.

Yang said: "I could not sleep a few nights, because so many things were in my mind and I worried so much since I did not know what would happen in the new, strange land in Hawaii. I did not know how to speak English and I did not know anything about sugar plantation work either." He remembered that about one hundred immigrants, including women and children, landed in Honolulu in January 1903. A few days later he found that he had been assigned to work at a sugar plantation on Oahu Island.

Then he described plantation camp life and the general working conditions of the plantation fields in Hawaii. "During these early days on the plantation, we all lived in one big camp; the married family men were given small houses for themselves, but the single men lived in the big barracks, which had one big square sleeping room, where there was no privacy. There was one large community kitchen. Those who wanted to cook their own meals, they could do that, but most of the people hired one cook paying six dollars a month, and the cook got free meals. We ate together in one big kitchen. The menus of three meals were almost the same: rice, soup, *kimchi* (Korean hot pickles), and sometimes dry fish or cooked vegetables. The working pattern was the same, day in and day out. We got up early in the morning, about five o'clock, and after eating breakfast everybody went to the plantations by motor-trailer which was driven by a white driver.

"As soon as we arrived on the fields we started to work under the supervision of a *luna* (supervisor) until lunch time, without break. They gave us only a half hour lunch. Then we started again until four-thirty. This meant that we worked ten hours a day and six days a week. Our monthly wage averaged eighteen dollars, but women's average wage was fifteen dollars a month." He added: "It was hard work, but some Korean farmers thought the plantation work was easier than working in the native Korean farm fields, because the plantation owners supplied all necessary tools to do the job."

Yang also recalled that some of the Korean immigrants wore native Korean costumes on the plantation fields in order to save money. The plantation worker's clothes consisted of a white jacket and baggy trousers, which had to be bought by the individual worker with his own money. Yang said that a few Koreans also refused to cut their hair and kept their native hair style, a tied knot with the hair on top of the head. Yang remembers one interesting episode that led Koreans to cut their hair. One of his friends always wore a native hat when he went to work. One morning his hat was blown away by the wind while he was riding the motor-trailer. He tried desperately to catch his hat, and the motor-trailer went off the track. Everybody on the motor-trailer was scared, and the driver threatened to sue him. So all the Koreans offered the driver an apology. Soon after this incident, Koreans who kept their hair and wore native costumes started to have their hair cut and began to wear Western clothes. Within ten days, native Korean costumes had completely disappeared on the working camps.

Yang remembers another episode, which might be called "How to Buy Eggs Without Speaking English." He and his friends wanted to buy eggs from the neighborhood grocery store, but none of them knew the word *eggs*. One of his friends volunteered to try to buy the eggs by using gestures. He took his white handkerchief out of his pocket and put it around his left fist so that it looked like a very large egg. He moved the fist behind his buttocks, and made the sound of a hen that has laid an egg. The grocery clerk understood the gesture and the sound, and brought out a dozen eggs, which Yang's friend thereupon bought.

Yang also remembered a sad story. The medical care on the plantation was very poor, although it was free. When someone got sick, he did not want to go to the doctor because he did not know English and did not know how to explain his trouble to the doctor. The interpreter often made mistakes or could not explain the nature of the illness to the doctor because of his own limitations in speaking English. Most of the doctors who took care of the immigrants were not kind and did not really care about their patients. In short, no real communication was possible between doctors and patients. Yang said, "I saw with my eyes some of my good friends die in the plantation camps. In fact, one of them died in my lap with an unknown illness after he got back from his doctor." He added that "it was a great shock to my life on the plantation camp in the strange land."

As far as Yang knew, every Korean immigrant on his plantation completed three years of labor and repaid the one hundred dollar loan for the steamship fare from Inchon to Hawaii. After three years of working on the plantation, Yang felt free, and he decided to come to San Francisco. He had heard there were plenty of job opportunities and a good community leader, Ahn Ch'ang-ho.

On the matter of racial discrimination, Yang said: "We worked like draft animals, cows and horses, in the plantation fields, and were treated like animals by the *lunas* or foremen during work, even not allowing us to talk or smoke with each other. We lived also like animals in the working camps, which were similar to barns. But we Korean immigrants did not protest against the inhumane treatment by the plantation owners, because first, we did not know enough language to express our hardships to the superiors, and second, we were always in fear of losing our jobs in case we complained against their treatment. Third, the interpreters and foremen had a tendency of taking sides with the plantation owners because they were paid well. Under these given circumstances, we thought that we were just helpless human beings in the white man's society."

However, Yang said that the Koreans were strongly anti-Japanese while working on the sugar plantation fields. Koreans hated working with the Japanese on the same plantations, but occasionally the foremen ordered everybody to work together in order to get the work done at one time. Often fist fights took place between Japanese and Koreans. Most of the time Koreans won the fight, because many Koreans were ex-soldiers who knew how to subdue the enemy. Because of such unfortunate incidents, the Japanese consul-general in Hawaii advised the Japanese to stay away from the Koreans as much as possible and to avoid any physical violence with them. The anti-Japanese feelings within the Korean community in Hawaii became even stronger when news came that Japan had forced the Korean government to sign the Protectorate Treaty soon after the Russo-Japanese War. Some ex-soldiers wanted to return to Korea in order to clean up the pro-Japanese Korean leaders in Seoul.

Yang saved enough money to pay his steamship fare from Hawaii to San Francisco and landed there in April 1906. He met Ahn Ch'ang-ho, whom he respected as a patriotic leader, and told him that he would like to study at an American institution of higher education. In the meantime, he wanted to help Ahn with his community work. Unfortunately, the San Francisco earthquake occurred even before Yang had a chance to settle down. As he recalls, there were about fifty Korean residents in San Francisco. Fortunately none were killed and only one was injured when the quake threw him to the ground. As an emergency measure, all Koreans moved to Oakland to set up relief headquarters there. Yang remembers that the relief goods including money, clothes, food, and other articles came not only from Korean communities in the United States but also from Mexico, Cuba, and Korea as well as from American relief organizations.

Yang also told of one previously unknown episode that happened during this period. Perhaps as a good-will gesture, the Japanese consul-general in San Francisco sent relief goods, including clothing, food, and money. But the Koreans agreed to reject the Japanese offer because accepting it would have political implications and would harm the cause of the national independence movement. However, one Korean leader, Mr. X, who had started Christian church services in 1903 in a private home on Ellis Street, received the Japanese relief goods in secret and used them for himself. When this affair became known to other Korean leaders, he was advised to return the goods to the Japanese authorities. He refused to do so; whereupon a few concerned Koreans threatened to bring the matter before the Korean community and to try him as a traitor in front of a Korean people's jury. The frightened Mr. X. fled from the Korean community, and nobody knows what has happened to him since.

Yang became a charter member of the Korean Methodist Church (now called San Francisco Unified Korean Methodist Church, located at 1123 Powell Street), which was formally established on April 15, 1906, with the approval of the Board of Mission of the Southern Methodist Church. At first the congregation rented a house on California Street. Later, worship was conducted at the Korean National Building on Oak Street. The present church building was constructed in 1928 at a cost of eighteen thousand dollars. Yang remembers the names of all the ministers who served in the Korean church: Mr. Ryang Ju-sam, Mr. Yun Byong-koo, Mr. Lee Dae-wii (David Lee), Mr. Wahng Sa-sun, Mr. Kim Ha-tai, Mr. Lim Doo-wha, Mr. Ahn Byong-joo, and Mr. Song Jeung-neul (Charles Song), the present pastor. Yang became a local preacher of the church in 1915 and still (February 27, 1974) holds that title.

Today, Yang is the only living eyewitness of the sensational Stevens assassination, which took place in front of the San Francisco Ferry Building on March 23, 1908. As discussed in detail in Chapter 8, Durham W. Stevens was a pro-Japanese Korean government foreign officer. At an interview with American news correspondents in San Francisco, he asserted that Japanese control of Korea was working for the benefit of the country. The Korean community was outraged by his statement and sent its delegates, headed by Choy Chung-ik, to meet Stevens at the Fairmont Hotel to demand an apology. When Stevens refused to retract his statement, Chung Chae-kwan, one of the delegates, attacked Stevens.

The Koreans held a second meeting to discuss the next step to be taken against Stevens. Yang attended that meeting. As he recalls, Chun Myung-woon, a member of the Mutual Cooperation Association, said: "I will take care of that pro-Japanese on my own." Every Korean knew Chun as a man of action and expected him to take violent action against Stevens. At this meeting, Yang noticed that another man, Chang In-hwan, was also present. Chang, however, was known as a very quiet and shy Christian gentleman. As far as Yang recalls, Chang did not speak even one word at the meeting. Since at that time no Oriental was able to buy a gun, Chun purchased a toy gun with which to attack Stevens. However, Chang In-hwan secured a real gun from his roommate and took it with him to the Ferry Building where Stevens was to leave for Washington, D.C., by train from Oakland. Yang and other Korean residents were assembled in front of the Ferry Building when Stevens arrived in a limousine provided by the Japanese consul-general. At once, Chun Myung-woon struck Stevens with his toy gun, and the two men engaged in a fight. At this juncture, Chang fired three shots. The first struck Chun by mistake; the second and third shots hit Stevens's chest, and he fell to the ground. Yang recalls that it was about 9:30 A.M. on March 23, 1908.

He heard a crowd of white people shouting "Lynch the Oriental devils."
Stevens was taken to Saint Francis Hospital by ambulance. Chang and
Chun were apprehended by the police.

The crowd was angry at the violent action taken by Koreans against the
white American. At this confused and emotional moment, Lee Hak-hyun,
who was one of the delegates of the Korean community, appealed to the
public: "We Koreans had to take this kind of action, because Mr. Stevens
has been pro-Japanese for many years and he even justifies the Japanese
domination of Korea. We Korean residents in San Francisco, who escaped
from the Japanese barbarous rule, knew that hundreds and thousands of
Koreans have been persecuted by Japanese military and police forces,
because they have advocated freedom and liberty as you Americans did
during the Independence War against Great Britain." After Lee finished his
speech, the crowd began to calm down and break up.

The ninety-seven-year-old Yang concluded his account of this incident
by saying that "I have still one regret, because I was not fast enough to pick
up Stevens's briefcase that was left on the ground when he got shot." It was
picked up by the Japanese consul-general. Yang said that had a Korean
grabbed the briefcase, we might have been able to know about some of the
secret documents that Stevens had planned to present to the State Department or to the president of the United States about the future of Korea.

Yang talked about the Korean language schools. "Many immigrants
who came to Hawaii did not know even the Korean alphabet, and evening
and Saturday Korean schools were established in every Korean community
to teach adults as well as immigrant children." At this time, "every Korean
overseas thought that Japan would destroy the Korean history and culture,
so that we Koreans in America thought we should preserve our culture and
urged Koreans to support the Korean school financially." This news reached
Korean government diplomatic offices overseas. Yang remembers that one
Korean diplomatic officer, Lee Byum-chin, who was then working at the
Korean Embassy in Moscow, sent a donation of one hundred dollars to the
Korean language school. Lee committed suicide in 1910 as a sign of protest
against the Japanese annexation of Korea.

Yang also remembers a Japanese atrocity which was never known to the
general public. A Korean patriot named Namkung Kwan planted the Rose
of Sharon, the Korean national flower, in his back yard in Seoul. The
Japanese police discovered it and beat him to death. Yang was so upset by
this inhuman act that he never forgot it. About twenty years later, he came
across ten Rose of Sharon plants at a neighborhood nursery in San Francisco. He bought them all, and in memory of Namkung, divided them
among his friends. He planted one in the yard of the Korean Methodist
Church and another in the front yard of the Korean consulate at 3500 Clay

Street. He still has a few Rose of Sharon plants at his apartment. He kindly gave one to this author when this interview took place.

After Yang landed in San Francisco, he had two different occupations: farming in Sacramento for a few years, and a restaurant business for forty years until his retirement. He married Jae-hyun in 1913 and has three children. The late Mrs. Yang was very active in the Korean community as a lifetime member of the Korean Methodist Church, the Korean National Association, and the Korean Women's Patriotic Association. Yang is one of the two original members of the Korean National Association, founded in 1909, and a loyal subscriber to *New Korea*, the only surviving Korean-language weekly newspaper from the period of the early immigrants. He had a complete file of issues dating from 1909. He donated the entire collection to the Korean National Library in Seoul in 1961. He was also one of the eight original members of the *Hung Sa Dan* (Young Korean Academy), which was established in 1913 by Ahn Ch'ang-ho.

When asked about his independence movement activities, Yang said, "I never have been, so to speak, a 'front man'; I have always worked behind the scenes by helping leaders and young students who have been fighting for the restoration of national independence." He said that he helped hundreds of young Korean students who came to America for their studies. Almost all of them ate free meals at his restaurant for a few days or even weeks until they departed on their way. Some did not have any money, and he and his wife prepared lunches and dinners that they could eat on the train or bus. Some did not have proper clothing to wear at school. So the Yangs bought them such items as underwear, shirts, and shoes.

Yang said somewhat proudly, "Dr. Syngman Rhee stayed in my home for three months after he was married, because they did not have enough money and weren't able to afford staying at a hotel. I served my home cooking to them after closing the restaurant. I still remember that Dr. and Mrs. Rhee liked my cooking and said, 'We never have had such delicious soup anywhere in the United States.'" He also mentioned that Dr. Kim Kiusic stayed at the Yang home for a few months. He did not have any money to buy a train ticket to go to Washington, D.C., to attend an important conference on the Korean independence movement. Yang said that "After I had a talk with my wife, we borrowed $150 from our life insurance company and bought the train ticket for Dr. Kim." He added: "I never have been a rich man, but I donated hundreds and thousands of dollars to the Korean community and independence movement as well as the Korean church activities. I think I used my money for worthy causes."

Yang visited South Korea twice. In 1961, the South Korean government invited him as an official guest. In 1973, the Korean Air Lines (KAL) extended a special invitation to him to be a guest of honor for the line's first anniversary. He said: "I saw many changes in South Korea, new buildings, new highways, schools, and hospitals. I felt that I was in a foreign land, because it was my first visit since I left Korea in 1902 as an immigrant to Hawaii." He continued by saying, "I have met many old friends and many new people. I was overwhelmed with their kindness and expressions of appreciation for what I have done for them when they were in America." His most happy occasion was a visit to his old friend, Park Induk, at his school in Seoul, where he sent all his collections, papers, and pictures in hopes of establishing some kind of memorial library. He said that "more than eight hundred students greeted me and they treated me like some kind of home-coming hero or high government official."

He sadly said, "I had hoped to visit my hometown, Kaesong, but this time I just looked at the city from afar because it is under the North Korean regime. . . . Next time I hope I can go over there and see my birthplace."

When this author asked him what his last wish was, he replied: "Reuni-fication of the country; as far as I am concerned, there is no reason to remain a divided country. After all, we are all Koreans, whether Communists or non-Communists."

As a final question, I asked, "What kind of advice would you like to pass on to the new generation in the Korean community in America?" Yang took a moment, then he said, "Well, it would seem that the younger genera-tion knows everything; they are better educated and they might not need my advice. But I want to say that they should first take care of themselves and their families financially. Some of them look to me and try to show off by buying expensive homes, furniture, and cars, even without much money or savings in their own hands. Their life styles and ways of thinking are markedly different from that of my generation. My generation had always thought about our motherland, how to restore the national independence, and we spent our money and energy for that cause. Today's new generation does not need to think about that problem; instead, they have to think of how to reunite the divided motherland without war. In the meantime, I wish that the new generation should become more community-conscious and do something about improving the Korean community here. They should par-ticipate in the community affairs; after all, this is their community to live in America."

At the time of this writing (1974), Yang was still in good health and his memories were clear. Every Korean in the Bay Area knows him and calls him Yang *harabaji* ("great grandpa" Yang). He lives alone in an apartment, takes daily walks, and goes to church every Sunday.

THE REVEREND MR. WHANG SA-SUN[2]

The Reverend Mr. Whang Sa-sun was born October 18, 1885, in

Wiwha-myun, Eiju-kun, Pyongan Pukdo (North Korea). He was the youngest son of Mr. and Mrs. Whang Kae-chung. His father died in 1895, when Sa-sun was nine years of age, and his mother died the following year. He had three older brothers and four sisters.

Sa-sun was raised in the home of his oldest brother, Sa-yung. He was influenced toward Christianity at an early age by his older sister, Sa-sung. He studied Chinese literature and the Chinese classics for about eight years in an old Confucian-type school. When he was sixteen years old, he entered Sung Sill High School on the advice of his older sister. It was a Presbyterian missionary school located in Pyongyang, the present capital of North Korea. There he received a Christian education under the guidance of Dr. William Baird, the principal. Later, he graduated from Sung Sill College, the only Christian college in North Korea. He taught at Sin Sung High School for two years and then at Yung Sill High School for two years (both Christian missionary schools).

As a high school teacher, he joined the secret patriotic society *Sinmin-hoe* (New People's Society), formed to combat Japanese domination of Korea. When the Japanese began to arrest members of the *Sinmin-hoe*, he was forced to leave Korea. In order to disguise himself, he put on Western clothes, and he and his wife crossed the Yalu River during the night. He remembers that it was risky, because the river wasn't quite frozen. From Manchuria, they travelled to Shanghai by train; this time they wore Chinese clothes to conceal themselves from the eyes of the Japanese secret police.

From Shanghai they boarded the *Mongolia* and landed in San Francisco on April 12, 1913, without a passport but under the sponsorship of the Reverend Lee Dae-wii (David Lee). Mr. Lee was a representative of the Korean National Association, which was recognized by the U.S. government as a sort of unofficial consulate for Koreans in America. Upon their arrival, they were supposed to go to Upland, California, to work for the Korean community. This had been arranged by Sa-sun's older brother, the Reverend Whang Sa-yong, who had come to America in 1904 as a student. Lacking money for the trip, Sa-sun went instead to a farm in Stockton. It was a tomato farm, and this work was his first experience with manual labor. "My first work assignment was to plant tomatoes. Three men worked as a team; the first man [dug] the hole, the second planted tomato seeds, and the third covered the hole and watered it. I was assigned to plant the tomato seeds." He continued: "Everybody was working faster than I was, and I had a hard time following the other two. I waited for lunch time to come so that I could rest for awhile. When lunch time came, I did not eat my lunch, because the weather was so hot and I was very tired and lost my appetite. Instead of eating my lunch, I laid down on the ground and rested until the others finished their lunch. When I finished my day's work, I hardly could walk back to my rooming house. . . . During the night I was unable to sleep, because my whole body was sore and I felt pains all over." The Reverend Whang said with a big smile, "I returned to San Francisco after one day of work on the tomato farm."

In San Francisco, he held all kinds of odd jobs before starting his own business, a tailoring and cleaning shop on Mason Street. The Reverend Whang said that during this period, the Alien Land Act made it impossible for Asians to buy real estate. When he started business, he even had a hard time renting a store because of the anti-Asian feeling among white landowners. However, with financial help from his brother and other friends, he was finally able to open the cleaning and tailoring shop.

Immediately upon his arrival in San Francisco, he became a member of the Korean National Association and the *Hung Sa Dan* (Young Korean Academy), organizations in which he retained his membership until his death. He also joined the Korean Methodist Church and studied at the Pacific School of Religion in Berkeley. In 1915, he was appointed a local preacher in the church. In 1920, Bishop H.W. Duboce ordained him as an associate minister, and in 1928, Bishop Sam Hay appointed him the minister of the church and ordained him an elder. Mr. Whang then served for fourteen years as minister of the Korean Methodist Church. In 1930, he had the privilege of helping dedicate the present building at 1123 Powell Street for the Korean community as its first edifice on the mainland. Mr. Whang served as vice-chairman of the Korean National Association and as chairman of the *Hung Sa Dan*.

During his service as minister, hundreds of Korean students and political refugees received advice, counsel, and help in securing jobs. Many stayed at his home until they found a place to live or secured employment.

Mr. Whang was a man of integrity and high ideals. He never compromised the principles in which he believed. He possessed keen judgment, and always made clear distinctions between private and community interests. He gave no attention to his own personal gain or glory but always concerned himself with the welfare and interests of others.

He retired from the ministry in 1942, because he thought that someone with more contact with American society and a higher academic background could better serve the growing Korean community and the second and third generations. Another instance of his humble attitude took place when he was awarded a citation by the Korean Residents' Association in San Francisco for his service to the Korean community and to the national independence movement. He refused the award, saying, "I have not done enough for the independence of Korea; there were many patriots who gave their lives during the Japanese occupation and they are the ones to be honored." He went on to say, "The struggle for independence has been every Korean's duty and I have done merely that."

The Reverend Whang was a faithful Christian servant. He served twenty-seven years as a servant of God in the Korean Methodist Church. He believed that the Bible was the spiritual food for his daily life. After he retired from the ministry, he read the Bible every day and prayed for the reunification of Korea. He felt that the Korean War was a tragedy in human history, and he believed that reunification could be achieved through peaceful means.

His unselfish, humble, and kind example influenced many Koreans in America as well as members of his own family. Many of his friends and relatives believe that although the Reverend Whang has departed from the Korean community, his noble ideals and principles will remain in their minds. One of his grandchildren wrote: "Through his quiet and perservering example, my grandfather, Reverend Whang Sa-sun, has influenced me and has given me strength, for he could have allowed the drudgery of running a cleaning shop, which he had to do in order to survive, [to] defeat him; and he could have given in to the disappointment of not continuing his education and not fulfilling his intellectual potentials. Instead, he sustained himself through his Christian beliefs, his patriotic spirit and his personal ideals and values." His final advice to his children and grandchildren was: "Keep your Koreanness, although you are an American citizen."

KIM HYUNG-SOON[3]

Kim was eighty-nine years old in 1975 and one of the most successful businessmen in the Korean community. He was born on May 4, 1886, in Tong-gun, Korea. He came to Hawaii in 1903 as an interpreter on a plantation. He had learned English at the American missionary school, *Paejae Haktang*, in Seoul. He worked three years as an interpreter on Maui and was paid well, seventy-five dollars per month. He thinks the plantation owners treated Korean workers no better than cows or horses, as animals rather than as human beings. Every worker was called by number, never by name. During working hours, nobody was allowed to talk, smoke, or even stretch his back. A foreman kept his eyes on his workers at all times. When he found anyone violating working regulations, he whipped the violator without mercy. If the worker showed any signs of resistance, he would be fired at once. Working hours were from six o'clock in the morning to half-past four in the afternoon. Kim said that "the plantation work was very hard work but some of the Koreans did not know how to work." He also noticed that "some of the Koreans were lazy and wanted to live without hard work." He remembers the condition of the living quarters of the plantation workers;

there were wood floors, and the workers had to sleep on the floor with one blanket. There was only one toilet and one kitchen in each camp. No separate facilities were provided for male and female workers. The inside of the camp was dirty and was full of bad odors.

Kim returned to Korea in 1909 with some money he had saved but came back for a second time to the United States in 1913 because he could not stand Japanese rule. He finished high school in Los Angeles and then started to work as a farmer in Dinuba. In 1916, he settled down in Reedley and concentrated on the orchard and nursery businesses. In 1921, he established the Kim Brothers Company with his friend Kim Ho (Charles Kim) as a partner.

Since they did not have much capital, they began as trucking wholesalers of fruit and nursery products. Then they gradually expanded into orchards, fruit packing houses, and nurseries. Kim Hyung-soon and his American friend, Anderson, who had been one of his employees, began developing new varieties of fruit trees. They worked mainly with peaches and nectarines. It took about ten years to produce a "fuzzless peach," which today is sold on the market as "Le Grand" and "Sun Grand." The year of success for this new fruit was 1952, when the Kim Brothers Company obtained a patent for it. Kim said: "We felt that we were the first Orientals who invented a new fruit for the American people and would be the first Korean millionaires in the Korean community." Kim mentioned that since 1952, average net profit ran from $250,000 to $1 million per year. They had two fruit-packing houses, one in Reedley and the other in Fresno. The nursery business also became prosperous, and they installed a new nursery at a cost of $500,000. Kim recalled the cold facts of business life in America. Once, his company was sued over the issue of the patent by a competitive firm owned by Caucasian businessmen. Kim Brothers offered a compromise settlement outside of court, but the other company refused to accept the offer. Kim believes the company's owners thought they would win in court because they were white and their opponents were Oriental. Kim Brothers hired the best qualified lawyers in town and finally won the case. As far as Kim's memory goes, it was the first case in a California court where Orientals won against white businessmen.

Kim described the living conditions and wages of employees. When they started the orchard business in the 1920s, the hourly wage ranged from twenty to twenty-three cents for a ten-hour day. After the Second World War, the hourly wage averaged from seventy-five cents to one dollar. There were six working days per week and during the busy season, seven days a week with no overtime pay. Work started at six o'clock in the morning and ended at five o'clock in the afternoon with a one hour break for lunch. Living quarters were provided free by the company. Some of the workers lived in the camp, while others lived in rooming houses run by Koreans.

Average living expenses in the 1920s ranged from ten to fifteen dollars; during the war, from twenty to twenty-five dollars. The total number of employees had also varied throughout the years depending on the season and business outlook, but the average number was two hundred and fifty. As far as the nationality of workers was concerned, Mexicans were predominant, because they were hard workers and more obedient than the other nationalities. Koreans, including students during the summer vacations, usually numbered between fifty and seventy. According to Kim's experience, the Korean students were rather poor workers. Some had no physical work experience at all, while many left their jobs after only a few hours or two or three days. Kim said that the Koreans complained most; they expected better pay and better treatment than other nationalities from Korean employers. But Kim added that he never treated Koreans differently because they were Koreans. "When you are in business you have to treat the employees equally," he said. He also found that Korean women were better workers than Korean men. The women made more money than the men doing piece-work.

It would seem that Kim learned a great deal about business management from the Hawaiian plantation owners when he worked as an interpreter for Korean immigrants. For example, he provided free living quarters for the workers; he used white foremen instead of Koreans or other Orientals to supervise the workers; and he did not pay any overtime.

After more than forty years in the orchard and nursery business, the Kim Brothers Company was sold in 1962 for $1.4 million. Kim and his partner retired and took on a more active role in Korean community affairs. Kim joined the Korean National Association and at one time served as chairman of its executive committee. He also established a Korean church in Reedley and financed all its expenses. He was one of the founders of the Korean Foundation, which provided scholarships to needy Korean students. He donated $10,000 to set up the Korean community center in Los Angeles. He was interested in helping Korean orphanages and donated $750 annually until 1974.

After the Korean War, Kim visited South Korea twice. In 1966, he was one of the overseas Korean leaders invited by the South Korean government to attend the National Liberation Day celebration on August 15. In 1974, he visited Seoul to join his present wife.

Kim has never applied for naturalization to be an American citizen. He wants to die as a Korean, since he fought for the restoration of national independence and Korea now is independent, although divided in two. When this author asked, "What is your last wish?" Kim replied with a smile, "I would like to go back to Korea and work for the country. . . . Perhaps I will run for election as a national assemblyman."

WARREN Y. KIM (KIM WON-YONG)[4]

Kim Won-yong was born in Seoul on December 25, 1896. He studied Chinese literature and the classics. He joined a guerrilla group that was fighting against the Japanese. He escaped from Korea in 1917 and came to the United States to study Western government, especially the judicial system. He attended several universities, including the University of Southern California, but was forced to give up his studies because of financial difficulties. Like other Korean intellectuals, he did all kinds of odd jobs. Sometimes he ventured into small businesses but without success.

After 1930, Kim was interested in Korean community affairs and devoted his time and energy to the cause of national independence. "I served for many decades for the restoration of Korean independence and I am glad I did," he said. Then he read a prepared text listing all the public positions he held from 1930 to 1957.

In July 1930, he went to Honolulu to attend the All-Korean Unity Conference as the representative of Koreans on the mainland. In January 1931, he was appointed to the editorial staff of the *Korean National Herald* in Honolulu (now defunct). In January 1933, he served as general secretary of the Korean National Association of Hawaii. In January 1936, he became an editor of the *Korean National Herald*. In April 1941, he was appointed a delegate from Hawaii to the All-Korean Unity Conference. In August 1941, he was elected secretary of the board of directors and a member of the executive board of the United Korean Committee in America. In April 1945, he was elected chairman of the board of directors of the United Korean Committee in America. In October 1945, he went to Seoul as vice-chairman of the Korean delegation team from the United States. In December 1946, he was appointed by General John R. Hodge, the commander of United States armed forces in South Korea, to be an interim national assemblyman; he served as vice-chairman of the Judicial Committee of the National Assembly. In January 1951, he was elected a member of the central committee of the Korean National Association of North America. In December 1957, he published *Chaemi Hanin Osipnyon-sa* (A Fifty Year History of the Koreans in America).

Kim recalled three unforgettable events in which he was directly involved. The first was his attempt to bring about unity among Korean factional leaders. When Japan invaded Manchuria in the 1930s, the Korean leaders in America resumed their independence movement activities. However, they had been divided since the 1919 national uprising. About this time, Syngman Rhee came to the mainland and appealed to Korean leaders to patch up their differences and to work for independence. As a result, the Korean leaders met in Chicago, chose Warren Kim as a mediator to settle factional disputes, and sent him to Hawaii. As Kim recalls, the unity confer- ence was held on July 16, 1930, in Honolulu, and most of the organizational leaders agreed in principle to the necessity for unity in the Korean community.

However, in the midst of negotiation, Rhee changed his mind and issued a statement demanding unity on his own terms. The leaders thought this meant accepting his policy unconditionally, and therefore rejected it. Rhee then asked Kim Hyun-ku, editor of the *Korean National Herald*, to publish his article. Kim refused and said that such an article would be detri- mental to the unity movement. Rhee then began attacking both Warren Kim and the editor of the *Korean National Herald*. He labeled them undesirable characters in the Korean community who wanted to destroy the unity effort. And in fact, the unity attempt was aborted.

Warren Y. Kim's second task was to establish the Korean Foundation. He returned to California from South Korea in 1948 just before Rhee came into power. A few Korean leaders thought that future activities in the United States should center on the field of higher education by providing financial aid to needy young Korean students. Finally, in May 1957, the three Kims of Reedly—Kim Ho (Charles H. Kim), Kim Hyung-soon (Harry Kim), and Warren Kim—and other Korean businessmen established the Korean Foun- dation as a non-profit organization. The Kim Brothers Corporation donated a half million dollars worth of real estate. Warren Kim served as treasurer of the Foundation. He said that 226 students received scholarship funds at three Korean universities, Kunkook, Ewha Women's University, and Chungnam University. The Foundation paid out more than three hundred thousand dollars before being dissolved in 1968.

The last major activity in which Warren Y. Kim was involved was the unsuccessful effort to reform the Korean National Association. Some of the Association's leaders, including Warren Kim himself, thought that the objec- tives of the Association no longer served the interests of the Korean com- munity since its main objective—restoration of national independence—had been achieved when Japan was defeated by the Allied powers. Therefore, the Association had to adopt new guidelines and principles in conformity with the needs of the Korean community in America.

The leadership of the traditional generation was more or less out of date in terms of age as well as intellectual scholarship. The reform movement was launched by the three Kims, known as the Reedley group. Among other things, they proposed a policy of democratization of the Korean commu- nity and promotion of higher education. These measures, they argued, would serve to recruit younger members into the Association. But the reform measures were rejected by the majority of the members of the Asso- ciation at the annual conference held in 1959 in Los Angeles. The majority believed that the 1937 constitution of the Association contained principles similar to those of the reform. They also wanted to retain the name—Korean National Association—which had a more than fifty-year history in the United States. Warren Y. Kim said that "no compromise was possible with the so-called majority members of the traditional association, and we withdrew our membership from the Association altogether."

In 1963, the three Kims and Song Chul, one of the charter members of the *Tongji-hoe*, established the Korean Center in Los Angeles to be used as a meeting place. Then, in 1965, they organized the *Hanin-hoe* (Korean Association) of California. Many new intellectuals joined and became leaders. The Korean Center building was purchased with a seventy thousand dollar donation from the Reedley Kims, Song Chul, South Korean President Park Chung-hee, and many others. The organization changed its name twice; today it is called the Korean Association of Southern California.

Warren Y. Kim concluded by saying that "I retired actually in 1968, and now live quietly here, at 4609 6th Avenue, Los Angeles, with my wife." He was a living political historian of the Korean community in America, and his death was a great loss. Many Koreans admired him as a man of principle and a patriot who served the community well.

GLORIA HAHN TELLS ABOUT "MY MOTHER, HELEN KIM"[5]

"My mother was born in Chul San, Pyongan Pukdo, Korea. She says that she was born in 1899, but I'm not sure that she means 1898 or 1900, because a child born in Korea is cosidered to be a year old at birth. She can't remember now; besides, it doesn't really matter.

"Her name is Helen Kim. There are several Helen Kims. My mother is the one who wrote a series of columns on Korean history in *New Korea* and throughout the years contributed various articles and poems to the same newspaper. Her childhood name is Pahl Bok (Eight Blessings) but when she grew up, she took on the name Helen. She liked the sound of it and associated the name with Helen of Troy.

"When she was sixteen, my mother was betrothed to my father, Kim Lhrong Sun. My mother wasn't interested in marriage; she wanted to be one of those women who were beginning to break away from the traditional role of Korean women. She'd rather pursue an education, perhaps even a career. The idea had been stimulated by missionaries from the West.

"At that time, 1916, my mother and her family lived in Sun Chun where Presbyterian missionaries from the United States had become respected members of the community. When they were among themselves, the Koreans made fun of the large nose and peculiar odor of the foreigners; still, they respected the missionaries because the missionaries brought new learning and a chance at an education. The only other choice the Koreans had for schooling was under the Japanese, and patriotic Koreans would not subject themselves to any message delivered by Japanese educators.

"My father attended the missionary high school and worked in the home of the school's president. When he sought my mother's hand in marriage, my father asked the president to speak to my grandmother on his behalf. My grandmother couldn't say no to the esteemed president of the high school and agreed to the betrothal. Any aspirations my mother had for her own future were thus aborted and, in spite of her protests to my grandparents, she conformed to tradition and did as her parents bade her to do.

"By 1916, Koreans had already begun to leave Korea for political or economic reasons or both. The same reasons that drew other immigrants to the United States drew Koreans.

"In my father's case, his family owned the land they farmed, but there wasn't enough of it to go around. The only other experience he had was that of a student. As poorly prepared as he was, encouraged by his missionary employer, he decided to leave Korea to try his luck in a new society on the other side of the world. My father left for the United States. The plan was to have my mother join him when he had earned and sent the money for her passage. They weren't married yet, but he wasn't worried, the marriage agreement had been made.

"While she waited for my father to send for her, my mother went to P'yongyang to attend a school where she would learn Japanese and earn the *hun-do* certificate. The certificate was designed to enable the recipient to apply for a civil-service job. I asked her why she did that when she knew she was going to be married. 'I just wanted to,' she replied.

"In Los Angeles, my father landed a job as a dishwasher. From his meager earnings, he saved enough money to send for my mother. It must have taken almost every penny he earned.

"On July 19, 1917, my mother arrived in San Francisco aboard the S.S. *China*. She was detained on Angel Island for two days. 'I was really lucky,' she recalled, 'some Koreans were kept there for weeks.' She was met by Mr. Suh, a friend of the family, who escorted her to Los Angeles where she was met by my father. My mother stayed with the Suhs. Mrs. Suh was from my mother's hometown and she called my mother 'sister.'

"Although my mother never had to work in Korea, she felt that she should earn some money before getting married, so she took what she thought was to be a live-in job as a domestic in a Christian family's home. According to my mother: 'Mr. Park, who ran an employment service, told me it was a permanent job. He thought it was. I packed a suitcase and he took me to work. They told me to clean the stove. It was so dirty that I got all black myself. I worked and scrubbed so hard. . . . I never worked like that before. After they made me work all day, the lady said she didn't need me anymore, and then paid me two dollars. Can you imagine! What could I do? I just called Mr. Park to come and get me and take me home. He was really surprised and when we were going home we were both disgusted and said, "What a good Christian home!"'

"My mother tried other domestic work and found she hated it, especially cleaning toilets. There was no point in delaying the wedding any longer; she borrowed twenty dollars for a wedding outfit and set the date. Mr. Lee, the friend who loaned the twenty dollars, offered to pay for the reception.

"It rained on the wedding day and in the excitement, my father forgot to take off his galoshes. Around eighty Korean friends and a couple of Caucasians from my father's place of work had gathered for the ceremony. They all laughed about the galoshes afterwards. My mother still laughs when she tells about it, some sixty years after it happened.

"The Korean community was small then and everyone knew everyone else. They helped each other whenever they could, so my parents lived with the Suhs until my mother became pregnant. My mother and father moved into a rooming house and my mother, knowing she could never work for anyone and knowing that there was little future in dishwashing, suggested that they start their own business. She convinced my father.

"Filled with anxiety but greatly excited, they carefully set up boxes of fruit on a street corner and waited to see what fortune had in store for them. They had become their own boss and thrown their lot into the capitalistic society. That was in 1918.

"By 1927, my father had moved in and out of partnerships in the retail produce business, building up his capital with each move, finally settling into his own wholesale produce business. He began to make a lot of money.

"My mother stayed home to raise a family, breaking the monotony of homemaking by being a charter member of the Women's Patriotic League, writing for Korean newspapers, and working actively in her church.

"Her children grew up in the Korean community, going to Korean language schools along with attending American schools. They spoke Korean at home and, when they were old enough, dated Koreans their own age. They were sent to Korean churches and taken to Korean independence meetings on March First. Life for my mother's family was an amalgamation of things Korean and things American, but mostly Korean.

"It was all working out fine as long as my father provided for his family, a wife and six children, sheltering them with financial security. But he became careless with his money and when he died in 1937, he had lost his business, all his money, leaving my mother nothing.

"My mother was faced with raising six children alone with no help in sight. It was the hardest time of her life. The independence she cherished with a passion was threatened by her need to turn to friends for help. Finally, she had no choice but seek help from the state itself. I remember the first time she went to pick up her allotment of food; she came home and cried. As soon as she could, she went off welfare. She was ashamed to be on it and was determined to manage without it.

"She survived and kept her family intact. She took in sewing and stayed her own boss. A try at a second marriage, this time with a man of her own choice, failed. Finding herself alone the second time was easier than the first; the children were growing up, working, or getting married. Throughout the difficult times, she remained her own boss. After her children married and left her to start a family of their own, she lived by herself as long as she could.

"My mother is in her late seventies now [1975]. Her family has grown to include twenty grandchildren. Her children have all but forgotten how to speak Korean. Of her twenty grandchildren, only one speaks Korean. My mother has to use her broken English to communicate with her family.

"Many of her friends have died, and she doesn't know who of her family in Korea lives. Does she want to return to Korea? 'Only for a visit,' she says. 'My home is with my children.'

"As have other Koreans, my mother has lived through the admixture of patriotic fervor for Korea while adapting to American ways. She shared a sense of community and knew the comradeship of steadfast friends apart from the mainstream of American society. If the measure of one's life is in his response to the human condition under ordinary circumstances, the measure of my mother's life is in her response under extraordinary circumstances. Her response has been heroic. She can claim experiences her children and grandchildren will never have."

HANNAH SURH'S LIFE IN THE UNITED STATES[6]

"I came to the United States in 1948 on a student visa, obtained my citizenship in 1964, and retired in 1975 from a sixteen-year social work career in the YWCA of San Francisco, and my life in the United States can [be] said to consist solely of my life in the YWCA and the years I spent attending college. Thus it is with some pride and satisfaction that I review my experiences during the nearly thirty years that I have lived in this country as I believe I have made a few lasting contributions that affect the lives of people for the better.

"Actually, it had been far from my intention to join the YWCA when I received my graduate degree in social work from the University of Michigan in 1957. Having majored in community organization, my first attempts to find employment were with community organization agencies in New York City and in Washington, D.C. New York I gave up in one week. I was staying with a friend who lived in a cold-water flat in Greenwich Village—noisy and crowded—and after fighting my way in subway travel in the summer heat and being rejected at one agency after another, I suddenly decided that New York City was not a place in which I wanted to live. In Washington, D.C., the employment situation was as discouraging, though the counselor at the employment service agency made every effort to please me. The problem seemed to be that because community organization as a social work discipline was fairly new, community organization agencies would not employ a major in the field without some previous social work experience, and neither would case work or group work agencies employ someone who had not majored in their fields. I was in Washington for nearly two years, earning my keep as a bookkeeping machine operator for a real estate firm while waiting for opportunities in my profession.

"I came to San Francisco in May 1959 to the National Conference of Social Work which usually has [an] extensive employment service at which jobs from throughout the country are registered. I also applied at local community organizations and other agencies, but met with the same responses that I had in Washington. It was the director of a case work agency who suggested that I go to the YWCA where she felt I might find some help, though she did not know that they were employing at that time. I was still reluctant to go to the YWCA. I believed that their services were hotels for girls and swimming and adult classes. I did not want to be a hotel keeper, nor was I interested in becoming a teacher. But I was desperate, and I did go. The then executive greeted me with open arms once she saw my resume. She offered me immediate appointment to my choice of one of the two positions she had vacant—the directorships at their center in Chinatown and their center in the Western Addition area in San Francisco. It seemed like a miracle. I could not believe that someone had at least recognized that in my forty-nine years of life, I had gained some life experiences that could be useful in addition to my professional training. My undergraduate degree had been in economics and business administration with a strong concentration in accounting. I had had business experiences before I came to this country, both as an employee and as a proprietor. As I listened to the executive outline the responsibilities of a center director in the YWCA and what the work of the YWCA was all about, I realized how wrong I had been about the organization and felt that here I could truly be useful.

"I chose to work in Chinatown because I knew little about the Japanese, though I spoke the language, and less about the blacks, while I knew the Chinese much better. I had lived all my life in China and spoke both Mandarin and Cantonese. I have never regretted the choice, of both my employer and the location. There [has] been much frustration which is a natural part of working with people, but there have also been great satisfactions which, though rare, compensated for every disappointment. China-town has changed greatly since I left the community in 1968 but when I joined the YWCA center there in 1959, it was still much the old closed community dominated by the local politics of a few so-called Chinatown leaders, where social problems were rarely aired in public and where, it was said, there were no juvenile delinquents. Yet the stirrings could be felt. The recent admission of families of old-time residents and GI brides to this country created problems within families, cultural conflicts between generations and among siblings where there were foreign-born older siblings and native-born younger ones. Scarce and underpaying jobs were made even scarcer, with non-English speaking immigrants locked into the crowded ghetto because of language difficulties. Youngsters were floundering in schools and developing psychological problems because of the pressures at home to do well in school, yet there were no special programs to help them in the public school system.

"When the immigration laws were liberalized late in 1965, to admit up to twenty thousand immigrants to the United States from any one country each year, the flood gates were loosened and there [was a] huge influx into San Francisco's Chinatown that did not level off for many years. There were secondary school age children, too, coming in large numbers, who had substandard schooling and far fewer number of years than that of youngsters of the same age in this country. They had no hope of graduating from high school here within the two or three years left till they would no longer be eligible to attend public schools. As a consequence, large numbers dropped out as soon as they could, and some of these eventually became the gang of foreign-born youth about which much has been written elsewhere.

"Clearly, the existing conditions called for far greater effort than was being exerted in the community in behalf of immigrants with their multiple problems. That is not to say that no services were being provided for some of their needs, but they were scattered among traditional settings in traditional agencies doing traditional programs. I envisioned a massive effort, particularly in the area of language training among non-English speaking newcomers.

"The YWCA is an excellent organization for staff with innovative ideas. So long as those ideas do not conflict with its overall policy, staff in each center are given every opportunity to be flexible and innovative in programming to meet the needs of the community in which it is located. The YWCA function, it was seen, is to be a catalyst and enabler, using its skills to bring programs not only into the YWCA but to help local communities to acquire the services they need. Thus, I began introducing special programs at my center for foreign-born youngsters—club and interest groups, tutorial service, basic English programs in which whole families participated together, and a series of orientation sessions for everyone dealing with everyday problems of living in a new country with its unfamiliar customs and regulations.

"As I became familiar with the community and learned to work with the various community groups and organizations, both formally and informally, and to find my way around community power groups, I was able to initiate, over the years, several programs that are now well established, permanent institutions in Chinatown. One of these is the present Chinatown Resources Development Center, of which the Korean English Language and Job Training Program is a unit. Originally named the Chinatown-North Beach Community English Language Center, the proposal for the program was based on one that I had written for the YWCA but which had not yet been funded. Convinced that non-English speakers should be taught English as a second language, I had visited the Defense Language Institute in Monterey and had been much impressed with the effectiveness of the techniques they used.

"When Chinatown was declared a poverty area under the Economic Opportunity Act and became eligible for anti-poverty funds, I re-wrote my original proposal in collaboration with a specialist in linguistics who had extensive experience in teaching English as a second language (ESL), and included it in the package of Community Action Programs (CAP) submitted from Chinatown for funding by the Economic Opportunity Council of San Francisco. The program was designed not only to teach English to adult immigrants but also to develop materials and train volunteers that could be used throughout the community. But soon the funding source was changed to the Department of Labor with their own guidelines that precluded training volunteers for community use.

"Another of the agencies with the creation of which I was much involved is the Newcomer Services Center. I was becoming increasingly concerned with the plight of non-English speaking immigrants arriving in this country willy-nilly in the belief that in a land paved with gold, all that was necessary to succeed was hard work. They had no notion of the realities of life in a crowded ghetto to which most were headed. I felt that perhaps if they could be forewarned before they left home and had some idea of what awaited them and where they might turn in case of need, and if they could be persuaded to learn some English before their departure, it might help to alleviate some of the hardships and frustrations they were bound to face once they were in this country. I took the opportunity of a summer vacation in 1965 to visit Hong Kong and arrange cooperative effort with an agency there and the United States consul in Hong Kong. The consul agreed to permit the International Social Service (ISS) to set up a desk at the consulate to register visa applicants for orientation sessions and English classes, and to send me their monthly list of visa approvals with their addresses and sponsors in San Francisco. For a period, I personally met the immigrants at the airport and called on the sponsors to determine what services were most needed. It seemed that there had to be a receiving agent at this end, one central agency to which all newcomers could turn for information and referral, provide transportation and interpretation services, and be able to do follow-up work. I turned over my findings to the International Institute as the most appropriate agency to undertake this task. The Immigration and Immigrants Committee of the District Council, of which I was chairman, acted as the advisory council to the Institute while they sought funds for the project. The San Francisco Foundation ultimately approved the funds for a Newcomer Services Center in Chinatown, but instead of granting the funds to the Institute, the grant was given to the Immigration and Immigrants Committee, which then became the board of directors of the new program.

"The program of which I am the proudest to have had a part in originating is the Chinese Education Center (CEC) established within the Unified School District. The CEC is a special school that grew out of my concept of a centralized facility for all immigrants who needed language training in Chinatown, from pre-schoolers to adults. It is a school in which all primary grade, zero-English youngsters are enrolled as they arrive in San Francisco for an intensive program of bilingual/bicultural education with ESL. Staff counselors work closely with them and their families to help them with adjustment problems and referrals to community health and other services. The students remain at the center for one semester to rarely more than a year, when they are assigned to their regular schools as soon as they are deemed ready to participate in them.

"I had first proposed this concept of a centralized facility as a member of a small group of concerned individuals who had been given a small grant by the Rosenberg Foundation to develop a comprehensive program of teaching English to the language handicapped Chinese. I had felt that concentrating all elements of an ESL program at one location would provide flexibility in both programming and ability grouping, efficiency in training, and capacity utilization of the meager supply of skills, talents, and materials then existing. Based on this concept, the group eventually produced an overview which was written in components that could be implemented one unit at a time as funds became available.

"The principals of elementary schools in the area who had participated in all of our deliberations saw the merit of my idea and cooperatively proposed to the School District to establish a centralized elementary school in Chinatown, and the CEC was born even before the overview was completed.

"Today, there are two other such facilities, one in the Spanish speaking community and one in the Filipino community. These were proposed by the Citizens Advisory Committee to the Board of Education on Desegregation and Integration, of which I was a member of the Bilingual Committee that originated the proposal. The Bilingual Committee was also instrumental in preventing the dispersal of enrollment at the CEC in the busing program and keeping it intact for non-English speaking youngsters.

"In 1970, the Rosenberg Foundation gave a sizable grant to the group that produced the overview to implement the objectives contained in it. Till the group received the grant and became incorporated as the Education Center for Chinese (ECC), a non-profit charitable organization, and I became a board member and its vice-chairman, I had performed all the secretarial and clerical chores for the group. But with the grant we were able to employ a proposal writer and secretarial help. The ECC has sponsored several funded projects, but the largest and [the] one with the greatest impact was the Asian Newcomer Parent Program. We received three one-year grants from the Department of Education of HEW and, working with parents of youngsters enrolled in CEC and with teachers supplied by the Community College District, teaching materials for adults were developed that are being used by ESL programs across the country, including New York and Los Angeles.

"What changes I might believe I had helped to bring about, certainly, could not have been possible single handed. No community work is a one-man job. It was only through, and working with, the numerous organizations, agencies, and groups that ideas could be tested, nurtured, and finally implemented. Without the support, encouragement, and cooperation of such groups, nothing would have been possible. Some of the organizations and groups with whom I have worked that have not yet been mentioned are the Chinatown-North Beach Area Board of the San Francisco Economic Opportunity Council to which I was elected and on whose Program Committee I served, the Youth and Education Committee of the Human Rights Commission to which I was appointed by then Mayor Shelley, the Citizens Advisory Committee to the Board of Education on Quality/Equality Education, the Bilingual/Bicultural Committee of the Board of Education to which I was appointed as the president's representative, and the Board of Regents of Lone Mountain College.

"My involvement in the problems of the Korean community dates back only to the spring of 1974, when a member of the community approached me for assistance in establishing an English language and job training program for Korean immigrants similar to that of the Chinese Resources Development Center for Chinese immigrants. I was able to be of service by producing a fundable proposal for a federal grant which, on the advice of the funding source, was written as a unit of the Chinatown program to be administered by them. To be funded, it was necessary that there be a Korean community group to be advisory to the Chinatown board, and I was elected to chair this group shortly after the program got underway in September of that year. This advisory group was incorporated in 1975 as the Multi-Services Center for Koreans, a non-profit charitable organization. While the language and job training program will remain under the aegis of the Chinatown program through fiscal year 1975-76, we will be funded as an independent agency for fiscal 1976-77, and we hope that as an independent agency, we will seek other funds to provide some of the many other services that our immigrants need.

"Often I am asked whether I was born in the United States, or whether I still speak Korean when I have been in this country for so long, and why do I not really look like a Korean.

"I was born in Seoul, Korea, of Korean parents who were then living in Antung, Manchuria, just across the Yalu River. My mother had returned home to her parents when I was expected, to await my arrival, and rejoined father when I was three weeks old. My father, Beung Kiu Surh, was serving with the Chinese Maritime Customs Service at the time and remained with them till his retirement in 1936. Father was an 1898 graduate of Roanoke College in Salem, Virginia, the first Korean to obtain a college [degree] in the United States. He took his master's degree in 1899 in jurisprudence and political science at Princeton University under Professor Woodrow Wilson. He returned home to Korea soon thereafter and held various offices in the Korean imperial government, including the mayoralty of Chemulpo (Inchon), and was largely responsible for Korean emigration to Hawaii.

"The course of political events following the Treaty at Shimonoseki in 1895 and the establishment of a Japanese protectorate over Korea in 1905 led my father to the realization that ultimate annexation was inevitable. Preferring to make his home elsewhere than to live under the Japanese rule, he left home in 1907 to join the Chinese Customs in Antung. In 1911, when I was but a year old, he was transferred to Hunchun, Manchuria, to establish a customs service there. We lived in Hunchun till I was five years of age and had acquired a brother and a sister. It is of this period that I have the fondest memories, and it is during this time that I learned my Korean alphabet, sitting on father's knees while he had his lunch.

"My primary education took place in Japanese, in Antung when my father was transferred back there in 1916. There he built a permanent home on an estate on the outskirts of the city to which we returned for summer vacations whenever possible. I had not quite completed my sixth grade when father was transferred to Pakhoi in the province of Canton on the Gulf of Tonkin, and four of us children were dropped off in boarding schools in

Hong Kong on his way to his new assignment. My secondary education, therefore, was acquired in English, first in an all-English speaking girls' school and then in one in which the student body was almost entirely Cantonese. I matriculated with honors in the winter of 1926 and entered the Hong Kong University in the following January to major in pure mathematics. I dropped out of college when I went home for my summer vacation in 1928, this time to Shanghai to which father had been transferred in 1926, and the summer job I had was offered to me on a permanent basis.

"In 1937, . . . only we children, by then nine of us, were left in Shanghai while my parents, who had returned home to Antung after father's retirement, had added a tenth who was then not yet a year old. When the Shanghai incident occurred in the fall of 1937 in the undeclared war between China and Japan, all of us except one sister were with our parents in Manchuria. When Shanghai was bombed, my sister and our Korean woman servant were evacuated by the Japanese and sent with other refugees to Korea, and they made their way to join the family in Antung. Two of my sisters returned to Shanghai the following year, and I joined them in the winter of 1939 and found employment with the Shanghai Telephone Company, a subsidiary of the Bell Telephone System, where one of my sisters was already working. Both my sister and I were service representatives, but my primary responsibilities were translation of Japanese letters and dealing with Japanese subscribers, including the military.

"Pearl Harbor brought Japanese occupation of the company, where gendarmes were placed as supervisors with final authority on all company matters. Through the year of 1942, eleven of the company employees were taken in one by one for interrogation and detention at the Gendarmerie Detention Center. In October, my sister, I, and a Korean young man who had only recently been employed to help me with my Japanese work, were also taken and detained. My brother, who is a radio expert, had already been there since August. All four of us were released 2 days before Christmas, my brother after 105 days of confinement, and my sister and I after 69 days. Each of us had been grilled once in the middle of the night. I was called at 3:00 A.M. and told to confess, and they had gone to our apartment on the day we were taken and had gone through all our papers so that they already knew who our friends were and the contents of our correspondence. Foreign nationals, we later learned, were subsequently transferred to war detention camps.

"In April 1943, I left to join my parents in Antung. I could no longer endure the constant visits by the gendarmes, always asking if I had any information on any possible subversive activities in the telephone company and whether I would not confess.

"We were again all in Antung when the Japanese surrendered, except the two sisters who had preceded me to Shanghai after the bombing. My father was away in the country on one of his numerous trips to promote home industries among farmers when the Korean Residents Association elected him, in absentia, to head the Association. On his return about a month later, he undertook the task of caring for the hundreds upon hundreds of refugees from the interior of Manchuria who wanted to return to Korea and flocked to Antung. With no adequate facilities and not enough food, illnesses were breaking out in serious proportions, but the train service to Korea had been cut when the Russians occupied North Korea. Father finally obtained a train to transport the refugees by stationing himself at the Russian headquarters for three days till they relented. The proudest day of my life came when father, in his capacity as president of the Korean Residents Association, met the train bringing the first contingent of Korean soldiers who had fought against the Japanese and were returning home, with my brother carrying the Korean flag.

"When the Chinese Communist Army arrived in October and took control of Antung, they supplied father with bodyguards on his travels between home and office. But as time went on, we found our friends not returning when one by one they were called in for questioning. It seemed that our own safety was without doubt in jeopardy and that it was only father's usefulness among the refugees that kept us safe. On the other hand, father would not leave before his work was done. But one day in November, two carloads of Communist soldiers invaded our home, to search for arms, they said, and took two of my brothers with them when they left. My brothers escaped two days later by a clever ruse, and we left for South Korea immediately. We crossed the 38th parallel by night and on foot and arrived in Seoul on December 16, one week after we left home.

"In Seoul I found employment as chief clerk at the Chosun Hotel, which was being used by the military government as their field officers' billet. In January 1948, I was made Korean manager of the hotel prepared to house the United Nations Temporary Commission on Korea, who were to oversee our first presidential election. I left for the United States in September 1948 after my mother's funeral. She had passed away earlier that month. I attended Roanoke College in Salem, Virginia, my father's alma mater, on a full tuition and board scholarship while I worked in the bursar's office for my room and pocket money. Because of an illness during my last semester that kept me away from school for a year and a half, I did not graduate till 1955, with a bachelor's degree in economics and business administration.

"I had intended to do graduate work in institutional accounting at the Wharton School of Business Administration at the University of Pennsylvania and had already been granted a scholarship for the 1953-1954 session when I became ill and had ample time to do some thinking. After all, my father had ever been concerned for the welfare of people and believed that the poor should be helped to earn their own living so that they may gain a sense of dignity as individuals rather than having them dependent on charity handouts, and had undertaken numerous projects out of his own funds to give them the opportunity. Would I not be more useful as a social worker whether I remained in this country or returned to Korea, which I would have done had he been still living? I decided that perhaps, in some little way, I could follow in his footsteps.

"I was fortunate to be granted the Barbour Scholarship for Oriental Women at the University of Michigan. I enrolled in the School of Social Work to major in community organization. The scholarship provided me with full tuition and a small allowance, which I supplemented with work for one of my professors, and I earned my degree in 1957 and went to Washington, D.C., to seek employment.

"While in Washington, I became associated with a nonprofit cultural project which qualified me for a first preference status immigrant. The sponsor of the project has always said that even though the project had to be abandoned, it had to its credit the fact that it had enabled me to become a United States citizen. Thanks to the project, I am now a San Franciscan as this is the city I had chosen in which to live and the city in which I had become a United States citizen."

THE AUTOBIOGRAPHY OF ANNA CHOI[7]

"I came to Hawaii as a picture bride not due to the fact that my family was poor but because I had heard so many times about an uncle on my mother's side who was doing quite well for himself in Hawaii. It just sounded like a dreamland to me.

"In 1915, I decided to go to Hawaii and asked my mother whether I could be a picture bride, since my uncle's family in Korea knew of a man there looking for a wife. My mother thought I was crazy and tried to persuade me to abandon such a notion, but in vain. So, when I was fifteen, equipped with an introduction and a photograph, I boarded a ship at the Pusan port with five other girls, despite my family's disapproval of my departure. We boarded another ship in Yokohama after physical examinations, and three long months later we finally arrived at our destination.

"We were kept in the immigration quarantine quarters until we were cleared. The other five girls were cleared after three days and left with their grooms-to-be. Feeling awfully cheated and left behind, I spent most of my time crying. Finally, after five days, I was cleared of immigrations with the help of not my fiance but my uncle. My uncle advised me not to marry this man I had not even met, since I was only fifteen and had a long life ahead of me. He advised me to get an education.

"When I first saw my fiancé, I could not believe my eyes. His hair was grey and I could not see any resemblance to the picture I had. He was a lot older than I had imagined. I had a very big decision to make of whether or not to listen to my uncle. If my fiancé had been a little bit younger, I would have listened to my uncle readily, but I did not have it in my heart to disappoint or hurt such a middle-aged man like him.

"He drove me in an old car which he had borrowed to a hotel where I stayed two nights and prepared for my wedding. On the third day I met him, he brought me a bouquet, and we were married in a church. I found then that he was forty-six years old. He was more like a father than my husband and he did treat me more like a daughter. However, his age did not bother me too much. I felt I could trust and lean on him.

"We settled on the big island of Hawaii where my husband had been working. A month after we were settled, my uncle gave us a visit, wondering how I was doing. I told him that I was fine and did not regret my doings.

"I had heard in Korea that Hawaii was a paradise. People spoke of clothing that grew on trees, free to be picked, and the abundance of fruits and all kinds of foods. Money, they said, was not necessary for survival and could be saved for future use. I heard only of prosperity and wealth in the islands.

"I found the situation quite to the contrary. Hawaii was definitely not a paradise of luxury. After our honeymoon, I decided to work, since I had heard that my husband had spent one month's worth of his earnings on our wedding. When I told my husband of my intentions to work, he was not surprised at all but seemed to have expected it all along. It was very hard work for me. I arose at four o'clock in the morning and we took a truck to the sugarcane fields, eating breakfast on the way. Work in the sugar plantation was back-breaking. It involved cutting sugarcanes, watering, and pulling out weeds. All the work at that time was accomplished with manpower, for tractors and farming machinery were not in use like they are today. The sugarcane fields were endless and twice the height of myself. Now that I look back, I thank goodness for the height, for if I had seen how far the fields stretched, I probably had fainted from knowing how much work was ahead. My waistline got slimmer and my back ached from bending over all the time to cut the sugarcanes. Sometimes I wished I was a dwarf so that I would not have to bend down constantly. During the coffee breaks the majority of the workers drank coffee with their snacks, but I could not drink the bitter coffee and could not help but think of our native drinks and foods I used to have back home in Korea. Since food was supplied at the plantations, we could only have Korean food on Sundays. Since there were quite a few Japanese workers, I could find rice in the market and also *toran*, which was called taro in Hawaii. I felt so much pleasure when I cooked Korean food that I felt like a woman again. Women were not paid as much for our work on the sugar plantations, so I decided to do some laundry work for our fellow plantation workers. An average man's salary was forty-five cents per day and my total income, including the small profit from my laundry job, was less than that of my husband's.

"Six months of my life in Hawaii had passed, but I had no correspondence with my family back home in Korea. In those days, it took six months for a letter to cross the ocean. I was discouraged and found it useless to write home. Besides, I did not want to have to lie about the rough life I was leading. However, I was becoming envious of my fellow workers who were receiving letters from home. The night I finally wrote to my mother, I saw her in my dreams.

"My husband being thirty years my senior, I definitely looked upon him more as my father than my husband. We were meant to work, I believe, rather than to enjoy our life together. There was absolutely no time to relax. The only time we had together in peace was between nine in the evening and four in the morning every day. We lived in a one-room studio apartment with an adjoining kitchen. The old bed in the corner of the living room was about the only piece of furniture that belonged to us.

"I do not ever recall using or hearing the word love between us. Life was so dry and routine that any sort of warm feelings were out of the question.

"Sundays were days of rest, but I always awoke at four in the morning out of habit. The only pleasures I got on Sunday mornings were watching the rainbows which reminded me of the *saektong*, the traditional multi-colored striped fabric worn by children during festivities, and having papayas with my husband. We also attended church every Sunday.

"In three years I had two sons, which gave me much joy and made me feel like I was truly a woman. Since then, I had something to live for. It was disappointing to see how my children grew up to be Hawaiians, though. It made me very sad to hear them speak Hawaiian English much more fluently than our native tongue. Watching the children grow up, however, was very rewarding to me, and it made me forget about being homesick. I believe that the times I spent with my children were the happiest moments of my life. When I became twenty-two years of age, I was already a mother of five.

"There was a terrible turning point in my life during my seventh year in Hawaii. My husband had passed away after being ill for two whole years and left me behind with five young children. It was very sad and depressing, but I could not spare the time and energy for crying. I was faced with a dilemma. I had all my children and myself to support. I worked without rest, straight through the week. There were no more Sundays to look forward to. I did any kind of work I could lay my hands on. I drew water from the well, carried sugarcanes, did other people's laundry, and so on. Fortunately, my children were taken care of by some church people during the daytime so that I could work. We moved from our apartment to an abandoned house on the hill in order to save rent. I had a little further to walk to work, but I had to do anything to save money. After a while, my body could not keep up with this sort of hard work and routine. One day when I was drawing water from the well, I was thrown into the well and lost all consciousness. I believe I was very lucky to have ever regained my consciousness, for when I came to, I learned that I was in a coma for twenty days, and I found myself on the island of Oahu. I believe that it was quite a miracle that I was alive, and I thanked God for saving me. When I first regained my consciousness, I could only think of my children's welfare. The woman who was apparently taking care of me informed me of their well-being and told me not to worry about them. Later, I learned that she was Japanese and had taken care of me all along. She worked in the hospital and moonlighted by making Japanese socks. While I was recovering in the hospital, she taught me how to make the socks, and I helped her out in return by making some socks for her. She advised me to make them after I returned home, and helped me purchase a sewing machine with monthly payments. All hospital expenses had been covered by the health insurance I had been paying all along, so I was able to pay for the sewing machine. After a total of forty days, I returned home to the island of Hawaii and was surprised to find a sewing machine waiting for me at home. I started making the socks right away. A collector came to take the finished socks and supplied me with more fabric and materials. It was not bad work at all. I could earn a little money without doing the backbreaking work on the sugar plantations. So our life was finally becoming more stable financially.

"One day, three years after my husband's death, my uncle and minister visited me with a proposition to remarry. They introduced me to a Mr. Choi, who was ten years older than I was. I took a liking to him since he was not a plantation worker. I thought about it over and over again until finally I decided to remarry after I received an encouraging letter from my mother.

"After we were married, we moved into town and bought a house. This was only the beginning of a new life for me. Then, I had things I had never had for ten years. I acquired friends and neighbors, and I had a whole life ahead to learn. My second husband lost his first wife before we were married and was a lot different from my first. He was not such a homely type. He did not make too much money, but with my income from my sewing, baby-sitting, and laundry work, we could make ends meet and more. We made more of our lives. On Sundays we went on picnics and traveled around the island with our children. I had another son and when he was fifteen years old, I became a widow for the second time. My second marriage lasted fifteen years, but when I was widowed again, I was not left with such an empty feeling as the first time. The children were all grown, and I had only a feeling of satisfaction of witnessing their success.

"Since my early forties, I devoted myself to church work. I helped create the Youngnam Women's Club, which consisted of seventy-nine members. We invited speakers to hear about the Korean independence movement.

"I moved to Honolulu after I retired, and I had an opportunity to visit Korea just a few years ago to visit my parent's graves. I was surprised by how much she had changed and was especially surprised to see how many people there were. Seoul and Pusan were much larger than Honolulu, but I felt very uncomfortable to see that the living standards of the people were not proportional to the size and growth of the cities."

A Sketch of the Author's Life Story

I was born on May 25, 1914, the Year of the Tiger in the lunar calendar, in the small farming village of Ja-dong, Eiju-kun, in the northwestern part of Korea. I was the seventh of nine children of the Choy family. My father was a farmer cultivating his own land, but he was too poor to send all his children to the Japanese-established elementary school located in the city Consequently, I attended a Confucian-type private institute in the village where the lesson of the first school year was to learn the one thousand Chinese characters (*chunja-mun*). When I was fourteen years old, I began to learn some of the Chinese classics.

My father's original plan for me was that when I reached the age of fifteen, I was to become a farmer like him so that my older and younger brothers could go to the public school for more formal, advanced studies. However, I was able to persuade my father to send me to the public school by suggesting that I could work my way through if he would provide me with financial help for the first two or three years. I was admitted to the Yungsan elementary school located about thirty miles from my home. Before graduating from this elementary school, I took four different high school entrance examinations. I passed the one for the last school, Sungin Commercial School in P'yongyang, the capital of present-day North Korea.

About this time, I was converted to Christianity and attended church every Sunday. I was very active in church work, teaching a Sunday school class (I later became the superintendent) and working for the YMCA of the Sungin Commercial School as the head of the religious section. I had an opportunity to become acquainted with some of the outstanding national and Christian leaders like Cho Man-sik, known as the Korean Gandhi; the Reverend Hahn Kyung-chik; the Reverend Kim Chai-choon; Dr. Song Chang-keun; and the famous patriot Ahn Ch'ang-ho, who had just been released from a Japanese prison. They were my heroes, and I was inspired by their Christian faith and patriotism. I often thought that I should like to follow in their footsteps myself and work for the cause of Korean national independence.

Sungin Commercial School was one of the institutions established by the Korean people themselves without financial support from foreign missionaries. A few of the teachers including the principal, Kim Hang-bok, belonged to a patriotic organization called *Suyang Dongu-hoe* (*Hung Sa Dan*), which was organized by Ahn Ch'ang-ho.

Some of the teachers gave lectures on Korean history and the nationalist movement to the classes once or twice during the semester, although such lectures were prohibited by the Japanese authorities in Korea. I was an honor student, but I had decided not to apply for a job after graduation, which was contrary to·my father's expectations. I completed the school courses by earning my school expenses as a tutor.

In March 1934, I applied for admission to Aoyama Gakuin in Tokyo, even though I had no idea where my school expenses would be coming from. It seemed almost a miracle to me when I heard from a woman evangelist, Mrs. Kim Duk-young, who said, "I will send you twenty won [about $6.50] per month until your college graduation."

I arrived in Tokyo in April and lived first in a dormitory. The cost of room and board at that time was about fifteen won, so I could get along reasonably well with twenty won. Aoyama Gakuin was one of the best Christian colleges in Japan, but I did not feel that I was learning much in the classes. Most of the class lectures were on Bible studies, and I had to spend too much time learning foreign languages (German, Greek, and Hebrew), since they were required for graduation. I had noticed that Japanese society was becoming more and more militaristic and totalitarian. Government control began to penetrate even academic circles. The Japanese national police suspected every Korean resident. At least once every month, plain-clothesmen "visited" me and asked all kinds of questions. Public meetings, even though non-political in nature, were not permitted to Korean residents in Japan.

In addition to class studies, I concentrated on reading about Japanese history, especially Japanese nationalism and militarism. I also attended political meetings and mass rallies, most of which were extremely nationalistic and militaristic in tone. I was an eyewitness to the military coup d'etat known as "2, 26 Jiken (incident)." During my four-year stay in Tokyo, I faithfully carried on my Christian work in the Korean community there. When I finished my third year of college, I began to prepare myself to go to the United States for advanced study.

It took me about three months to secure a student passport from the Japanese government in Tokyo. I was overwhelmed with news that Cho Man-sik and the Reverend Hahn Kyung-chik were going to help me to obtain enough money for the steamship fare from Yokohama to Los Angeles. It was the middle of April 1938 when I set out on my first trip across the Pacific. Naturally I was thrilled and excited. I was full of ambition as a young man, because I was about to arrive in my dream world, the land of freedom!

During the first six months in this country, I spent most of my time learning English in night school. I attended Pasadena College for one semester, transferred to Los Angeles City College, then to Los Angeles Junior College. After graduating from City College, I enrolled in Chapman College. My wife came to the United States as a student in 1941, and she also attended Chapman College.

The Japanese attack on Pearl Harbor interrupted my studies for one semester because I was asked to work for the U.S. government as an interpreter of Japanese.

I graduated from Chapman College with B.A. in political science and a minor in history. In 1942, I was appointed an instructor in Oriental languages at the University of California in Berkeley. The following six years were the busiest ones of my whole life. In addition to my full-time teaching schedule, I had to teach university extension language courses in Oakland and San Francisco two nights a week. I enrolled as a graduate student in the university to work for my master's degree. I also worked with the Office of War Information in San Francisco on Saturdays and Sundays as a broadcaster to Korea. I delivered lectures on Korean and Japanese politics to the Office of War Information for three months. In addition, I was asked to teach Japanese to the special Army Training Program classes. I was often called by the federal court to translate Japanese documents in connection with Japanese property.

Since no Korean language courses had ever been given in any American university in the past, I offered Korean language courses for the first time in the Department of Oriental Languages. In 1943 I published *The Korean Reader*, a textbook for beginners. During the war I worked from eight o'clock in the morning to eleven o'clock in the evening, seven days a week. My monthly income was well over five hundred dollars.

When the Japanese government accepted the unconditional surrender terms of the Allied powers, I decided to return to Korea and work for the reconstruction of the country. I had the opportunity to express my desire to Dr. Monroe E. Deutsch, then vice-president and provost of the university. He agreed with me and wrote a letter of recommendation to General Archer L. Lerch, governor of the American military government in South Korea. Part of his letter stated:

> All members of the Oriental Department have the highest respect for Mr. Choy's well-proven integrity and can testify as to his devotion to his work, his loyalty, and his pleasing personality. . . . . During that period he has been working hard completing his education and has made an excellent record as a graduate student in the Department of Political Science.

I landed at Inchon Harbor in June 1946, and a GI driver drove me to the Banto Hotel in Seoul, where my relatives and friends were anxiously awaiting my arrival. My family had to remain in San Francisco until civilian dependents were permitted to join their overseas husbands.

I had mixed feelings about my homeland, which had been emancipated from Japanese domination but divided into two occupation zones by the Allied powers. The general conditions of the country at that time could be characterized as political confusion, economic chaos, and social disorder. The outlook was dark.

After consultation with Colonel Gail Cleland, my superior officer, I set up my working schedule as a political education specialist. I concentrated on training teams of speakers, setting up programs, and interpreting the democratic ideology. My articles on democracy and comparative government appeared in the daily newspapers and academic monthly magazines. In the meantime, I was assigned to install a Department of Political Science in Seoul National University.

Dr. Chang Lee-wook, president of the university, said in his letter that "Professor Choy was with us for the last two years and contributed a great deal toward building up the Department of Political Science to a degree that we are well proud of."

I was soon promoted to deputy director of the Department of Public Information in the American military government. Thus I was able to meet many different social and political leaders in Korea, including rightists, leftists, and middle-of-the-road groups. I also attended various political meetings and conferences such as the United States and Soviet Union Joint Conference and the United Nations Temporary Commission meeting.

The possibility of Korean unification became remote when the United Nations General Assembly authorized the Temporary Commission to supervise general elections in the area accessible to them, that is, South Korea, and the Soviet Union rejected the United Nations resolution. I was profoundly disappointed with the failure of unification of my native land. I could see nothing but the possibility of a tragic civil war. I felt that my services were no longer necessary or useful in Korea.

When Syngman Rhee seized power in South Korea, I prepared to leave with my family. At that time General William F. Dean, the last American military governor, said in his letter to me, "You proved yourself to be [a] very capable leader and performed your duties in a superior manner."

On August 2, 1948, my family of five boarded an army transport ship at Inchon. We docked at San Francisco on August 17, and I had to start all over again as a newcomer in the United States. This time I settled down in Seattle, Washington. First I went into the hotel business with one of my friends. A few months later, I was invited to teach political science and Far Eastern history at Seattle Pacific College, where I immensely enjoyed my teaching profession for two years. The members of the faculty and the students alike were just one big family.

Dr. Hoyt Watson, president of the college, wrote me a complimentary letter, stating, "We have greatly enjoyed your presence and feel that you are making a real contribution to the collegiate atmosphere and the real education of Seattle Pacific College."

It was at this time that I had trouble with the Immigration Service, primarily because of my strong stand against Rhee's regime, which was an ironfisted one-man rule. I left teaching and came back to the Berkeley campus for further studies. Receiving unforgettable moral and financial help from the late Mrs. Henriette Lehman, I had a golden opportunity to concentrate on research in the fields of political science and history for more than five years. During this period, I had time to prepare a manuscript entitled *Korea: A History*, which was published by Charles E. Tuttle Company. My wife also wrote a book, *The Art of Oriental Cooking*, published by Ward Ritchie Press.

During the next several years, I worked as a house painter and then went into the restaurant business. When my wife passed away, I sold the business and went back again to teaching. I am now semi-retired. However, I would like to continue my academic work, teaching part-time and writing books on Korea.

I am grateful that all my children have grown up, are happily married, and have become professionals.

My first job in the United States was as a Korean language teacher to American-born Koreans (*iise*) sponsored by the Korean National Association in Los Angeles. I thought that teaching the Korean language to American-born Koreans was exciting and challenging as well as self-educational. First, I was employed as a part-time teacher, teaching two hours a day for five days a week, every afternoon from three-thirty to five-thirty. My monthly salary was twenty-five dollars. Most of the students were of elementary and junior high school age and were more or less forced by their parents to attend language school after returning from their American schools.

Since no adequate and proper teaching materials and textbooks existed, I had to prepare all the teaching materials needed for the study of the Korean language, history, culture, and music. I noticed that many of the students were not interested in learning about Korea. Some did not even bother to open their books, while some talked to each other in English during the class. I also felt that I could not communicate freely with my students because my English was very poor and when I spoke in Korean, they did not understand a word. I was discouraged and on many occasions thought that I should leave the job. But I had to stay since I did not have the confidence to look for another job outside the Korean community.

During the summer of 1938, a Korean language summer school was opened for two and a half months. I and another teacher (a woman) were appointed on a full-time basis. The classes ran from eight o'clock in the morning until noon, five days a week. The summer school curriculum covered the Korean language, history, culture, and folk songs and dances. The classes were divided into four levels: kindergarten, elementary, junior high, and senior high. More than fifty students were enrolled, and the Korean National Association and the Korean Presbyterian Church on West Jefferson Blvd. became the classrooms. Almost every Korean child attended the summer school. During this period, there were about five hundred Korean residents in the Los Angeles area. Some of the parents came with their children and sat in on the classes. Many parents rendered help, providing transportation, needed classroom equipment, and money. Thus the summer school became a center of Korean community activities for two and one-half months.

The program held on the last day of summer school was a big event in the Korean community. Every class put on its best program to show the Korean public how much they had learned about Korea during the summer. More than two hundred Korean residents came to see the summer school show (festival). I acted as chairman of the program, and was overwhelmed by the remarks made by the head of the Education Department of the Korean National Association. Among other things, he said that "it was one of the best summer school programs in the Korean community history in Los Angeles ever since the summer school started."

I also still remember a remark made by one of my students. One day I was very tired and was resting on a chair during intermission. A student passed by me and asked, "What is the matter with you, teacher?" I replied, "I am very tired." She said, "Well, you get paid for teaching us." I was quite surprised at the attitude of the student, because in Korea students do not express such views to their teachers. There the teaching profession is considered one of the most respectable positions and is not considered a money-making occupation. Nevertheless, the remark was my first lesson in understanding the values of American culture. American society places a great deal of emphasis on money, whereas Korean society emphasizes cultivation of the beauty of life.

My next summer job was at a Korean-owned vegetable store. This was my first experience with physical labor. Because of my language difficulty, I was assigned to work at the "warehouse" located in the back of the store, washing and cleaning the vegetables, such as carrots, celery, lettuce, and cabbage. My work started at seven o'clock in the morning and ended at eight or nine o'clock in the evening. Therefore I had to get up about five o'clock every morning, eat breakfast, and take the bus to the store. I had half an hour for lunch. This meant that I worked an average of thirteen hours a day, six days a week. My first hourly wage was twenty-five cents for an eight-hour day; we were not paid at all for overtime. I usually got home around ten or eleven o'clock at night and often went to bed without even taking a shower, because I was so tired. Sunday was my day off. During the school season, I worked three days a week (Saturday, Sunday, and one week day) and attended school three or four days a week.

There are two unforgettable working experiences in my life. One Saturday, I was called to work at an American supermarket because an employee was sick. When I arrived at the store, the foreman told me that I was going to work with a Chinese man at the warehouse. He also said that Saturday was the busiest day of the week and work had to be done fast. The American-born Chinese told me that he had been working for more than two years there. He was a fast worker, and white people did not like this kind of work. Soon the foreman came back to the "warehouse" (vegetable washing room) and said, "Get busy, boys." I started to wash the vegetables with a water hose with my bare hands, without gloves or rubber boots. Once I started, I had no chance to rest until lunch time, because the Chinese man kept saying "Hurry, hurry, we are behind." I had half an hour for lunch and started again to wash the vegetables. I quit at eight o'clock in the evening. When I left the warehouse, I found that my whole body was wet; my shirt, pants, shoes, socks and underwear were soaked with water. I took the bus and returned to my apartment. My physical appearance shocked my wife, who was waiting for my return. With tears in her eyes, she said to me, "Please don't go back to work there tomorrow." I was speechless for a moment. Then I said, "Well, we have to overcome these kinds of difficulties in order to survive in this society."

After I resigned from my teaching position at Seattle Pacific College in 1951, I was employed as a house painter by a black contractor. Since I had no experience in painting homes, I began as an apprentice. My hourly wage was $1.45, which was half that of a regular painter's wage according to the union wage scale at the time. On the first day of my job, I did not wear a painter's uniform; I did not even know all the names of the tools. I went to the place of work, a three-story apartment building, at seven-thirty in the morning with only a lunch box in my hands, and waited for my foreman, who was also black. My boss and the foreman came with a truck loaded with painting equipment—ladders, ladder jacks, painting buckets, and brushes. I helped with the unloading and set the scaffold against the apartment building. The boss told the foreman that Bong Choy is a new member of our crew and to take good care of him, since he does not have any previous experience in painting. Then the boss left for another job site. I told the foreman that "I do not know anything about painting, and I need your help and patience." He looked at me with somewhat surprised eyes and said, "Bong, I will tell you something. I have been a painter for more than thirty years, and I know young men like you can become good painters." He also said that he knew a few Chinamen and that he liked Chinese food, especially chop suey. I said that I was not Chinese, I was a Korean. He said, "Oh, you are a Korean. I never know the difference between a Chinese, Japanese, and Korean."

The foreman gave me a big paint brush, a half-full bucket of paint, a caulking gun, one spackling paste can, and other tools. Then he said, "Now we are in business. You climb up the ladder on the left side of the building while I do the right side." When I held the bucket in my right hand and started to climb up the ladder, I felt that I was climbing up the Golden Gate Bridge to commit suicide. It took me a few minutes to reach the top of the painting board. As I stood up straight on the board and looked down to the ground, I felt very dizzy. I immediately grabbed the ladder with my left hand and closed my eyes. After a few minutes, I took a deep breath, but I still continued to grab the ladder with my right hand. I painted the same place over many times because I was afraid to move. While I was doing this, the foreman came to me and said: "Bong, what are you doing?" and "What is the matter with you?" I said, "Don't ask me anything now! I'm scared to death." Then he told me to come down from the ladder and to paint the building from the ground level. I followed his instructions and finally finished my longest day's work. At the end of the day, I noticed that my whole body was white, covered all over with paint from top to bottom. I said to myself, "I don't know whether I painted the building or my body." Even today, whenever I pass that apartment building, I feel kind of dizzy.

One day when I was painting a house alone, I was so lonely that I started whistling and continued to do so for two or three hours, repeating the same melody all the way through. Suddenly, the landlady opened her window and yelled in an angry voice, "Can't you stop that whistling? It's driving me crazy!'" I stopped immediately and thought to myself that I had even lost my freedom to whistle in this country.

I have had three different kinds of businesses: a produce store, a hotel, and a restaurant. In the summer of 1940, my wife and I opened a vegetable store with fifty dollars in capital which I borrowed from one of my friends in Los Angeles. The rent was twenty-five dollars per month, and the store was located in front of the corner grocery building. My wife and I worked from seven o'clock in the morning to ten o'clock in the evening, seven days a week. At that time I did not know how to drive a car and had no money to buy a truck for business purposes. Lim Song-taik, a seventy-year-old elder of the Korean church, bought our produce from the wholesale market every other day.

When I started the business, some of my friends were very skeptical about it, because I had no capital or business experience, and competition in the vegetable business was very acute in that particular area. Just across from my store, there was already a supermarket. But I knew that any business in this country would require some risk and competition. I worked out my business guidelines: honesty and hard work.

On opening day, two friends came to help us. The first day, business was good, We sold about forty dollars in goods. Thereafter, average daily business ran from twenty-five to thirty-five dollars, and our net profit was five to seven dollars. I thought such an income was not bad at all and better than working for someone else. I sold the business to another Korean after two and one-half months because I had to return to school in the fall. I made enough money for one semester's living and school expenses.

I had a shocking experience toward the end of the business venture. I had rented a small cottage, which had been converted from a garage, near my store. The rent was ten dollars per month, and it was unfurnished. I bought a used stove and installed it at my own expense. Therefore, when I moved out from the cottage, I expected to take the stove with me. To my surprise, the landlord said that I could not take the stove with me because it belonged to the cottage. Naturally I ignored his false claim and tried to take the stove with me after I moved all the other furniture. Suddenly, the landlord grabbed me, threw me out of the cottage, and warned me by saying that, "If you try again to take the stove from the cottage, I am going to shoot you." I was frightened and never went back to that place again.

My second business venture was a hotel operation in Seattle. Because I did not receive sufficient income from teaching at Seattle Pacific College, I formed a hotel partnership with an old friend, Lee Chang-hee, who was one of the early Korean students in America and a gentleman scholar. Lee and I ran the hotel business for two and one-half years. We did all kinds of work, acting as anything from chambermaids to janitors. The business was not too bad, but we had to sell it as I planned to move to Berkeley in 1952.

My third business venture was the Korean Inn Restaurant and Oriental Cooking School in Berkeley. First my late wife and I thought that we would open an oriental cooking school since no such establishment existed and many Americans were interested in oriental cookery. But we also decided to open a restaurant to the general public because there were no authentic Korean restaurants in the Bay Area. We formed a partnership with one of my friends, but he withdrew after six months.

As guidelines for the restaurant business, I applied the following principles: serve quality food; give good service to the customers; create a pleasant and friendly atmosphere; and charge moderate prices. We soon found that the restaurant business was one of the hardest businesses, but a rewarding one. My wife was the master chef and I was the manager, doing everything from marketing to janitorial work. My two sons, David and Francis, who were still in public school, helped us as dishwashers and waiters. Both of them were very good workers and became valuable assets to the business. My daughter, Cora, also helped whenever she visited us. The restaurant was open six days a week, and every Tuesday night my wife conducted cooking classes.

We worked from fourteen to sixteen hours a day. During the first six months, we lost a little money because we did not know how to run the restaurant and lacked customers. When my partner indicated his desire to withdraw, I was in trouble because our payment was late and the outlook was still questionable. I asked myself, "Why did I start this and why do I face this kind of trouble?" But we had no choice, so we determined to carry on the business, doing the best we could. Fortunately, business began to pick up the second six months, and every week the number of customers increased. After one year, the restaurant business, as well as the cooking class, doubled. Every weekend the restaurant was full, and customers without reservations had to wait from ten to thirty minutes. The Korean Inn Restaurant became popular in the Bay Area, and many well-known community and academic leaders and their families became patrons. Various parties and wedding receptions, including the International Film Festival and the World Anthropology Conference, took place at the Korean Inn Restaurant.

A few professional writers on the restaurant business wrote articles about the Korean Inn. R. B. Read, the author of *The San Francisco Underground Gourmet*, said, "The Restaurant (Korean Inn) is authentically but not richly decorated, and the air is one of quiet good taste—very much what one would expect of academicians turned restauranteurs in any country. . . . With her training and temperament, Mrs. Choy is particularly adept at adjusting her native cuisine to the exigencies of the American market and the American palate."

After seven years of business, we had to sell when Mrs. Choy found that she had a terminal illness (cancer). The success of this business was the fruit of Mrs. Choy's infinite efforts based on her philosophy of life: "Human life is an endless struggle and one should fight for the principle of justice as one's conscience dictates. . . . One should find a high purpose no matter where you are and build your life around it, then give yourself to it with all your heart. Success or failure of your life is not to be measured by *how long you lived but how you lived*: the ultimate judgment of your life is in the hands of God."

She has gone, but her philosophy of life remains with members of my family. Recently our family pledged ten thousand dollars to the newly built Center for Korean Studies in Hawaii to dedicate an office room in memory of Mrs. Choy and a dear family friend, Mrs. Henriette Lehman.

Notes

Chapter 1
Korea: The Land, the People,
the Culture, and the History

[1]For further information, see Shannon McCune, *Korea's Heritage: A Regional and Social Geography* (Rutland, Vt.: Charles E. Tuttle Co., 1956), pp. 3-24.

[2]McCune, op cit., p. 24.

[3]Korea is the world's fifth largest producer of gold and also has considerable deposits of iron, coal, and copper. Its extensive water resources for generating electricity put Korea in a rather favorable position with respect to power potential. See George M. McCune, *Korea Today* (Cambridge, Mass.: Harvard University Press, 1950), pp. 16-21.

[4]Until recently, South Korean government documents used the Korean calendar. For example, the year 1955 is referred to as the year 4288 after Tan'gun. One of the best books on Tan'gun is Choy Dong, *Choson Sangko Minchok-sa* [The ancient history of the Korean people] (Seoul: Tonkkook Munhwa-sa, 1966), pp. 81-264.

[5]Cornelius Osgood, *The Koreans and Their Culture* (New York: Ronald Press, 1951), p. 160.

[6]William E. Henthorn, *A History of Korea* (New York: Free Press, 1971), pp. 18-32.

[7]Ibid., p. 25.

[8]For further information, see Henthorn, op cit., pp. 6-17; and Osgood, op. cit., pp. 213-28.

[9]One of the best books on Korean art is Evelyn McCune, *The Arts of Korea: An Illustrated History* (Rutland, Vt.: Charles Tuttle Co., 1962).

[10]For a detailed pattern of Korean house structure, see Osgood, op. cit., pp. 24-36.

[11]There are two good books on Korean clothes: Kwan Kae-soor, *Uriot Byungchun kwa Chaebong* [Changing of our clothing and sewing] (Seoul: Shuhak-sa, 1965) and Kim Boon-ok, *Hanbok Sanghwal* [Wearing of Korean clothes] (Seoul: Shuhak-sa, 1969).

[12]Korean women wear their native dresses on special occasions.

[13]For further information on Korean cooking, see Choy Jung-suck, *The Art of Oriental Cooking* (Los Angeles: Ward Ritchie Press, 1964), pp. 3-69.

[14]Homer B. Hulbert, *The Passing of Korea* (New York: Young People's Missionary Movement of the United States, 1906), p. 69.

[15] For further accounts of the legendary history of Korea, see Choi Nam-son, *Kookmin Choson Yok-sa* [A history of Koreans] (Seoul: Illu-sa, 1947); Choy Dong, op. cit., pp. 3-50 of the English translation; and Ahn Chae-hong, *Choson Sangko Sakam* [Outline of ancient Korean history], two volumes (Seoul: Minu-sa, 1947 and 1948).

[16] For a detailed analysis of the land system, see Choy Bong-youn, *Korea: A History*, (Rutland, Vt. and Tokyo: Charles E. Tuttle Co., 1971), pp. 37-38.

[17] Ibid., pp. 45-47.

[18] For an analysis of the Confucian economic system and its consequences, see Ibid., pp. 63-78.

[19] Ibid., p. 79.

[20] For a further analysis of the destruction of Korea's independence, see Eugene C. I. Kim and Kim Han-kyo, *Korea and the Politics of Imperialism (1876-1910)* (Berkeley and Los Angeles: University of California Press, 1967), pp. 61-223.

Chapter 2
Korea in the 19th and Early 20th Centuries

[1] For additional information on the social structure of the Yi dynasty, see Sohn Pow-kye, "Social History of the Early Yi Dynasty with Emphasis on the Functional Aspects of Government Structure," Ph. D. dissertation, University of California, Berkeley, 1963. See also Choy Bong-youn, *Korea: A History* (Rutland, Vt., and Tokyo: Charles E. Tuttle, 1971), pp. 78-80.

[2] For a history and an analysis of the factionalism, see Choy, op. cit., pp. 80-86.

[3] Eugene C. I. Kim, and Kim Han-kyo, *Korea and the Politics of Imperialism (1876-1910)* (Berkeley and Los Angeles: University of California Press, 1967), p. 14.

[4] Hilary Conroy, *The Japanese Seizure of Korea, 1868-1910* (Philadelphia: University of Pennsylvania Press, 1960), pp. 18-77. Many experts do not agree with Conroy's interpretations.

[5] For the full text of the treaty, see Henry Chung, *Korean Treaties* (New York: H. S. Nichols, 1921), pp. 194-204.

[6] For further information, see Kim and Kim, op. cit., pp. 16-19.

[7] Ibid., p. 69.

[8] For detailed figures on imports and exports, see Ichitaro Shiokar, *Chosen Tsusho Jijo* [The condition of Korean commerce] (Tokyo: Yao Shoten, 1895), pp. 56-63; and Choy, op. cit., pp. 110-11.

[9] For different views on the matter, see Conroy, op. cit., pp. 221-29; and Kim and Kim, op. cit., p. 79.

[10] Choy, op cit., pp. 111-12.

[11] Ibid., p. 113.

[12] For a more detailed analysis of the Treaty of Shimonoseki, see Kim and Kim, op. cit., pp. 84-85, and Conroy, op. cit., pp. 285-90.

[13] Spencer J. Palmer, *The Period of Growing Influence, 1887-1895, Korean-American Relations: Documents Pertaining to the Far Eastern Diplomacy of the United States*, vol. 2 (Berkeley and Los Angeles: University of California Press, 1963), p. 7.

[14] Ibid.

[15] Fred H. Harrington, *God, Mammon, and the Japanese* (Madison: University of Wisconsin Press, 1944), p. 256.

[16] Conroy, op. cit., pp. 304-5.

[17] Palmer, op. cit., pp. 6-7.

[18] Harrington, op. cit., p. 252.

[19] Kim and Kim, op. cit., pp. 87-88. See also Harrington, op. cit., pp. 270-271; Conroy, op.

cit., pp. 268, 303, and 306-9; and Frederick M. Nelson, *Korea and the Old Order in East Asia* (Baton Rouge, La.: Louisiana State University Press, 1946), pp. 228-29.

[20]Harrington, op. cit., pp. 288-90.

[21]Ibid., p. 283.

[22]For the Japanese text of the memorandum, see Hyaku Nan-wun and others, *Chosen Minjok Kaiho Toso-shi* [History of the liberation struggle of the Korean people] (Tokyo: Matsuzaki-kaisha, 1954), pp. 171-72.

[23]Nelson, op. cit., p. 236.

[24]Choy, op. cit., p. 115.

[25]Harrington, op. cit., p. 296.

[26]Ibid., pp. 298-99.

[27]Choy, op. cit., p. 115-16.

[28]Nelson, op. cit., pp. 249-50.

[29]Actually, in August 1903, Korea formally requested the Japanese and Russian governments to consider it a neutral in the event of war and to spare it from the hostile military operations of either belligerent. For Russia's counterproposals and the Japanese reaction, see Kim and Kim, op. cit., pp. 101-2.

Chapter 3
The Korean-American Treaty

[1]Eugene C. I. Kim and Kim Han-kyo, *Korea and the Politics of Imperialism 1876-1910* (Berkeley and Los Angeles: University of California Press, 1967), p. 19.

[2]Frederick M. Nelson, *Korea and the Old Order in East Asia* (Baton Rouge, La.: Louisiana State University, 1946), pp. 137-38.

[3]For detailed information, see Ibid., pp. 119-63.

[4]Kim and Kim, op. cit., p. 23.

[5]Ibid., pp. 23-24.

[6]For the full text of the treaty, see Henry Chung, *Treaty and Conventions Between Corea and Other Powers* (New York: H. S. Nichols Co., 1919), pp. 197-204.

[7]Nelson, op. cit., p. 145.

[8]Kim and Kim, op. cit., p. 25. For a textual analysis of different English translations of the king's letter, see Nelson, op. cit., pp. 145-49.

[9]George McCune and John A. Harrison, ed., *The Initial Period, 1883-1886, Korean-American Relations: Documents Pertaining to the Far Eastern Diplomacy of the United States,* vol. 1. (Berkeley and Los Angeles: University of California Press, 1951), p. 25.

[10]Hilary Conroy, *The Japanese Seizure of Korea, 1868-1910* (Philadelphia: University of Pennsylvania Press, 1960), p. 121.

[11]There are two views about Japan's policy toward the Korean-American Treaty. Nelson felt that the "Japanese government hesitated to render her aid to Commodore Shufeldt when he asked the Japanese government to deliver the State Department letter to the Korean King." See Nelson, op. cit., pp. 139-40. Conroy believed that "the Japanese government supported the treaty, because the Japanese Foreign Minister, Inoue Kaoru, advised the Korean government by stating that "the American motive is nothing but friendly foreign trade. Your persistence in isolation is bad. It will invite unexpected harm. Therefore, accept the American offer."

[12]The United States government's current policy of "give away" dollar diplomacy to underdeveloped countries in order to keep them from becoming Communist is analogous to the Chinese policy of financial aid to Korea in the 1880s.

[13]Fred H. Harrington, *God, Mammon, and the Japanese* (Madison: University of Wisconsin Press, 1944), pp. 125-26.

[14]For detailed information on the contract, see ibid., pp. 144-69.

[15]Harrington, op. cit., pp. 163-64.

[16]Ibid., pp. 285-86.

[17]Ibid.

[18]Ibid., p. 193.

[19]Ibid.

[20]Ibid., p. 327.

[21]Ibid.

[22]George L. Paik, *The History of Protestant Mission in Korea (1882-1910)* (Pyongyang: Union Christian College Press, 1929), p. 180.

[23]Andrew J. Grajdanzev, *Modern Korea* (New York: John Day Co., 1944), p. 34.

[24]Kim and Kim, op. cit., pp. 190-91.

[25]For a detailed description of the incident, see Harrington, op. cit., pp. 265-82.

[26]Ibid., pp. 274-75.

[27]Ibid., p. 276.

[28]Ibid., p. 275.

[29]Harrington, op. cit., p. 215.

[830]Harrington, op. cit., pp. 281-82.

[31]For a detailed analysis of the reform movement, see Choy Bong-youn, *Korea: A History* (Rutland, Vt., and Tokyo: Charles E. Tuttle Co., 1971), pp. 132-36. See also Kim and Kim, op. cit., pp. 108-18.

[32]Harrington, op. cit., p. 317.

[33]Ibid., p. 316.

[34]Ibid., p. 320.

[35]Ibid., p. 322.

[36]Ibid., p. 323.

[37]Ibid., p. 324.

[38]Nelson, op. cit., p. 258.

[39]Paul H. Clyde, *The Far East: A History of the Impact of the West on the East Asia* (New York: Prentice Hall, 1949), p. 355.

[40]D. G. Tewksbury, *Source Materials on Korean Politics and Ideologies* (New York: Institute of the Pacific Relations, 1950), p. 22.

[41]For the full text of the letters, see ibid., pp. 23-25.

[42]Ibid., pp. 25-26.

[43]For the full text of the treaty, see ibid., pp. 28-29.

[44]Grajdanzev, op. cit., pp. 34-35.

[45]Ibid., p. 36.

[46]For a further analysis of the Korean people's reform movement, see Choy, op. cit., pp. 133-36 and pp. 168-69. See also Frajdanzev, op. cit., pp. 38-39.

Chapter 4
The Pioneer Period

[1]Noh Chae-yon, *Chaemi Hanin Saryak* [A short history of Koreans in America], vol. 1 (Los Angeles: American Publishing Co., 1951), p. 1.

[2]Fred H. Harrington, *God, Mammon, and the Japanese* (Madison: University of Wisconsin Press, 1944), pp. 233-34.

[3]Ibid., p. 235.

[4]"Encountering Allen's opposition, the Chinese diplomat was satisfied with a conversation with Secretary of State Bayard, in which he tried to connect the Chinese government with

Korea . . . to suggest a certain supervision as if the thing had been done with the consent of the Chinese government." Ibid., pp. 238-39.

[5]For comments on Allen's action, see Frederick M. Nelson, *Korea and the Old Order in East Asia* (Baton Rouge: Louisiana State University Press, 1946), pp. 176-77. See also Eugene C. I. Kim and Kim Han-kyo, *Korea and the Politics of Imperialism (1876-1910)* (Berkeley and Los Angeles: University of California Press, 1967), pp. 125-88.

[6]So Kwang-woon, *Miju Hanin Chi'lsipnyon-sa* [A seventy-year history of Koreans in America] (Seoul: Haewaikyopo Munjae Yonku-so, 1971), p. 25.

[7]Kim Hyung-chan and Wayne Patterson, *The Koreans in America (1882-1974)* (Dobbs Ferry, N.Y.: Oceana Publications, 1974), p. 2.

[8]Ibid.

[9]Andrew W. Lind, *Hawaii's People* (Honolulu: University of Hawaii Press, 1955), p. 175. See also Koh Sung-che, *Hankook Imin-sa Yonku* [Study of Korean emigration history] (Seoul: Changmun-kak, 1973), pp. 119-230.

[10]Harrington, op. cit., p. 186.

[11]Kim and Patterson, op. cit., pp. 85-86.

[12]So, op. cit., p. 22.

[13]Yun Yo-chon, "Minu Imin Chil'sipnyon" [Seventy years of emigration to America], *Kyonghyang Sinmun,* No. 3, December 29, 1973.

[14]The total number of Korean immigrants to Hawaii varies from author to author. This discrepancy is caused by the failure of the authors to take into account the number of people who were sent back to Korea because they failed to pass the physical examination of the American immigration office.

[15]For the full text, see Kim and Patterson, op. cit., pp. 87-89.

[16]Henry Chung, *Korean Treaties* (New York: Fleming, 1919), pp. 197-98.

[17]Kim Won-yong, *Chaemi Hanin Osipnyon-sa* [A fifty-year history of the Koreans in America] (Reedley: Charles Kim Ho, 1959), pp. 6-7.

[18]Warren Y. Kim, *Koreans in America* (Seoul: Chin Chai Printing Co., 1971), p. 23.

[19]Yang Yu-sin, "Toknip Sinmun kwa So Chae-p'il." This account was found in Yang Choo-en's personal files and no name of publication was recorded.

[20]For further information about Ahn's work, see Lee Kwang-su, *Tosan, Ahn Ch'ang-ho* [Biography of Ahn Ch'ang-ho] (Seoul: Tosan Kirum Saop-sa, 1967), pp. 24-34.

[21]The objectives and activities of the Hun Sa Dan are well analyzed in Chu Yo-han, *Hung Sa Dan Osipnyon-sa* [Fifty years of Hung Sa Dan] (Seoul: Taesong Munhwa-sa, 1965), p. 348.

[22]Chae-soon Kim, ed., "Yaksok ul Jikko ra" [Keeping promises], *Samtoh,* Vol. 5, No. 9, September 1973, p. 124.

[23]For a detailed biography of Rhee, see Robert T. Oliver, *Syngman Rhee: The Man Behind the Myth* (New York: Dodd Mead and Co., 1954).

[24]*Honolulu Star-Bulletin,* July 22, 1965.

[25]For a detailed analysis of Rhee's rule and politics, see Choy Bong-youn, *Korea: A History* (Rutland, Vt., and Tokyo: Charles E. Tuttle Co., 1971), pp. 248-86.

[26]*Honolulu Star-Bulletin,* July 22, 1965.

[27]A brief biography of Park Yong-man can be found in Kim Won-yong, op. cit., pp. 193-95.

[28]Warren Y. Kim, op. cit., p. 87-89.

[29]Practically no material existed on the Reverend Lee Dai-wu, although Warren Y. Kim described his work very briefly. Thus, this author depended heavily on interviews with Yang Choo-en and the late Mr. Whang Sa-sun, who were close friends of Mr. Lee.

[30]Kim Won-yong, op. cit., pp. 27-29.

Chapter 5
The Koreans in Hawaii

[1]Robert M. C. Little, *The Government of Hawaii: A Study in Territorial Administration* (Stanford, Calif. Stanford University Press, 1929), p. 144.

[2]Koh Song-che, *Hankook Imin-sa Yonku* [A study of the history of Korean emigration] (Seoul: Changmun-kak, 1973), pp. 196 and 205.

[3]This information was obtained from Yang Choo-en, the only surviving early Korean immigrant in San Francisco today (1976).

[4]This information is based on interviews with early Korean immigrants, including Yang Choo-en, Kim Hyong-soon (Harry Kim), and others.

[5]So Kwang-woon, *Miju Hanin Chilsipnyon-sa* [A seventy-year history of Koreans in America] (Seoul: Haewaikyopo Munjae Yonku-sa, 1973), pp. 27-30.

[6]*Hapsong Sinpo* (a weekly newspaper), December 2, 1908.

[7]*Hankook Ilbo*, January 12, 1973, p. 5. This was a special edition to mark the seventieth anniversary of the first Korean migration to Hawaii.

[8]George H. Jones, "The Koreans in Hawaii," *Korean Review,* November 1906, pp. 404-5.

[9]For a further analysis of primitive Korean democracy, see Choy Bong-youn, *Korea: A History* (Rutland, Vt., and Tokyo: Charles E. Tuttle Co., 1971), p. 25.

[10]Warren Y. Kim, *Koreans in America* (Seoul: Po Chin Chai Printing Co., 1971) p. 38.

[11]Ibid.

[12]Arthur L. Gardner, *The Koreans in Hawaii: An Annotated Bibliography* (Honolulu: University of Hawaii Press, 1970), p. 4.

[13]*Dong-A Ilbo,* December, 26, 1974, p. 9.

[14]*Center for Korean Studies* (Honolulu: University of Hawaii, 1975), p. 1.

Chapter 6.
Koreans on the Mainland

[1]According to Yang Choo-en, the Reverend Whang Sa-sun, and other early immigrants, the working guidelines were written by Ahn Ch'ang-ho and issued in the name of the Kognip Hyop-hoe.

[2]Kim Hyung-chan and Wayne Patterson, *The Koreans in America (1882-1974)* (Dobbs Ferry, N.Y.: Oceana Publications, 1974), p. 11.

[3]*Yang Choo-en's Personal File Documents,* pp. 90-91. See also Kim Won-yong, *Chiemi Hanin Osipnyon-sa* [A fifty year history of the Koreans in America] (Reedley: Charles Kim Ho, 1959), pp. 80-81.

[4]Chang, Lee-wook. "Sesang un dalrajiko itta" [The world is changing] *Samtoh,* Vol. 3, No. 12, December 1972, pp. 36-37.

[5]Chang, Lee-wook. "Ijulsu opnun sedae ka itts" [There is an unforgetable generation], *Samtoh,* Vol. 4, No. 1, January 1973, pp. 44-45.

[6]This story is based on the tape recording made by this author and his wife at the home of Mrs. Roh Jung-soon in Berkeley, California, on February 6, 1974. This author has known Mrs. Roh and her family for more than thirty years.

[7]For further information about Korean social and political organizations, see Kim, op. cit., pp. 83-241.

[8]The first constitution of the Korean National Association consisted of four articles. For additional information, see ibid., pp. 113-14.

[9]For the full text, see ibid., pp. 122-25. For the English translation, see Kim and Patterson, op. cit., p. 114.

[10]Chu Yoo-han, "My Autobiography," *Hankook Ilbo,* September 23, 1975, p. 4.

[11]The constitution of the *Hung Sa Dan* contained twenty-seven articles. It was translated by Kang Young-kak, Cha Sang-dal, Chang Lee-wook, and Frank Yerjeh Kim. See *Hung Sa Dan Osipnyon-sa* [A fifty-year history of the *Hung Sa Dan*], compiled by the Society of the Hung Sa Dan History Committee, Seoul, 1964.

[12]Kim, op. cit., pp. 187-95.

[13]Kim Hyung-chan, "Korean Community Organizations in America: Their Characteristics and Problems," *Korea Journal,* Vol. 15, No. 11, 1975, p. 34.

[14]Kim Won-yong, op. cit., p. 199. See also Noh Chae-yon *Chaemi Hanin Saryak* [A short history of Koreans in America] (Los Angeles: American Publishing Co., 1951), p. 105.

[15]For the Korean text, see Kim Won-yong, op. cit., pp. 203-4. For the English translation, see Kim and Patterson, op. cit., p. 105.

[16]Kim Won-yong, op. cit., pp. 224-29.

[17]Ibid., pp. 217-19.

Chapter 7
The Economic Life of Koreans
in the United States

[1]*New Korea,* May 16, 1921. See also Warren Y. Kim, *Koreans in America* (Seoul: Po Chin Chai Printing Co., 1971), p. 13.

[2]Kim, op. cit., p. 14.

[3]Arthur L. Gardner, *The Koreans in America: An Annotated Bibliography* (Honolulu: University of Hawaii, 1970), p. 4.

[4]Kim Won-yong, *Chaemi Hanin Osipnyon-Sa* [A fifty year history of the Koreans in America] (Reedley: Charles Kim Ho, 1959), pp. 299-301.

[5]Ibid., p. 299.

[6]Michael Park, "Three Generations of Koreans in America," mimeographed, University of California, Berkeley, 1974, pp. 42-44.

[7]Kim Won-yong, *Chaemi Hanin Osipnyon-Sa,* p. 302.

[8]In Los Angeles county in 1939 there were thirty-three fruit and vegetable stores, nine grocery stores, five wholesale produce companies, five restaurants, one employment agency, eight pressing and laundry shops, six trucking companies, three beer stores, three hat shops, and one rooming house. For a detailed analysis, see Kim Hyung-chan, "Ethnic Enterprises Among Korean Immigrants in America," mimeographed.

[9]Kim Hyung-chan and Wayne Patterson, *Koreans in America (1882-1974)* (Dobbs Ferry, N.Y.: Oceana Publications, Inc., 1974), p. 16. See also Kim Won-yong, op. cit., pp. 285-93.

[10]Ibid., pp. 302-5.

[11]Ibid., pp. 305-6.

[12]Ibid., pp. 306-8.

[13]Ibid., p. 292.

[14]Ibid., p. 308.

[15]Kim and Patterson, op. cit., p. 25.

[16]This author's personal observation.

[17]Kim and Patterson, op. cit., p. 37.

[18]The report was published in *New Korea,* March 24, 1975.

[19]*Dong-A Ilbo,* March 21, 1975, in the section "News of Koreans in America" *(Miju Dong-A),* p. 2.

[20]*Hankook Ilbo,* October 25, 1975, in the section "Korean News in America" *(Mikook Sosik),* p. 1.

[21]Ibid., January 21, 1976.

[22]South Korea's deficit jumped from $1 billion in 1973 to $2.4 billion in 1974 and is estimated at $2 billion for 1975. See *Korea Link,* Fall, 1975, p. 5. Los Angeles imported nearly $3 billion worth of Korean goods in 1975; New York was second with imports valued at $2.5 billion.

[23]See David Kim, "Korean to Win: U.S.A.," mimeographed, University of California at Los Angeles, 1975, p. 80.

[24]For more detailed information, see ibid., pp. 16-45.

[25]*Hankook Ilbo,* June 12, 1975, in the section "Korean News in America" *(Mikook Sosik),* p. 1.

[26]*Dong-A Ilbo,* June 23, 1975, in the section "News of Koreans in America" *(Miju-Dong-A),* p. 4.

Chapter 8
The Korean Independence Movement
in America: 1905-1930

[1]Noh Chae-yon, *Chaemi Hanin Saryak* [A short history of Koreans in America], Vol. 1. (Los Angeles: American Publishing Co., 1951), pp. 6 and 8.

[2]The Mutual Association headquarters building was destroyed in 1906 during the San Francisco earthquake.

[3]There are conflicting reports about Rhee's selection as a delegate to the peace conference. Oliver stated that Rhee was elected by the Koreans in Hawaii; Warren Y. Kim said that Rhee was chosen to serve as an interpreter for the delegate; Shin Hung-woo wrote that Rhee was elected as a delegate by Korean students. See the series of articles on Syngman Rhee entitled "Inkan Rhee Syngman Paik-nyon" [Human being Rhee Syngman—one hundred years] in *Hankook Ilbo,* May 19, 1975.

[4]*Hankook Ilbo,* June 3, 1975.

[5]For the full text, see D. C. Tewksbury, *Source Materials on Korean Politics and Ideologies* (New York: Institute of Pacific Relations, 1950), pp. 28-29.

[6]Warren Y. Kim, *Koreans in America* (Seoul: Po Chin Chai Printing Co., 1971), p. 75.

[7]Ibid., pp. 76-77.

[8]For the full text of the petition, see Tewksbury, op. cit., pp. 34-35.

[9]F. A. MacKenzie, *Korea's Fight for Freedom* (New York: F. H. Revell Co., 1920), pp. 136-137.

[10]Kim Won-yong, *Chaemi Hanin Osipnyon-sa* [A fifty year history of the Koreans in America] (Reedley: Charles Kim Ho, 1959), pp. 317-18.

[11]For a more detailed article, see *San Francisco Chronicle,* March 22, 1908.

[12]See also Kim, *Koreans In America,* pp. 78-84.

[13]Kim did not mention the toy gun in his book. He stated that "the weapon did not work and failed to discharge, as the Korean rushed forward and struck Stevens a vicious blow on the face."

[14]Kim, *Koreans in America,* pp. 81-82.

[15]Ibid., pp. 82-83. For information in Korean, see Kim, *Chaemi Hanin Osipnyon-sa,* pp. 317-30. See also Noh, op. cit., pp. 44-46. Noh also did not mention the toy gun but did mention a gun that failed to work. The *San Francisco Chronicle* of March 24, 1908, reported the incident under the headline "Korean Youths Attempt the Assassination of D. W. Stevens," with pictures of Stevens and two Koreans.

[16]Kim, *Koreans in America,* pp. 82-83.

[17]More than ninety Korean residents in the Bay Area attended the memorial service held at the United Korean Methodist Church before Chang's body was flown to Korea. Among those paying their final respects was Yang Choo-en, the only surviving eyewitness of the incident.

[18]Kim, *Chaemi Hanin Osipnyon-sa,* pp. 341-42.

[19]For further information, see Ibid., pp. 342-51.

[20]Ibid., p. 348.

[21]*New York Times,* February 18, 1919.

[22]Ibid., March 17, 1919.

[23]Kim Kiusic was a graduate of Roanoke College, Virginia. He served in the Korean provisional government as minister of education, minister of foreign affairs, and vice-chairman. After the liberation of Korea in 1945, he returned to South Korea and served as chairman (speaker) of the Interim National Assembly. In 1948, he attended the conference of southern and northern political leaders. He was captured during the Korean War and died in North Korea.

[24]C. W. Kendall, *The Truth About Korea* (San Francisco: Korean National Association, 1919), pp. 59 and 71-93.

[25]Ibid., p. 68.

[26]Kim, *Chaemi Hanin Osipnyon-sa,* pp. 363-64.

[27]Ibid., pp. 365-67.

[28]Lee Chong-sik, *The Politics of Korean Nationalism* (Berkeley and Los Angeles: University of California Press, 1965), p. 142.

[29]For the full text, see ibid., p. 143.

[30]Kendall, op. cit., p. 34.

[31]Lee, op. cit., p. 145.

[32]Ibid., p. 133.

[33]For detailed information on the structure and activities of the Commission, see Kim, *Chaemi Hanin Osipnyon-sa,* pp. 376-387.

[34]Lee, op. cit., pp. 146-47.

[35]Kim Hyung-chan and Wayne Patterson, *The Koreans in America 1882-1974* (Dobbs Ferry, N. Y.: Oceana Publications, 1974), pp. 31-33; see also Kim, op. cit., pp. 12-13.

[36]An actual copy of the bond certification appeared on the cover of So Kwang-woon's book *Miju Hanin Chilsipnyon-sa* [A seventy-year history of Koreans in America] (Seoul: Haewai Kyopo Munjae Yonku-so, 1973). It read as follows:

$50.00   No. 108

Republic of Korea: Certificate of Indebtedness

This certifies that there is due from the Republic of Korea to the Bearer, the sum of Fifty Dollars, of standard of value, weight and fineness of gold coin of the United States of America, for redemption of which we pledge the good faith and credit of the Republic of Korea upon presentation to the Minister of Finance, at Seoul, Korea, within one year after the recognition of the Republic of Korea by the United States of America: the original holder hereof having loaned the amount of this certificate of indebtedness to the Republic of Korea. Redemption shall be made either in cash or in authorized bonds to the Republic of Korea drawing not less than four per cent per annum as the said Minister of Finance, acting for the said Republic of Korea, by proper authority shall direct. This certificate shall draw interest at six percent per annum until time for redemption as above specified.

Done and certified by and for the Republic of Korea this first day of September, A.D., 1919. Attest.

Kiusic Kim
Chairman of the Korean Commission
Syngman Rhee
President of the Republic of Korea

[37]Kim, *Chaemi Hanin Osipnyon-sa,* pp. 379-86.

[38]Ibid., pp. 389-93.

[39]Kim, *Koreans in America,* pp. 132-33.

[40]For further information on the factionalism, see Kim, *Chaemi Hanin Osipnyon-sa,* pp. 137-64.

[41]So, op. cit., pp. 98-101.

[42]For the full text of the suicide note, see Kim, op. cit., pp. 147-48.

[43]Ibid., pp. 187-91.

[44]Ibid., pp. 201-2. See also *Hankook Ilbo,* August 1, 1975.

[45]Kim, op. cit., pp. 202-3.

[46]*Pacific Times,* August 1, 1921.

[47]So, op. cit., p. 139. See also Kim, op. cit., pp. 191-93, and *Hankook Ilbo,* August 5 and 6, 1975.

Chapter 9
The Korean Independence Movement
in America Since 1930

[1]For a further analysis of the student uprising, see Choy Bong-youn, *Korea: A History* (Rutland, Vt. and Tokyo: Charles E. Tuttle Co., 1971), pp. 185-86.

[2]So Kwang-woon, *Miju Hanin Chilsipnyon-sa* [A seventy-year history of Koreans in America] (Seoul: Haewai Kyopo Munjae Yonku-so, 1973), p. 150.

[3]Whitney Griswood said that the Lytton Commission's report is "possibly the most careful and objective conerancous investigation of the origin of war in history." *The Far East Policy of the United States* (New York: Harcourt, Brace, and Co., 1938) p. 403 ff.

[4]For further information, see Robert T. Oliver, *Syngman Rhee: The Man Behind the Myth* (New York: Dodd Mead and Co., 1954), pp. 163-64.

[5]Nym Wales and Kim San, *Song of Ariran* (San Francisco: Ramparts Press, 1872), p. 16.

[6]One of the best accounts of the Communists in Korea can be found in Lee, Chong-sik and Robert A. Scalapino, *Communism in Korea,* Vols. I and II (Berkeley and Los Angeles: University of California Press, 1973), pp. 3-65.

[7]Choy, op. cit., p. 189.

[8]Oliver, op. cit., p. 174.

[9]Kim Hyung-chan and Wayne Patterson, *The Koreans in America (1882-1974)* (Dobbs Ferry, N.Y.: Oceana Publication, Inc., 1974), p. 44.

[10]For the full text in Korean, see Kim Won-yong, *Chaemi Hanin Osipnyon-sa* [A fifty year history of the Koreans in America] (Reedley: Charles Ho Kim, 1959), pp. 403-5.

[11]Ibid., pp. 405-10.

[12]The Los Angeles branch of the Korean National Revolutionary Party in the United States published a weekly newspaper called *Independence.* Some of the leaders of this group were Rev. Lee Kyung-sun, Kim Kang, Shin Doo-sik, and Pyun Jun-ho. Two of them went to North Korea. They were later purged by the North Korean regime on charges of being American spies.

[13]This author participated in the play as a master-ceremony, or priest. Winifred Lee was the bride and En Kim was the bridegroom. See *Los Angeles Times,* December 8, 1941. The show was held at Hollywood Legion Hall. The chairman of the program was Mayor Brown. The vice-chairmen were T. K. Chang, the Chinese consul, and Key H. Chang, pastor of the Korean Methodist Church.

[14]Kim, *Koreans in America,* pp. 138-39.

[15]This author joined the Korean military units in both Los Angeles and San Francisco

between 1941 and 1944. Much of this section is based on this author's personal experiences and observations.

[16]Kim, *Chaemi Hanin Osipnyon-sa,* p. 424.

[17]Oliver, op. cit., p. 176.

[18]Ibid., p. 178.

[19]Ibid., pp. 179-80.

[20]George M. McCune, *Korea Today* (Cambridge: Harvard University Press, 1950): p. 41.

[21]Ibid.

[22]Oliver, op. cit., p. 182. Haan was one of Rhee's students at the Korean language school (then called the Korean compound) in Hawaii. He belonged to an anti-Rhee political group, the Sino-Korean People's League of Hawaii.

[23]Kim, *Chaemi Hanin Osipnyon-sa,* pp. 428-30.

[24]Kim and Patterson, op. cit p. 46.

[25]Warren Y. Kim, *Koreans in America,* (Seoul: Po Chin Chai Printing Co., 1971), p. 137.

[26]Ibid., pp. 144-45.

[27]Oliver, op cit., p. 207.

[28]For a more detailed account of Rhee's return to Korea and some of his difficulties with the State Department see Oliver, op. cit., pp. 208-25.

[29]*Top Secret* (defunct), Vol. 1, No. 18 (1956), pp. 24-25 and 49-50.

[30]The resolution was drafted by this author. For a further analysis of the idea of permanent Korean neutrality, see Choy, op. cit., Chapter 19.

[31]The Korean text of this statement was filed in this author's private documentary collections titled "My Activities During the Student Revolution, April 20-29, 1960."

[32]*San Francisco Chronicle,* April 24, 1960.

[33]The text of the note was reported in *Yunhap Shinmoon* (defunct), April 30, 1960. Rev. and Mrs. Whang Sa-sun and this author's late wife and myself visited most of the Koreans in the Bay Area to collect donations for the Chin family. Mrs. Whang sent the money to Mrs. Chin in Seoul.

[34]Much of this information was obtained by this author during the summer of 1974 when he visited Los Angeles. He interviewed most of the Korean community leaders, including both the old and the new generation. Kim Won-yong (Warren Y. Kim) was the most informed person on Korean community affairs; he was one of the leaders for many years, as well as the author of *Chaemi Hanin Osipnyon-sa* [A fifty year history of Koreans in America]. The informal conversation at his home on the general subject of Korean community problems lasted more than four hours. See also *Korean Directory of Southern California,* 1972, pp. 8-9.

Chapter 10
Divided Korea

[1]The division of Korea was initiated by the United States government. See Harry S. Truman, *Memoirs, Vol. 1: Year of Decisions* (New York: Doubleday, 1955), pp. 444-45. See also L. M. Goodrich, *Korea: A Study of U.S. Policy in the United Nations* (New York: Council on Foreign Relations, 1956), pp. 12-13.

[2]*San Francisco Chronicle,* July 5, 1972. For the Korean text, see *Tong-A Ilbo,* July 6, 1972.

[3]The three books are: *Kookka wa Hyongmyong Kwa Na* [Nation, revolution, and I] (Seoul: Hyangmun-sa, 1962); *Uriminjok Ui Nakal Kil* [Our nation's path] (Seoul: Donga-sa, 1962); and *Chidojaui Do* [The road to leadership] (Seoul: Chimoon-sa, 1969).

[4]Park Chung-he, *Our Nation's Path* (Seoul: Hollym Corp., 1970), pp. 188-89.

[5]Park, *Chidoja ui Do.,* pp. 345-59.

[6]*Drafted Amendment to the Constitution of the Republic of Korea* (Seoul: Korean Overseas Information Services, 1972), p. 11.

[7]For the Korean text of the reformation program, see *Tong-A Ilbo*, January 4, 1974.

[8]The new constitution contains 126 articles and 11 chapters of supplementary rules.

[9]Kim Sei-jin, *The Politics of Military Revolution in Korea* (Chapel Hill: University of North Carolina Press, 1971), pp. 89-91.

[10]Robert A. Scalapino, "The Erosion of Democracy in South Korea," September 7, 1973, *Yomiuri Shimbun*, Tokyo.

[11]Kim, op. cit., pp. 145-47.

[12]*Tong-A Ilbo*, August 14, 1973, and *New York Times*, August 13, 1973.

[13]*Washington Post*, November 2, 1973.

[14]*San Francisco Chronicle*, December 15, 1975.

[15]For the full text, see "Excerpts from Kim Chi Ha's Declaration of Conscience," published by Korean Link Committee for the Support of Human Rights in South Korea, San Francisco, September 5, 1975.

[16]*Los Angeles Times*, November 9, 1975.

[17]Ibid.

[18]*New Korea*, November 6, 1975.

[19]The expelled American missionaries are the Reverend George E. Ogle and Father James Sinnot, a Catholic priest. Both said that they did not violate any laws in South Korea. See *New Korea*, December 19, 1974, and January 15, 1976.

[20]For the Korean text of the emergency measure, see *Tong-A Ilbo*, January 9, 1975.

[21]*Tong-A Ilbo*, May 14, 1975.

[22]*New York Times*, September 25, 1975.

[23]Cha Chi-son, *Taetongnung Tansang* [Birth of president] (Seoul: Sinhyonsil-sa, 1971), p. 53.

[24]Paik Du-jin, Minjok ui Tungbul [Limelight of the nation] (Seoul: Naekak kefoik chochongsil-pon, 1971), p. 79.

[25]Kim, op. cit., pp. 89 and 134.

[26]Kim Chong-shin, *Seven Years with Korea's Park Chung-hee* (Seoul: Hollym Co., 1967), p. 199.

[27]Yun Po-sun, *Kukook ui kasibal-kil: Na ui Foiko* [Thorny road of country and my memo] (Seoul: Han'kook ohongkyong-sa, 1967), p. 171.

[28]Kim Chung-rak, "Death of Democracy in South Korea," *Christian Century*, December, 1972.

[29]Park, *Our Nation's Path*, p. 193.

[30]Irma Adelman et al., *Practical Approaches to Development Planning: Korea's Second Five-year Plan (1967-1971)* (Baltimore: Johns Hopkins Press, 1969), p. 304.

[31]*Korean Journal*, February 28, 1974.

[32]Institute for International Policy, "Economic Crisis Looms for South Korea," International Policy Report, Washington, D. C., December 1975, p. 3.

[33]Ibid.

[34]Robert Shaplen, "A Report At Large: New Chapter in Korea," *New Yorker*, November and December, 1972.

[35]See the South Korean government publication entitled *Saemaol: 1973* [New community movement: 1973].

[36]Institute for International Policy, op. cit., p. 8.

[37]Ibid., p. 7.

[38]*Wall Street Journal*, December 16, 1975.

[39]Institute for International Policy, op. cit., p. 3.

[40]Shaplen, op. cit., p. 143.

[41]Institute for International Policy, op. cit., pp. 1 and 8.

[42]*Wall Street Journal*, December 16, 1975.

[43] Ibid.

[44] Nam Duck-woo, head of the government's economic planning board, thought that the wholesale price increase in 1976 could be held to 10 percent. *Wall Street Journal,* December 16, 1975.

[45] The *San Francisco Chronicle* reports that "the country's astonishing average annual rate of nine per cent in the past decade had brought real improvements in living standards or work conditions for the work force. Wages are low and work hours outrageously long by European or American standards. Strikes are illegal, the unions are controlled by the government and collective bargaining exists in name only." A female factory worker said: "I just wonder why I was born in this country." She continued by saying: "We work a week of nights from 8:00 P.M. to 8:00 A.M., then a week of days and we have about fifteen days off a year." For the full story, see ibid., February 15, 1976.

[46] Institute for International Policy, op. cit., pp. 2-3.

[47] Ibid.

[48] One of the best known poets in South Korea, Kim Chi-ha, wrote "Five Thieves" (top government officials, generals, political party leaders, big businessmen, and cabinet ministers). The poem was banned by the government.

[49] Kim Chung-rak, op. cit., pp. 161-64.

[50] Ibid., pp. 111-18.

[51] *New York Times,* August 20, 1973.

[52] Ibid.

[53] Ibid., August 15, 1973.

[54] *Free Republic* (defunct), July 1, 1973. This author was one of the eyewitnesses of the incident.

[55] *New York Times,* August 13, 1973.

[56] For the text of the student statement, see *Free Republic,* November 1, 1973.

[57] *Christian Science Monitor,* November 28, 1973.

[58] For the full text, see *Free Republic,* December 15, 1973.

[59] Ibid., November 1, 1973.

[60] *Korean Journal,* January 18, 1974.

[61] *New Korea,* December 18, 1975.

[62] For the full testimony, see *New Korea,* March 25 and April 8, 1976. See also *Washington Post,* March 18, 1976.

Chapter 11
Postwar Korean Emigration

[1] Kim Bok-lim and Margaret E. Condon, *A Study of Asian Americans in Chicago: Their Socio-Economic Characteristics, Problems and Service Needs,* (Urbana-Champaign: National Institute of Mental Health, U.S. Department of Health, Education and Welfare, 1975), pp. 40-53.

[2] Im Sung-bin, "Historical View on the Korean Community Structure," *Hankook Ilbo,* January 1, 1976.

[3] See also Kim Hyung-chan, "Some Aspects of Social Demography of Korean Americans," *International Migration Review,* Vol. 8, No. 1, 1974, p. 26, and *Hankook Ilbo,* February 19, 1976.

[4] *Hankook Shinmoon,* April 24, 1976.

[5] The inadequacy of government data on Koreans in the United States was discussed by H. Cooke Sunoo in "Koreans in Los Angeles; Employment and Education," a paper read at the 94th annual conference of the Association of Korean Christian Scholars in the United States.

⁶At present it is difficult, if not impossible, to make an adequate statistical analysis of Koreans in the United States. Even the total number of Koreans is in dispute. For example, in 1975, the official figure was about 161,000. Unofficial estimates ranged up to 200,000, while newspaper subscriptions were over 220,000. According to a report in the *Tong-A Ilbo,* January 1, 1976, the Korean population in eleven major American areas was as follows: Los Angeles— 60,000; New York—35,000; Chicago—30,000; Washington, D. C.—20,000; Hawaii and San Francisco—15,000; Baltimore—10,000; San Diego—4,500; Philadelphia—4,000; Tacoma— 3,500; and Seattle and Detroit—3,000. Three cities—St. Louis, Atlanta, and Cleveland—had 2,000 each. Two cities, Dallas and Houston, had 1,500 each; five cities—Boston, Milwaukee, Monterey, Las Vegas, and Denver—had 1,000 each. Eleven cities had fewer than 1,000 Koreans each: Indianapolis—800; Minneapolis and Kansas City—700; Cincinnati—600; Portland—400; Sacramento, Tampa, Toledo, and Columbus—300; Miami—150; and New Orleans—100. This report was far from complete, because it failed to include such communities as San Jose and Oakland, in California, where several thousand Koreans lived.

⁷California Advisory Committee to the U.S. Commission on Civil Rights, *Asian-Americans and Pacific People: A Case of Mistaken Identity,* Los Angeles, 1975, pp. 39-40.

⁸*Hankook Shinmoon,* Oct. 10, 1973. See also Park Yong-shin and Park Eun-he, "What is Wrong with Korean Intellectuals," mimeographed, Berkeley, 1974.

⁹Koh Kwang-lim and Koh Hesung, ed., *Koreans and Korean-Americans in the United States; Their Problems and Perspectives* (New Haven: East Rock Press, 1974), p. 35.

¹⁰Kim Hyung-chan, "Ethnic Enterprises Among Korean Immigrants in America," mimeographed, Western Washington State College, Bellingham, Washington, 1976.

¹¹Ibid., pp. 13-19.

¹²Ibid., pp. 19-27. See also Kim David, *Korean to Win: U.S.A.,* mimeographed, Los Angeles, University of California at Los Angeles, 1975.

¹³*Hankook Ilbo,* in the section "Korean News in America" (*Mikook Sosik*), carried a series of articles from March 5, 1976 through May 1976 on successful Korean businessmen.

¹⁴Ibid., December 4, 1975.

¹⁵*Los Angeles Times,* February 1, 1976.

¹⁶This author has served as a member of the Advisory Board Committee of the Center since 1975; this material is based on his personal observations.

¹⁷California Advisory Committee to the U.S. Commission on Civil Rights, op. cit., p. 42.

¹⁸*Hankook Ilbo,* in the section "Korean News in America" *(Mikook Sosik),* February 28, 1975.

¹⁹See Kim Hyung-chan's classification in "Korea Community Organizations in America: Their Characteristics and Problems," *Korea Journal,* Vol. 15, No. 11, 1975, p. 36.

²⁰*Joong Ang Ilbo,* June 26, 1975.

²¹*Tong-A Ilbo,* December 31, 1975.

²²*Hankook Ilbo,* December 19, 1975.

²³For detailed reports on the controversy over the community building, see *Hankook Ilbo,* October 10-15, 1975.

²⁴*Tong-A Ilbo,* November 17, 1975.

²⁵For additional details, see *Hankook Ilbo,* November 20 and December 12, 1975, and *New Korea,* December 4, 1975.

²⁶*Hankook Ilbo,* December 8, 1975.

²⁷Ibid., December 2, 1975.

²⁸*New Korea,* December 4, 1975.

²⁹Ibid., December 11, 1975.

[30]This author closely observed the procedures of the election and filed the detailed reports on the election that appeared in the Korean daily newspapers in his personal files. See *Tong-A Ilbo*, and *Hankook Ilbo* from December 29, 1976 to June 18, 1976. The files contain the campaign speeches of both teams, statements of the election platforms, and other materials. This author also attended the court hearings and obtained a copy of the temporary restraining order, findings of facts, and conclusions of law.

Chapter 12
Characteristics and Problems
of the Korean Immigrants

[1]For Jaisohn's political reforms, see Eugene C. I. Kim and Kim Han-kyo, *Korea and the Politics of Imperialism (1876-1910)* (Berkeley and Los Angeles: University of California Press, 1967, pp. 103-6 and 110-11. See also Choy Bong-youn, *Korea: A History* (Rutland, Vt. and Tokyo: Charles E. Tuttle Co., 1971), pp. 99, 132-35, and 169.

[2]Between 1965 and 1976, the average number of yearly immigrants has been over 15,000. See *Hankook Ilbo*, February 19, 1976, and *Dong-A Ilbo*, February 13, 1976.

[3]Robert Shaplen, "A Report At Large: New Chapter in Korea," *New Yorker*, November 25, 1972, p. 144.

[4]Kim Hyung-chan, "Some Aspects of Social Demography of Koreans in America," *International Migration Review*, Vol. 1, No. 8, 1974, p. 28.

[5]See Choy, op. cit., Chapter 19 for a discussion of Korean unification problems.

[6]George M. McCune, *Korea Today* (Cambridge: Harvard University Press, 1950), p. 62.

[7]For a detailed analysis of the role of Christian churches in the Korean community, see Chapter 13 of this book.

[8]*Hankook Ilbo*, December 11, 1975.

[9]Melanie Hahn, ed., *The Fallen Egg: A Portrayal of the Korean Experience*, San Francisco Unified School District, 1974, p. 7.

[10]For detailed information, see *Asian American Bilingual Newsletter*, March 1976.

[11]This author learned this fact when he worked with the Richmond Unified School District of California, in 1974.

[12]Hahn and others, op. cit., p. 7.

[13]Won Yong, *Ibang-in* [A stranger], San Francisco, 1973. The poem is an unpublished work written in Korean.

[14]Kim Ha-tai, "Koreans in Southern California," *New Korea*, March 6, 1975.

[15]For detailed information, see Kim Hyung-chan, "Ethnic Enterprises Among the Korean Immigrants in America," *Korean Journal*, March 1976, pp. 40-52. See also chapters 7 and 11 of this book.

[16]California Advisory Committee to the U.S. Commission on Civil Rights, *Asian-American and Pacific People: A Case of Mistaken Identity*, Los Angeles, 1975, p. 44.

[17]Ibid., pp. 41-42.

[18]Ibid.

[19]This author has served as a member of the Board of Trustees Multi-Service Center for Koreans since 1974.

[20]For more information, see "Demonstration Project for Asian Americans Research Demonstration of P3 (Push, Pull, Put Together)." 1608 East Jefferson, Seattle, Washington, 1976. This is an unpublished work written by Sil Kim under a grant from the United States Department of Health, Education and Welfare.

Chapter 13
Korean Religious and Cultural Activities
in the United States

[1]Kim Hyung-chan and Wayne Patterson, *The Koreans in America (1882-1974)* (Dobbs Ferry, N.Y.: Oceana Publications, 1974), p. 125.

[2]George Heber Jones, "Koreans in Hawaii," *Korea Review*, Vol. 6, No. 2, 1906, pp. 4-5.

[3]Kim Won-yong, *Chaemi Hanin Osipnyon-sa* [A fifty-year history of Koreans in America] (Reedley: Charles Ho Kim, 1959), p. 40.

[4]Ibid., pp. 47-50.

[5]Ibid., pp. 57-58.

[6]*Tong-A Ilbo*, April 18, 1974.

[7]Kim, op. cit., p. 63.

[8]For a further brief history of the Korean Christian churches in America, see Kim, op. cit., pp. 47-78.

[9]Kim and Patterson, op. cit., p. 127.

[10]Kim, op. cit., p. 244.

[11]Ibid., p. 42.

[12]Ibid., pp. 42-43.

[13]Kim and Patterson, op. cit., p. 131.

[14]Ibid., p. 132. See also Kim, op. cit., pp. 44 and 56.

[15]Kim, op. cit., pp. 44-45.

[16]*Hankook Ilbo*, December 11, 1975.

[17]*New York Times*, November 30, 1973. "Reverend Moon has one million followers and a $10 million annual income. What compels these followers, called 'Moonies,' to live in communal centers, renounce all ties to society and work from dawn to dusk peddling candles, peanuts, dried flowers and whatever else the Church feels will inspire donations?"

The San Francisco Chronicle, February 2, 1976. "It is also reported that the Internal Revenue Service is investigating the Unification Church of America on the matter of tax-exempt status, whether it is a religious movement or a political organization and qualified for tax-exempt status." See also ibid., February 5, 1976.

[18]For the full text of the Korean Christian Manifesto, see *Free Republic* (defunct), July 1, 1973, and "Christianity and Crisis," *A Christian Journal of Opinion*, July 9, 1973.

[19]*Free Republic*, May 15, 1974.

[20]For the full text of the testimony, see the Reverend Cary's unpublished manuscript, August 5, 1974.

[21]*New Korea*, October 31, 1975.

[22]For the full text of the resolution (in Korean), see *New Korea*, May 1, 1975.

[23]*Korean Link*, San Francisco, November 4, 1974, p. 7.

[24]*New Korea*, January 15, 1976.

[25]Ibid., January 22, 1976.

[26]Ibid., January 15, 1976.

[27]Ibid., January 22, 1976.

[28]Ahn Byong-mu, "Inkwan kwa Chungchi ui Kuwon" [Human rights and political salvation], *Ssi-al ii Sori* [Voice of the people], March 3, 1975, pp. 9-16.

[29]Gregory Henderson, "The New Korean Migration," *Koreans and Korea: Americans in the United States* (New Haven: East Rock Press, 1974), pp. 34-35.

[30]*Washington Post*, May 24, 1974.

[31]*Tong-A Ilbo*, December 26, 1975.

[32]For more detailed information on the educational and cultural activities of the early Koreans, see Kim Won-yong, op. cit., pp. 242-82.

[33]San Francisco Unified School District, "Selected Data for Study in the Challenge to Effect a Better Racial Balance in San Francisco Public Schools 1974–75," September 1974.

[34]*Los Angeles Times,* February 1, 1976.

Chapter 14
Korean Contributions to America

[1]Koh Sung-che, *Han'kook Imin-sa Yonku* [A study of the history of Korean emigration], (Seoul: Changmui-kak, 1973), p. 189.

[2]Andrew W. Lind, *Hawaii's People* (Honolulu: University of Hawaii Press, 1954), p. 4.

[3]George H. Jones, "Koreans in Hawaii," *Korea Review,* Vol. 6, No. 11, 1906, pp. 401-6.

[4]Ibid.

[5]Kim Won-yong, *Chaemi Hanin Osipnyon-sa* [A fifty year history of the Koreans in America] (Reedley: Charles Ho Kim, 1959), p. 350.

[6]Ibid., p. 300.

[7]Ibid., pp. 80-81.

[8]Ibid., pp. 303-5.

[9]For the full text of the petition, see Henry Chung, *The Oriental Policy of the United States* (New York and London: Fleming H. Revell Co., 1919), pp. 241-45.

[10]Kim Hyung-chan and Wayne Patterson, *The Koreans in America (1882-1974)* (Dobbs Ferry, N.Y.: Oceana Publications, 1974), pp. 99-100.

[11]Kim, op. cit., pp. 417-20.

[12]This author attended the meeting and heard the speech.

[13]See *Who's Who in America,* 38th ed. (Chicago: Marquis' Who's Who Inc., 1975) and David Hsin-Fu Wand, ed., *Asian-American Heritage* (New York: Washington Square Press, 1974). The author's personal interviews, biographical materials including newspaper articles, and other information obtained through correspondence are used here. This author has also known several of the individuals on a close personal basis for many years.

Chapter 15
Oral History of Early Koreans in America

[1]This author interviewed Yang Choo-en on February 27, 1974.

[2]This author has known the Whang family for more than thirty-five years. The interview took place on February 18, 1974.

[3]This author interviewed Kim Hyung-soon on March 3, 1975.

[4]The interview between Kim Won-yong (Warren Y. Kim) and this author took place on July 2, 1974, in Los Angeles.

[5]This story was written by Gloria Hahn at the request of this author. In 1938, Mrs. Hahn was one of his students at the Korean language school in Los Angeles.

[6]This author has known Hannah Surh for more than twenty-five years. She wrote her life story at his request.

[7]Anna Choi is an assumed name. Her life story is a summary translation from the Korean text, which appeared in *Shin-Dong-A,* April 1974, pp. 286-305.

Bibliography

Annotated Bibliographical Works on Koreans in America

Gardner, Arthur L. (comp.). *The Koreans in Hawaii: An Annotated Bibliography*. Honolulu: Social Science Research Institute, University of Hawaii, 1970.

Henthron, William E. (comp.). *Korean Views of America 1954-1964: An Annotated Bibliography*. Honolulu: Research Translations Institute of Advanced Projects, East-West Center, 1965.

Kim, Christopher (comp.). "Annotated Bibliography." Unpublished manuscript. Los Angeles: Asian Studies Center, University of California of Los Angeles, 1975.

General Bibliographical Works

McCune, Shannon B. (comp.). *Bibliography of Western Language Materials on Korea*. New York: International Secretary, Institute of Pacific Relations, 1950.

United States Library of Congress. *Korea: An Annotated Bibliography*. 3 vols. Washington, D.C., 1950. Vol. I: Publications in Western Languages. Vol. II and III: Publications in Far Eastern Languages.

University of California, Institute of East Asiatic Studies. *Korea Studies Guide*. Compiled by B. H. Harzard, Jr., H. T. Kim, and H. Smith. Edited by Richard Marcus. Berkeley and Los Angeles: University of California Press, 1954.

Books in Korean

Ahn, Chae-hong. *Choson Sangko Sakam* [Outline of ancient Korean history]. Seoul: Minu-sa, 1947.

Chaemi Hanjok Yonhap Wiwon-hoe (The United Korean Committee in America), ed. *Haebang Choson* [Liberated Korea]. Los Angeles: Wiwon-hoe Chibang-bu, 1948.

Chang, Lee-wook. *Na ui Foiko-rok* [My memoir—biography]. Seoul: Samtoh-sa, 1975.

Choi, Nam-son. *Kookmin Choson Yoksa* [A Korean national history]. Seoul: Tongkook Munhwa-sa, 1947.

Choy, Dong. *Choson Sangko Minjok-sa* [The ancient history of the Korean people]. Seoul: Tongkook Munhwa-sa, 1966.

Han, Seung-jo. *Han'kook Minjujuii wa Chungchi Balchon* [The Korean way to democracy.]. Seoul: Popmin-sa, 1975.

Hong, Yi-sup. *Han'kook-sa Bangbop* [Method of the Korean history study]. Seoul: Ilcho-sa, 1966.

Kim, Won-yong. *Chaemi Hanin Osipnyon-sa* [A fifty-year history of the Koreans in America]. Reedley, Calif.: Charles Ho Kim, 1959.

Koh, Sung-che. *Han'kook Imin-sa Yonku* [A study of the history of Korean emigration]. Seoul: Changmun-kak, 1973

Lee, In-yong. *Kooksa Kam* [Outline of Korean history]. Seoul: Ilmun-sa, 1949.

Lee, Kang-hun. *Minju Hyokmyong ui Baljachwi* [Footsteps of democratic revolution]. Seoul: The Dong-A Ilbo-sa, 1960.

Lee, Ki-paik. *Han'kook-sa Sinron* [New theory of Korean history]. Seoul: Ilcho-sa, 1966.

Lee, Kwang-su. *Dosan: Ahn Ch'ang-ho* [Bibliography of Ahn Ch'ang-ho]. Seoul: Tosan Kiron Saop-sa, 1947.

Lee, Song-keun. *Dae Han'kook-sa* [A great history of Korea], 12 vols. Seoul: Chongum-sa, 1973.

Noh, Chae-yon. *Chaemi Hanin Saryak* [A short history of Koreans in America]. 2 vols. Los Angeles: American Publishing Co., 1951 and 1963.

Oaemubu Oaekyo Yonku-won (Institute of Foreign Policy Study of the Foreign Affairs Department), ed. *Hank'kook Oaekyo ui Isipnyon* [Twenty years of Korean foreign policy]. Seoul: Oaemu Chulpan-bu, 1976.

———— *Collection of Multilateral Treaties: 1965-71.* Seoul: 1971.

Park, Chung-hee. *Chidoja ui Do* [The road of leadership]. Seoul: Hyangmun-sa, 1962.

———— *Kookka wa Hyokmyong kwa Na* [Nation, revolution and I]. Seoul: Donga-sa, 1963.

———— *Uri Minjok ui Nakalkil* [Our nation's path]. Seoul: Hollym, 1969.

Park, Un-sik. *Han'kook Doknip Undong-ji Hol-sa* [Bloody history of the Korean independence movement]. Seoul: Seoul Sinmun-sa, 1946.

So, Kwang-woon. *Miju Hanin Chilsipnyon-sa* [A seventy year history of Koreans in America]. Seoul: Haewai Kyopo Munjae Yonku-sa, 1973.

Yun, Po-sun. *Kukook ui Kasibal: Na ui Foiko* [Thorny road of country and my memo.]. Seoul: Han'kook Chongkyong-sa, 1967.

Books in English

Adelman, Irma, ed. *Practical Approaches to Development Planning: Korea's Second Five-Year Plan.* Baltimore: Johns Hopkins Press, 1969.

Allen, Horace N. *Korea: Fact and Fancy.* Seoul: Methodist Publishing House, 1904.

———— *Things Korean.* New York: Fleming H. Revell Co., 1908.

Asakawa, K. *The Russo-Japanese Conflict.* Boston and New York: Houghton Mifflin and Co., 1904.

Bishop, Isabella B. *Korea and Her Neighbor.* New York: Fleming H. Revell Co., 1898.

Buck, Pearl S. *The Living Reed.* New York: John Day Co., 1963.

Cho, Soon-sung. *Korea in World Politics: 1940-1950.* Berkeley and Los Angeles: University of California Press, 1967.

Choy, Bong-youn, *Korea: A History.* Rutland, Vt. and Tokyo: Charles E. Tuttle Co., 1971.

Choy, Bong-youn and Lee, Olinda. *Asian American Studies Project: Korean-American Experience.* Secondary level guide-grade 8. Richmond Unified School District, California, 1975. Mimeographed Asian-American curriculum guide.)

Choy, Jung-suck. *The Art of Oriental Cooking.* Los Angeles: Ward Ritchie Press, 1964.

Chung, Henry. *The Case of Korea.* New York: Fleming H. Revell Co., 1921.

———— *Oriental Policy of the United States.* New York: Fleming H. Revell Co., 1919.

———— *Korean Treaties.* New York: H. S. Nichols, 1921.

Chung, Kyung-cho. *Korea: The Third Republic.* New York: MacMillan, 1971.

Conroy, Hilary. *The Japanese Seizure of Korea, 1868-1910.* Philadelphia: University of Pennsylvania Press, 1960.

Dong, Chon. *Can Aggression Be Justified and Imperialism Rationalized by Realism? A Review of Hilary Conroy's* The Japanese Seizure of Korea, 1919-1968. Seoul: Korean Research Center, n.d.

———— *Japanese Annexation of Korea: A Study of Korean-Japanese Relations.* Boulder: Colorado University Press, 1955.

Given, Helen L. *The Korean Community in Los Angeles (1939)*. San Francisco: R and E Research Association, 1974.

Goodrich, Leland M. *Korea: A Study of U.S. Policy in the United Nations*. New York: Council on Foreign Relations, 1956.

Grajdanzev, Andrew J. *Modern Korea*. New York: Institute of Pacific Relations, 1944.

Griffins, William E. *Korea, the Hermit Nation*. New York: C. Scribner's Sons, 1907.

Hahn, Melanie, ed. *The Fallen Egg: A Portrayal of the Korean Experience*. San Francisco Unified School District, California, 1974. (Mimeographed Asian-American curriculum guide).

Han, Sungjoo. *The Failure of Democracy in South Korea*. Berkeley and Los Angeles: University of California Press, 1974.

Harrington, Fred H. *God, Mammon, and the Japanese*. Madison: University of Wisconsin Press, 1944.

Hawaii Korean Golden Jubilee Committee. *Fifty Years of Progress: Hawaii Korean Golden Jubilee Celebration*. Unpublished manuscript prepared by Korean Golden Jubilee Celebration Committee, Honolulu, 1953.

Henderson, Gregory. *Korea: The Politics of the Vortex*. Cambridge: Harvard University Press, 1968.

Henthron, William E. *A History of Korea*. New York and London: Free Press, 1971.

Hulbert, Homer B. *The Passing of Korea*. New York: Young People's Missionary Movement of the United States and Canada, 1906.

———. *The History of Korea*. Seoul: Methodist Publishing House, 1905.

Kang, Younghill. *The Grass Roof*. New York: C. Scribner's Sons, 1931.

———. *East Goes West*. New York: C. Scribner's Sons, 1937.

———. *The Happy Grove*. New York: C. Scribner's Sons, 1933.

Kendall, C. W. *The Truth About Korea*. San Francisco: Korean National Association, 1919.

Kim, Agnes D. *I Married a Korean*. New York: John Daily, 1953.

Kim, Bok-lim, and Condon, Margaret E. *A Study of Asian-Americans in Chicago: Their Socio-Economic Characteristics, Problems and Services*. Urbana-Champaign: National Institute of Mental Health, U. S. Department of Health, Education and Welfare, 1975.

Kim, Byong Sik. Modern Korea: The Socialist North, Revolutionary Perspective in the South. New York: International Pub., 1970.

Kim, Changsoon, ed. *The Culture of Korea*. Honolulu: Korean-American Cultural Association, 1946.

Kim, Chong-shin. *Seven Years with Korea's Park Chung-hee*. Seoul: Hollyum Co., 1967.

Kim. Eugene C. I., and Kim, Han-kyo. *Korea and the Politics of Imperialism (1876-1910)*. Berkeley, University of California Press, 1967.

Kim, Hyung-chan, ed. *The Korean Diaspora*. Santa Barbara, Cal.: ABC-Clio, Inc., 1977.

Kim, Hyung-chan, and Patterson, Wayne. *The Koreans in America (1882-1974)*. Dobbs Ferry, N.Y.: Oceana Publications, 1974.

Kim, Il-song. *Revolution and Social Construction in Korea: Selected Writings of Kim Il-song*. New York: International Pub. 1971.

Kim, Richard E. *The Martyred*. New York: Pocket Books, 1965.

———. *The Innocent*. New York: Ballantine Books, 1968.

———. *Lost Names*. New York: Praeger Co., 1970.

Kim, Sei-jin. *The Politics of Military Revolution in Korea*. Chapel Hill: University of North Carolina Press, 1971.

Kim, Sei-jin, and Chang Hyun Cho, ed. *Government and Politics of Korea*. Silver Springs, Md.: The Research Institute on Korean Affairs, 1971.

Kim, Warren Y. *Koreans in America*. Seoul: Po Chin Chai Printing Co., 1971.

Kim, Yong-ik. *Blue in the Seed*. Boston: Little, Brown, 1974.

———. *The Moons of Korea*. Washington, D. C.: Korean Information Services, 1959.

Koh, Kwang-lim, and Koh, Seung-chun, ed. *Koreans and Korean-Americans in the United States*. New Haven: East Rock Press, 1974.

Kuno, Yoshi S. *Japanese Expansion on the Asiatic Continent*, 2 vols. Berkeley and Los Angeles: University of California Press, 1937.

Lee, Chong-sik. *The Politics of Korean Nationalism.* Berkeley and Los Angeles: University of
   California Press, 1965.
Lee, Chong-sik, and Scalapino, Robert A. *Communism in Korea,* 12 vols. Berkeley and Los Angeles:
   University of California Press, 1973.
Lee, David Y., Report on Korean-American Community in Los Angeles for Demonstration Project.
   Unpublished manuscript, Korean Association of Southern California, Los Angeles, 1972.
Lee, Hoon-koo. *Korean Immigrants in Manchuria.* Pyongyang: Union Christian College Press, 1931.
Liem, Channing. *America's Finest Gift to Korea.* New York: William-Frederick Press, 1952.
McCune, Evelyn. *The Arts of Korea: An Illustrated History.* Rutland, Vt., and Tokyo: Charles
   E. Tuttle Co., 1962.
McCune, George M. *Korea Today.* Cambridge: Harvard University Press, 1950.
McCune, George M., and Harrison, John A. *Korean-American Relations: Documents Pertaining to the Far
   Eastern Diplomacy of the United States, Vol. 1, The Initial Period, 1883-1886.* Berkeley and
   Los Angeles: University of California Press, 1951.
McCune, Shannon. *Korea's Heritage: A Regional and Social Geography.* Rutland, Vt., and Tokyo:
   Charles, E. Tuttle Co., 1956.
McKenzie, F. A. *The Tragedy of Korea.* London: Hodder and Soughton Co., 1909.
_____ *Korea's Fight for Freedom.* London: F. H. Revell Co., 1920.
Nam, Andrew. *Kim Ok-kyun and the Korean Progressive Movement.* Stanford: Stanford
   University Press, 1961.
Nelson, M. Frederick. *Korea and the Old Order in East Asia.* Baton Rouge, La.: Louisiana State
   University Press, 1946.
Oliver, Robert T. *Syngman Rhee: The Man Behind the Myth.* New York: Dodd Mead and Co., 1954.
Osgood, Cornelius. *The Koreans and Their Culture.* New York: Ronald Press Co., 1951.
Paik, L. George. *The History of Protestant Mission in Korea (1882-1910).* Pyongyang: Union
   Christian College Press, 1929.
Palmer, Spencer J. *Korean-American Relations Documents Pertaining to the Far Eastern Diplomacy of
   the United States, Vol. 11; The Period of Growing Influence, 1887-1895.* Berkeley and Los Angeles:
   University of California Press, 1963.
Rudolph, Philip. North Korea's Political and Economic Structure. Mimeographed, Institute of Pacific
   Relations, New York, 1959.
Sohn, Pow-key, ed. *History of Korea.* Seoul: UNESCO, 1970.
Stone, I. F. *The Hidden History of the Korean War.* New York: Monthly Review Press, 1952.
Suh, Dae-sook. *The Korean Communist Movement 1918-1948.* Princeton, N.J.: Princeton
   University Press, 1968.
Sunoo, Brenda Paik. *Korean-American Writings.* New York: Insight, 1975.
Tachiki, Amy, ed. *Roots: An Asian-American Reader.* Los Angeles: UCLA Asian-American
   Studies Center, 1971.
Tewksbury, D. G. Source Materials on Korean Politics and Ideologies. Mimeographed, Institute of
   Pacific Relations, New York, 1950.
Truman, Harry S. *Memoirs, Vol. 1: Year of Decisions.* New York: Doubleday, 1946.
Wales, Nym. *Song of Ariran.* San Francisco: Ramparts Press, 1971.
Wright, Edward R., ed. *Korean Politics in Transition.* Seattle and London: University of
   Washington Press, 1975.
Zanizi, A. W. Economic Reconstruction Problems in South Korea. Mimeographed, Institute of
   Pacific Relations, New York, 1954.

Articles in Korean

"Byonyong eui Kisu-dol" [Pioneers of the successful businessmen]. *Hankook Ilbo,* March 5,
   1976-April 28, 1976.
Chang, Lee-wook. "Miju Hanin Doknip-sa" [A history of independence movement of Koreans in
   America]. *Dong-A Ilbo,* March 14, 1973-March 21, 1973.
Chong, Du-ok. "Chaemi Hanjok Doknip Undong Silki" [A record of the independence movement of Koreans
   in America]. *Hankook Ilbo,* February 28, 1961-March 3, 1961.
Han, Chang-ho. "Dosan Sonsang ul Kirin-da" [I picture Dosan: Ahn Chang-ho]. *Dong-A Ilbo,* March
   25, 1975-April 1, 1975.

"Hanin Sahoe Udekaji" [How far has the Korean society in America come?]. *Hankook Ilbo,* Janaury 1, 1976-February 28, 1976.
"Inkan Rhee Syngman" [Human being: Syngman Rhee]. *Hankook Ilbo,* May 29, 1975-August 14, 1975.
Shin, Hung-woo. "Miju ui P'alchun Dongpo Kunwhang" [Present situation of our eight thousand countrymen in America]. In *Pyongwha wa Chayou* [Peace and freedom], edited by Kim Dong-whan, pp. 287-90. Seoul: Kundae-sa, 1932.
Song, Chull. "Miju Hanin Doknip Undong-sa" [A history of independence movement of Koreans in America]. *Dong-A Ilbo,* February 6, 1973-March 10, 1973.
————. "Na eui Imin Sanghwal" [My immigrant life]. *Joong-Ang Ilbo,* November 20, 1974-November 29, 1974
Yun, Yo-chon. "Miju Imin Ch'ilsipnyon" (Seventy years of emigration to America). *Kyonghyang Sinmun,* October 6, 1973-December 27, 1973.

Articles, Dissertations, Unpublished Studies, and Pamphlets in English

Ahn, Ch'ang-ho. "A Korean Appeal to America." *The Nation,* April 19, 1919, pp. 638-39.
"American Sympathy for Korea." *Korea Review,* Vol. 1, No. 9 (1919): 11-13.
"An Appeal from the Korean Mission to the Washington Conference." *Korea Review,* Vol. 3, No. 8 (1921): 608-9.
"An Appeal to America by Korean Congress in U. S., Philadelphia, April 14-16, 1919." In *Source Materials on Korean Politics and Ideologies,* edited by D. G. Tewkbury. New York: Institute of Pacific Relations, 1950.
Appenzeller, Alice R. "A Generation of Koreans in Hawaii." *Paradise of the Pacific,* Vol. 56, No. 12 (1944): 81-83.
Asian American Students at Antioch College and the Institute for Study of Social Problems. "Asians In America: A Chronology of Early Immigrants." Antioch, 1973.
Bae, Chung-keun. "The Effects of Traditionalism on Social Adjustment and Brain-Drain: A Study of Korean Students at the University of Wisconsin." Ph.D. dissertation, University of Wisconsin, 1972.
Brudnoy, David. "Race and the San Francisco School Board Incident: Contemporary Evaluation." *California Historical Quarterly,* Vol. 1 (1971): 295-312.
Cary, Sterling W. "Limitation of Military Aid to Korea." U. S. Congress, House Committee on Foreign Affairs, 93rd Cong., 2d sess., August 5, 1974.
Chai, Allice Yun. "Attitude of American-Educated Korean Students Toward America and Americanization " Master's thesis, Ohio State University, 1957.
Chang, Won Ho. "Communication and Acculturation: A Case Study of Koreans In Los Angeles." Ph.D. dissertation, University of Iowa, 1972.
Chun, Lowell K. Y. "Teaching the Asian-American Experience." In *Teaching Ethnic Studies.* Washington, D. C.: National Council for the Social Studies, 1973.
Church, Deborah. "Korean Emigration to Hawaii: An Aspect of U. S.-Japanese Relations." Mimeographed. Honolulu: University of Hawaii, 1971.
Desmond, Gail Whang. "Korean-Mexican Experience." *Insight,* Vol. 2, No. 2 (1973); 6.
Dunn, J. Kyuang. "Progress of Koreans in Hawaii." *Paradise of the Pacific,* Vol. 58, No. 12 (1946): 90-91.
"Economic Crisis Looms for South Korea." *International Policy Report,* Vol. 1 (1975): 1-20.
"First Korean Students' Conference in Dinuba, California." *Korea Review,* Vol. 1, No. 7 (1919): 15.
"First National Meeting of the Asian Presbyterian Caucus." Paper read March 16-19, 1972.
Gregor, Kyung Sook Cho. "Korean Immigrants in Gresham, Oregon: Community Life and Social Adjustment." Master's thesis, University of Oregon, 1963.
Griffis, William E. "The First Koreans in America." *Korea Review,* Vol. 4, No. 3 (1922): 11-15.
————. "Americans Interested in Korea." *Korea Review,* Vol. 2, No. 6 (1920): 5.
Han, Sang-en. "A Study of Social and Religious Participation in Relationship to Occupational Mobility and Self-Esteem Among Korean Immigrants in Chicago." Ph.D. dissertation, Northwestern University, 1973.
Jaisohn, Philip. "An Open Letter." *Korea Review,* Vol. 2, No. 10 (1920): 1-6.
Jhung, Walter. "Korean Independence Activities of Overseas Koreans" *Korean Survey,* Vol. 1, No. 4 (1952): 7-10.

———— "Koreans and the New U. S. Immigration Quota." *Korean Survey*, Vol. 2, No. 6 (1953): 5-7.

Kang, Donald. "The Koreans in Hawaii." *New Pacific*, Vol. 11, No. 11 (1944): 4-5.

Kang, Shin-pyo: "The East Asian and His Transformation in the West: A Cognitive Approach to Changing Views Among East-Asian Americans in Hawaii." Ph.D. dissertation, University of Hawaii, 1973.

Kim, Bernice Dong-hee: "The Koreans in Hawaii," *Social Science*, Vol. 9 (1934): 409-13.

Kim, Bok Lim. "Service Needs of Asian Immigrants as Seen by the Ethnic Churches: Korean Example." Mimeographed. Champaign-Urbana: University of Illinois, 1973.

———— "Koreans in the U. S. A." Unpublished paper, prepared at the Cultural Seminar of Social Rehabilitation Service in Washington, D. C., 1973.

Kim, David S. "Koreans to Win: U. S. A." Prepared with the support of Korean Town Development Association and Korean Chamber of Commerce of Los Angeles. Mimeographed. Los Angeles: University of California at Los Angeles, 1975.

Kim, Ha Tae. "The Koreans and Their Problems in Southern California." *The New Korea*, March 6-March 20, 1975.

Kim, Hyun-tae. "Relationship Between Personal Characteristics of Korean Students in Pennsylvania and Their Attitude Toward the Christian Churches in America." Ph.D. dissertation, University of Pittsburgh, 1966.

Kim, Kyung-chan. "Korean Emigration to the U. S. A., 1959-1969." *Korean Journal*, Vol. 11, No. 9 (1971): 16-24.

———— "Some Aspects of Social Demography of Korean-Americans." International Migration Review, Vol. 8, No. 1 (1974): 23-42.

———— "Korean Community Organizations in America: Their Characteristics and Problems." *Korea Journal*, Vol. 15, No. 11 (1975: 99-42.

———— "Ethnic Enterprises Among Korean Immigrants in America." Mimeographed. Bellingham, Wash. 1976.

———— "Korean's View of America: Reflection on American Character and Culture." *Korean Journal*, Vol. 12, No. 5 (1972): 12-19.

———— "History and Role of the Church in the Korean-American Community." In *The Koreans in America: (1882-1974)*. New York: Oceana Publications, 1974.

Kim, Ms. "The Life of Korean Women in America." *Insight*, Vol. 2, No. 1 (1973): 3-5.

Kim, Sando Joseph. "A Study of the Korean Church and Her People in Chicago, Illinois." Master's thesis, McCormick Theological Seminary, 1968.

Kim, Sil Dong. "Demonstration Project for Asians: An Analysis of Problems of Asian Wives of U. S. Servicemen." Mimeographed. Seattle, 1975.

"Korean Celebration March First." *Korean Review*, Vol. 4, No. 2 (1922): 15-16.

"Korean Women Write to American Congressmen." *Korean Review*, Vol. 2, No. 8 (1920): 1-2.

Lee, David Y. "Organizational Activities of Korean Community." Master's thesis, University of California at Los Angeles, 1974.

Lee, Dong-chang. "Acculturation of Korean Residents in Georgia." Ph.D. dissertation, University of Georgia, 1972.

Lee, Ha-jin. "Survey Reports 10,000 Korean Families in L. A.: Evidence Gross Undercut by U. S. Government," *The New Korea*, December 5, 1974.

Lee, Houchins and Chang-su Houchins: "The Korean Experience in America, 1903-1924." *Pacific Historical Review*, Vol. 18, No. 15, (1974): 548-72.

Lee, Kyung. "Settlement Patterns of Los Angeles Koreans." Master's thesis, University of California at Los Angeles, 1968.

Lyu, Kingsley K. "Korean Nationalist Activities in Hawaii and America." Mimeographed. Honolulu: University of Hawaii, 1950.

Mullen, Anne. "Korean Nursing Assistants Are Training in Danger." *Fresno Bee*, July 8, 1974.

O'Connell, James T. "Korean Nationalist Movement." Master's thesis, University of California at Los Angeles, 1938.

Oh, Hyun-sik. "Church Work with Oriental Youth," Ph.D. dissertation, California Graduate School of Theology, 1971.

Pang, Morris. "A Korean Immigrant." *Social Forces in Hawaii*, Vol. 13, (1949): 19-24.

Shin, Ku-bom. "The Post Graduation Residency Plans of Korean Students Attending University of Michigan." Ph.D. dissertation, Michigan State University, 1972.

Shin, Linda. "Koreans in America: 1903-1945." In Taichiki, A. (ed.), *Roots: An Asian American Reader.* Los Angeles: U.C.L.A. Asian Studies Center, 1971. Pp. 200-206.
_____. "A Note on Koreans in the United States." Mimeographed. Los Angeles: University of California at Los Angeles, 1970.
Shular, Helen. "Halmune with a Korean Accent." *Paradise of the Pacific,* Vol. 69, No. 3 (1957): 22-24.
Sunoo, Cooke H. "Koreans in Los Angeles: Employment and Education." Paper read at the Annual Conference of the Korean Christian Scholars in the United States, 1974, at St. Louis.
Sur, William. "Korean Ethnic Nationalism." *Hawaii Pono Journal,* Fourth Quarter (1970): 17-31.
Thames, John A. "Korean Students in Southern California: Factors Influencing Their Plans Toward Returning Home." Ph.D. dissertation, University of Southern California, 1971.
Wong, Ken. "Koreans: The Invisible Americans." *San Francisco Examiner,* December 18, 1972.
Wong, Paul. "The Emergence of the Asian-American Movement," *Bridge,* Vol. 2, No. 1 (1972): 32-36.
Yim, Sun Bin. "Mate Selection and Marriage as Perceived by Native Americans and Immigrant Koreans." Master's thesis, University of California, Santa Barbara, 1974.
Yoo, Jai-kun. "The Correlates of Cultural Assimilation of Korean Immigrants in the United States." *Korea Observer,* Vol. 1, No. 4: 88-97.
Yoshihara, Nancy. "Koreans Find Riches, Faded Dreams in L. A." *Los Angeles Times,* February 1, 1976.
Young, Sandra. "Families Open Homes, Hearts to Adopted Korean Children." *Fresno Bee,* January 1, 1974.
Yun, Yo-jun. "Early History of Korean Emigration to America (1)." *Korea Journal,* Vol. 14, No. 6 (1974): 21-26.
_____. "Early History of Korean Emigration to America (2)." *Korea Journal,* Vol. 14, No. 7 (1974): 40-45.

Official Documents

Annual Report of the Commissioner-General of Immigration: Washington, D. C.: Government Printing Office, 1899-1976.
California Advisory Committee to the U. S. Commission on Civil Rights: "Asian-Americans and Pacific People: A Case of Mistaken Identity," Washington, D. C., U. S. Government Printing Office, 1975.
Department of Health, Education, and Welfare: "A Summary of Asian-American Health, Education, and Welfare Problems," Washington, D.C., Government Printing Office, 1974.
Korean Directory of Northern California. San Francisco: The Center for Korean Studies, 1975.
Korean Directory of Southern California. Los Angeles: Korean Association of Southern California, 1976.
Korean Scientists and Engineers in America. Bethesda, Md.: The Korean Scientists and Engineers Association in America, Inc., 1974.
Office of Planning and Coordination of the Prime Minister, Republic of Korea: "Evaluation of the First Five Year Program: the Third Five Year Economic Development Plan," Seoul, 1973.
_____. "Evaluation Report of the Second Five Year Economic Development Plan (1967-71)," Seoul, 1972.
Urban Association, Inc.: "A Study of Selected Socio-Economic Characteristics of Ethnic Minorities based on 1970 Census, Vol. 11, Asian Americans," Washington, D. C., Government Printing Office, 1974.
U. S. Bureau of the Census: "Census of Population: 1970. Subject Reports, Final Report PC-1G., Japanese, Chinese, Filipinos, and Others in the U. S.," Washington, D. C., Government Printing Office, 1973.

Korean-American Journals

In Korean:
   Chayu Konghwa Kook [The free republic]. weekly (defunct)
   Dong-A Ilbo
   Hankook Ilbo
   Hankook Shinmoon (weekly)
   Hanmi Shinbo (weekly)

Joong Ang Ilbo
Korea Journal (defunct)
New Korea (weekly)

In English:
Korea Review (defunct)
Korea Survey (defunct)
Korea Times
Korea Week
Korean Commission to America and Europe (defunct)
Korean Information Bulletin (defunct)
Korean Research Bulletin (defunct)
Pan-Asia Times

Index